THEODORE ROOSEVELT ON HUNTING

THEODORE ROOSEVELT
ON HUNTING

Edited and with an introduction by
LAMAR UNDERWOOD

THE LYONS PRESS

Guilford, Connecticut
An imprint of The Globe Pequot Press

The Lyons Press is an imprint of The Globe Pequot Press.

10 9 8 7 6 5 4 3 2 1

Printed in the United States of America

ISBN 1–59228–021–8

Library of Congress Cataloging-in-Publication data is available on file.

Contents

Contents

PART TWO: SAFARI

Selections from *African Game Trails*

I am enamour'd of growing out-doors,
Of men that live among cattle or taste of the ocean or woods,
Of the builders and steerers of ships and the wielders of axes
        and mauls, and the drivers of horses,
I can eat and sleep with them week in and week out.

—Walt Whitman
Song of Myself

Alone far in the wilds and mountains I hunt,
Wandering amazed at my own lightness and glee,
In the late afternoon choosing a safe spot to pass the night,
Kindling a fire and broiling the fresh-kill'd game,
Falling asleep on the gather'd leaves with my dog and gun by
        my side.

—Walt Whitman
Song of Myself

No one, but he who has partaken thereof, can understand the keen delight of hunting in lonely lands. For him is the joy of the horse well ridden and the rifle well held; for him the long days of toil and hardship, resolutely endured, and crowned at the end with triumph. In after years there shall come forever to his mind the memory of endless prairies shimmering in the bright sun, of vast snow-clad wastes lying desolate under gray skies; of the melancholy marshes; of the rush of mighty rivers; of the breath of evergreen forest in summer; of the crooning of ice-armored pines at the touch of the winds of winter; of cataracts roaring between hoary mountain masses; of all the innumerable sights and sounds of the wilderness; of its immensity and mystery; and of the silences that brood in its still depths.

—Theodore Roosevelt
The Wilderness Hunter

Life is a great adventure, and the worst of all fears is the fear of living.

—Theodore Roosevelt

Introduction

To know something is not as good as loving it; to love something is not as good as rejoicing in it.

—Confucius

In living and rejoicing in the bold outdoor life he led throughout his sixty years, Theodore Roosevelt (1858–1919) probably reflected on the wisdom of Confucius from time to time, among other philosophers, scholars, and writers whose works he devoured as avidly as he did the call of the wild. Many of the twenty-sixth president's books were as important a part of his hunting kit as were his guns and loads, and he turned their pages by flickering firelight in places ranging from his ranch house to campfires on the prairie to tent camps on the African veldt. TR touches on his passion for reading being intertwined with his love of the outdoors in his autobiography (*Theodore Roosevelt: An Autobiography*, Scribner's, 1913): "There are men who love out-of-doors who yet never open a book, and other men who love books but to whom the great book of nature is a sealed volume, and the lines written therein blurred and illegible. Nevertheless among those men whom I have known the love of books and the love of outdoors, in their highest expressions, have usually gone hand in hand. . . . Usually the keenest appreciation of what is seen in nature is to be found of those who have also profited by the hoarded and recorded wisdom of their fellow men. . . . Personally the books by which I have profited infinitely more than by any others have been those in which profit was a by-product of the pleasure; this is, I read them because I enjoyed them, because I liked reading them, and the profit came in as part of the experience."

The strenuous outdoor life . . . the inquiring mind of a scholar. Mix these with potent measures of creativity and talent, and in Theodore Roosevelt you have a writer whose books about his experiences form a true literary treasure from which we all may "profit," as he used the word. And if you are a hunter, passionately committed to the spirit of the chase as TR himself, then Roosevelt's books can represent a true mother lode of reading pleasure. Never mind the stereotyped images (we've all seem them) of TR that come to mind: the flashing teeth, the political bully pulpit, the big stick, the wire-rimmed glasses, the Rough Riders and San Juan Hill. All these are but temporary masks for Theodore Roosevelt, the dedicated outdoorsman, the man who savored every moment afield and then wrote about them in some of the most engaging prose ever put onto paper.

Roosevelt's overall literary output was prodigious, a staggering forty-two volumes plus countless articles. His chosen subjects ranged from such expected areas as politics to history, biography, philosophy, and what clearly was his favorite—the outdoors and hunting. Unlike most dedicated and active hunters, Roosevelt did not seize upon this activity through the influence of his father or grandfather. He came to love hunting as part of the outdoor life he embraced on his own initiative, striving as a youngster to overcome a plethora of illnesses, such as asthma, that made him frail and weak. Although he would downplay the fact all his life, TR was born into a New York family of great wealth and privilege, with opportunities to enjoy life to the fullest while experiencing education, travel, and many activities not available to the average American in the latter part of the nineteenth century. He made the most of his birthright, especially in reading and embracing the vigorous outdoor life encouraged by his father to build up his body. Whenever he was outdoors, Roosevelt's asthma was held at bay. This, coupled with his acute interest in nature and natural history, led Roosevelt to glean every moment and experience possible from the great outdoors. Riding, rowing, and swimming were favorite activities when he attended Harvard, but he had also started doing some shooting and small game hunting. He was befriended by a Maine guide named Bill Sewall, who showed the youngster the ways of woodsmanship, accompanying him over lakes and trails of many adventures, including the climbing of Maine's highest peak, Mount Katahdin, 5,267 feet.

Shortly before TR's graduation from Harvard, reveals Nathan Miller in his excellent biography of Roosevelt, *Theodore Roosevelt: A Life*, an event occurred that shows exactly the kind of man young Roosevelt had become. In a checkup a doctor told Roosevelt that he had detected an irregular heartbeat, a condition he attributed to Roosevelt's vigorous lifestyle at the time. He advised a sedentary occupation and to avoid stairs. Miller reports Roosevelt's reaction: "'Doctor,' he said, 'I am going to do all the things you tell me not to do. If I've got to live the sort of life you have described, I don't care how short it is.'" Miller writes that Roosevelt kept this conversation secret until nearly the end of his life. One wonders today what the good doctor would have thought had he a glimpse of Roosevelt's future. Stairs? Just a few years later Roosevelt was to climb Switzerland's famed Matterhorn mountain, 15,000 feet.

By the time he was twenty-three, Roosevelt had studied law at Columbia, married, and written his first book—*The Naval War of 1812*—and he had expanded his hunting horizons to the great American heartland. With his brother Elliott, Roosevelt hunted waterfowl and grouse in the Red River country of Minnesota and saw, for the first time, the great prairie country he would come to love in his adventures even farther west. Then, in 1883, while his wife was four months pregnant, he answered the siren call urged upon him by his years of reading and confirmed by his visit to Minnesota: The far west, the great "Bad Lands" he longed to see, were beckoning and his life would never be the same.

A camp for wealthy hunters had opened on the Little Missouri River just east of the Montana line, and with it the opportunity to hunt buffalo, survivors of the vast herds that once roamed the West but were no more. Invited by an acquaintance, Roosevelt eagerly seized the chance and in late September arrived at the town of Little Missouri, in the badlands of Dakota. There he lived in a bunkhouse, like the other hunters, and with a guide stalked and bagged a buffalo in the wilderness. By the time he returned home, he was so deeply impressed by what he had seen of the cattle and ranching life that he committed some $14,000 to starting a herd of his own. Little did he realize that the badlands and the ranching life were about to become an island of escape from a sea of despair.

At age twenty-two, Roosevelt's wife Alice died in the hours after giving birth to a daughter on February 14, 1884. (Nathan Miller writes that Bright's disease, a kidney ailment, was undetected during her pregnancy.) The baby, christened Alice Lee, lived, but tragedy continued to stalk the house on New York's Fifty-seventh Street. Ill with a severe cold in the same house, Roosevelt's mother died within hours of Alice.

Roosevelt's life was shattered by heartbreak. Later, ending a tribute to Alice in his autobiography, TR said, "And when my heart's dearest died, the light went from my life for ever."

In the months that followed the double funeral, Roosevelt tried to be stalwart but was a dazed and bruised man. Political setbacks followed, and finally he decided to try to start a new life elsewhere. The Fifty-seventh Street house was sold and he headed for the Dakota badlands.

Introduction

Now began the ranching and western hunting years, destined to inspire so many books and to build the TR legend of the robust cowboy and hunter. So prolific was TR on writing about this portion of his life that one's immediate impression is that many, many years were involved. In fact, he was immersed in the ranching/hunting life for only three years, and even those were broken by trips back east when business, family, and politics dictated. Eventually, Roosevelt made more money writing about his western experiences than he did as a cattleman. His trilogy of books on western ranch life and hunting were well received by both the public and critics captivated by prose that transcended the hunting story genre of that time by their deep layers of natural history and illuminating portraits of the western lifestyle.

Already a successful writer with *The Naval War of 1812* under his belt, Roosevelt turned to his western experiences for his second book, *Hunting Trips of a Ranchman* (1885). This would be followed by *Ranch Life and the Hunting Trail* in 1888 and *The Wilderness Hunter* in 1893. Even this great trilogy could not contain all his thoughts and affection for western life. He also wrote four volumes of the great history, *The Winning of the West,* and continued to write about western game and hunting in *Some America Game* (1897), *Outdoor Pastimes of an American Hunter* (1905), and *Good Hunting* (1907). All these amid his unbelievable literary production of other books on history, politics, and philosophy. How did the man do it? Truly, he was amazing.

My role in bringing you the pleasure of reading TR's best stories in a single volume requires somewhat of a leap of faith on your part. TR has penned so many great pages of hunting prose that, to reap the full reward of the man's work, one must simply take the time to read them all. Obviously, we cannot do that here. However, the pieces I have selected for this book, though but a sampling of TR's hunting works, are enduring and timeless. They capture the hunting scene as TR lived it with prose that is alive with vivid detail and feeling. From the choking dust on the trail, to the keen blast of icy air as you top a steep ridgeline among the mighty peaks, the sense of place and action with TR is irresistible. Listen as he describes taking to the hunting trail, absorbing and reveling in all the natural world of his surroundings:

> Nowhere, not even at sea, does a man feel more lonely than when riding over the far-reaching, seemingly never-ending plains; and after a man has lived a little while on or near them, their very vastness and loneliness and their melancholy monotony have a strong fascination for him. . . . As far as the eye can see there is no break; either the prairie stretches out into perfectly level flats, or else there are gentle, rolling slopes, whose crests mark the divides between the drainage systems of the different creeks; and when one of these is ascended, immediately another precisely like it takes its place in the distance, and so roll succeeds roll in a succession as interminable as that of the waves of the ocean.

Another:

> After securing the buck's hams and head (the latter for the sake of the horns, which were unusually long and fine), I pushed rapidly on without stopping to hunt, to reach some large creek which should contain both wood and water, for even in summer a fire adds greatly to the comfort and coziness of a night camp. When the sun had nearly set we went over a divide and came in sight of a creek fulfilling the required conditions. It wound its way through a valley of rich bottom land, cotton-wood trees of no great height in size growing in thick groves along its banks, while its bed contained many deep pools of water, some of it fresh and good. I rode into a great bend, with a grove of trees on its right and containing excellent feed. Manitou was loosed, with the lariat round his neck, to feed where he wished until I went to bed, when he was to be taken to a place where the grass was thick and succulent, and tethered out for the night. There was any

amount of wood with which a fire was started for cheerfulness, and some of the coals were soon raked off apart
to cook over. The horse blanket was spread on the
ground, with the oil-skin over it as a bed, underneath a
spreading cotton-wood tree, while the regular blanket
served as covering. The metal cup was soon filled with
water and simmering over the coals to make tea, while
an antelope steak was roasting on a forked stick. It is
wonderful how cozy a camp, in clear weather, becomes if
there is a good fire and enough to eat, and how sound the
sleep is afterwards in the cool air, with the brilliant stars
glimmering through the branches overhead.

Reading passages like this, I sometimes reflect on the fact
that Ernest Hemingway, as a young man, read Roosevelt's prose
with great relish and idolized his lifestyle, especially the places
TR's hunts took him, the West and Africa. He began to dream of
his own hunts, in the high country of the West he longed to see,
and in Africa. Like Goethe's mythical "young man," he got what
he wished for—in fact being guided on safari in Africa by the
legendary Philip Percival, who had been one of Roosevelt's
"white hunters." Not lost on Hemingway in his enthrallment
with Roosevelt's hunting adventures was his exposure to interesting, quiet aspects of TR's nature. A hunter, yes, dedicated to the
chase. But a naturalist as well, interested in wildlife in all its
forms, and a sensitive observer of the habits and habitat of all
birds and animals.

Roosevelt, the naturalist, is particularly evident in his *African
Game Trails*, which he subtitled "An Account of the African Wanderings of an American Hunter-Naturalist." With his son Kermit
on the 1909 safari, Roosevelt shot and collected a great deal of
game for the Smithsonian and National Museums and was a keen
observer and recorder of everything he saw. His account of the safari has its share of the exciting, dangerous moments expected in
this type of big game hunting, but the two-volume work is rich

with descriptions of the quieter pleasures of safari life, from camp-fire scenes to reflections on bird watching.

Roosevelt shot a great deal of game. There is no arguing that. But for his time of abundance, and for his missions of gathering food and collecting museum specimens, he was not excessive. That he was a true conservationist, as most good hunters are, there is no doubt. He became friends with George Grinnell, editor of *Forest & Stream* magazine, who was instrumental in shoring up some of Roosevelt's outdated, flakier notions on wildlife and habitat. Both participated in the foundation of the Boone & Crockett Club. And Roosevelt continued to speak about and write on conversation issues throughout his life.

Roosevelt's wilderness adventures abroad continued in 1913, when he embarked on his now famous journey of exploration down the Rio da Divuda, the River of Doubt, a tributary of the Amazon, in the Mato Grosso region of Brazil. Finding the river and running it was a harrowing experience that nearly cost Roosevelt his life and left him drained and ill. The story is well told in his *Through the Brazilian Wilderness*, 1914.

Personal tragedy struck Roosevelt once again in 1918 when his son Quentin was shot down and killed in a dogfight with German planes while flying for the U.S. Army Air Corps in the First World War. Roosevelt himself did not last much longer. He had been very ill and feeble with the ravages of rheumatic fever, thought later to have possibly been complicated by diseases from his South American and African experiences. Early on the morning of January 6, 1919, at his Oyster Bay home, Sagamore Hill, Theodore Roosevelt breathed his last.

The hunter was home from the hill.

Lamar Underwood
May 2003

Part One

The Western Years

Selections from

Hunting Trips of a Ranchman

Sketches of Sport on the Northern Cattle Plains

&

The Wilderness Hunter

An Account of the Big Game of the United States

and Its Chase with Horse, Hound and Rifle

Wilderness Hunters and Wilderness Game

(From *The Wilderness Hunter*)

Manifold are the shapes taken by the American wilderness. In the east, from the Atlantic coast to the Mississippi valley, lies a land of magnificent hardwood forest. In endless variety and beauty, the trees cover the ground, save only where they have been cleared away by man, or where towards the west the expanse of the forest is broken by fertile prairies. Towards the north, this region of hardwood trees merges insensibly into the southern extension of the great subarctic forest; here the silver stems of birches gleam against the sombre background of coniferous evergreens. In the southeast again, by the hot, oozy coasts of the south Atlantic and the Gulf, the forest becomes semi-tropical; palms wave their feathery fronds, and the tepid swamps teem with reptile life.

Some distance beyond the Mississippi, stretching from Texas to North Dakota, and westward to the Rocky Mountains, lies the plains country. This is a region of light rainfall, where the ground is clad with short grass, while cottonwood trees fringe the courses of the winding plains streams; streams that are alternately turbid torrents and mere dwindling threads of water. The great stretches of natural pasture are broken by gray sage-brush plains, and tracts of strangely shaped and colored Bad Lands; sun-scorched wastes in summer, and in winter arctic in their iron desolation. Beyond the plains rise the Rocky Mountains, their flanks covered with coniferous woods; but the trees are small, and do not ordinarily grow very closely together. Towards the north the forest becomes denser, and the peaks higher; and glaciers creep down towards the valleys from the fields of everlasting snow. The brooks are brawling, trout-filled torrents; the swift rivers foam over rapid and cataract, on their way to one or the other of the two great oceans.

Southwest of the Rockies evil and terrible deserts stretch for leagues and leagues, mere waterless wastes of sandy plain and barren mountain, broken here and there by narrow strips of fertile ground. Rain rarely falls, and there are no clouds to dim the brazen sun. The rivers run in deep canyons, or are swallowed by the burning sand; the smaller watercourses are dry throughout the greater part of the year.

Beyond this desert region rise the sunny Sierras of California, with their flower-clad slopes and groves of giant trees; and north of them, along the coast, the rain-shrouded mountain chains of Oregon and Washington, matted with the towering growth of the mighty evergreen forest.

The white hunters, who from time to time first penetrated the different parts of this wilderness, found themselves in such hunting grounds as those wherein, long ages before, their Old-World forefathers had dwelt; and the game they chased was much the same as that their lusty barbarian ancestors followed, with weapons of bronze and of iron, in the dim years before history dawned. As late as the end of the seventeenth century the turbulent village nobles of Lithuania and Livonia hunted the bear, the bison, the elk, the wolf, and the stag, and hung the spoils in their smoky wooden palaces; and so, two hundred years later, the free hunters of Montana, in the interludes between hazardous mining quests and bloody Indian campaigns, hunted game almost or quite the same in kind, through the cold mountain forests surrounding the Yellowstone and Flathead lakes, and decked their log cabins and ranch houses with the hides and horns of the slaughtered beasts.

Zoölogically speaking, the north temperate zones of the Old and New Worlds are very similar, differing from one another much less than they do from the various regions south of them, or than these regions differ among themselves. The untrodden American wilderness resembles both in game and physical character the forests, the mountains, and the steppes of the Old World as it was at the beginning of our era. Great woods of pine and fir, birch and beech, oak and chestnut; streams where the chief game fish are spotted trout and silvery salmon; grouse of various kinds as the most common game birds; all these the hunter finds as characteristic of the New World as of the Old. So it is with most of the beasts of the chase, and so also with the fur-bearing animals that furnish to the trapper alike his life work and his means of livelihood. The bear, wolf, bison, moose, caribou, wapiti, deer, and bighorn, the lynx, fox, wolverine, sable, mink, ermine, beaver, badger, and otter of both worlds are either identical or more or less closely kin to one another. Sometimes of the two forms, that found in the Old World is the largest. Perhaps more often the reverse is true, the American beast being superior in size. This is markedly the case with the wapiti, which is merely a giant brother of the European stag, exactly as the fisher is merely a very large cousin of the European sable or marten. The extraordinary prong-buck, the only hollow-horned ruminant which sheds its horns annually, is a distant representative of the Old-World antelopes of the steppes; the queer white antelope-goat has for its nearest kinsfolk certain Himalayan species. Of the animals commonly known to our hunters and trappers, only a few, such as the cougar, peccary, raccoon, possum (and among birds the wild turkey), find their nearest representatives and type forms in tropical America.

Of course this general resemblance does not mean identity. The differences in plant life and animal life, no less than in the physical features of the land, are sufficiently marked to give the American wilderness a character distinctly its own. Some of the most characteristic of the woodland animals, some of those which have most vividly impressed themselves on the imagination of the hunters and pioneer settlers, are the very ones which have no Old-World representatives. The wild turkey is in every way the king of American game birds. Among the small beasts the coon and the possum are those which have left the deepest traces in the humbler lore of the frontier; exactly as the cougar—usually under the name of panther or mountain lion—is a favorite figure in the wilder hunting tales. Nowhere else is there anything to match the wealth of the eastern hardwood forests, in number, variety, and beauty of trees; nowhere else is it possible to find conifers approaching in size the giant redwoods and sequoias of the Pacific slope. Nature here is generally on a larger scale than in the Old-World home of our race. The lakes are like inland seas, the rivers like arms of the sea. Among stupendous mountain chains there are valleys and canyons of fathomless depth and incredible beauty and majesty. There are tropical swamps, and sad, frozen marshes; deserts and Death Valleys, weird and evil, and the strange wonderland of the Wyoming geyser region. The waterfalls are rivers rushing over precipices; the prairies seem without limit, and the forest never ending.

At the same time when we first became a nation, nine tenths of the territory now included within the limits of the United States was wilderness. It was during the stirring and troubled years immediately preceding the outbreak of the Revolution that the most adventurous hunters, the vanguard of the hardy army of pioneer settlers, first crossed the Alleghenies, and roamed far and wide through the lonely, danger-haunted forests which filled the No-man's-land lying between the Tennessee and the Ohio. They waged ferocious warfare with Shawnee and Wyandott and wrought huge havoc among the herds of game with which the forests teemed. While the first Continental Congress was still sitting, Daniel Boone, the archetype of the American hunter, was leading his bands of tall backwoods riflemen to settle in the beautiful country of Kentucky, where the red and the white warriors strove with such obstinate rage that both races alike grew to know it as "the dark and bloody ground."

Boone and his fellow-hunters were the heralds of the oncoming civilization, the pioneers in that conquest of the wilderness which has at last been practically achieved in our own day. Where they pitched their camps and built their log huts or stockaded hamlets, towns grew up, and men who were tillers of the soil, not mere wilderness wanderers, thronged in to take and hold the land. Then, ill-at-ease among the settlements for which they had themselves made ready the way, and fretted even by the slight restraints of the rude and uncouth semi-civilization of the border, the restless hunters moved onward into the yet unbroken wilds where the game dwelt and the red tribes marched forever to war and hunting. Their untamable souls ever found something congenial and beyond measure attractive in the lawless freedom of the lives of the very savages against whom they warred so bitterly.

Step by step, often leap by leap, the frontier of settlement was pushed westward; and ever from before its advance fled the warrior tribes of the red men and the scarcely less intractable array of white Indian fighters and game hunters. When the Revolutionary war was at its height, George Rogers Clarke, himself a mighty hunter of the old backwoods type, led his handful of hunter-soldiers to the conquest of the French towns of the Illinois. This was but one of the many notable feats of arms performed by the wild soldiery of the backwoods. Clad in their fringed and tasseled hunting shirts of buckskin or homespun, with coonskin caps and deer-hide

7

leggings and moccasins, with tomahawk and scalping knife thrust into their bead-worked belts, and long rifles in hand, they fought battle after battle of the most bloody character, both against the Indians, as at the Great Kanawha, at the Fallen Timbers, and at Tippecanoe, and against more civilized foes, as at King's Mountain, New Orleans, and the River Thames.

Soon after the beginning of the present century Louisiana fell into our hands, and the most daring hunters and explorers pushed through the forests of the Mississippi valley to the great plains, steered across these vast seas of grass to the Rocky Mountains, and then through their rugged defiles onwards to the Pacific Ocean. In every work of exploration, and in all the earlier battles with the original lords of the western and southwestern lands, whether Indian or Mexican, the adventurous hunters played the leading part; while close behind came the swarm of hard, dogged, border-farmers,—a masterful race, good fighters and good breeders, as all masterful races must be.

Very characteristic in its way was the career of quaint, honest, fearless Davy Crockett, the Tennessee rifleman and Whig Congressman, perhaps the best shot in all our country, whose skill in the use of his favorite weapon passed into a proverb, and who ended his days by a hero's death in the ruins of the Alamo. An even more notable man was another mighty hunter, Samuel Houston, who when a boy ran away to the Indians; who while still a lad returned to his own people to serve under Andrew Jackson in the campaigns which that greatest of all the backwoods leaders waged against the Creeks, the Spaniards, and the British. He was wounded at the storming of one of the strongholds of Red Eagle's doomed warriors, and returned to his Tennessee home to rise to high civil honor, and become the foremost man of his State. Then, while Governor of Tennessee, in a sudden fit of moody anger, and of mad longing for the unfettered life of the wilderness, he abandoned his office, his people and his race, and fled to the Cherokees beyond the Mississippi. For years he lived as one of their chiefs; until one day, as he lay in ignoble ease and sloth, a rider from the south, from the rolling plains of the San Antonio and Brazos, brought word that the Texans were up, and in doubtful struggle striving to wrest their freedom from the lancers and carbineers of Santa Anna. Then his dark soul flamed again into burning life; riding by night and day he joined the risen Texans, was hailed by them as a heaven-sent leader, and at the San Jacinto led them on to the overthrow of the Mexican host. Thus the stark hunter, who had been alternately Indian fighter and Indian chief, became the President of the new Republic, and, after its admission into the United States, a Senator at Washington; and, to his high honor, he remained to the end of his days staunchly loyal to the flag of the Union.

By the time that Crockett fell, and Houston became the darling leader of the Texans, the typical hunter and Indian fighter had ceased to be a backwoodsman; he had become a plains-man, or mountain-man; for the frontier, east of which he never willingly went, had been pushed beyond the Mississippi. Restless, reckless, and hardy, he spent years of his life in lonely wanderings through the Rockies as a trapper; he guarded the slow-moving caravans, which for purposes of trade journeyed over the dangerous Santa Fé trail; he guided the large parties of frontier settlers who, driving before them their cattle, with all their household goods in their white-topped wagons, spent perilous months and seasons on their weary way to Oregon or California. Joining in bands, the stalwart, skin-clad riflemen waged ferocious war on the Indians scarcely more savage than themselves, or made long raids for plunder and horses against the outlying Mexican settlements. The best, the bravest, the most modest of them all was the renowned Kit Carson. He was not only a mighty hunter, a daring fighter, a finder of trails, and maker of roads through the unknown, untrodden wilderness, but also a real leader of men. Again and again he crossed and recrossed the continent, from the Mississippi to the Pacific; he guided many of the earliest military and exploring expeditions of the United States Government; he himself led the troops in

9

victorious campaigns against Apache and Navahoe; and in the Civil War he was made a colonel of the Federal army.

After him came many other hunters. Most were pureblooded Americans, but many were Creole Frenchmen, Mexicans, or even members of the so-called civilized Indian tribes, notably the Delawares. Wide were their wanderings, many their strange adventures in the chase, bitter their unending warfare with the red lords of the land. Hither and thither they roamed, from the desolate, burning deserts of the Colorado to the grassy plains of the Upper Missouri; from the rolling Texas prairies, bright beneath their sunny skies, to the high snow peaks of the northern Rockies, or the giant pine forests, and soft rainy weather, of the coasts of Puget Sound. Their main business was trapping, furs being the only articles yielded by the wilderness, as they knew it, which were both valuable and portable. These early hunters were all trappers likewise, and, indeed, used their rifles only to procure meat or repel attacks. The chief of the fur-bearings animals they followed was the beaver, which abounded in the streams of the plains and mountains; in the far north they also trapped otter, mink, sable, and fisher. They married squaws from among the Indian tribes with which they happened for the moment to be at peace; they acted as scouts for the United States troops in their campaigns against the tribes with which they happened to be at war.

Soon after the Civil War the life of these hunters, taken as a class, entered on its final stage. The Pacific coast was already fairly well settled, and there were a few mining camps in the Rockies; but most of this Rocky Mountains region, and the entire stretch of plains country proper, the vast belt of level or rolling grass land lying between the Rio Grande and the Saskatchewan, still remained primeval wilderness, inhabited only by roving hunters and formidable tribes of Indian nomads, and by the huge herds of game on which they preyed. Beaver swarmed in the streams and yielded a rich harvest to the trapper; but trapping was no longer the mainstay of the adventurous plainsmen. Foremost among the beasts of the chase, on account of its numbers, its size, and its economic importance, was the bison or American buffalo: its innumerable multitudes darkened the limitless prairies. As the transcontinental railroads were pushed towards completion, and the tide of settlement rolled onwards with ever increasing rapidity, buffalo robes became of great value. The hunters forthwith turned their attention mainly to the chase of the great clumsy beasts, slaughtering them by hundreds of thousands for their hides; sometimes killing them on horseback, but more often on foot, by still-hunting, with the heavy long-range Sharp's rifle. Throughout the fifteen years during which this slaughter lasted, a succession of desperate wars was waged with the banded tribes of the Horse Indians. All the time, in unending succession, long trains of big white-topped wagons crept slowly westward across the prairies, marking the steady oncoming of the frontier settlers.

By the close of 1883 the last buffalo herd was destroyed. The beaver were trapped out of all the streams, or their numbers so thinned that it no longer paid to follow them. The last formidable Indian war had been brought to a successful close. The flood of the incoming whites had risen over the land; tongues of settlement reached from the Mississippi to the Rocky Mountains, and from the Rocky Mountains to the Pacific. The frontier had come to an end; it had vanished. With it vanished also the old race of wilderness hunters, the men who spent all their days in the lonely wilds, and who killed game as their some means of livelihood. Great stretches of wilderness still remain in the Rocky Mountains, and here and there in the plains country, exactly as much smaller tracts of wild land are to be found in the Alleghenies and northern New York and New England; and on these tracts occasional hunters and trappers still linger; but as a distinctive class, with a peculiar and important position in American life, they no longer exist.

There were other men beside the professional hunters, who lived on the borders of the wilderness, and followed hunting, not only as a pastime, but also as yielding an important portion of their

11

subsistence. The frontier farmers were all hunters. In the eastern backwoods, and in certain places in the west, as in Oregon, these adventurous tillers of the soil were the pioneers among the actual settlers; in the Rockies their places were taken by the miners, and on the great plains by the ranchmen and cowboys, the men who lived in the saddle, guarding their branded herds of horses and horned stock. Almost all of the miners and cowboys were obliged on occasions to turn hunters.

Moreover, the regular army which played so important a part in all the later stages of the winning of the west produced its full share of mighty hunters. The later Indian wars were fought principally by the regulars. The West Point officer and his little company of trained soldiers appeared abreast of the first hardy cattlemen and miners. The ordinary settlers rarely made their appearance until in campaign after campaign, always inconceivably wearing and harassing, and often very bloody in character, the scarred and tattered troops had broken and overthrown the most formidable among the Indian tribes. Faithful, uncomplaining, unflinching, the soldiers wearing the national uniform lived for many weary years at their lonely little posts, facing unending toil and danger with quiet endurance, surrounded by the desolation of vast solitudes, and menaced by the most merciless of foes. Hunting was followed not only as a sport, but also as the only means of keeping the posts and the expeditionary trains in meat. Many of the officers became equally proficient as marksmen and hunters. The three most famous Indian fighters since the Civil War, Generals Custer, Miles, and Crook, were all keen and successful followers of the chase.

Of American big game the bison, almost always known as the buffalo, was the largest and most important to man. When the first white settlers landed in Virginia the bison ranged east of the Alleghenies almost to the seacoast, westward to the dry deserts lying beyond the Rocky Mountains, northward to the Great Slave Lake and southward to Chihuahua. It was a beast of the forests and mountains, in the Alleghenies no less than in the Rockies; but its true home was on the prairies, and the high plains. Across these it roamed, hither and thither, in herds of enormous, or incredible magnitude; herds so large that they covered the waving grass land for hundreds of square leagues, and when on the march occupied days and days in passing a given point. But the seething myriads of shaggy-maned wild cattle vanished with remarkable and melancholy rapidity before the inroads of the white hunters, and the steady march of the oncoming settlers. Now they are on the point of extinction. Two or three hundred are left in that great national game preserve, the Yellowstone Park; and it is said that others still remain in the wintry desolation of Athabasca. Elsewhere only a few individuals exist—probably considerably less than half a hundred all told—scattered in small parties in the wildest and most remote and inaccessible portions of the Rocky Mountains. A bison bull is the largest American animal. His huge bulk, his short, curved black horns, the shaggy mane clothing his great neck and shoulders, give him a look of ferocity which his conduct belies. Yet he is truly a grand and noble beast, and his loss from our prairies and forest is as keenly regretted by the lover of nature and of wild life as by the hunter.

Next to the bison in size, and much superior in height to it and to all other American game—for it is taller than the tallest horse—comes the moose, or broad-horned elk. It is a strange, uncouth-looking beast, with very long legs, short thick neck, a big, ungainly head, a swollen nose, and huge shovel horns. Its home is in the cold, wet pine and spruce forests, which stretch from the sub-arctic region of Canada southward in certain places across our frontier. Two centuries ago it was found as far south as Massachusetts. It has now been exterminated from its former haunts in northern New York and Vermont, and is on the point of vanishing from northern Michigan. It is still found in northern Maine and northeastern Minnesota and in portions of northern Idaho and Washington; while along the Rockies it extends its range southward through western

Montana to northwestern Wyoming, south of the Tetons. In 1884 I saw the fresh hide of one that was killed in the Bighorn Mountains.

The wapiti, or round-horned elk, like the bison, and unlike the moose, had its centre of abundance in the United States, though extending northward into Canada. Originally its range reached from ocean to ocean and it went in herds of thousands of individuals; but it has suffered more from the persecution of hunters than any other game except the bison. By the beginning of this century it had been exterminated in most localities east of the Mississippi; but a few lingered on for many years in the Alleghenies. Col. Cecil Clay informs me that an Indian whom he knew killed one in Pennsylvania in 1869. A very few still exist here and there in northern Michigan and Minnesota, and in one or two spots on the western boundary of Nebraska and the Dakotas; but it is now properly a beast of the wooded western mountains. It is still plentiful in western Colorado, Wyoming, and Montana, and in parts of Idaho, Washington, and Oregon. Though not as large as the moose it is the most beautiful and stately of all animals of the deer kind, and its antlers are marvels of symmetrical grandeur.

The woodland caribou is inferior to the wapiti both in size and symmetry. The tips of the many branches of its long, irregular antlers are slightly palmated. Its range is the same as that of the moose, save that it does not go so far southward. Its hoofs are long and round; even larger than the long, oval hoofs of the moose, and much larger than those of the wapiti. The tracks of all three can be told apart at a glance, and cannot be mistaken for the footprints of other game. Wapiti tracks, however, look much like those of yearling and two-year-old cattle, unless the ground is steep or muddy, in which case the marks of the false hoofs appear, the joints of the wapiti being more flexible than those of domestic stock.

The whitetail deer is now, as it always has been, the best known and most abundant of American big game, and thought its numbers have been greatly thinned it is still found in almost every State of the Union. The common blacktail or mule deer, which has likewise been sadly thinned in numbers, though once extraordinarily abundant, extends from the great plains to the Pacific; but is supplanted on the Puget Sound coast by the Columbian blacktail. The delicate, heart-shaped footprints of all three are nearly indistinguishable; when the animal is running the hoof prints are of course separated. The track of the antelope is more oval, growing squarer with age. Mountain sheep leave footmarks of a squarer shape, the points of the hoof making little indentations in the soil, well apart, even when the animal is only walking; and a yearling's track is not unlike that made by a big prong-buck when striding rapidly with the toes well apart. White-goat tracks are also square, and as large as those of the sheep; but there is less indentation of the hoof points, which come nearer together.

The antelope, or prong-buck, was once found in abundance from the eastern edge of the great plains to the Pacific, but it has everywhere diminished in numbers, and has been exterminated along the eastern and western borders of its former range. The bighorn, or mountain sheep, is found in the Rocky Mountains from northern Mexico to Alaska; and in the United States from the Coast and Cascade ranges to the Bad Lands of the western edges of the Dakotas, wherever there are mountains chains or tracts or rugged hills. It was never very abundant, and, though it has become less so, it has held its own better than most game. The white goat, however, alone among our game animals, has positively increased in numbers since the advent of settlers; because white hunters rarely follow it, and the Indians who once sought its skin for robes now use blankets instead. Its true home is in Alaska and Canada, but it crosses our borders along the lines of the Rockies and Cascades, and a few small isolated colonies are found here and there southward to California and New Mexico.

The cougar and wolf, once common throughout the United States, have now completely disappeared from all save the wildest regions. The black bear holds its own better; it was never found on the great plains. The huge grisly ranges from the great plains to the

Pacific. The little peccary or Mexican wild hog merely crosses our southern border.

The finest hunting ground in America was, and indeed is, the mountainous region of western Montana and northwestern Wyoming. In this high, cold land, of lofty mountains, deep forests, and open prairies, with its beautiful lakes and rapid rivers, all the species of big game mentioned above, except the peccary and Columbian blacktail, are to be found. Until 1880 they were very abundant, and they are still, with the exception of the bison, fairly plentiful. On most of the long hunting expeditions which I made away from my ranch, I went into this region.

The bulk of my hunting has been done in the cattle country, near my ranch on the Little Missouri, and in the adjoining lands round the lower Powder and Yellowstone. Until 1881 the valley of the Little Missouri was fairly thronged with game, and was absolutely unchanged in any respect from its original condition of primeval wildness. With the incoming of the stockmen all this changed, and the game was wofully slaughtered; but plenty of deer and antelope, a few sheep and bear, and an occasional elk are still left.

Since the professional hunters have vanished, with the vast herds of game in which they preyed, the life of the ranchman is that which yields most chance of hunting. Life on a cattle ranch, on the great plains or among the foothills of the high mountains, has a peculiar attraction for those hardy, adventurous spirits who take most kindly to a vigorous out-of-doors existence, and who are therefore most apt to care passionately for the chase of big game. The free ranchman lives in a wild, lonely country, and exactly as he breaks and tames his own horses, and guards and tends his own branded herds, so he takes the keenest enjoyment in the chase, which is to him not merely the pleasantest of sports but also a means of adding materially to his comforts, and often his only method of providing himself with fresh meat.

Hunting in the wilderness is of all pastimes the most attractive, and it is doubly so when not carried on merely as a pastime. Shooting over a private game preserve is of course in no way to be compared to it. The wilderness hunter must not only show skill in the use of the rifle and address in finding and approaching game, but he must also show the qualities of hardihood, self-reliance, and resolution needed for effectively grappling with his wild surroundings. The fact that the hunter needs the game, both for its meat and for its hide, undoubtedly adds a zest to the pursuit. Among the hunts which I have most enjoyed were those made when I was engaged in getting in the winter's stock of meat for the ranch, or was keeping some party of cowboys supplied with game from day to day.

Hunting from a Bad Lands Ranch
(From *Hunting Trips of a Ranchman*)

My own ranches, the Elkhorn and the Chimney Butte, lie along the eastern border of the cattle country, where the Little Missouri flows through the heart of the Bad Lands. This, like most other plains rivers, has a broad, shallow bed, through which in times of freshets runs a muddy torrent, that neither man nor beast can pass; at other seasons of the year it is very shallow, spreading out into pools, between which the trickling water may be but a few inches deep. Even then, however, it is not always easy to cross, for the bottom is filled with quicksands and mud-holes. The river flows in long sigmoid curves through an alluvial valley of no great width. The amount of this alluvial land enclosed by a single bend is called a bottom, which may be either covered with cotton-wood trees or else be simply a great grass meadow. From the edges of the valley the land rises abruptly in steep high buttes whose crests are sharp and jagged. This broken country extends back from the river for many miles, and has been called always, by Indians, French voyageurs, and American trappers alike, the "Bad Lands," partly from its dreary and forbidding aspect and partly from the difficulty experienced in travelling through it. Every few miles it is crossed by creeks which open into the Little Missouri, of which they are simply repetitions in miniature, except that during most of the year they are almost dry, some of them having in their beds here and there a never-failing spring or muddy alkaline-water hole. From these creeks run coulies, or narrow, winding valleys, through which water flows when the snow melts; their bottoms contain patches of brush, and they lead back into the heart of the Bad Lands. Some of the buttes spread out into level plateaus, many miles in extent; others form chains, or rise as steep isolated masses. Some are of volcanic origin, being composed of masses of scoria; the others, of sandstone or clay, are worn by water into the most fantastic shapes. In coloring they are as bizarre as in form. Among the level, parallel strata which make up the land are some of coal. When a coal vein gets on fire it makes what is called a burning mine, and the clay above it is turned into brick; so that where water wears away the side of a hill sharp streaks of black and red are seen across it, mingled with the grays, purples, and browns. Some of the buttes are overgrown with gnarled, stunted cedars or small pines, and they are all cleft through and riven in every direction by deep narrow ravines, or by canyons with perpendicular sides.

In spite of their look of savage desolation, the Bad Lands make a good cattle country, for there is plenty of nourishing grass and excellent shelter from the winter storms. The cattle keep close to them in the cold months, while in the summer time they wander out on the broad prairies stretching back of them, or come down to the river bottoms.

My home ranch-house stands on the river brink. From the low, long veranda, shaded by leafy cotton-woods, one looks across sand bars and shallows to a strip of meadowland, behind which rises a line of sheer cliffs and grassy plateaus. This veranda is a pleasant place in the summer evenings when a cool breeze stirs along the river and blows in the faces of the tired men, who loll back in their rocking-chairs (what true American does not enjoy a rocking-chair?), book in hand—though they do not often read the books, but rock gently to and fro, gazing sleepily out at the weird-looking buttes opposite, until their sharp outlines grow indistinct and purple in the after-glow of the sunset. The story-high house of hewn logs is clean and neat, with many rooms, so that one can be alone if one wishes to. The nights in summer are cool and pleasant, and there are plenty of bear-skins and buffalo robes, trophies of our own skill, with which to bid defiance to the bitter cold of winter. In summer time we are not much within doors, for we rise before dawn and work hard enough to be willing to go to bed soon after nightfall. The long winter evenings are spent sitting round the hearthstone, while the pine logs roar and crackle, and the men play checkers or chess, in the fire light. The rifles stand in the corners of the room or rest across the elk antlers which jut out from over the fireplace. From the deer horns ranged along the walls and thrust into the beams and rafters hang heavy overcoats of wolf-skin or coon-skin, and otter-fur or beaver-fur caps and gauntlets. Rough board shelves hold a number of books, without which some of the evenings would be long indeed. No ranchman who loves sport can afford to be without Van Dyke's "Still Hunter," Dodge's "Plains of the Great West," or Caton's "Deer and Antelope of America"; and Coues' "Birds of the Northwest" will be valued if he cares at all for natural history. A western plainsman is reminded every day, by the names of the prominent landmarks among which he rides, that the country was known to men who spoke French long before any of his own kinsfolk came to it, and hence he reads with a double in-terest Parkman's histories of the early Canadians. As for Irving, Hawthorne, Cooper, Lowell, and the other standbys, I suppose no man, east of west, would willingly be long without them; while for lighter reading there are dreamy Ike Marvel, Burroughs' breezy pages, and the quaint, pathetic character-sketches of the Southern writers—Cable, Cradock, Macon, Joel Chandler Harris, and sweet

Sherwood Bonner. And when one is in the Bad Lands he feels as if they somehow *look* just exactly as Poe's tales and poems *sound*.

By the way, my books have some rather unexpected foes, in the shape of the pack rats. These are larger than our house rats, with soft gray fur, big eyes, and bushy tails, like a squirrel's; they are rather pretty beasts and very tame, often coming into the shacks and log-cabins of the settlers. Woodmen and plainsmen, in their limited vocabulary, make great use of the verb "pack," which means to carry, more properly to carry on one's back; and these rats were christened pack rats, on account of their curious and inveterate habit of dragging off to their holes every object they can possibly move. From the hole of one, underneath the wall of a hut, I saw taken a small revolver, a hunting-knife, two books, a fork, a small bag, and a tin cup. The little shack mice are much more common than the rats, and among them there is a wee pocket-mouse, with pouches on the outside of its little cheeks.

In the spring, when the thickets are green, the hermit thrushes sing sweetly in them; when it is moonlight, the voluble, cheery notes of the thrashers or brown thrushes can be heard all night long. One of our sweetest, loudest songsters is the meadow-lark; this I could hardly get used to at first, for it looks exactly like the eastern meadow-lark, which utters nothing but a harsh, disagreeable chatter. But the plains air seems to give it a voice, and it will perch on the top of a bush or tree and sing for hours in rich, bubbling tones. Out on the prairie there are several kinds of plains sparrows which sing very brightly, one of them hovering in the air all the time, like a bobolink. Sometimes in the early morning, when crossing the open, grassy plateaus, I have heard the prince of them all, the Missouri skylark. The skylark sings on the wing, soaring over head and mounting in spiral curves until it can hardly be seen, while its bright, tender strains never cease for a moment. I have sat on my horse and listened to one singing for a quarter of an hour at a time without stopping. There is another bird also which sings on the wing, though I have not seen the habit put down in the books. One bleak March day, when snow covered the ground and the shaggy ponies crowded about the empty corral, a flock of snow-buntings came familiarly round the cow-shed, clambering over the ridge-pole and roof. Every few moments one of them would mount into the air, hovering about with quivering wings and warbling a loud, merry song with some very sweet notes. They were a most welcome little group of guests, and we were sorry when, after loitering around a day or two, they disappeared toward their breeding haunts.

In the still fall nights, if we lie awake we can listen to the clanging cries of the water-fowl, as their flocks speed southward; and in cold weather the coyotes occasionally come near enough for us to hear their uncanny wailing. The larger wolves, too, now and then join in, with a kind of deep dismal howling; but this melancholy sound is more often heard when out camping than from the ranch-house.

The charm of ranch life comes in its freedom, and the vigorous, open-air existence it forces a man to lead. Except when hunting in bad ground, the whole time away from the house is spent in the saddle, and there are so many ponies that a fresh one can always be had. These ponies are of every size and disposition, and rejoice in names as different as their looks. Hackamore, Wire Fence, Steel-Trap, War Cloud, Pinto, Buckskin, Circus, and Standing Jimmie are among those that, as I write, are running frantically round the corral in the vain effort to avoid the rope, wielded by the dexterous and sinewy hand of a broad-hatted cowboy.

A ranchman is kept busy most of the time, but his hardest work comes during the spring and fall round-ups, when the calves are branded or the beeves gathered for market. Our round-up district includes the Beaver and Little Beaver creeks (both of which always contain running water, and head up toward each other), and as much of the river, nearly two hundred miles in extent, as lies between their mouths. All the ranches along the line of these two creeks and the river space between join in sending from one to three or four men to the round-up, each man taking eight ponies; and for every six or seven men there will be a four-horse wagon to carry the blankets and mess kit. The whole, including perhaps forty or fifty cowboys, is under the head of one first-class foreman, styled the captain of the round-up. Beginning at one end of the line the round-up works along clear to the other. Starting at the head of one creek, the wagons and the herd of spare ponies go down it ten or twelve miles, while the cowboys, divided into small parties, scour the neighboring country, covering a great extent of territory, and in the evening come into the appointed place with all the cattle they have seen. This big herd, together with the pony herd, is guarded and watched all night, and driven during the day.

At each home-ranch (where there is always a large corral fitted for the purpose) all the cattle of that brand are cut out from the rest of the herd, which is to continue its journey and the cows and calves are driven into the corral, where the latter are roped, thrown, and branded. In throwing the rope from horseback, the loop, held in the right hand, is swung round and round the head by a motion of the wrist; when on foot, the hand is usually held by the side, the loop dragging on the ground. It is a pretty sight to see a man who knows how, use the rope; again and again an expert will catch fifty animals by the leg without making a mis-throw. But unless practice is begun very young it is hard to become really proficient.

Cutting out cattle, next to managing a stampeded herd at night, is that part of the cowboy's work needing the boldest and most skillful horsemanship. A young heifer or steer is very loath to leave the herd, always tries to break back into it, can run like a deer, and can dodge like a rabbit; but a thorough cattle pony enjoys the work as much as its rider, and follows a beast like a four-footed fate through every double and turn. The ponies for the cutting-out or afternoon work are small and quick; those used for the circle-riding in the morning have need rather to be strong and rangey.

The work on a round-up is very hard, but although the busiest it is also the pleasantest part of a cowboy's existence. His food is good, though coarse, and his sleep is sound indeed; while the work is very exciting and is done in company, under the stress of an intense rivalry between all the men, both as to their own skill, and as to the speed and training of their horses. Clumsiness, and still more the slightest approach to timidity, expose a man to the roughest and most merciless raillery; and the unfit are weeded out by a very rapid process of natural selection. When the work is over for the day the men gather round the fire for an hour or two to sing songs, talk, smoke, and tell stories; and he who has a good voice, or better still, can play a fiddle or banjo, is sure to receive his meed of most sincere homage.

Though the ranchman is busiest during the round-up, yet he is far from idle at other times. He rides round among the cattle to see if any are sick, visits any outlying camp of his men, hunts up any band of ponies which may stray—and they are always straying—superintends the haying, and, in fact, does not often find that he has too much leisure time on his hands. Even in winter he has work which must be done. His ranch supplies milk, butter, eggs, and potatoes, and his rifle keeps him, at least intermittently, in fresh meat; but coffee, sugar, flour, and whatever else he may want, has to be hauled in, and this is generally done when the ice will bear. Then firewood must be chopped; or, if there is a good coal vein, as on my ranch, the coal must be dug out and hauled in. Altogether, though the ranchman will have time enough to take shooting trips, he will be very far from having time to make shooting a business, as a stranger who comes for nothing else can afford to do.

There are now no Indians left in my immediate neighborhood, though a small party of harmless Grosventres occasionally passes through; yet it is but six years since the Sioux surprised and killed five men in a log station just south of me, where the Fort Keogh trail crosses the river; and, two years ago, when I went down on the prairies toward the Black Hills, there was still danger from Indians. That summer the buffalo hunters had killed a couple of Crows, and while we were on the prairie a long-range skirmish occurred near us between some Cheyennes and a number of cowboys. In fact, we ourselves were one day scared by what we thought to be a party of Sioux; but on riding toward them they proved to be half-breed Crees, who were more afraid of us than we were of them.

During the past century a good deal of sentimental nonsense has been talked about our taking the Indians' land. Now, I do not mean to say for a moment that gross wrong has not been done the Indians, both by government and individuals, again and again. The government makes promises impossible to perform, and then fails to do even what it might toward their fulfilment; and where brutal and reckless frontiersmen are brought into contact with a set of treacherous, revengeful, and fiendishly cruel savages a long series of outrages by both sides is sure to follow. But as regards the taking the land, at least from the western Indians, the simple truth is that the latter never had any real ownership in it at all. Where the game was plenty, there they hunted; they followed it when it moved away to new hunting-grounds, unless they were prevented by stronger rivals; and to most of the land on which we found them they had no stronger claim than that of having a few years previously butchered the original occupants. When my cattle came to the Little Missouri the region was only inhabited by a score or so of white hunters; their title to it was quite as good as that of most Indian tribes to the lands they claim; yet nobody dreamed of saying that these hunters owned the country. Each could eventually have kept his own claim of 160 acres, and no more. The Indians should be treated in just the same way that we treat the white settlers. Give each his little claim; if, as would generally happen, he declined this, why then let him share the fate of the thousands of white hunters and trappers who have lived on the game that the settlement of the country has exterminated, and let him, like these whites, who will not work, perish from the face of the earth which he cumbers.

The doctrine seems merciless, and so it is; but it is just and rational for all that. It does not do to be merciful to a few, at the cost of justice to the many. The cattle-men at least keep herds and build houses on the land; yet I would not for a moment debar settlers from the right of entry to the cattle country, though their coming in means in the end the destruction of us and our industry.

For we ourselves, and the life that we lead, will shortly pass away from the plains as completely as the red and white hunters who have vanished from before our herds. The free, open-air life of the ranchman, the pleasantest and healthiest life in America, is from its very nature ephemeral. The broad and boundless prairies have already been bounded and will soon be made narrow. It is scarcely a figure of speech to say that the tide of white settlement during the last few years has risen over the west like a flood; and the cattle-men are but the spray from the crest of the wave, thrown far in advance, but soon to be overtaken. As the settlers throng into the lands and seize the good ground, especially that near the streams, the great fenceless ranches, where the cattle and their mounted herdsmen wandered unchecked over hundreds of thousands of acres, will be broken up and divided into corn land, or else into small grazing farms where a few hundred head of stock are closely watched and taken care of. Of course, the most powerful ranches, owned by wealthy corporations or individuals and already firmly rooted in the soil, will long resist this crowding; in places, where the ground is not suited to agriculture, or where, through the old Spanish land-grants, title has been acquired to a great tract of territory, cattle ranching will continue for a long time, though in a greatly modified form; elsewhere I doubt if it outlasts the present century. Immense sums of money have been made at it in the past, and it is still fairly profitable; but the good grounds (aside from those reserved for the Indians) are now almost all taken up, and it is too late for new men to start at it on their own account, unless in exceptional cases, or where an Indian reservation is thrown open. Those that are now in will continue to make money; but most of those who hereafter take it up will lose.

The profits of the business are great; but the chances for loss are great also. A winter of unusual severity will work sad havoc among the young cattle, especially the heifers; sometimes a disease like the Texas cattle fever will take off a whole herd; and many animals stray and are not recovered. In fall, when the grass is like a mass of dry and brittle tinder, the fires do much damage, reducing the prairies to blackened deserts as far as the eye can see, and destroying feed which would keep many thousand head of stock during winter. Then we hold in about equal abhorrence the granger who may come in to till the land, and the sheep-owner who drives his flocks over it. The former will gradually fill up the country to our own exclusion, while the latter's sheep nibble the grass off so close to the ground as to starve out all other animals.

Then we suffer some loss—in certain regions very severe loss—from wild beasts, such as cougars, wolves, and lynxes. The latter, generally called "bob-cats," merely make inroads on the hen-roosts (one of them destroyed half my poultry, coming night after night with most praiseworthy regularity), but the cougars and wolves destroy many cattle.

The wolf is not very common with us; nothing like as plentiful as the little coyote. A few years ago both wolves and coyotes were very numerous on the plains, and as Indians and hunters rarely molested them, they were then very unsuspicious. But all this is changed now. When the cattle-men came in they soon perceived in the wolves their natural foes, and followed them unrelentingly. They shot at and chased them on all occasions, and killed great numbers by poisoning; and as a consequence the comparatively few that are left are as wary and cunning beasts as exist anywhere. They hardly ever stir abroad by day, and hence are rarely shot or indeed seen. During the last three years these brutes have killed nearly a score of my cattle, and in return we have poisoned six or eight wolves and a couple of dozen coyotes; yet in all our riding we have not seen so much as a single wolf, and only rarely a coyote. The coyotes kill sheep and occasionally very young calves, but never meddle with any thing larger. The stockman ears only the large wolves.

According to my experience, the wolf is rather solitary. A single one or a pair will be found by themselves, or possibly with one or more well-grown young ones, and will then hunt over a large tract where no other wolves will be found; and as they wander very far, and as their melancholy howlings have most ventriloquial effect, they are often thought to be much more plentiful than they are. During the daytime they lie hid in caves or in some patch of bush, and will let a man pass right by them without betraying their presence. Occasionally somebody runs across them by accident. A neighboring ranchman to me once stumbled, while riding an unshod pony, right into the midst of four wolves who were lying in some tall, rank grass, and shot one with his revolver and crippled another before they could get away. But such an accident as this is very rare; and when, by any chance, the wolf is himself abroad in the daytime he keeps such a sharp look-out, and is so wary, that it is almost impossible to get near him, and he gives every human being a wide berth. At night it is different. The wolves then wander far and wide, often coming up round the outbuildings of the ranches; I have seen in light snow the tracks of two that had walked round the house within fifty feet of it. I have never heard of an instance where a man was attacked or threatened by them, but they will at times kill every kind of domestic animal. They are fond of trying to catch young foals, but do not often succeed, for the mares and foals keep together in a kind of straggling band, and the foal is early able to run at good speed for a short distance. When attacked, the mare and foal dash off towards the rest of the band, which gathers together at once, the foals pressing into the middle and the mares remaining on the outside, not in a ring with their heels out, but moving in and out, and forming a solid mass into which the wolves do not venture. Full-grown horses are rarely molested, while a stallion becomes himself the assailant.

In early spring when the cows begin to calve the wolves sometimes wait upon the herds as they did of old on the buffalo, and snap up any calf that strays away from its mother. When hard

pressed by hunger they will kill a steer or a heifer, choosing the bit-
terest and coldest night to make the attack. The prey is invariably
seized by the haunch or flank, and its entrails afterwards torn out;
while a cougar grasps the neck or throat. Wolves have very strong
teeth and jaws and inflict a most severe bite. They will in winter
come up to the yards and carry away a sheep, pig, or dog without
much difficulty; I have known one which had tried to seize a sheep
and been prevented by the sheep dogs to canter off with one of the
latter instead. But a spirited dog will always attack a wolf. On the
ranch next below mine there was a plucky bull terrier, weighing
about twenty-five pounds, who lost his life owing to his bravery.
On one moonlight night three wolves came round the stable, and
the terrier sallied out promptly. He made such a quick rush as to
take his opponents by surprise, and seized one by the throat; nor
did he let go till the other two tore him almost asunder across the
loins. Better luck attended a large mongrel called a sheep dog by
his master, but whose blood was apparently about equally derived
from collie, Newfoundland, and bulldog. He was a sullen, but very
intelligent and determined brute, powerfully built and with strong
jaws, and though neither as tall nor as heavy as a wolf he had yet
killed two of these animals single-handed. One of them had come
into the farm-yard at night, and had taken a young pig, whose squeals
roused everybody. The wolf loped off with his booty, the dog
running after and overtaking him in the darkness. The struggle
was short, for the dog had seized the wolf by the throat and the
latter could not shake him off, though he made the most desperate
efforts, rising on his hind legs and pressing the dog down with his
fore paws. This time the victor escaped scatheless, but in his second fight, when he strangled a still larger wolf, he was severely
punished. The wolf had seized a sheep, when the dog, rushing on
him, caused him to leave his quarry. Instead of running he turned
to bay at once, taking off one of the assailant's ears with a rapid
snap. The dog did not get a good hold, and the wolf scored him
across the shoulders and flung him off. They then faced each other

for a minute and at the next dash the dog made good his throat hold, and throttled the wolf, though the latter contrived to get his foe's foreleg into his jaws and broke it clear through. When I saw the dog he had completely recovered, although pretty well scarred.

On another neighboring ranch there is a most ill-favored hybrid, whose mother was a Newfoundland and whose father was a large wolf. It is stoutly built, with erect ears, pointed muzzle, rather short head, short bushy tail and of a brindled color; funnily enough it looks more like a hyena than like either of its parents. It is familiar with people and a good cattle dog, but rather treacherous; it both barks and howls. The parent wolf carried on a long courtship with the Newfoundland. He came round the ranch, regularly and boldly, every night, and she would at once go out to him. In the daylight he would lie hid in the bushes at some little distance. Once or twice his hiding place was discovered and then the men would amuse themselves by setting the Newfoundland on him. She would make at him with great apparent ferocity; but when they were a good way from the men he would turn round and wait for her and they would go romping off together, not to be seen again for several hours.

The cougar is hardly ever seen round my ranch; but toward the mountains it is very destructive both to horses and horned cattle. The ranchmen know it by the name of mountain lion; and it is the same beast that in the east is called panther or "painter." The cougar is the same size and build as the Old World leopard, and with very much the same habits. One will generally lie in wait for the heifers or young steers as they come down to water, and singling out an animal, reach it in a couple of bounds and fasten its fangs in the throat or neck. I have seen quite a large cow that had been killed by a cougar; and on another occasion, while out hunting over light snow, I came across a place where two bucks, while fighting, had been stalked up to by a cougar which pulled down one and tore him in pieces. The cougar's gait is silent and stealthy to an extraordinary degree; the look of the animal when creeping up to his prey has been wonderfully caught by the sculptor, Ke-meys, in his bronzes: "The Still Hunt" and "The Silent Footfall."

I have never myself killed a cougar, though my brother shot one in Texas, while still-hunting some deer, which the cougar it-self was after. It never attacks man, and even when hard pressed and wounded turns to bay with extreme reluctance, and at the first chance again seeks safety in flight. This was certainly not the case in old times, but the nature of the animal has been so changed by constant contact with rifle-bearing hunters, that timidity toward them has become a hereditary trait deeply en-grained in its nature. When the continent was first settled, and for long afterward, the cougar was quite as dangerous an antagonist as the African or Indian leopard, and would even attack men unpro-voked. An instance of this occurred in the annals of my mother's family. Early in the present century one of my ancestral relatives, a Georgian, moved down to the wild and almost unknown country bordering on Florida. His plantation was surrounded by jungles on which all kinds of wild beasts swarmed. One of his negroes had a sweetheart on another plantation, and in visiting her, instead of going by the road he took a short cut through the swamps, heed-less of the wild beasts, and armed only with a long knife—for he was a man of colossal strength, and of fierce and determined tem-per. One night he started to return late, expecting to reach the plantation in time for his daily task on the morrow. But he never reached home, and it was thought he had run away. However, when search was made for him his body was found in the path through the swamp, all gashed and torn, and but a few steps from him the body of a cougar, stabbed and cut in many places. Cer-tainly that must have been a grim fight, in the gloomy, lonely re-cesses of the swamp, with no one to watch the midnight death struggle between the powerful, naked man and the ferocious brute that was his almost unseen assailant.

When hungry, a cougar will attack any thing it can master. I have known of their killing wolves and large dogs. A friend of mine, a ranchman in Wyoming, had two grizzly bear cubs in his possession at one time, and they were kept in a pen outside the ranch. One night two cougars came down, and after vain efforts to catch a dog which was on the place, leaped into the pen and carried off the two young bears!

Two or three powerful dogs, however, will give cougar all he wants to do to defend himself. A relative of mine in one of the Southern States had a small pack of five blood-hounds, with which he used to hunt the canebrakes for bear, wildcats, etc. On one occasion they ran across a cougar, and after a sharp chase treed him. As the hunters drew near he leaped from the tree and made off, but was overtaken by the hounds and torn to pieces after a sharp struggle in which one or two of the pack were badly scratched.

Cougars are occasionally killed by poisoning, and they may be trapped much more easily than a wolf. I have never known them to be systematically hunted in the West, though now and then one is accidentally run across and killed with the rifle while the hunter is after some other game.

As already said, ranchmen do not have much idle time on their hands, for their duties are manifold, and they need to be ever on the watch against their foes, both animate and inanimate. Where a man has so much to do he cannot spare a great deal of his time for any amusement; but a good part of that which the ranchman can spare he is very apt to spend in hunting. His quarry will be one of the seven kinds of plains game—bear, buffalo, elk, bighorn, antelope, blacktail or whitetail deer. Moose, caribou, and white goat never come down into the cattle country; and it is only on the southern ranches near the Rio Grande and the Rio Colorado that the truculent peccary and the great spotted jaguar are found.

Until recently all sporting on the plains was confined to army officers, or to men of leisure who made extensive trips for no other purpose; leaving out of consideration the professional hunters, who trapped and shot for their livelihood. But with the incoming of the cattle-men, there grew up a class of residents, men with a stake in the welfare of the country, and with a regular business carried on in it, many of whom were keenly devoted to sport,—a class whose members were in many respects closely akin to the old Southern planters. In this book I propose to give some description of the kind of sport that can be had by the average ranchman who is fond of the rifle. Of course no man with a regular business can have such opportunities as fall to the lot of some who pass their lives in hunting only; and we cannot pretend to equal the achievements of such men, for with us it is merely a pleasure to be eagerly sought after when we have the chance, but not to be allowed to interfere with our business. No ranchmen have time to make such extended trips as are made by some devotees of sport who are so fortunate as to have no every-day work to which to attend. Still, ranch life undoubtedly offers more chance to a man to get sport than is now the case with any other occupation in America, and those who follow it are apt to be men of game spirit, fond of excitement and adventure, who perforce lead an open-air life, who must needs ride well, for they are often in the saddle from sunrise to sunset, and who naturally take kindly to that noblest of weapons, the rifle. With such men hunting is one of the chief of pleasures; and they follow it eagerly when their work will allow them. And with some of them it is at times more than a pleasure. On many of the ranches—on my own, for instance—the supply of fresh meat depends mainly on the skill of the riflemen, and so, both for pleasure and profit, most ranchmen do a certain amount of hunting each season. The buffalo are now gone forever, and the elk are rapidly sharing their fate; but antelope and deer are still quite plenty, and will remain so for some years; and these are the common game of the plainsman. Nor is it likely that the game will disappear much before ranch life itself is a thing of the past. It is a phase of American life as fascinating as it is evanescent, and one well deserving an historian. But in these pages I propose to dwell on only one of its many pleasant sides, and to give some idea of the game shooting which forms perhaps the chief of the cattle-man's pleasures, aside from those more strictly connected with his actual work. I have to tell of no unusual adventures, but merely of just such hunting as lies within reach of most of the sport-loving ranchmen whose cattle range along the waters of the Powder and the Bighorn, the Little Missouri and the Yellowstone.

Of course I have never myself gone out hunting under the direction of a professional guide or professional hunter, unless it was to see one of the latter who was reputed a crack shot; all of my trips have been made either by myself or else with one of my cowboys as a companion. Most of the so-called hunters are not worth much. There are plenty of men hanging round the frontier settlements who claim to be hunters, and who bedizen themselves in all the traditional finery of the craft, in the hope of getting a job at guiding some "tender-foot"; and there are plenty of skin-hunters, or meat-hunters, who, after the Indians have been driven away and when means of communication have been established, mercilessly slaughter the game in season and out, being too lazy to work at any regular trade, and keeping on hunting until the animals become too scarce and shy to be taken without more skill than they possess; but these are all mere temporary excrescences, and the true old Rocky Mountain hunter and trapper, the plainsman, or mountain-man, who, with all his faults, was a man of iron nerve and will, is now almost a thing of the past. In the place of these heroes of a bygone age, the men who were clad in buckskin and who carried long rifles, stands, or rather rides, the bronzed and sinewy cowboy, as picturesque and self-reliant, as dashing and resolute as the saturnine Indian fighters whose place he has taken; and, alas that it should be written! he in his turn must at no distant time share the fate of the men he has displaced. The ground over which he so gallantly rides his small, wiry horse will soon know him no more, and in his stead there will be the plodding grangers and husbandmen. I suppose it is right and for the best that the great cattle country, with its broad extent of fenceless land, over which the ranchman rides as free as the game that he follows or the horned herds that he guards, should be in the end broken up into small patches of fenced farm land and grazing land; but I hope against hope that I myself shall not live to see this take place, for when it does one of the pleasantest and freest phases of western American life will have come to an end.

The old hunters were a class by themselves. They penetrated, alone or in small parties, to the farthest and wildest haunts of the animals they followed, leading a solitary, lonely life, often never seeing a white face for months and even years together. They were skilful shots, and were cool, daring, and resolute to the verge of recklessness. On any thing like even terms they very greatly over-matched the Indians by whom they were surrounded, and with whom they waged constant and ferocious war. In the government expeditions against the plains tribes they were of absolutely in-valuable assistance as scouts. They rarely had regular wives or white children, and there are none to take their places, now that the greater part of them have gone. For the men who carry on hunting as a business where it is perfectly safe have all the vices of their prototypes, but, not having to face the dangers that beset the latter, so neither need nor possess the stern, rough virtues that were required in order to meet and overcome them. The ranks of the skin-hunters and meat-hunters contain some good men; but as a rule they are a most unlovely race of beings, not excelling even in the pursuit which they follow because they are too shiftless to do any thing else; and the sooner they vanish the better.

A word as to weapons and hunting dress. When I first came to the plains I had a heavy Sharps rifle, 45–120, shooting an ounce and a quarter of lead, and a 50-calibre, double-barrelled English ex-press. Both of these, especially the latter, had a vicious recoil; the former was very clumsy; and above all they were neither of them repeaters; for a repeater or magazine gun is as much superior to a single- or double-barrelled breech-loader as the latter is to a muz-zle-loader. I threw them both aside: and have instead a 40–90 Sharps for very long range work; a 50–115 6-shot Bullard express, which has the velocity, shock, and low trajectory of the English gun; and, better than either, a 45–75 half-magazine Winchester. The Winchester, which is stocked and sighted to suit myself, is by all odds the best weapon I ever had, and I now use it almost exclusively, having killed every kind of game with it, from a grizzly bear to a big-horn. It is as handy to carry, whether on foot or on horseback, and comes up to the shoulder as readily as a shot-gun; it is absolutely sure, and there is no recoil to jar and disturb the aim, while it caries accurately quite as far as a man can aim with any degree of certainty; and the bullet, weighing three quarters of an ounce, is plenty large enough for any thing on this continent. For shooting the very large game (buffalo, elephants, etc) of India and South Africa, much heavier rifles are undoubtedly necessary; but the Winchester is the best gun for any game to be found in the United States, for it is as deadly, accurate, and handy as any, stands very rough usage, and is unapproachable for the rapidity of its fire and the facility with which it is loaded.

Of course every ranchman carries a revolver, a long 45 Colt or Smith & Wesson, by preference the former. When after game a hunting-knife is stuck in the girdle. This should be stout and sharp, but not too long with a round handle. I have two double-barrelled shot-guns: a No. 10 choke-bore for ducks and geese, made by Thomas of Chicago; and a No. 16 hammerless, built for me by Kennedy of St. Paul, for grouse and plover. On regular hunting trips I always carry the Winchester rifle; but in riding around near home, where a man may see a deer and is sure to come across ducks and grouse, it is best to take the little ranch gun, a double-barrel No. 16, with a 40–70 rifle underneath the shot-gun barrels.

As for clothing, when only off on a day's trip, the ordinary ranchman's dress is good enough: flannel shirt, and overalls tucked into alligator boots, the latter being of service against the brambles, cacti, and rattlesnakes. Such a costume is good in warm weather. When making a long hunting trip, where there will be much rough work, especially in the dry cold of fall and winter, there is nothing better than a fringed buckskin tunic or hunting-shirt, (held in at the waist by the cartridge belt,) buckskin trowsers, and a fur cap, with heavy moccasins for use in the woods, and light alligator-hide shoes if it is intended to cross rocks and open ground. Buckskin is most durable, keeps out wind and cold, and is the best possible color for the hunter—no small point in approaching game. For wet it is not as good as flannel, and it is hot in warm weather. On very cold days, fur gloves and either a cook-skin overcoat or a short riding jacket of fisher's fur may be worn. In cold weather, if travelling light with only what can be packed behind the horse, I sleep in a big buffalo-robe, sewed up at the sides and one end into the form of a bag, and very warm. When, as is sometimes the case, the spirit in the thermometer sinks to negative 60°–65° Fahrenheit, it is necessary to have more wraps and bedding, and we use beaver-robes and bear-skins. An oilskin "slicker" or waterproof overcoat and a pair of shaps keep out the rain almost completely.

Where most of the hunting is done on horseback the hunting-pony is a very important animal. Many people seem to think that any broken-down pony will do to hunt, but this seems to me a very great mistake. My own hunting-horse, Manitou, is the best and most valuable animal on the ranch. He is stoutly built and strong, able to carry a good-sized buck behind his rider for miles at a lope without minding it in the least; he is very enduring and very hardy, not only picking up a living but even growing fat when left to shift for himself under very hard conditions; and he is perfectly surefooted and as fast as any horse on the river. Though both willing and spirited, he is very gentle, with an easy mouth, and will stay grazing in one spot when left, and will permit himself to be caught without difficulty. Add to these virtues the fact that he will let any dead beast or thing be packed on him, and will allow a man to shoot off his back or right by him without moving, and it is evident that he is as nearly perfect as can be the case with hunting-horseflesh. There is a little sorrel mare on the ranch, a perfect little pet, that is almost as good, but too small. We have some other horses we frequently use, but all have faults. Some of the quiet ones are slow, lazy, or tire easily; others are gun shy; while others plunge and buck if we try to pack any game on their backs. Others cannot be left standing untied, as they run away; and I can imagine few forms of exercise so soul-harrowing as that of spending an hour or two in running, in shaps, top boots, and spurs over a broken prairie, with the thermometer at 90°, after an escaped horse. Most of the hunting-horses used by my friends have one or more of these tricks, and it is rare to find one, like Manitou, who has none of them. Manitou is a treasure and I value him accordingly. Besides, he is a sociable old fellow, and a great companion when off alone, coming up to have his head rubbed or to get a crust of bread, of which he is very fond.

To be remarkably successful in killing game a man must be a good shot; but a good target shot may be a very poor hunter, and a fairly successful hunter may be only a moderate shot. Shooting well with the rifle is the highest kind of skill, for the rifle is the queen of weapons; and it is a difficult art to learn. But many other qualities go to make up the first-class hunter. He must be persevering, watchful, hardy, and with good judgment; and a little dash and energy at the proper time often help him immensely. I myself am not, and never will be, more than an ordinary shot; for my eyes are bad and my hand not over-steady; yet I have killed every kind of game to be found on the plains, partly because I have hunted very perseveringly, and partly because by practice I have learned to shoot about as well at a wild animal as at a target. I have killed rather more game than most of the ranchmen who are my neighbors, though at least half of them are better shots than I am.

Time and again I have seen a man who had, as he deemed, practised sufficiently at a target, come out "to kill a deer," hot with enthusiasm; and nine out of ten times he has gone back unsuccessful, even when deer were quite plenty. Usually he has been told by the friend who advised him to take the trip, or by the guide who inveigled him into it, that "the deer were so plenty you saw them all round you," and, this not proving quite true, he lacks perseverance to keep on; or else he fails to see the deer at the right time; or else if he does see it he misses it, making the discovery that to shoot at a gray object, not overdistinctly seen, at a distance merely guessed at, and with a background of other gray objects, is very different from firing into a target, brightly painted and a fixed number of yards off. A man must be able to hit a bull's-eye eight inches across every time to do good work with deer or other game; for the spot around the shoulders that is fatal is not much bigger than this; and a shot a little back of that merely makes a wound which may in the end prove mortal, but which will in all probability allow the animal to escape for the time being. It takes a good shot to hit a bull's-eye off-hand several times in succession at a hundred yards, and if the bull's-eye was painted the same color as the rest of the landscape, and was at an uncertain distance, and, moreover, was alive, and likely to take to its heels at any moment, the difficulty of making a good shot would be greatly enhanced. The man who can kill his buck right along at a hundred yards has a right to claim that he is a good shot. If he can shoot off-hand standing up, that is much the best way, but I myself always drop on one knee, if I have time, unless the animal is very close. It is curious to hear the nonsense that is talked and to see the nonsense that is written about the distances at which game is killed. Rifles now carry with deadly effect the distance of a mile, and most middle-range hunting-rifles would at least kill at half a mile; and in war firing is often begun at these ranges. But in war there is very little accurate aiming, and the fact that there is a variation of thirty or forty feet in the flight of the ball makes no difference; and, finally, a thousand bullets are fired for every man that is killed—and usually many more than a thousand. How would that serve for a record on game? The truth is that three hundred yards is a very long shot, and that even two hundred yards is a long shot. On looking over my gamebook I find that the average distance at which I have killed game on the plains is less than a hundred and fifty yards. A few years ago, when the buffalo would stand still in great herds, half a mile from the hunter, the latter, using a long-range Sharp's rifle, would often, by firing a number of shots into the herd at that distance, knock over two or three buffalo; but I have hardly ever known single animals to be killed six hundred yards off, even in antelope hunting, the kind in which most long-range shooting is done; and a half that distance a very good shot, with all the surroundings in his favor, is more apt to miss than to hit. Of course old hunters—the most inveterate liars on the face of the earth—are all the time telling of their wonderful shots at even longer distances, and they do occasionally, when shooting very often, make them, but their performances, when actually tested, dwindle amazingly. Others, amateurs, will brag of their rifles. I lately read in a magazine about killing antelopes at eight hundred yards with a Winchester express, a weapon which cannot be depended upon at over two hundred, and is wholly inaccurate at over three hundred, yards.

The truth is that, in almost all cases the hunter merely guesses at the distance, and, often perfectly honestly, just about doubles it in his own mind. Once a man told me of an extraordinary shot by which he killed a deer at four hundred yards. A couple of days afterward we happened to pass the place, and I had the curiosity to step off the distance, finding it a trifle over a hundred and ninety. I always make it a rule to pace off the distance after a successful shot, whenever practicable—that is, when the animal has not run too far before dropping,—and I was at first both amused and somewhat chagrined to see how rapidly what I had supposed to be remarkably long shots shrank under actual pacing. It is a good rule always to try to get as near the game as possible, and in most cases it is best to risk startling it in the effort to get closer rather than to risk missing it by a shot at long range. At the same time, I am a great believer in powder-burning, and if I cannot get near, will generally try a shot anyhow, if there is a chance of the rifle's carrying to it. In this way a man will now and then, in the midst of many misses, make a very good long shot, but he should not try to deceive himself into the belief that these occasional long shots are to be taken as samples of his ordinary skill. Yet it is curious to see how a really truthful man will forget his misses, and his hits at close quarters, and, by dint of constant repetition, will finally persuade himself that he is in the habit of killing his game at three or four hundred yards. Of course in different kinds of ground the average range for shooting varies. In the Bad Lands most shots will be obtained much closer than on the prairie, and in the timber they will be nearer still.

Old hunters who are hardy, persevering, and well acquainted with the nature of the animals they pursue, will often kill a great deal of game without being particularly good marksmen; besides, they are careful to get up close, and are not flurried at all, shooting as well at a deer as they do at a target. They are, as a rule, fair shots—that is, they shoot a great deal better than Indians or soldiers, or than the general run of Eastern amateur sportsmen; but I have never been out with one who has not missed a great deal, and the "Leather-stocking" class of shooting stories are generally untrue, at least to the extent of suppressing part of the truth—that is, the number of misses. Beyond question our Western hunters are, as a body, to the full as good marksmen as, and probably much better than, any other body of men in the world, not even excepting the Dutch Boers or Tyrolese Jägers, and a certain number of them who shoot a great deal at game, and are able to squander cartridges very freely, undoubtedly become crack shots, and perform really wonderful feats. As an instance there is old "Vic," a former scout and Indian fighter, and concededly the best hunter on the Little Missouri; probably there are not a dozen men in the West who are better shots or hunters than he is, and I have seen him do most skilful work. He can run the muzzle of his rifle through a board so as to hide the sights, and yet do quite good shooting at some little distance; he will cut the head off a chicken at eighty or ninety yards, shoot a deer running through brush at that distance, kill grouse on the wing early in the season, and knock over antelopes when they are so far off that I should not dream of shooting. He firmly believes, and so do most men that speak of him, that he never misses. Yet I have known him to make miss after miss at game, and some that were not such especially difficult shots either. One secret of his success is his constant practice. He is firing all the time, at marks, small birds, etc., etc., and will average from fifty to a hundred cartridges a day; he certainly uses nearly twenty thousand a year, while a man who only shoots for sport, and that occasionally, will, in practising at marks and every thing else, hardly get through with five hundred. Besides, he was cradled in the midst of wild life, and has handled a rifle and used it against both brute and human foes almost since his infancy; his nerves and sinews are like iron, and his eye is naturally both quick and true.

Vic is an exception. With practice an amateur will become nearly as good as the average hunter; and, as I said before, I do not myself believe in taking out a professional hunter as a shooting companion. If I do not go alone I generally go with one of my foremen, Merrifield, who himself came from the East but five years ago. He is a good-looking fellow, daring and self-reliant, a good rider and first-class shot, and a very keen sportsman. Of late years he has been my *fidus Achates* of the hunting field. I can kill more game with him than I can alone; and in hunting on the plains there are many occasions on which it is almost a necessity to have a companion along.

It frequently happens that a solitary hunter finds himself in an awkward predicament, from which he could be extricated easily enough if there were another man with him. His horse may fall into a washout, or may get stuck in a mud-hole or quicksand in such a manner that a man working by himself will have great difficulty in getting it out; and two heads often prove better than one in an emergency, especially if a man gets hurt in any way. The first thing that a western plainsman has to learn is the capacity for self-help, but at the same time he must not forget that occasions may arise when the help of others will be most grateful.

Hunting the Grisly

(From *The Wilderness Hunter*)

If out in the late fall or early spring, it is often possible to follow a bear's trail in the snow; having come upon it either by chance or hard hunting, or else having found where it leads from some carcass on which the beast has been feeding. In the pursuit one must exercise great caution, as at such times the hunter is easily seen a long way off, and game is always especially watchful for any foe that may follow its trail.

Once I killed a grisly in this manner. It was early in the fall, but snow lay on the ground, while the gray weather boded a storm. My camp was in a bleak, wind-swept valley, high among the mountains which form the divide between the head-waters of the Salmon and Clarke's Fork of the Columbia. All night I had lain in my buffalo-bag, under the lea of a windbreak of branches, in the clump of fir-trees, where I had halted the preceding evening. At my feet ran a rapid mountain torrent, its bed choked with ice-covered rocks; I had been lulled to sleep by the stream's splashing

45

murmur, and the loud moaning of the wind along the naked cliffs. At dawn I rose and shook myself free of the buffalo robe, coated with hoarfrost. The ashes of the fire were lifeless; in the dim morning the air was bitter cold. I did not linger a moment, but snatched up my rifle, pulled on my fur cap and gloves, and strode off up a side ravine; as I walked I ate some mouthfuls of venison, left over from supper.

Two hours of toil up the steep mountain brought me to the top of a spur. The sun had risen, but was hidden behind a bank of sullen clouds. On the divide I halted, and gazed out over a vast landscape, inconceivably wild and dismal. Around me towered the stupendous mountain masses which make up the backbone of the Rockies. From my feet, as far as I could see, stretched a rugged and barren chaos of ridges and detached rock masses. Behind me, far below, the stream wound like a silver ribbon, fringed with dark conifers and the changing, dying foliage of poplar and quaking aspen. In front the bottoms of the valley were filled with the sombre evergreen forest, dotted here and there with black, ice-skimmed tarns; and the dark spruces clustered also in the higher gorges, and were scattered thinly along the mountain sides. The snow which had fallen lay in drifts and streaks, while, where the wind had scope it was blown off, and the ground left bare.

For two hours I walked onwards across the ridges and valleys. Then among some scattered spruces, where the snow lay to the depth of half a foot, I suddenly came on the fresh, broad trail of a grisly. The brute was evidently roaming restlessly about in search of a winter den, but willing, in passing, to pick up any food that lay handy. At once I took the trail, travelling above and to one side, and keeping a sharp look-out ahead. The bear was going across wind, and this made my task easy. I walked rapidly, though cautiously; and it was only in crossing the large patches of bare ground that I had to fear making a noise. Elsewhere the snow muffled my footsteps, and made the trail so plain that I scarcely had to waste a glance upon it, bending my eyes always to the front.

At last, peering cautiously over a ridge crowned with broken rocks, I saw my quarry, a big, burly bear, with silvered fur. He had halted on an open hill-side, and was busily digging up the caches of some rock gophers or squirrels. He seemed absorbed in his work, and the stalk was easy. Slipping quietly back, I ran towards the end of the spur, and in ten minutes struck a ravine, of which one branch ran past within seventy yards of where the bear was working. In this ravine was a rather close growth of stunted evergreens, affording good cover, although in one or two places I had to lie down and crawl through the snow. When I reached the point for which I was aiming, the bear had just finished rooting, and was starting off. A slight whistle brought him to a standstill, and I drew a bead behind his shoulder, and low down, resting the rifle across the crooked branch of a dwarf spruce. At the crack he ran off at speed, making no sound, but the thick spatter of blood splashes, showing clear on the white snow, betrayed the mortal nature of the wound. For some minutes I followed the trail; and then, topping a ridge, I saw the dark bulk lying motionless in a snow drift at the foot of a low rock-wall, down which he had tumbled.

The usual practice of the still-hunter who is after grisly is to toll it to baits. The hunter either lies in ambush near the carcass, or approaches it stealthily when he thinks the bear is at its meal.

One day while camped near the Bitter Root Mountains in Montana I found that a bear had been feeding on the carcass of a moose which lay some five miles from the little open glade in which my tent was pitched, and I made up my mind to try to get a shot at it that afternoon. I stayed in camp till about three o'clock, lying lazily back on the bed of sweet-smelling evergreen boughs, watching the pack ponies as they stood under the pines on the edge of the open, stamping now and then, and switching their tails. The air was still, the sky a glorious blue; at that hour in the afternoon even the September sun was hot. The smoke from the smouldering logs of the campfire curled thinly upwards. Little chipmunks scuttled out from their holes to the packs, which lay in a heap on the ground, and then scuttled madly back again. A couple of drab-colored whisky-jacks, with bold mien and fearless bright eyes, hopped and fluttered round, picking up the scraps, and uttering an extraordinary variety of notes, mostly discordant; so tame were they that one of them lit on my outstretched arm as I half dozed, basking in the sunshine.

When the shadows began to lengthen, I shouldered my rifle and plunged into the woods. At first my route lay along a mountain side; then for half a mile over a windfall, the dead timber piled about in crazy confusion. After that I went up the bottom of a valley by a little brook, the ground being carpeted with a sponge of soaked moss. At the head of this brook was a pond covered with water-lilies; and a scramble through a rocky pass took me into a high, wet valley, where the thick growth of spruce was broken by occasional strips of meadow. In this valley the moose carcass lay, well at the upper end.

In moccasined feet I trod softly through the soundless woods. Under the dark branches it was already dusk, and the air had the cool chill of evening. As I neared the clump where the body lay, I walked with redoubled caution, watching and listening with strained alertness. Then I heard a twig snap; and my blood leaped, for I knew the bear was at his supper. In another moment I saw his shaggy, brown form. He was working with all his awkward giant strength, trying to bury the carcass, twisting it to one side and the other with wonderful ease. Once he got angry and suddenly gave it a tremendous cuff with his paw; in his bearing he had something half humorous, half devilish. I crept up within forty yards; but for several minutes he would not keep his head still. Then something attracted his attention in the forest, and he stood motionless looking towards it, broadside to me, with his fore-paws planted on the carcass. This gave me my chance. I drew a very fine bead between his eye and ear, and pulled trigger. He dropped like a steer when struck with a pole-axe.

If there is a good hiding-place handy it is better to lie in wait at the carcass. One day on the head-waters of the Madison, I found that a bear was coming to an elk I had shot some days before; and I at once determined to ambush the beast when he came back that evening. The carcass lay in the middle of a valley a quarter of a mile broad. The bottom of this valley was covered by an open forest of tall pines; a thick jungle of smaller evergreens marked where the mountains rose on either hand. There were a number of large rocks scattered here and there, one, of very convenient shape, being only some seventy or eighty yards from the carcass. Up this I clambered. It hid me perfectly, and on its top was a carpet of soft pine needles, on which I could lie at my ease.

Hour after hour passed by. A little black woodpecker with a yellow crest ran nimbly up and down the tree trunks for some time and then flitted away with a party of chickadees and nut-hatches. Occasionally a Clarke's crow soared about overhead or clung in any position to the swaying end of a pine branch, chattering and screaming. Flocks of cross-bills, with wavy flight and plaintive calls, flew to a small mineral lick near by, where they scraped the clay with their queer little beaks.

As the westering sun sank out of sight beyond the mountains these sounds of bird-life gradually died away. Under the great pines the evening was still with the silence of primeval desolation. The sense of sadness and loneliness, the melancholy of the wilderness, came over me like a spell. Every slight noise made my pulses throb as I lay motionless on the rock gazing intently into the gathering gloom. I began to fear that it would grow too dark to shoot before the grisly came.

Suddenly and without warning, the great bear stepped out of the bushes and trod across the pine needles with such swift and silent footsteps that its bulk seemed unreal. It was very cautious, continually halting to peer around; and once it stood up on its hind legs and looked long down the valley towards the red west. As it reached the carcass I put a bullet between its shoulders. It rolled over, while the woods resounded with its savage roaring. Immediately it struggled to its feet and staggered off; and fell again to the next shot, squalling and yelling. Twice this was repeated; the brute being one of those bears which greet every wound with a great outcry, and sometimes seem to lose their feet when hit—although they will occasionally fight as savagely as their more silent brethren. In this case the wounds were mortal, and the bear died before reaching the edge of the thicket.

I spent much of the fall of 1889 hunting on the headwaters of the Salmon and Snake in Idaho, and along the Montana boundary line from the Big Hole Basin and the head of the Wisdom River to the neighborhood of Red Rock Pass and to the north and west of Henry's Lake. During the last fortnight my companion was the old mountain man, already mentioned, named Griffeth or Griffin—I cannot tell which, as he was always called either "Hank" or "Griff." He was a crabbedly honest old fellow, and a very skilful hunter; but he was worn out with age and rheumatism, and his temper had failed even faster than his bodily strength. He showed me a greater variety of game that I had ever seen before in so short a time; nor did I ever before or after make so successful a hunt. But he was an exceedingly disagreeable companion on account of his surly, moody ways. I generally had to get up first, to kindle the fire and make ready breakfast, and he was very quarrelsome. Finally, during my absence from camp one day, while not very far from Red Rock pass, he found my whiskey flask, which I kept purely for emergencies, and drank all the contents. When I came back he was quite drunk. This was unbearable, and after some high words I left him, and struck off homeward through the woods on my own account. We had with us four pack and saddle horses; and of these I took a very intelligent and gentle little bronco mare, which possessed the invaluable trait of always staying near camp, even when not hobbled. I was not hampered with much of an outfit, having only my buffalo sleeping-bag, a fur coat, and my washing kit, with a couple of spare pairs of socks and some handkerchiefs. A frying-pan, some salt, flour, baking-powder, a small chunk of salt pork, and a hatchet, made up a light pack, which with the bedding, I fastened across the stock saddle by means of a rope and a spare packing cinch. My cartridges and knife were in my belt; my compass and matches, as always, in my pocket. I walked, while the little mare followed almost like a dog, often without my having to hold the lariat which served as halter.

The country was for the most part fairly open, as I kept near the foot-hills where glades and little prairies broke the pine forest. The trees were of small size. There was no regular trail, but the course was easy to keep, and I had no trouble of any kind save on the second day. That afternoon I was following a stream which at last "canyoned up," that is, sank to the bottom of a canyon-like ravine impassable for a horse. I started up a side valley, intending to cross from its head coulies to those of another valley which would lead in below the canyon.

However, I got enmeshed in the tangle of winding valleys at the foot of the steep mountains, and as dusk was coming on I halted and camped in a little open spot by the side of a small, noisy brook, with crystal water. The place was carpeted with soft, wet, green moss, dotted red with the kinnikinnic berries, and at its edge, under the trees where the ground was dry, I threw down the buffalo bed on the mat of sweet-smelling pine needles. Making camp took but a moment. I opened the pack, tossed the bedding on a smooth spot, knee-haltered the little mare, dragged up a few dry logs, and then strolled off, rifle on shoulder, through the frosty gloaming, to see if I could pick up a grouse for supper.

For half a mile I walked quickly and silently over the pine needles, across a succession of slight ridges separated by narrow, shallow valleys. The forest here was composed of lodge-pole pines, which on the ridges grew close together, with tall slender trunks, while in the valleys the growth was more open. Though the sun was behind the mountains there was yet plenty of light by which to shoot, but it was fading rapidly.

At last, as I was thinking of turning towards camp, I stole up the crest of one of the ridges, and looked over into the valley some sixty yards off. Immediately I caught the loom of some large, dark object; and another glance showed me a big grisly walking slowly off with his head down. He was quartering to me, and I fired into his flank, the bullet, as I afterwards found, ranging forward and piercing one lung. At the shot he uttered a loud, moaning grunt and plunged forward at a heavy gallop, while I raced obliquely down the hill to cut him off. After going a few hundred feet he reached a laurel thicket, some thirty yards broad, and two or three times as long which he did not leave. I ran up to the edge and there halted, not liking to venture into the mass of twisted, close-growing stems and glossy foliage. Moreover, as I halted, I heard him utter a peculiar, savage kind of whine from the heart of the brush. Accordingly, I began to skirt the edge, standing on tiptoe and gazing earnestly to see if I could not catch a glimpse of his hide. When I was at the narrowest part of the thicket, he suddenly left it directly opposite, and then wheeled and stood broadside to me on the hill-side, a little above. He turned his head stiffly towards me; scarlet string of froth hung from his lips; his eyes burned like embers in the gloom.

I held true, aiming behind the shoulder, and my bullet shattered the point or lower end of his heart, taking out a big nick. Instantly the great bear turned with a harsh roar of fury and challenge, blowing the bloody foam from his mouth, so that I saw the gleam of his white fangs; and then he charged straight at me, crashing and bounding through the laurel bushes, so that it was hard to aim. I waited until he came to a fallen tree, raking him as he topped it with a ball, which entered his chest and went through the cavity of his body, but he neither swerved nor flinched, and at the moment I did not know that I had stuck him. He came steadily on, and in another second was almost upon me. I fired for his forehead, but my bullet went low, entering his open mouth, smashing his lower jaw and going into the neck. I leaped to one side almost as I pulled trigger; and through the hanging smoke the first thing I saw was his paw as he made a vicious side blow at me. The rush of his charge carried him past. As he struck he lurched forward, leaving a pool of bright blood where his muzzle hit the ground; but he recovered himself and made two or three jumps onwards, while I hurriedly jammed a couple of cartridges into the magazine, my rifle holding only four, all of which I had fired. Then he tried to pull up, but as he did so his muscles seemed suddenly to give way, his head drooped, and he rolled over and over like a shot rabbit. Each of my first three bullets had inflicted a mortal wound.

It was already twilight, and I merely opened the carcass, and then trotted back to camp. Next morning I returned and with much labor took off the skin. The fur was very fine, the animal being in excellent trim, and unusually bright-colored. Unfortunately, in packing it out I lost the skull, and had to supply its place with one of plaster. The beauty of the trophy, and the memory of the circumstances under which I procured it, make me value it perhaps more highly than any other in my house.

This is the only instance in which I have been regularly charged by a grisly. On the whole, the danger of hunting these great bears has been much exaggerated. At the beginning of the present century, when white hunters first encountered the grisly, he was doubtless an exceedingly savage beast, prone to attack without provocation, and a redoubtable foe to persons armed with the clumsy, small-bore, muzzle-loading rifles of the day. But at present bitter experience has taught him caution. He has been hunted for sport, and hunted for his pelt, and hunted for the bounty, and hunted as a dangerous enemy to stock, until, save in the very wildest districts, he has learned to be more wary than a deer, and to avoid man's presence almost as carefully as the most timid kind of game. Except in rare cases he will not attack of his own accord, and, as a rule, even when wounded his object is escape rather than battle.

Still, when fairly brought to bay, or when moved by a sudden fit of ungovernable anger, the grisly is beyond per-adventure a very dangerous antagonist. The first shot, if taken at a bear a good distance off and previously unwounded and unharried, is not usually fraught with much danger, the startled animal being at the outset bent merely on flight. It is always hazardous, however, to track a wounded and worried grisly into thick cover, and the man who habitually follows and kills this chief of American game in dense timber, never abandoning the bloody trail whithersoever it leads, must show no small degree of skill and hardihood, and must not too closely count the risk to life or limb. Bears differ widely in temper, and occasionally one may be found who will not show fight, no matter how much he is bullied; but, as a rule, a hunter must be cautious in meddling with a wounded animal which has retreated into a dense thicket, and has been once or twice roused; and such a beast, when it does turn, will usually charge again and again, and fight to the last with unconquerable ferocity. The short distance at which the bear can be seen through the underbrush, the fury of his charge, and his tenacity of life make it necessary for the hunter on such occasions to have steady nerves and a fairly quick and accurate aim. It is always well to have two men in following a wounded bear under such conditions. This is not necessary, however, and a good hunter, rather than lose his quarry, will, under ordinary circumstances, follow and attack it no matter how tangled the fastness in which it has sought refuge; but he must act warily and with the utmost caution and resolution, if he wishes to escape a terrible and probably fatal mauling. An experienced hunter is rarely rash, and never heedless; he will not, when alone, follow a wounded bear into a thicket, if by the exercise of patience, skill, and knowledge of the game's habits he can avoid the necessity; but it is idle to talk of the feat as something which ought in no case to be attempted. While danger ought never to be needlessly incurred, it is yet true that the keenest zest in sport comes from its presence, and from the consequent exercise of the qualities necessary to overcome it. The most thrilling moments of an American hunter's life are those in which, with every sense on the alert, and with nerves strung to the highest point, he is following alone into the heart of its forest fastness the fresh and bloody footprints of an angered grisly; and no other triumph of American hunting can compare with the victory to be thus gained.

These big bears will not ordinarily charge from a distance of over a hundred yards; but there are exceptions to this rule. In the fall of 1890 my friend Archibald Rogers was hunting in Wyoming, south of the Yellowstone Park, and killed seven bears. One, an old he, was out on a bare table-land, grubbing for roots, when he was spied. It was early in the afternoon, and the hunters, who were on a high mountain slope, examined him for some time through their powerful glasses before making him out to be a bear. They then stalked up to the edge of the wood which fringed the table-land on one side, but could get no nearer than about three hundred yards, the plains being barren of all cover. After waiting for a couple of hours Rogers risked the shot, in despair of getting nearer, and wounded the bear, though not very seriously. The animal made off, almost broadside to, and Rogers ran forward to intercept it. As soon as it saw him it turned and rushed straight for him, not heeding his second shot, and evidently bent on charging home. Rogers then waited until it was within twenty yards, and brained it with his third bullet.

In fact bears differ individually in courage and ferocity precisely as men do, or as the Spanish bulls, of which it is said that no more than one in twenty is fit to stand the combat of the arena. One grisly can scarcely be bullied into resistance; the next may fight to the end, against any odds, without flinching, or even attack unprovoked. Hence men of limited experience in this sport, generalizing from the actions of the two or three bears each has happened to see or kill, often reach diametrically opposite conclusions as to the fighting temper and capacity of the quarry. Even old hunters—who indeed, as a class, are very narrow-minded and opinionated—often generalize just as rashly as beginners. One will portray all bears as very dangerous; another will speak and act as if he deemed them of no more consequence than so many rabbits. I knew one old hunter who had killed a score without ever seeing one show fight. On the other hand, Dr. James C. Merrill, U.S.A., who has had about as much experience with bears as I have had, informs me that he has been charged with the utmost determination three times. In each case the attack was delivered before the bear was wounded or even shot at, the animal being roused by the approach of the hunters from his day bed, and charging headlong at them from a distance of twenty or thirty paces. All three bears were killed before they could do any damage. There was a very remarkable incident connected with the killing of one of them. It occurred in the northern spurs of the Bighorn range. Dr. Merrill, in company with an old hunter, had climbed down into a deep narrow canyon. The bottom was threaded with well-beaten elk trails. While following one of these the two men turned a corner of the canyon and were instantly charged by an old she-grisly, so close that it was only by good luck that one of the hurried shots disabled her and caused her to tumble over a cut bank where she was easily finished. They found that she had been lying directly across the game trail, on a smooth well beaten patch of bare earth, which looked as if it had been dug up, refilled, and trampled down. Looking curiously at this patch they saw a bit of hide only partially covered at one end; digging down they found the body of a well grown grisly cub. Its skull had been crushed, and the brains licked out, and there were signs of other injuries. The hunters pondered long over this strange discovery, and hazarded many guesses as to its meaning. At last they decided that probably the cub had been killed, and its brains eaten out, either by some old male-grisly or by a cougar, that the mother had returned and driven away the murderer, and that she had then buried the body and lain above it, waiting to wreak her vengeance on the first passer-by.

Old Tazewell Woody, during his thirty years' life as a hunter in the Rockies and on the great plains, killed very many grislies. He always exercised much caution in dealing with them; and, as it happened, he was by some suitable tree in almost every case when he was charged. He would accordingly climb the tree (a practice of which I do not approve however); and the bear would look up at him and pass on without stopping. Once, when he was hunting in the mountains with a companion, the latter, who was down in a valley, while Woody was on the hill-side, shot at a bear. The first thing Woody knew the wounded grisly, running up-hill, was almost on him from behind. As he turned it seized his rifle in its jaws. He wrenched the rifle round, while the bear still gripped it, and pulled trigger, sending a bullet into its shoulder; whereupon it struck him with its paw, and knocked him over the rocks. By good luck he fell in a snow bank and was not hurt in the least. Meanwhile the bear went on and they never got it.

Once he had an experience with a bear which showed a very curious mixture of rashness and cowardice. He and a companion were camped in a little tepee or wigwam, with a bright fire in front of it, lighting up the night. There was an inch of snow on the ground. Just after they went to bed a grisly came close to camp. Their dog rushed out and they could hear it bark round in the darkness for nearly an hour; then the bear drove it off and came right into camp. It went close to the fire, picking up the scraps of meat and bread, pulled a haunch of venison down from a tree, and passed and repassed in front of the tepee, paying no heed whatever to the two men, who crouched in the doorway talking to one another. Once it passed so close that Woody could almost have touched it. Finally his companion fired into it, and off it ran, badly wounded, without an attempt at retaliation. Next morning they followed its tracks in the snow, and found it a quarter of a mile away. It was near a pine and had buried itself under the loose earth, pine needles, and snow; Woody's companion almost walked over it, and putting his rifle to its ear blew out its brains.

In all his experience Woody had personally seen but four men who were badly mauled by bears. Three of these were merely wounded. One was bitten terribly in the back. Another had an arm partially chewed off. The third was a man named George Dow, and the accident happened to him on the Yellowstone, about the year 1878. He was with a pack animal at the time, leading it on a trail through a wood. Seeing a big she-bear with cubs he yelled at her; whereat she ran away, but only to cache her cubs, and in a minute, having hidden them, came racing back at him. His pack animal being slow he started to climb a tree; but before he could get far enough up she caught him, almost biting a piece out of the calf of his leg, pulled him down, bit and cuffed him two or three times, and then went on her way.

The only time Woody ever saw a man killed by a bear was once when he had given a touch of variety to his life by shipping on a New Bedford whaler which had touched at one of the Puget Sound ports. The whaler went up to a part of Alaska where bears were very plentiful and bold. One day a couple of boats' crews landed; and the men, who were armed only with an occasional harpoon or lance, scattered over the beach, one of them a Frenchman, wading into the water after shell-fish. Suddenly a bear emerged from some bushes and charged among the astonished sailors, who scattered in every direction; but the bear, said Woody, "just had it in for that Frenchman," and went straight at him. Shrieking with terror he retreated up to his neck in the water, but the bear plunged in after him, caught him, and disembowelled him. One of the Yankee mates then fired a bomb lance into the bear's hips, and the savage beast hobbled off into the dense cover of the low scrub, where the enraged sailor folk were unable to get at it.

The truth is that while the grisly generally avoids a battle if possible, and often acts with great cowardice, it is never safe to take liberties with him; he usually fights desperately and dies hard when wounded and cornered, and exceptional individuals take the aggressive on small provocation.

During the years I lived on the frontier I came in contact with many persons who had been severely mauled or even crippled for life by grislies; and a number of cases where they killed men outright were also brought under my ken. Generally these accidents, as was natural, occurred to hunters who had roused or wounded the game.

A fighting bear sometimes uses his claws and sometimes his teeth. I have never known one to attempt to kill an antagonist by hugging, in spite of the popular belief to this effect; though he will sometimes draw an enemy towards him with his paws the better to reach him with his teeth, and to hold him so that he cannot escape from the biting. Nor does the bear often advance on his hind legs to the attack; though, if the man has come close to him in thick underbrush, or has stumbled on him in his lair unawares, he will often rise up in this fashion and strike a single blow. He will also rise in clinching with a man on horseback. In 1882 a mounted Indian was killed in this manner on one of the river bottoms some miles below where my ranch house now stands, not far from the function of the Beaver and Little Missouri. The bear had been hunted into a thicket by a band of Indians, in whose company my informant, a white squaw-man, with whom I afterward did some trading, was travelling. One of them in the excitement of the pursuit rode across the end of the thicket; as he did so the great beast sprang at him with wonderful quickness, rising on its hind legs, and knocking over the horse and rider with a single sweep of his terrible fore-paws. It then turned on the fallen man and tore him open, and though the other Indians came promptly to his rescue and slew his assailant, they were not in time to save their comrade's life.

A bear is apt to rely mainly on his teeth or claws according to whether his efforts are directed primarily to killing his foe or to making good his own escape. In the latter event he trusts chiefly to his claws. If cornered, he of course makes a rush for freedom, and in that case he downs any man who is in his way with a sweep of his great paw, but passes on without stopping to bite him. If while sleeping or resting in thick brush some one suddenly stumbles on him close up he pursues the same course, less from anger than from fear, being surprised and startled. Moreover, if attacked at close quarters by men and dogs he strikes right and left in defence.

Sometimes what is called a charge is rather an effort to get away. In localities where he has been hunted, a bear, like every other kind of game, is always on the look-out for an attack, and is prepared at any moment for immediate flight. He seems ever to have in his mind, whether feeding, sunning himself, or merely roaming around, the direction—usually towards the thickest cover or most broken ground—in which he intends to run if molested. When shot at he instantly starts towards this place; or he may be so confused that he simply runs he knows not whither; and in either event he may take a line that leads almost directly to or by the hunter, although he had at first no thought of charging. In such a case he usually strikes a single knock-down blow and gallops on without halting, though that one blow may have taken life. If the claws are long and fairly sharp (as in early spring, or even in the fall, if the animal has been working over soft ground) they add immensely to the effect of the blow, for they cut like blunt axes. Often, however, late in the season, and if the ground has been dry and hard, or rocky, the claws are worn down nearly to the quick, and the blow is then given mainly with the under side of the paw; although even under this disadvantage a thumb from a big bear will down a horse or smash in a man's breast. The hunter Hofer once lost a horse in this manner. He shot at and wounded a bear which rushed off, as ill luck would have it, past the place where his horse was picketed; probably more in fright than in anger it struck the poor beast a blow which, in the end, proved mortal.

If a bear means mischief and charges not to escape but to do damage, its aim is to grapple with or throw down its foe and bite him to death. The charge is made at a gallop, the animal sometimes coming on silently, with the mouth shut, and sometimes with the jaws open, the lips drawn back and teeth showing, uttering at the same time a succession of roars or of savage rasping snarls. Certain bears charge without any bluster and perfectly straight; while others first threaten and bully, and even when charging stop to growl, shake the head, and bite at a bush or knock holes in the ground with their fore-paws. Again, some of them charge home with a ferocious resolution which their extreme tenacity of life renders especially dangerous; while others can be turned or driven back even by a shot which is not mortal. They show the same variability in their behavior when wounded. Often a big bear, especially if charging, will receive a bullet in perfect silence, without flinching or seeming to pay any heed to it; while another will cry out and tumble about, and if charging, even though it may not abandon the attack, will pause for a moment to whine or bite at the wound.

Sometimes a single bite causes death. One of the most successful bear hunters I ever knew, an old fellow whose real name I never heard as he was always called Old Ike, was killed in this way in the spring or early summer of 1886 on one of the head-waters of the Salmon. He was a very good shot, had killed nearly a hundred bears with the rifle, and, although often charged, had never met with any accident, so that he had grown somewhat careless. On the day in question he had met a couple of mining prospectors and was travelling with them, when a grisly crossed his path. The old hunter immediately ran after it, rapidly gaining, as the bear did not hurry when it saw itself pursued, but slouched slowly forwards, occasionally turning its head to grin and growl. It soon went into a dense grove of young spruce, and as the hunter reached the edge it charged fiercely out. He fired one hasty shot, evidently wounding the animal, but not seriously enough to stop or cripple it; and as his two companions ran forward they saw the bear seize him with is wide-spread jaws, forcing him to the ground. They shouted and fired, and the beast abandoned the fallen man on the instant and sullenly retreated into the spruce thicket, whither they dared not follow it. Their friend was at his last gasp; for the whole side of the chest had been crushed in by the one bite, the lungs showing between the rent ribs.

Very often, however, a bear does not kill a man by one bite, but after throwing him lies on him, biting him to death. Usually, if no assistance is at hand, such a man is doomed; although if he pretends to be dead, and has the nerve to lie quiet under very rough treatment, it is just possible that the bear may leave him alive, perhaps after half burying what it believes to be the body. In a very few exceptional instances men of extraordinary prowess with the knife have succeeded in beating off a bear, and even in mortally wounding it, but in most cases a single-handed struggle, at close quarters, with a grisly bent on mischief, means death.

Occasionally the bear, although vicious, is also frightened, and passes on after giving one or two bites; and frequently a man who is knocked down is rescued by his friends before he is killed, the big beast mayhap using his weapons with clumsiness. So a bear may kill a foe with a single blow of its mighty fore-arm, either crushing in the head or chest by sheer force of sinew, or else tearing open the body with its formidable claws; and so on the other hand he may, and often does, merely disfigure or maim the foe by a hurried stroke. Hence it is common to see men who have escaped the clutches of a grisly, but only at the cost of features marred beyond recognition, or a body rendered almost helpless for life. Almost every old resident of western Montana or northern Idaho has known two or three unfortunates who have suffered in this manner. I have myself met one such man in Helena, and another in Missoula; both were living at least as late as 1889, the date at which I last saw them. One had been partially scalped by a bear's teeth; the animal was very old and so the fangs did not enter the skull. The other had been bitten across the face, and the wounds never entirely healed, so that his disfigured visage was hideous to behold.

Most of these accidents occur in following a wounded or worried bear into thick cover; and under such circumstances an animal apparently hopelessly disabled, or in the death throes, may with a last effort kill one or more of its assailants. In 1874 my wife's uncle, Captain Alexander Moore, U.S.A., and my friend Captain Bates, with some men of the 2d and 3d Cavalry, were scouting in Wyoming, near the Freezeout Mountains. One morning they roused a bear in the open prairie and followed it at full speed as it ran towards a small creek. At one spot in the creek beavers had built a dam, and as usual in such places there was a thick growth of bushes and willow saplings. Just as the bear reached the edge of this little jungle it was struck by several balls, both of its fore-legs being broken. Nevertheless, it managed to shove itself forward on its hind-legs, and partly rolled, partly pushed itself into the thicket, the bushes though low being so dense that its body was at once completely hidden. The thicket was a mere patch of brush, not twenty yards across in any direction. The leading troopers reached the edge almost as the bear tumbled in. One of them, a tall and powerful man named Miller, instantly dismounted and prepared to force his way in among the dwarfed willows, which were but breast-high. Among the men who had ridden up were Moore and Bates, and also the two famous scouts, Buffalo Bill—long a companion of Captain Moore,—and California Joe, Custer's faithful follower. California Joe had spent almost all his life on the plains and in the mountains, as a hunter and Indian fighter; and when he saw the trooper about to rush into the thicket he called out to him not to do so, warning him of the danger. But the man was a very reckless fellow and he answered by jeering at the old hunter for his over-caution in being afraid of a crippled bear. California Joe made no further effort to dissuade him, remarking quietly: "Very well, sonny, go in; it's your own affair." Miller then leaped off the bank on which they stood and strode into the thicket, holding his rifle at the port. Hardly had he taken three steps when the bear rose in front of him, roaring with rage and pain. It was so close that the man had no chance to fire. Its fore-arms hung useless and as it reared unsteadily on its hind-legs, lunging forward at him, he seized it by the ears and strove the hold it back. His strength was very great, and he actually kept the huge head from his face and braced himself so that he was not overthrown; but the bear twisted its muzzle from side to side, biting and tearing the man's arms and shoulders. Another soldier jumping down slew the beast with a single bullet, and rescued his comrade; but though alive he was too badly hurt to recover and died after reaching the hospital. Buffalo Bill was given the bear-skin, and I believe has it now.

The instances in which hunters who have rashly followed gris-lies into thick cover have been killed or severely mauled might be multiplied indefinitely. I have myself known of eight cases in which men have met their deaths in this manner.

It occasionally happens that a cunning old grisly will lie so close that the hunter almost steps on him; and he then rises sud-denly with a loud, coughing growl and strikes down or seizes the man before the latter can fire off his rifle. More rarely a bear which is both vicious and crafty deliberately permits the hunter to ap-proach fairly near to, or perhaps pass by, its hiding-place, and then suddenly charges him with such rapidity that he has barely time for the most hurried shot. The danger in such a case is of course great.

Ordinarily, however, even in the brush, the bear's object is to slink away, not to fight, and very many are killed even under the most unfavorable circumstances without accident. If an un-wounded bear thinks itself unobserved it is not apt to attack; and in thick cover it is really astonishing to see how one of these large animals can hide, and how closely it will lie when there is danger. About twelve miles below my ranch there are some large river bot-toms and creek bottoms covered with a matted mass of cotton-wood, box-alders, bullberry bushes, rose-bushes, ash, wild plums, and other bushes. These bottoms have harbored bears ever since I first saw them; but though, often in company with a large party, I have repeatedly beaten through them, and though we must at times have been very near indeed to the game, we never so much as heard it run.

When bears are shot, as they usually must be, in open timber or on the bare mountain, the risk is very much less. Hundreds may thus be killed with comparatively little danger; yet even under these circumstances they will often charge, and sometimes make their charge good. The spice of danger, especially to a man armed with a good repeating rifle, is only enough to add zest to the chase, and the chief triumph is in outwitting the wary quarry and getting within range. Ordinarily the only excitement is in the stalk, the bear doing nothing more than keep a keen lookout and manifest the utmost anxiety to get away. As is but natural, accidents occasionally occur; yet they are usually due more to some failure in man or weapon than to the prowess of the bear. A good hunter whom I once knew, at a time when he was living in Butte, received fatal injuries from a bear he attacked in open woodland. The beast charged after the first shot, but slackened its pace on coming almost up to the man. The latter's gun jammed, and as he was endeavoring to work it he kept stepping slowly back, facing the bear which followed a few yards distant, snarling and threatening. Unfortunately while thus walking backwards the man struck a dead log and fell over it, whereupon the beast instantly sprang on him and mortally wounded him before help arrived.

On rare occasions men who are not at the time hunting it fall victims to the grisly. This is usually because they stumble on it unawares and the animal attacks them more in fear than in anger. One such case, resulting fatally, occurred near my own ranch. The man walked almost over a bear while crossing a little point of brush, in a bend of the river, and was brained with a single blow of the paw. In another instance which came to my knowledge the man escaped with a shaking up, and without even a fright. His name was Perkins, and he was out gathering huckleberries in the woods on a mountain side near Pend'Oreille Lake. Suddenly he was sent flying head over heels, by a blow which completely knocked the

65

breath out of his body; and so instantaneous was the whole affair that all he could ever recollect about it was getting a vague glimpse of the bear just as he was bowled over. When he came to he found himself lying some distance down the hill-side, much shaken, and without his berry pail, which had rolled a hundred yards below him, but not otherwise the worse for his misadventure; while the footprints showed that the bear, after delivering the single hurried stroke at the unwitting disturber of its day-dreams, had run off up-hill as fast as it was able.

A she-bear with cubs is a proverbially dangerous beast; yet even under such conditions different grislies act in directly opposite ways. Some she-grislies, when their cubs are young, but are able to follow them about, seem always worked up to the highest pitch of anxious and jealous rage, so that they are likely to attack unprovoked any intruder or even passer-by. Others when threatened by the hunter leave their cubs to their fate without a visible qualm of any kind, and seem to think only of their own safety.

In 1882 Mr. Caspar W. Whitney, now of New York, met with a very singular adventure with a she-bear and cub. He was in Harvard when I was, but left it and, like a good many other Harvard men of that time, took to cow-punching in the West. He went on a ranch in Rio Arriba County, New Mexico, and was a keen hunter, especially fond of the chase of cougar, bear, and elk. One day while riding a stony mountain trail he saw a little grisly cub watching him from the chaparral above, and he dismounted to try to capture it; his rifle was a 40–90 Sharp's. Just as he neared the cub, he heard a growl and caught a glimpse of the old she, and he at once turned up-hill, and stood under some tall, quaking aspens. From this spot he fired at and wounded the she, then seventy yards off; and she charged furiously. He hit her again, but as she kept coming like a thunderbolt he climbed hastily up the aspen, dragging his gun with him, as it had a strap. When the bear reached the foot of the aspen she reared, and bit and clawed the slender trunk, shaking it for moment, and he shot her through the eye. Off she sprang for a few yards, and then spun round a dozen times, as if dazed or partially stunned; for the bullet had not touched the brain. Then the vindictive and resolute beast came back to the tree and again reared up against it; this time to receive a bullet that dropped her lifeless. Mr. Whitney then climbed down and walked to where the cub had been sitting as a looker-on. The little animal did not move until he reached out his hand; when it suddenly struck at him like an angry cat, dove into the bushes, and was seen no more.

In the summer of 1888 an old-time trapper, named Charley Norton, while on Loon Creek, of the middle fork of the Salmon, meddled with a she and her cubs. She ran at him and with one blow of her paw almost knocked off his lower jaw; yet he recovered, and was alive when I last heard of him.

Yet the very next spring the cowboys with my own wagon on the Little Missouri round-up killed a mother bear which made but little more fight than a coyote. She had two cubs, and was surprised in the early morning on the prairie far from cover. There were eight or ten cowboys together at the time, just starting off on a long circle, and of course they all got down their ropes in a second, and putting spurs to their fiery little horses started toward the bears at a run, shouting and swinging their loops round their heads. For a moment the old she tried to bluster and made a half-hearted threat of charging; but her courage failed before the rapid onslaught of her yelling, rope-swinging assailants; and she took to her heels and galloped off, leaving the cubs to shift for themselves. The cowboys were close behind, however, and after a half a mile's run she bolted into a shallow cave or hole in the side of a butte, where she stayed cowering and growling, until one of the men leaped off his horse, ran up to the edge of the hole, and killed her with a single bullet from his revolver, fired so close that the powder burned her hair. The unfortunate cubs were roped, and then so dragged about that they were speedily killed instead of being brought alive to camp, as ought to have been done.

In the cases mentioned above the grisly attacked only after having been itself assailed, or because it feared an assault, for itself or for its young. In the old days, however, it may almost be said that a grisly was more apt to attack than to flee. Lewis and Clarke and the early explorers who immediately succeeded them, as well as the first hunters and trappers, the "Rocky Mountain Men" of the early decades of the present century, were repeatedly assailed in this manner; and not a few of the bear hunters of that period found that it was unnecessary to take much trouble about approaching their quarry, as the grisly was usually prompt to accept the challenge and to advance of its own accord, as soon as it discovered the foe. All this is changed now. Yet even at the present day an occasional vicious old bear may be found, in some far off and little trod fastness, which still keeps up the former habit of its kind. All old hunters have tales of this sort to relate, the prowess, cunning, strength, and ferocity of the grisly being favorite topics for campfire talk throughout the Rockies; but in most cases it is not safe to accept these stories without careful sifting.

Still, it is just as unsafe to reject them all. One of my own cowboys was once attacked by a grisly, seemingly in pure wantonness. He was riding up a creek bottom, and had just passed a clump of rose and bullberry bushes when his horse gave such a leap as almost to unseat him, and then darted madly forward. Turning round in the saddle to his utter astonishment he saw a large bear galloping after him, at the horse's heels. For a few jumps the race was close, then the horse drew away and the bear wheeled and went into a thicket of wild plums. The amazed and indignant cowboy, as soon as he could rein in his steed, drew his revolver and rode back to and around the thicket, endeavoring to provoke his late pursuer to come out and try conclusions on more equal terms; but prudent Ephraim had apparently repented of his freak of ferocious bravado, and declined to leave the secure shelter of the jungle.

Other attacks are of a much more explicable nature. Mr. Huffman, the photographer, of Miles City, informed me that once when butchering some slaughtered elk he was charged twice by a she-bear and two well-grown cubs. This was a piece of sheer bullying, undertaken solely with the purpose of driving away the man and feasting on the carcasses; for in each charge the three bears, after advancing with much bluster, roaring, and growling, halted just before coming to close quarters. In another instance a gentleman I once knew, a Mr. S. Carr, was charged by a grisly from mere ill temper at being disturbed at meal-time. The man was riding up a valley; and the bear was at an elk carcass, near a clump of firs. As soon as it became aware of the approach of the horseman, while he was yet over a hundred yards distant, it jumped on the carcass, looked at him a moment, and then ran straight for him. There was no particular reason why it should have charged, for it was fat and in good trim, though when killed its head showed scars made by the teeth of rival grislies. Apparently it had been living so well, principally on flesh, that it had become quarrelsome; and perhaps its not over sweet disposition had been soured by combats with others of its own kind. In yet another case, a grisly charged with even less excuse. An old trapper, from whom I occasionally bought fur, was toiling up a mountain pass when he spied a big bear sitting on his haunches on the hill-side above. The trapper shouted and waved his cap; whereupon, to his amazement, the bear uttered a loud "wough" and charged straight down on him—only to fall a victim to misplaced boldness.

I am even inclined to think that there have been wholly exceptional occasions when a grisly has attacked a man with the deliberate purpose of making a meal of him; when, in other words, it has started on the career of a man-eater. At least, on any other theory I find it difficult to account for an attack which once came to my knowledge. I was at Sand Point, on Pend'Oreille Lake, and met some French and Méti trappers, then in town with their bales of beaver, otter, and sable. One of them, who gave his name as Baptiste Lamoche, had his head twisted over to one side, the result of the bite of a bear. When the accident occurred he was out

69

on a trapping trip with two companions. They had pitched camp right on the shore of a cove in a little lake, and his comrades were off fishing in a dugout or pirogue. He himself was sitting near the shore, by a little lean-to, watching some beaver meat which was sizzling over the dying embers. Suddenly, and without warning, a great bear, which had crept silently up beneath the shadows of the tall evergreens, rushed at him, with a guttural roar, and seized him before he could rise to his feet. It grasped him with its jaws at the junction of the neck and shoulder, making the teeth meet through bone, sinew, and muscle; and turning, racked off towards the forest, dragging with it the helpless and paralyzed victim. Luckily the two men in the canoe had just paddled round the point, in sight of, and close to, camp. The man in the bow, seeing the plight of their comrade, seized his rifle and fired at the bear. The bullet went through the beast's lungs, and it forthwith dropped its prey, and running off some two hundred yards, lay down on its side and died. The rescued man recovered full health and strength, but never again carried his head straight.

Old hunters and mountain-men tell many stories, not only of malicious grislies thus attacking men in camp, but also of their even dogging the footsteps of some solitary hunter and killing him when the favorable opportunity occurs. Most of these tales are mere fables; but it is possible that in altogether exceptional instances they rest on a foundation of fact. One old hunter whom I knew told me such a story. He was a truthful old fellow, and there was no doubt that he believed what he said, and that his companion was actually killed by a bear; but it is probable that he was mistaken in reading the signs of his comrade's fate, and that the latter was not dogged by the bear at all, but stumbled on him and was slain in the surprise of the moment.

At any rate, cases of wanton assaults by grislies are altogether out of the common. The ordinary hunter may live out his whole life in the wilderness and never know aught of a bear attacking a man unprovoked; and the great majority of bears are shot under circumstances of no special excitement, as they either make no fight at all, or, if they do fight, are killed before there is any risk of their doing damage. If surprised on the plains, at some distance from timber or from badly broken ground, it is no uncommon feat for a single horseman to kill them with a revolver. Twice of late years it has been performed in the neighborhood of my ranch. In both instances the men were not hunters out after game, but simply cowboys, riding over the range in the early morning in pursuance of their ordinary duties among the cattle. I knew both men and have worked with them on the round-up. Like most cowboys they carried 44-calibre Colt revolvers, and were accustomed to and fairly expert in their use, and they were mounted on ordinary cow-ponies—quick, wiry, plucky little beasts. In one case the bear was seen from quite a distance, lounging across a broad table-land. The cowboy, by taking advantage of a winding and rather shallow coulie, got quite close to him. He then scrambled out of the coulie, put spurs to his pony, and raced up to within fifty yards of the astonished bear ere the latter quite understood what it was that was running at him through the gray dawn. He made no attempt at fight, but ran at top speed towards a clump of brush not far off at the head of a creek. Before he could reach it, however, the galloping horseman was alongside, and fired three shots into his broad back. He did not turn, but ran on into the bushes and then fell over and died.

In the other case the cowboy, a Texan, was mounted on a good cutting pony, a spirited, handy, agile little animal, but excitable, and with a habit of dancing, which rendered it difficult to shoot from its back. The man was with the round-up wagon, and had been sent off by himself to make a circle through some low, barren buttes, where it was not thought more than a few head of stock would be found. On rounding the corner of a small washout he almost ran over a bear which was feeding on the carcass of a steer that had died in an alkali hole. After a moment of stunned surprise the bear hurled himself at the intruder with furious impetuosity;

while the cowboy, wheeling his horse on its haunches and dashing in the spurs, carried it just clear of his assailant's headlong rush. After a few springs he reined in and once more wheeled half round, having drawn his revolver, only to find the bear again charging and almost on him. This time he fired into it, near the joining of the neck and shoulder, the bullet going downwards into the chest hollow; and again by a quick dash to one side he just avoided the rush of the beast and the sweep of its mighty fore-paw. The beast then halted for a minute, and he rode close by it at a run, firing a couple of shots, which brought on another resolute charge. The ground was somewhat rugged and broken, but his pony was as quick on its feet as a cat, and never stumbled, even when going at full speed to avoid the bear's first mad rushes. It speedily became so excited, however, as to render it almost impossible for the rider to take aim. Sometimes he would come up close to the bear and wait for it to charge, which it would do, first at a trot, or rather rack, and then at a lumbering but swift gallop; and he would fire one or two shots before being forced to run. At other times, if the bear stood still in a good place, he would run by it, firing as he rode. He spent many cartridges, and though most of them were wasted, occasionally a bullet went home. The bear fought with the most savage courage, champing its bloody jaws, roaring with rage, and looking the very incarnation of evil fury. For some minutes it made no effort to flee, either charging or standing at bay. Then it began to move slowly towards a patch of ash and wild plums in the head of a coulie, some distance off. Its pursuer rode after it, and when close enough would push by it and fire, while the bear would spin quickly round and charge as fiercely as ever, though evidently beginning to grow weak. At last, when still a couple of hundred yards from cover the man found he had used up all his cartridges, and then merely followed at a safe distance. The bear no longer paid heed to him, but walked slowly forwards, swaying its great head from side to side, while the blood streamed from between its half-opened jaws. On reaching the cover he could tell by the waving of the bushes that it walked to the middle and then halted. A few minutes afterwards some of the other cowboys rode up, having been attracted by the incessant firing. They surrounded the thicket, firing and throwing stones into the bushes. Finally, as nothing moved, they ventured in and found the indomitable grisly warrior lying dead.

Cowboys delight in nothing so much as the chance to show their skill as riders and ropers; and they always try to ride down and rope any wild animal they come across in favorable ground and close enough up. If a party of them meets a bear in the open they have great fun; and the struggle between the shouting, galloping rough-riders and their shaggy quarry is full of wild excitement and not unaccompanied by danger. The bear often throws the noose from his head so rapidly that it is a difficult matter to catch him; and his frequent charges scatter his tormentors in every direction while the horses become wild with fright over the roaring, bristling beast—for horses seem to dread a bear more than any other animal. If the bear cannot reach cover, however, his fate is sealed. Sooner or later, the noose tights over one leg, or perchance over the neck and fore-paw, and as the rope straightens with a "pluck," the horse braces itself desperately and the bear tumbles over. Whether he regains his feet or not the cowboy keeps the rope taut; soon another noose tightens over a leg, and the bear is speedily rendered helpless.

I have known of these feats being performed several times in northern Wyoming, although never in the immediate neighborhood of my ranch. Mr. Archibald Rogers' cowhands have in this manner caught several bears, on or near his ranch on the Gray Bull, which flows into the Bighorn; and those of Mr. G. B. Grinnell have also occasionally done so. Any set of moderately good ropers and riders, who are accustomed to back one another up and act together, can accomplish the feat if they have smooth ground and plenty of room. It is, however, indeed a feat of skill and daring for a single man; and yet I have known of more than one instance in which it has been accomplished by some reckless knight of the rope and the saddle. One such occurred in 1887 on the Flathead Reservation, the hero being a half-breed; and another in 1890 at the mouth of the Bighorn, where a cowboy roped, bound, and killed a large bear single-handed.

My friend General "Red" Jackson, of Bellemeade, in the pleasant mid-county of Tennessee, once did a feat which casts into the shade even the feats of the men of the lariat. General Jackson, who afterwards became one of the ablest and most renowned of the Confederate cavalry leaders, was at the time a young officer in the Mounted Rifle Regiment, now known as the 3d University States Cavalry. It was some years before the Civil War, and the regiment was on duty in the southwest, then the debatable land of Comanche and Apache. While on a scout after hostile Indians, the troops in their march roused a large grisly which sped off across the plain in front of them. Strict orders had been issued against firing at game, because of the nearness of the Indians. Young Jackson was a man of great strength, a keen swordsman, who always kept the finest edge on his blade, and he was on a swift and mettled Kentucky horse, which luckily had but one eye. Riding at full speed he soon overtook the quarry. As the horse hoofs sounded nearer, the grim bear ceased its flight, and whirling round stood at bay, raising itself on its hind-legs and threatening its pursuer with bared fangs and spread claws. Carefully riding his horse so that its blind side should be towards the monster, the cavalryman swept by at a run, handling his steed with such daring skill that he just cleared the blow of the dreaded fore-paw, while with one mighty sabre stroke he cleft the bear's skull, slaying the grinning beast as it stood upright.

The Deer of the River Bottoms
(From *Hunting Trips of a Ranchman*)

Of all the large game of the United States, the white-tail deer is the best known and the most widely distributed. Taking the Union as a whole, fully ten men will be found who have killed white-tail for one who has killed any other kind of large game. And it is the only ruminant animal which is able to live on in the land even when it has been pretty thickly settled. There is hardly a State wherein it does not still exist, at least in some out-of-the-way corner; and long after the elk and the buffalo have passed away, and when the big-horn and prong-horn have become rare indeed, the white-tail deer will still be common in certain parts of the country.

When, less than five years ago, cattle were first driven on to the northern plains, the white-tail were the least plentiful and the least sought after of all the large game; but they have held their own as none of the others have begun to do, and are already in certain lo-calities more common than any other kind, and indeed in many places are more common than all other kinds put together. The

75

ranchmen along the Powder River, for instance, now have to content themselves with white-tail venison unless they make long trips back among the hills. The same is rapidly getting to be true of the Little Missouri. This is partly because the skin and meat hunters find the chase of this deer to be the most tedious and least remunerative species of hunting, and therefore only turn their attention to it when there is nothing else left to hunt, and partly because the sheep and cattle and the herdsmen who follow them are less likely to trespass on their grounds than on the grounds of other game. The white-tail is the deer of the river bottoms and the large creeks, whose beds contain plenty of brush and timber running down into them. It prefers the densest cover, in which it lies hid all day, and it is especially fond of wet, swampy places, where a horse runs the risk of being engulfed. Thus it is very rarely jumped by accident, and when the cattle stray into its haunts, which is but seldom, the cowboys are not apt to follow them. Besides, unlike most other game, it has no aversion to the presence of cattle, and in the morning and evening will come out and feed freely among them.

This last habit was the cause of our getting a fine buck a few days before last Christmas. The weather was bitterly cold, the spirit in the thermometer sometimes going down at night to 50° below zero and never for over a fortnight betting above −10° (Fahrenheit). Snow covered the ground, to the depth, however, of but a few inches, for in the cattle country the snowfall is always light. When the cold is so great it is far from pleasant to be out-of-doors. Still a certain amount of riding about among the cattle and ponies had to be done, and almost every day was spent by at least one of us in the saddle. We wore the heaviest kind of all-wool under-clothing, with flannels, lined boots, and great fur coats, caps, and gauntlets or mittens, but yet after reach ride one or the other of us would be almost sure to come in with a touch of the frost somewhere about him. On one ride I froze my nose and one cheek, and each of the men froze his ears, fingers, or toes at least once during the fortnight. This generally happened while riding over a plain or plateau with a strong wind blowing in our faces. When the wind was on our backs it was not bad fun to gallop along through the white weather, but when we had to face it, it cut through us like a keen knife. The ponies did not seem to mind the cold much, but the cattle were very uncomfortable, standing humped up in the bushes except for an hour or two at mid-day when they ventured out to feed; some of the young stock which were wintering on the range for the first time died from the exposure. A very weak animal we would bring into the cow-shed and feed with hay; but this was only done in cases of the direst necessity, as such an animal has then to be fed for the rest of the winter, and the quantity of hay is limited. In the Bad Lands proper, cattle do not wander far, the deep ravines affording them a refuge from the bitter icy blasts of the winter gales; but if by any accident caught out on the open prairie in a blizzard, a herd will drift before it for maybe more than a hundred miles, until it finds a shelter capable of holding it. For this reason it is best to keep more or less of a look-out over all the bunches of beasts, riding about among them every few days, and turning back any herd that begins to struggle toward the open plains; though in winter, when weak and emaciated, the cattle must be disturbed and driven as little as possible, or the loss among them will be fearful.

One afternoon, while most of us were away from the ranch-house, one of the cowboys, riding in from his day's outing over the range, brought word that he had seen two white-tail deer, a buck and a doe, feeding with some cattle on the side of a hill across the river, and not much more than half a mile from the house. There was about an hour of daylight left, and one of the foremen, a tall, fine-looking fellow named Ferris, the best rider on the ranch but not an unusually good shot, started out at once after the deer; but in the late fall and early winter we generally kill a good deal of game, as it then keeps well and serves as a food supply through the cold months; after January we hunt as little as possible. Ferris found the deer easily enough, but they started before he could get a standing shot at them, and when he fired as they ran, he only broke one of the buck's hind legs, just above the ankle. He followed it in the snow for several miles across the river and down near the house to the end of the bottom, and then back toward the house. The buck was a cunning old beast, keeping in the densest cover, and often doubling back on his trail and sneaking off to one side as his pursuer passed by. Finally it grew too dark to see the tracks any longer, and Ferris came home.

Next morning early we went out to where he had left the trail, feeling very sure from his description of the place (which was less than a mile from the house) that we would get the buck; for when he had abandoned the pursuit the deer was in a copse of bushes and young trees some hundreds of yards across, and in this it had doubtless spent the night, for it was extremely unlikely that, wounded and tired as it was, it would go any distance after finding that it was no longer pursued.

When we got to the thicket we first made a circuit round it to see if the wounded animal had broken cover, but though there were fresh deer tracks leading both in and out of it, none of them were made by a cripple; so we knew he was still within. It would seem to be a very easy task to track up and kill a broken-legged buck in light snow; but we had to go very cautiously, for though with only three legs he could still run a good deal faster than either of us on two, and we were anxious not to alarm him and give him a good start. Then there were several well-beaten cattle trails through the thicket, and in addition to that one or two other deer had been walking to and fro within it; so that it was hard work to follow the tracks. After working some little time we hit on the right trail, finding where the buck had turned into the thickest growth. While Ferris followed carefully in on the tracks, I stationed myself farther on toward the outside, knowing that the buck would in all likelihood start up wind. In a minute or two Ferris came on the bed where he had passed the night, and which he had evidently just left; a shout informed me that the game was on foot, and immediately afterward the cracking and snapping of the branches were heard as the deer rushed through them. I ran as rapidly and quietly as possible toward the place where the sounds seemed to indicate that he would break cover, stopping under a small tree. A minute afterward he appeared, some thirty yards off on the edge of the thicket, and halted for a second to look round before going into the open. Only his head and antlers were visible above the bushes which hid from view the rest of his body. He turned his head sharply toward me as I raised the rifle, and the bullet went fairly into his throat, just under the jaw, breaking his neck, and bringing him down in his tracks with hardly a kick. He was a fine buck of eight points, unusually fat, considering that the rutting season was just over. We dressed it at once, and, as the house was so near, determined we would drag it there over the snow ourselves, without going back for a horse. Each took an antler, and the body slipped along very easily; but so intense was the cold that we had to keep shifting sides all the time, the hand which grasped the horn becoming numb almost immediately.

White-tail are very canny, and know perfectly well what threatens danger and what does not. Their larger, and to my mind nobler, relation, the black-tail, is if any thing easier to approach and kill, and yet is by no means so apt to stay in the immediate neighborhood of a ranch, where there is always more or less noise and confusion. The bottom on which my ranch-house stands is a couple of miles in length, and well wooded; all through last summer it was the home of a number of white-tails, and most of them are on it to this moment. Two fawns in especial were really amusingly tame, at one time spending their days hid in an almost impenetrable tangle of bullberry bushes, whose hither edge was barely a hundred yards from the ranch-house; and in the evening they could frequently be seen from the door, as they came out to feed. In walking out after sunset, or in riding home when night had fallen, we would often run across them when it was too dark to make out any thing but their flaunting white tails as they cantered out of the way. Yet for all

their seeming familiarity they took good care not to expose themselves to danger. We were reluctant to molest them, but one day,
having performed our usual weekly or fortnightly feat of eating up
about everything there was in the house, it was determined that
the two deer (for it was late in autumn and they were then well
grown) should be sacrificed. Accordingly one of us sallied out, but
found that the sacrifice was not to be consummated so easily, for
the should-be victims appeared to distinguish perfectly well between a mere pass-by, whom they regarded with absolute indifference, and any one who harbored sinister designs. They kept such a
sharp look-out, and made off so rapidly if any one tried to approach
them, that on two evenings the appointed hunter returned empty-
handed, and by the third some one else had brought in a couple of
black-tail. After that no necessity arose for molesting the two
"tame deer," for whose sound common-sense we had all acquired a
greatly increased respect.

When not much molested white-tail feed in the evening or late
afternoon; but if often shot at and chased they only come out at
night. They are very partial to the water, and in the warm summer
nights will come down into the prairie ponds and stand knee-deep
in them, eating the succulent marsh plants. Most of the plains rivers
flow through sandy or muddy beds with no vegetable growth, and
to these, of course, the deer merely come down to drink or refresh
themselves by bathing, as they contain nothing to eat.

Throughout the day the white-tails keep in the densest thickets, choosing if possible those of considerable extent. For this reason they are confined to the bottoms of the rivers and the mouths
of the largest creeks, the cover elsewhere being too scanty to suit
them. It is very difficult to make them leave one of their haunts
during the daytime. They lie very close, permitting a man to pass
right by them; and the twigs and branches surrounding them are so
thick and interlaced that they can hear the approach of any one
from a long distance off, and hence are rarely surprised. If they
think there is danger that the intruder will discover them, they

arise and skulk silently off through the thickest part of the brush. If followed, they keep well ahead, moving perfectly noiselessly through the thicket, often going round in a circle and not breaking cover until hard pressed; yet all the time stepping with such sharp-eyed caution that the pursuing hunter will never get a glimpse of the quarry, though the patch of brush may not be fifty rods across.

At times the white-tail will lie so close that it may almost be trodden on. One June morning I was riding down along the river, and came to a long bottom, crowded with rose-bushes, all in bloom. It was crossed in every direction by cattle paths, and a drove of long-horned Texans were scattered over it. A cow-pony gets accustomed to travelling at speed along the cattle trails, and the one I bestrode threaded its way among the twisted narrow paths with perfect ease, loping rapidly onward through a sea of low rose-bushes, covered with the sweet, pink flowers. They gave a bright color to the whole plain, while the air was filled with the rich, full songs of the yellow-breasted meadow larks, as they perched on the topmost sprays of the little trees. Suddenly a white-tail doe sprang up almost from under the horse's feet, and scudded off with her white flag flaunting. There was no reason for harming her, and she made a pretty picture as she bounded lightly off among the rose-red flowers, passing without heed through the ranks of the long-horned and savage-looking steers.

Doubtless she had a little spotted fawn not far away. These wee fellows soon after birth grow very cunning and able to take care of themselves, keeping in the densest part of the brush, through which they run and dodge like a rabbit. If taken young they grow very tame and are most dainty pets. One which we had round the house answered well to its name. It was at first fed with milk, which it lapped eagerly from a saucer, sharing the meal with the two cats, who rather resented its presence and cuffed it heartily when they thought it was greedy and was taking more than its share. As it grew older it would eat bread or potatoes from our hands, and was perfectly fearless. At night it was let go or put in the cow-shed, whichever was handiest, but it was generally round in time for breakfast next morning. A blue ribbon with a bell attached was hung around its neck, so as to prevent its being shot; but in the end it shared the fate of all pets, for one night it went off and never came back again. Perhaps it strayed away of its own accord, but more probably some raw hand at hunting saw it, and slaughtered it without noticing the bell hanging from its neck.

The best way to kill white-tail is to still-hunt carefully through their haunts at dusk, when the deer leave the deep recesses in which their day-beds lie, and come out to feed in the more open parts. For this kind of hunting, no dress is so good as a buckskin suit and moccasins. The moccasins enable one to tread softly and noiselessly, while the buckskin suit is of a most inconspicuous color, and makes less rustling than any other material when passing among projecting twigs. Care must be taken to always hunt up wind, and to advance without any sudden motions, walking close in to the edges of the thickets, and keeping a sharp look-out, as it is of the first importance to see the game before the game sees you. The feeding-grounds of the deer may vary. If they are on a bottom studded with dense copses, they move out on the open between them; if they are in a dense wood, they feed along its edges; but by preference, they keep in the little glades and among the bushes underneath the trees. Wherever they may be found, they are rarely far from thick cover, and are always on the alert, lifting up their heads every few bites they take to see if any danger threatens them. But, unlike the antelope, they seem to rely for safety even more upon escaping observation than upon discovering danger while it is still far off, and so are usually in sheltered places where they cannot be seen at any distance. Hence, shots at them are generally obtained, if obtained at all at a very much closer range than at any other kind of game; the average distance would be nearer fifty than a hundred yards. On the other hand, more of the shots obtained are running ones than is the case with the same number taken at antelope or black-tail.

If the deer is standing just out of a fair-sized wood, it can often be obtained by creeping up along the edge; if seen among the large trees, it is even more easily still-hunted, as a tree trunk can be readily kept in line with the quarry, and thus prevent its suspecting any approach. Bu only a few white-tail are killed by regular and careful stalking; in much the greater number of instances the hunter simply beats patiently and noiselessly from the leeward, carefully through the clumps of trees and bushes, always prepared to see his game, and with his rifle at the ready. Sooner or later, as he steals round a corner, he either sees the motionless form of a deer, not a great distance off, regarding him intently for a moment before taking flight; or else he hears a sudden crash, and catches a glimpse of the animal as it lopes into the bushes. In either case, he must shoot quick; but the shot is a close one.

If he is heard or seen a long way off, the deer is very apt, instead of running away at full speed, to skulk off quietly through the bushes. But when suddenly startled, the white-tail makes off at a great rate, at a rolling gallop, the long, broad tail, pure white, held up in the air. In the dark or in thick woods, often all that can be seen is the flash of white from the tail. The head is carried low and well forward in running; a buck, when passing swiftly through thick underbrush, usually throws his horns back almost on his shoulders, with his nose held straight in front. White-tail venison is, in season, most delicious eating, only inferior to the mutton of the mountain sheep.

Among the places which are most certain to contain white-tails may be mentioned the tracts of swampy ground covered with willows and the like, which are to be found in a few (and but a few) localities through the plains country; there are, for example, several such along the Powder River, just below where the Little Powder empties into it. Here there is a dense growth of slim-stemmed young trees, sometimes almost impenetrable, and in other places opening out into what seem like arched passageways, through which a man must at times go almost on all fours. The ground may be covered with rank shrubbery, or it may be bare mud with patches of tall reeds. Here and there, scattered through these swamps, are pools of water, and sluggish ditches occasionally cut their way deep below the surface of the muddy soil. Game trails are abundant all through them, and now and then there is a large path beaten out by the cattle; while at intervals there are glades and openings. A horse must be very careful in going through such a swamp or he will certainly get mired, and even a man must be cautious about his footing. In the morning or late afternoon a man stands a good chance of killing deer in such a place, if he hunts carefully through it. It is comparatively easy to make but little noise in the mud and among the wet, yielding swamp plants, and by moving cautiously along the trails and through the openings, one can see some little distance ahead; and toward evening the pools should be visited, and the borders as far back as possible carefully examined, for any deer that come to drink, and the glades should be searched through for any that may be feeding. In the soft mud, too, a fresh track can be followed as readily as if in snow, and without exposing the hunter to such probability of detection. If a shot is obtained at all, it is at such close quarters as to more than counterbalance the dimness of the light, and to render the chance of a miss very unlikely. Such hunting is for a change very pleasant, the perfect stillness of the place, the quiet with which one has to move, and the constant expectation of seeing game keeping one's nerves always on the stretch; but after a while it grows tedious, and it makes a man feel cramped to be always ducking and crawling through such places. It is not to be compared, in cool weather, with still-hunting on the open hills; nevertheless, in the furious heat of the summer sun it has its advantages, for it is not often so oppressingly hot in the swamp as it is on the open prairie or in the dry thickets.

The white-tail is the only kind of large game for which the shot-gun can occasionally be used. At times in the dense brush it is seen, if seen at all, at such short distances, and the shots have to be taken so hurriedly, that the shot-gun is really the best weapon wherewith to attempt its death. One method of taking it is to have trained dogs hunt through a valley and drive the deer to guns stationed at the opposite end. With a single slow hound, given to baying, a hunter can often follow the deer on foot in the method adapted in most of the Eastern States for the capture of both the gray and the red fox. If the dog is slow and noisy the deer will play round in circles and can be cut off and shot from a stand. Any dog will soon put a deer out of a thicket, or drive it down a valley; but without a dog it is often difficult to drive deer toward the runaway or place at which the guns are stationed, for the white-tail will often skulk round and round a thicket instead of putting out of it when a man enters; and even when started it may break back past the driver instead of going toward the guns.

In all these habits white-tail are the very reverse of such game as antelope. Antelope care nothing at all about being seen, and indeed rather court observation, while the chief anxiety of a white-tail is to go unobserved. In passing through a country where there are antelope, it is almost impossible not to see them; while where there are an equal number of white-tail, the odds are manifold against travellers catching a glimpse of a single individual. The prong-horn is perfectly indifferent as to whether the pursuer sees him, so long as in his turn he is able to see the pursuer; and he relies entirely upon his speed and wariness for his safety; he never trusts for a moment to eluding observation. White-tail on the contrary rely almost exclusively either upon lying perfectly still and letting the danger pass by, or else upon skulking off so slyly as to be unobserved; it is only when hard pressed or suddenly startled that they bound boldly and freely away.

In many of the dense jungles without any opening the brush is higher than a man's head, and one has then practically no chance at all of getting a shot on foot when crossing through such places. But I have known instances where a man had himself driven in a tall light wagon through a place like this, and got several snap shots at the deer, as he caught momentary glimpses of them stealing off through the underbrush; and another method of pursuit in these jungles is occasionally followed by one of my foremen, who, mounted on a quiet horse, which will stand fire, pushes through the bushes and now and then gets a quick shot at a deer from horseback. I have tried this method myself, but without success, for though my hunting-horse, old Manitou, stands as steady as a rock, yet I find it impossible to shoot the rife with any degree of accuracy from the saddle.

Except on such occasions as those just mentioned, the white-tail is rarely killed while hunting on horseback. This last term, by-the-way, must not be understood in the sense in which it would be taken by the fox-hunter of the South, or by the Californian and Texan horsemen who course hare, antelope, and wild turkey with their fleet greyhounds. With us hunting on horseback simply means that the horse is ridden not only to the hunting grounds, but also through them, until the game is discovered; then the hunter immediately dismounts, shooting at once if the animal is near enough and has seen him, or stalking up to it on foot if it is a good distance off and he is still unobserved. Where great stretches of country have to be covered, as in antelope shooting, hunting on horseback is almost the only way followed; but the haunts and habits of the white-tail deer render it nearly useless to try to kill them in this way, as the horse would be sure to alarm them by making a noise, and even if he did not there would hardly be time to dismount and take a snap shot. Only once have I ever killed a white-tail buck while hunting on horseback; and at that time I had been expecting to fall in with black-tail.

This was while we had been making a wagon trip to the westward, following the old Keogh trail, which was made by the heavy army wagons that journeyed to Fort Keogh in the old days when the soldiers were, except a few daring trappers, the only white men to be seen on the last great hunting-ground of the Indians. It was abandoned as a military route several years ago, and is now only rarely travelled over, either by the canvas-topped ranch-wagon of some wandering cattle-men—like ourselves,—or else by a small party of emigrants, in two or three prairie schooners, which contain all their household goods. Nevertheless, it is still as plain and distinct as ever. The two deep parallel ruts, cut into the sod by the wheels of the heavy wagon, stretch for scores of miles in a straight line across the level prairie, and take great turns and doublings to avoid the impassable portions of the Bad Lands. The track is always perfectly plain, for in the dry climate of the western plains the action of the weather tends to preserve rather than to obliterate it; where it leads downhill, the snow water has cut and widened the ruts into deep gullies, so that a wagon has at those places to travel alongside the road. From any little rising in the prairie the road can be seen, a long way off, as a dark line, which, when near, resolves itself into two sharply defined parallel cuts. Such a road is a great convenience as a landmark. When travelling along it, or one like it, the hunters can separate in all directions, and no matter how long or how far they hunt, there is never the least difficulty about finding camp. For the general direction in which the road lies, is, of course, kept in mind, and it can be reached whether the sun is down or not; then a glance tells if the wagon has passed, and all that remains to be done is to gallop along the trail until camp is found.

On the trip in question we had at first very bad weather. Leaving the ranch in the morning, two of us, who were mounted, pushed on ahead to hunt, the wagon following slowly, with a couple of spare saddle ponies leading behind it. Early in the afternoon, while riding over the crest of a great divide, which separates the drainage basins of two important creeks, we saw that a tremendous storm was brewing with the marvellous rapidity which is so marked a characteristic of weather changes on the plains. A towering mass of clouds gathered in the northwest, turning that whole quarter of the sky to an inky blackness. From there the storm rolled down toward us at a furious speed, obscuring by degrees the light of the sun, and extending its wings toward each side, as if to overlap any that tried to avoid its path. Against the dark background of the mass could be seen pillars and clouds of gray mist, whirled hither and thither by the wind, and sheets of level rain driven before it. The edges of the wings tossed to and fro, and the wind shrieked and moaned as it swept over the prairie. It was a storm of unusual intensity; the prairie fowl rose in flocks from before it, scudding with spread wings toward the thickest cover, and the herds of antelope ran across the plain like race-horses to gather in the hollows and behind the low ridges.

We spurred hard to get out of the open, riding with loose reins for the creek. The centre of the storm swept by behind us, fairly across our track, and we only got a wipe from the tail of it. Yet this itself we could not have faced in the open. The first gust caught us a few hundred yards from the creek, almost taking us from the saddle, and driving the rain and hail in stinging level sheets against us. We galloped to the edge of a deep wash-out, scrambled into it at the risk of our necks, and huddled up with our horses underneath the windward bank. Here we remained pretty well sheltered until the storm was over. Although it was August, the air became very cold. The wagon was fairly caught, and would have been blown over if the top had been on; the driver and horses escaped without injury, pressing under the leeward side, the storm coming so level that they did not need a roof to protect them from the hail. Where the centre of the whirlwind struck it did great damage, sheets of hailstones as large as pigeons' eggs striking the earth with the velocity of bullets; next day the hailstones could have been gathered up by the bushel from the heaps that lay in the bottom of the gullies and ravines. One of my cowboys was out in the storm, during whose continuance he crouched under his horse's belly; coming home he came across some antelope so numb and stiffened that they could barely limp out of the way.

Near my ranch the hail killed quite a number of lambs. These were the miserable remnants of a flock of twelve thousand sheep driven into the Bad Lands a year before, fourth fifths of whom had died during the first winter, to the delight of all the neighboring cattle-men. Cattle-men hate sheep, because they eat the grass so close that cattle cannot live on the same ground. The sheepherders are a morose, melancholy set of men, generally afoot and with no companionship except that of the bleating idiots they are hired to guard. No man can associate with sheep and retain his self-respect. Intellectually a sheep is about on the lowest level of the brute creation; why the early Christians admired it, whether young or old, is to a good cattle-man always a profound mystery.

The wagon came on to the creek, along whose banks we had taken shelter, and we then went into camp. It rained all night, and there was a thick mist, with continual sharp showers, all the next day and night. The wheeling was, in consequence, very heavy, and after striking the Keogh trail we were able to go along it but a few miles before the fagged-out look of the team and the approach of evening warned us that we should have to go into camp while still a dozen miles from any pool or spring. Accordingly we made what would have been a dry camp had it not been for the incessant downpour of rain, which we gathered in the canvas wagon-sheet and in our oilskin overcoats in sufficient quantity to make coffee, having with infinite difficulty started a smouldering fire just to leeward of the wagon. The horses, feeding on the soaked grass, did not need water. An antelope, with the bold and heedless curiosity sometimes shown by its tribe, came up within two hundred yards of us as we were building the fire; but though one of us took a shot at him, it missed. Our shaps and oilskins had kept us perfectly dry, and as soon as our frugal supper was over, we coiled up among the boxes and bundles inside the wagon and slept soundly till daybreak.

When the sun rose next day, the third we were out, the sky was clear, and we two horsemen at once prepared to make a hunt. Some three miles off to the south of where we were camped, the plateau on which we were sloped off into a great expanse of broken ground, with chains upon chains of steep hills, separated by deep valleys, winding and branching in every direction, their bottoms filled with trees and brushwood. Toward this place we rode, intending to go into it some little distance, and then to hunt along through it near the edge. As soon as we got down near the brushy ravine we rode along without talking, guiding the horses as far as possible on earthy places, where they would neither stumble nor strike their feet against stones, and not letting our rifle-barrels or spurs clink against any thing. Keeping outside of the brush, a little up the side of the hill, one of us would ride along each side of the ravine, examining intently with our eyes every clump of trees or brushwood. For some time we saw nothing, but, finally, as we were riding both together round the jutting spur of a steep hill, my companion suddenly brought his horse to a halt, and pointing across the shelving bend to a patch of trees well up on the opposite side of a broad ravine, asked me if I did not see a deer in it. I was off the horse in a second, throwing the reins over his head. We were in the shadow of the cliff-shoulder, and with the wind in our favor; so we were unlikely to be observed by the game. I looked long and eagerly toward the spot indicated, which was about a hundred and twenty-five yards from us, but at first could see nothing. By this time, however, the experienced plainsman who was with me was satisfied that he was right in his supposition, and he told me to try again and look for a patch of red. I saw the patch at once, just glimmering through the bushes, but should certainly never have dreamed it was a deer if left to myself. Watching it attentively I soon saw it move enough to satisfy me where the head lay; kneeling on one knee and (as it was a little beyond point-blank range) holding at the top of the portion visible, I pulled trigger, and the bright-colored patch disappeared from among the bushes. The aim was a good one, for, on riding up to the brink of the ravine, we saw a fine white-tail buck lying below us, shot through just behind the shoulder; he was still in the red coat, with his antlers in the velvet.

The Deer of the River Bottoms

A deer is far from being such an easy animal to see as the novice is apt to suppose. Until the middle of September he is in the red coat; after that he is in the gray; but it is curious how each one harmonizes in tint with certain of the surroundings. A red doe lying down is, at a little distance, undistinguishable from the soil on which she is while a buck in the gray can hardly be made out in dead timber. While feeding quietly or standing still, they rarely show the proud, free port we are accustomed to associate with the idea of a buck, and look rather ordinary, humble-seeming animals, not at all conspicuous or likely to attract the hunter's attention; but once let them be frightened, and as they stand facing the danger, or bound away from it, their graceful movements and lordly bearing leave nothing to be desired. The black-tail is a still nobler-looking animal; while an antelope, on the contrary, though as light and quick on its feet as is possible for any animal not possessing wings to be, yet has an angular, goat-like look, and by no means conveys to the beholder the same idea of grace that a deer does.

In coming home, on this wagon trip, we made a long moonlight ride, passing over between sunset and sunrise what had taken us three days' journey on the outward march. Of our riding horses, two were still in good condition and well able to stand a twenty-four hours' jaunt, in spite of hard work and rough usage; the spare ones, as well as the team, were pretty well done up and could get along but slowly. All day long we had been riding beside the wagon over barren sage-brush plains, following the dusty trails made by the beef-herds that had been driven toward one of the Montana shipping towns.

When we halted for the evening meal we came near learning by practical experience how easy it is to start a prairie fire. We were camped by a dry creek on a broad bottom covered with thick, short grass, as dry as so much tinder. We wished to burn a good circle clear for the campfire; lighting it, we stood round with branches to keep it under. While thus standing a puff of wind struck us; the fire roared like a wild beast as it darted up; and our hair and eyelashes were well singed before we had beaten it out. At one time it seemed as if, though but a very few feet in extent, it would actually get away form us; in which case the whole bottom would have been a blazing furnace within five minutes.

After supper, looking at the worn-out condition of the team, we realized that it would take three more days travelling at the rate we had been going to bring us in, and as the country was monotonous, without much game, we concluded we would leave the wagon with the driver, and taking advantage of the full moon, push through the whole distance before breakfast next morning. Accordingly, we at nine o'clock again saddled the tough little ponies we had ridden all day and loped off out of the circle of firelight. For nine hours we rode steadily, generally at a quick lope, across the moon-lit prairie. The hoof-beats of our horses rang out in steady rhythm through the silence of the night, otherwise unbroken save now and then by the wailing cry of a coyote. The rolling plains stretched out on all sides of us, shimmering in the clear moonlight; and occasionally a band of spectral-looking antelope swept silently away from before our path. Once we went by a drove of Texas cattle, who stared wildly at the intruders; as we passed they charged down by us, the ground rumbling beneath their tread, while their long horns knocked against each other with a sound like the clattering of a multitude of castanets. We could see clearly enough to keep our general course of the trackless plain, steering by the stars where the prairie was perfectly level and without landmarks; and our ride was timed well, for as we galloped down into the valley of the Little Missouri the sky above the line of level bluffs in our front was crimson with the glow of the unrisen sun.

The Black-Tail Deer
(From *Hunting Trips of a Ranchman*)

Far different from the low-scudding, brush-loving white-tail, is the black-tail deer, the deer of the ravines and the rocky uplands. In general shape and form, both are much alike; but the black-tail is the larger of the two, with heavier antlers, of which the prongs start from one another, as if each of the tines of a two-pronged pitchfork had bifurcated; and in some cases it looks as if the process had been again repeated. The tail, instead of being broad and bushy as a squirrel's, spreading from the base, and pure white to the tip, is round and close haired, with the end black, though the rest is white. If an ordinary deer is running, its flaunting flag is almost its most conspicuous part; but no one would notice the tail of a black-tail deer.

All deer vary greatly in size; and a small black-tail buck will be surpassed in bulk by many white-tails; but the latter never reaches the weight and height sometimes attained by the former. The same holds true of the antlers borne by the two animals; on the average those of the black-tail are the heavier, and exceptionally large antlers of this species are larger than any of the white-tail. Bucks of both kinds very often have, when full-grown, more than the normal number of ten points; sometimes these many-pronged antlers will be merely deformities, while in other instances the points are more symmetrical, and add greatly to the beauty and grandeur of the head. The venison of the black-tail is said to be inferior in quality to that of the white-tail; but I have never been able to detect much difference, though, perhaps, on the whole, the latter is slightly better.

The gaits of the two animals are widely different. The white-tail runs at a rolling gallop, striking the round with the forward feet first, the head held forward. The black-tail, on the contrary, holds it head higher up, and progresses by a series of prodigious bounds, striking the earth with all four feet at once, the legs held nearly stiff. It seems like an extraordinary method of running, and the violent exertion tires the deer sooner than does the more easy and natural gait of the white-tail; but for a mile or so these rapidly succeeding bounds enable the black-tail to get over the ground at remarkable speed. Over rough ground, along precipitous slopes, and among the boulders of rocky cliffs, it will go with surprising rapidity and surefootedness, only surpassed by the feats of the big-horn in similar localities, and not equalled by those of any other plains game.

One of the noticeable things in western plains hunting is the different zones or bands of territory inhabited by different kinds of game. Along the alluvial land of the rivers and large creeks is found the white-tail. Back of these alluvial lands generally comes a broad tract of broken, hilly country, scantily clad with brush in some places; this is the abode of the black-tail deer. And where these hills rise highest, and where the ground is most rugged and barren, there the big-horn is found. After this hilly country is passed, in travelling away from the river, we come to the broad, level plains, the domain of the antelope. Of course the habitats of the different species overlap at the edges; and this overlapping is most extended in the cases of the big-horn and the black-tail.

The Bad Lands are the favorite haunts of the black-tail. Here the hills are steep and rugged, cut up and crossed in every direction by canyon-like ravines and valleys, which branch out and subdivide in the most intricate and perplexing manner. Here and there are small springs, or pools, marked by the greener vegetation growing round them. Along the bottoms and sides of the ravines there are patches of scrubby undergrowth, and in many of the pockets or glens in the sides of the hills the trees grow to some little height. High buttes rise here and there, naked to the top, or else covered with stunted pines and cedars, which also grow in the deep ravines and on the edges of the sheer canyons. Such lands, where the ground is roughest, and where there is some cover, even though scattered and scanty, are the best places to find the black-tail. Naturally their pursuit needs very different qualities in the hunter from those required in the chase of the white-tail. In the latter case stealth and caution are the prime requisites; while the man who would hunt and kill the deer of the uplands has more especial need of energy, activity, and endurance, of good judgment and of skill with the rifle. Hunting the black-tail is beyond all comparison the nobler sport. Indeed, there is no kind of plains hunting, except only the chase of the big-horn, more fitted to bring out the best and hardiest of the many qualities which go to make up a good hunter.

It is still a moot question whether it is better to hunt on horseback or on foot; but the course of events is rapidly deciding it in favor of the latter method. Undoubtedly it is easier and pleasanter to hunt on horseback; and it has the advantage of covering a great deal of ground. But it is impossible to advance with such caution, and it is difficult to shoot as quickly, as when on foot; and where the deer are shy and not very plenty, the most enthusiastic must, slowly and reluctantly but surely, come to the conclusion that a large bag can only be made by the still-hunter who goes on foot. Of course, in the plains country it is not as in mountainous or thickly wooded regions and the horse should almost always be taken as a means of conveyance to the hunting-grounds and from one point to another; but the places where game is expected should, as a rule, be hunted over on foot. This rule is by no means a general one, however. There are still many localities where the advantage of covering a great deal of ground more than counterbalances the disadvantage of being on horseback. About one third of my hunts are still made on horseback; and in almost all the others I take old Manitou to carry me to and from the ground and to pack out any game that may be killed. A hunting-horse is of no use whatever unless he will permit a man to jump from his back and fire with the greatest rapidity; and nowhere does practice have more to do with success than in the case of jumping off a horse to shoot at game which has just been seen. The various movements take a novice a good deal of time; while an old hand will be off and firing with the most instantaneous quickness. Manitou can be left anywhere at a moments warning, while his rider leaps off, shoots at a deer from almost under his head, and perhaps chases the wounded animal a mile or over; and on his return the good old fellow will be grazing away, perfectly happy and contented, and nor making a movement to run off or evade being caught.

One method of killing deer on horseback is very exciting. Many of the valleys or ravines extend with continual abrupt turns and windings for several miles, the brush and young trees stretching with constant breaks down the middle of the bottom, and leaving a space on each side along which a surefooted horse can gallop at speed. Two men, on swift, hardy horses, can hunt down such a ravine very successfully at evening, by each taking a side and galloping at a good speed the whole length against the wind. The patter of the unshod hoofs over the turf makes but little noise; and the turns are so numerous and abrupt, and the horses go so swiftly, that the hunters come on the deer almost before the latter are aware of their presence. If it is so late in the day that the deer have begun to move they will find the horses close up before they have a suspicion of danger, while if they are still lying in the cover the suddenness of the appearance of their foe is apt to so startle them as to make them break out and show themselves instead of keeping hid, as they would probably do if they perceived the approach from afar. One thus gets a close running shot, or if he waits a minute he will generally get a standing shot at some little distance, owing to a very characteristic habit of the black-tail. This is its custom of turning round, apparently actuated simply by curiosity, to look at the object which startled it, after it has run off a hundred and fifty yards or so. It then stands motionless for a few seconds, and offers a chance for a steady shot. If the chance is not improved, no other will offer, for as soon as the deer has ended its scrutiny it is off again, and this time will not halt till well out of danger. Owing to its singular gait, a succession of buck jumps, the black-tail is a peculiarly difficult animal to hit while on the run; and it is best to wait until it stops and turns before taking the shot, as if fired at, the report will generally so alarm it as to make it continue its course without halting to look back. Some of the finest antlers in my possession come from bucks killed by this method of hunting; and it is a most exhilarating form of sport, the horse galloping rapidly over what is often very broken ground, and the senses being continually on the alert for any sign of game. The rush and motion of the horse, and the care necessary to guide it and at the same time be in constant readiness for a shot, prevent the chase having any of the monotony that is at times inseparable from still-hunting proper.

Nevertheless, it is by still-hunting that most deer are killed, and the highest form of hunting craft is shown in the science of the skilful still-hunter. With sufficient practice any man who possesses common-sense and is both hardy and persevering can become, to a certain extent, a still-hunter. But the really *good* still-hunter is born rather than made; though of course in addition to possessing the gifts naturally he must also have developed them, by constant practice, to the highest point possible. One of the foremen on my ranch is a really remarkably good hunter and game shot, and another does almost as well; but the rest of us are not, and never will be, any thing very much out of the common. By dint of practice we have learned to shoot as well at game as at a target; and those of us who are fond of the sport hunt continually and so get a good deal of game at one time or another. Hunting through good localities, up wind, quietly and perseveringly, we come upon quite a number of animals; and we can kill a standing shot at a fair distance and a running shot close up, and by good luck every now and then kill far off; but to much more than is implied in the description of such modest feats we cannot pretend.

After the disappearance of the buffalo and the thinning out of the elk, the black-tail was, and in most places it still is, the game most sought after by the hunters; I have myself shot as many of them as of all other kinds of plains game put together. But for this very reason it is fast disappearing; and bids fair to be the next animal, after the buffalo and elk, to vanish from the places that formerly knew it. The big-horn and the prong-horn are more difficult to stalk and kill, partly from their greater natural wariness, and partly from the kind of ground on which they are found. But it seems at first sight strange that the black-tail should be exterminated or driven away so much more quickly than the white-tail, when it has sharper ears and nose, is more tenacious of life, and is more wary. The main reason is to be found in the difference in the character of the hunts of the two creatures. The black-tail is found on much more open ground, where the animals can be seen farther off, where it is much easier to take advantage of the direction of the wind and to get along without noise, and where far more country can be traversed in a given time; and though the average length of the shots taken is in one case two or three times as great as in the other, yet this is more than counterbalanced by the fact that they are more often standing ones, and that there is usually much more time for aiming. Moreover, one kind of sport can be followed on horseback, while the other must be followed on foot; and then the chase of the white-tail, in addition, is by far the more tedious and patience-trying. And the black-tail are much the more easily scared or driven out of a locality by persecution or by the encroaching settlements. All these qualities combine to make it less able to hold its own against mankind than its smaller rival. It is the favorite game of the skin hunters and meat hunters, and has, in consequence, already disappeared from many places, while in others its extermination is going on at a frightfully rapid rate, owing to its being followed in season and out of season without mercy. Besides, the cattle are very fond of just the places to which it most often resorts; and wherever cattle go the cowboys ride about after them, with their ready six-shooters at their hips. They blaze away at any deer they see, of course, and in addition to now and then killing or wounding one, continually harry and disturb the poor animals. In the more remote and inaccessible districts the black-tail will long hold its own, to be one of the animals whose successful pursuit will redound most to the glory of the still-hunter; but in a very few years it will have ceased entirely to be one of the common game animals of the plains.

Its great curiosity is one of the disadvantages under which it labors in the fierce struggle for existence, compared to the white-tail. The latter, when startled, does not often stop to look round; but, as already said, the former will generally do so after having gone a few hundred feet. The first black-tail I ever killed—unfortunately killed for the body was not found until spoiled—was obtained owning solely to this peculiarity. I had been riding up along the side of a brushy coulie, when a fine buck started out some thirty yards ahead. Although so close, my first shot, a running one, was a miss; when a couple of hundred yards off, on the very crest of the spur up which he had run, he stopped and turned partially round. Firing again from a rest, the bullet broke his hind leg far up and went into his body. Off he went on three legs, and I after him as fast as the horse could gallop. He went over the spur and down into the valley of the creek from which the coulie branched up, in very bad ground. My pony was neither fast nor surefooted, but of course in half a mile overhauled the three-legged deer, which turned short off and over the side of the hill flanking the valley. Instead of running right up on it I foolishly dismounted and began firing; after the first shot—a miss—it got behind a boulder hitherto unseen, and thence over the crest. The pony meanwhile had slipped its hind leg into the rein; when, after some time, I got it out and galloped up to the ridge, the most careful scrutiny of which my unpractised eyes were capable failed to discover a track on the dry ground hard as granite. A day or two afterwards the place where the carcass lay was made known by the vultures, gathered together from all parts to feed upon it.

When fired at from a place of hiding, deer which have not been accustomed to the report of a gun will often appear confused and uncertain what to do. On one occasion, while hunting in the mountains, I saw an old buck with remarkably large horns, of curious and beautiful shape, more symmetrical than in most instances where the normal form is departed from. The deer was feeding in a wide, gently sloping valley, containing no cover from behind which to approach him. We were in no need of meat, but the antlers were so fine that I felt they justified the death of their bearer. After a little patient waiting, the buck walked out of the valley, and over the ridge on the other side, moving upwind; I raced after him, and crept up behind a thick growth of stunted cedars, which had started up from among some boulders. The deer was about a hundred yards off, down in the valley. Out of breath, and overconfident, I fired hastily, overshooting him. The wind blew the smoke back away from the ridge, so that he saw nothing, while the echo prevented his placing the sound. He took a couple of jumps nearer, when he stood still and was again overshot. Again he took a few jumps, and the third shot went below him; and the fourth just behind him. This was too much, and away he went. In despair I knelt down (I had been firing off-hand), took a steady aim well-forward on his body, and fired, bringing him down, but with small credit to the shot, for the bullet had gone into his hip, paralyzing his hind-quarters. The antlers are the finest pair I ever got, and form a magnificent ornament for the hall; but the shooting is hardly to be recalled with pleasure. Still, though certainly very bad, it was not quite as discreditable as the mere target shot would think. I have seen many a crack marksman at the target do quite as bad missing when out in the field, and that not once, but again and again.

Of course, in those parts of the wilderness where the black-tail are entirely unused to man, they are as easy to approach (from the leeward side) as is any and every other kind of game under like conditions. In lonely spots, to which hunters rarely or never penetrate, deer of this species will stand and look at a hunter without offering to run away till he is within fifty yards of them, if he will advance quietly. In a far-off mountain forest I have more than once shot a young buck at less than that distance as he stood motionless, gazing at me, although but little caution had been used in approaching him.

But a short experience of danger on the part of the black-tail changes all this; and where hunters are often afoot, he becomes as wild and wary as may be. Then the successful still-hunter shows that he is indeed well up in the higher forms of hunting craft. For the man who can, not once by accident, but again and again, as a regular thing, single-handed, find and kill his black-tail, has shown that he is no mere novice in his art; still-hunting the black-tail is a sport that only the skilful can follow with good results, and one which implies in the successful sportsman the presence of most of the still-hunter's rarest attributes. All of the qualities which a still-hunter should possess are of service in the pursuit of any kind of game; but different ones will be called into especial play in hunting different kinds of animals. Thus, to be a successful hunter after any thing, a man should be patient, resolute, hardy, and with good judgement; he should have good lungs and stout muscles; he should be able to move with noiseless stealth; and he should be keen-eyed, and a first rate marksman with the rifle. But in different kinds of shooting, the relative importance of these qualities varies greatly. In hunting white-tail deer, the two prime requisites are stealth and patience. If the quarry is a big-horn, a man needs especially to be sound in wind and limbs, and to be both hardy and resolute. Skill in the use of the long-range rifle counts for more in antelope hunting than in any other form of sport; and it is in this kind of hunting alone that good marksmanship is more important than any thing else. With dangerous game, cool and steady nerves are of the first consequence; all else comes after. Then, again, in the use of the rifle, the *kind* of skill—not merely the *degree* of skill—required to hunt different animals may vary greatly. In shooting white-tail, it is especially necessary to be a good snap shot at running game; when the distance is close, quickness is an essential. But at antelope there is plenty of time, and what is necessary is ability to judge distance, and capacity to hit a small stationary object at long range.

The different degrees of estimation in which the chase of the various kinds of plains game is held depend less upon the difficulty of capture than upon the nature of the qualities in the hunter which each particular form of hunting calls into play. A man who is hardy, resolute, and a good shot, has come nearer to realizing the ideal of a bold and free hunter than in the case with one who is merely stealthy and patient; and so, though to kill a white-tail is rather more difficult than to kill a black-tail, yet the chase of the latter is certainly the nobler form of sport, for it calls into play, and either develops or implies the presence of, much more manly qualities than does the other. Most hunters would find it nearly as difficult to watch in silence by a salt-lick throughout the night, and then to butcher with a shot-gun a white-tail, as it would be to walk on foot through rough ground from morning till evening, and to fairly approach and kill a black-tail; yet there is no comparison between the degree of credit to be attached to one feat and that to be attached to the other. Indeed, if difficulty in killing is to be taken as a criterion, a mink or even a weasel would have to stand as high up in the scale as a deer, were the animals equally plenty.

Ranged in the order of the difficulty with which they are approached and slain, plains game stand as follows: big-horn, antelope, white-tail, black-tail, elk, and buffalo. But, as regards the amount of manly sport furnished by the chase of each, the white-tail should stand at the bottom of the list, and the elk and black-tail abreast of the antelope.

Other things being equal, the length of an animal's stay in the land, when the arch foe of all lower forms of animal life has made his appearance therein, depends upon the difficulty with which he is hunted and slain. But other influences have to be taken into account. The big-horn is shy and retiring; very few, compared to the whole number, will be killed; and yet the others vanish completely. Apparently they will not remain where they are hunted and disturbed. With antelope and white-tail this does not hold; they will cling to a place far more tenaciously, even if often harassed. The former being the more conspicuous, and living in such open ground, is apt to be more persecuted; while the white-tail, longer than any other animal, keeps its place in the land in spite of the swinish game butchers, who hunt for hides and not for sport or actual food, and who murder the gravid doe and the spotted fawn with as little hesitation as they would kill a buck of ten points. No one who is not himself a sportsman and lover of nature can realize the intense indignation with which a true hunter sees these butchers at their brutal work of slaughtering the game, in season and out, for the sake of the few dollars they are too lazy to earn in any other and more honest way.

All game animals rely upon both eyes, ears, and nose to warn them of the approach of danger; but the amount of reliance placed on each sense varies greatly in different species. Those found out on the plains pay very little attention to what they hear; indeed, in the open they can hardly be approached near enough to make of much account any ordinary amount of noise caused by the stalker, especially as the latter is walking over little but grass and soft earth. The buffalo, whose shaggy frontlet of hair falls over his eyes and prevents his seeing at any great distance, depends mainly upon his exquisite sense of smell. The antelope, on the other hand, depends almost entirely on his great, bulging eyes, and very little on his nose. His sight is many times as good as that of deer, both species of which, as well as elk, rely both upon sight and hearing, but most of all upon their sense of smell, for their safety. The big-horn has almost as keen eyesight as an antelope, while his ears and nose are as sensitive to sound and scent as are those of an elk.

Black-tail, like other members of the deer family, do not pay much attention to an object which is not moving. A hunter who is standing motionless or squatting down is not likely to receive attention, while a big-horn or prong-horn would probably see him and take the alarm at once; and if the black-tail is frightened and running he will run almost over a man standing in plain sight, without paying any heed to him, if the latter does not move. But the very slightest movement at once attracts a deer's attention, and deer are not subject to the panics that at times overtake other kinds of game. The black-tail has much curiosity, which often proves fatal to it; but which with it is after all by no means the ungovernable passion that it is with antelope. The white-tail and the big-horn are neither over-afflicted with morbid curiosity, nor subject to panics or fits of stupidity; and both these animals, as well as the black-tail, seem to care very little for the death of the leader of the band, going their own ways with small regard for the fate of the chief, while elk will huddle together in a confused group, and remain almost motionless when their leader is struck down. Antelope and more especially elk are subject to perfect panics of unreasoning terror, during which they will often put themselves completely in the power of the hunter; while buffalo will frequently show a downright stupidity almost unequalled.

The Black-Tail Deer

The black-tail suffers from no such peculiarities. His eyes are good; his nose and ears excellent. He is every alert and wary; his only failing is his occasional over-curiosity; and his pursuit taxes to the utmost the skill and resources of the still-hunter.

By all means the best coverings for the feet when still-hunting are moccasins, as with them a man can go noiselessly through ground where hobnailed boots would clatter like the hoofs of a horse; but in hunting in winter over the icy buttes and cliffs it is best to have stout shoes, with nails in the soles, and if the main work is done on horseback it is best to wear high boots, as they keep the trousers down. Indeed in the Bad Lands boots have other advantages, for rattlesnakes abound, and against these they afford perfect protection—unless a man should happen to stumble on a snake while crawling along on all fours. But moccasins are beyond all comparison the best footgear for hunting. In very cold weather a fur cap which can be pulled down over the ears is a necessity; but at other times a brimmed felt halt offers better protection against both sun and rain. The clothes should be of some neutral tint— buckskin is on this account excellent—and very strong.

The still-hunter should be well acquainted with, at any rate, certain of the habit of his quarry. There are seasons when the black-tail is found in bands; such is apt to be the case when the rutting time is over. At this period, too, the deer wander far and wide, making what may almost be called a migration; and in rutting time the bucks follow the does at speed for miles at a stretch. But except at these seasons each individual black-tail has a certain limited tract of country to which he confines himself unless disturbed or driven away, not, of course, keeping in the same spot all the time, but working round among a particular set of ravines and coulies, where the feed is good, and where water can be obtained without going too far out of the immediate neighborhood.

Throughout the plains country the black-tail lives in the broken ground, seldom coming down to the alluvial bottoms or out on the open prairies and plateaus. But he is found all through this broken ground. Sometimes it is rolling in character with rounded hills and gentle valleys, dotted here and there with groves of trees; or the hills may rise into high chains, covered with an open pine forest, sending off long spurs and divided by deep valleys and basins. Such places are favorite resorts of this deer; but it is as plentiful in the Band Lands proper. There are tracts of these which are in part or wholly of volcanic origin; then the hills are called scoria buttes. They are high and very steep, but with rounded tops and edges, and are covered, as is the ground round about, with scoriac boulders. Bushes, and sometimes a few cedar, grow among them, and though they would seem to be most unlikely places for deer, yet black-tail are very fond of them, and are very apt to be found among them. Often in the cold fall mornings they will lie out among the boulders, on the steep side of such a scoria butte, sunning themselves, far from any cover except a growth of brushwood in the bottom on the dry creeks or coulies. The grass on top of and between these scoria buttes is often very nutritious, and cattle are also fond of it. The higher buttes are choice haunts of the mountain sheep.

Nineteen twentieths of the Bad Lands, however, owe their origin not to volcanic action but to erosion and to the peculiar weathering forces always at work in the dry climate of the plains. Geologically the land is for the most part composed of a set of parallel, perfectly horizontal strata, of clay, marl, or sandstone, which, being of different degrees of hardness, offer some more and some less resistance to the action of the weather. The table-lands, peaks, cliffs, and jagged ridges are caused solely by the rains and torrents cutting away the land into channels, which at first are merely washouts, and at last grow into deep canyons, winding valleys, and narrow ravines or basins. The sides of these cuts are at first perpendicular, exposing to view the various bands of soil, perhaps of a dozen different colors; the hardest bands resist the action of the weather best and form narrow ledges stretching along the face of the cliff. Peaks of the most fantastic shapes are formed in this manner, and where a ridge is worn away on each side its crest may be as sharp as a knife blade, but all notched and jagged. The peaks and ridges vary in height from a few feet to several hundred; the sides of the buttes are generally worn down in places so as to be steeply sloping instead of perpendicular. The long washouts and the canyons and canyon-like valleys stretch and branch out in every direction; the dryness of the atmosphere, the extremes of intense heat and bitter cold, and the occasional furious rain-storms keep the edges and angles sharp and jagged, and pile up boulders and masses of loose detritus at the foot of the cliffs and great lonely crags. Sometimes the valleys are quite broad, with steep sides and with numerous pockets, separated by spurs jutting out into the bottom from the lateral ridges. Other ravines or clefts taper down to a ditch, a foot or so wide, from which the banks rise at an angle of sixty degrees to the tops of the enclosing ridges.

The faces of the terraced cliffs and sheer crags are bare of all but the scantiest vegetation, and where the Bad Lands are most rugged and broken the big-horn is the only game found. But in most places the tops of the buttes, the sides of the slopes, and the bottoms of the valleys are more or less thickly covered with the nutritious grass which is the favorite food of the black-tail.

Of course, the Bad Lands grade all the way from those that are almost rolling in character to those that are so fantastically broken in form and so bizarre in color as to seem hardly properly to belong to this earth. If the weathering forces have not been active, the ground will look, from a little distance, almost like a level plain, but on approaching nearer, it will be seen to be crossed by straight-sided gullies and canyons, miles in length, cutting across the land in every direction and rendering it almost impassable for horsemen or wagon teams. If the forces at work have been more intense, the walls between the different gullies have been cut down to thin edges, or broken through, leaving isolated peaks of strange shape, while the hollows have been channeled out deeper and deeper; such places show the extreme and most characteristic Bad Lands formation. When the weathering has gone on further, the angles are rounded off, grass begins to grow, bushes and patches of small trees sprout up, water is found in places, and the still very rugged country becomes the favorite abode of the black-tail.

During the daytime, these deer lie quietly in their beds, which are sometimes in the brush and among the matted bushes in the bottoms of the small branching coulies, or heads of the crooked ravines. More often they will be found in the thickets of stunted cedars clothing the brinks of the canyons or the precipitous slopes of the great chasms into which the ground is cleft and rent; or else among the groves of gnarled pines on the sides of the buttes, and in the basins and pockets between the spurs. If the country is not much hunted over, a buck or old doe will often take its mid-day rest out in the open, lying down among the long grass or shrubbery on one of the bare benches at the head of a ravine, at the edge of the dense brush with which its bottom and sides are covered. In such a case, a position is always chosen from which a look-out can be kept all around; and the moment any suspicious object is seen, the deer slips off into the thicket below him. Perhaps the favorite resting-places are the rounded edges of gorges, just before the sides of the latter break sheer off. Here the deer lies, usually among a few straggling pines or cedars, on the very edge of the straight side-wall of the canyon, with a steep-shelving slope above him, so that he cannot be seen from the summit; and in such places it is next to impossible to get at him. If lying on a cedar-grown spur or ridge-point, the still-hunter has a better chance, for the evergreen needles with which the ground is covered enable a man to walk noiselessly, and, by stopping or going on all fours, he can keep under the branches. But it is at all times hard and unsatisfactory work to find and successfully still-hunt a deer that is enjoying its day rest. Generally, the only result is to find the warm, fresh bed from which the deer has just sneaked off, the blades of grass still slowly rising, after the hasty departure of the weight that has flattened them down; or else, if in dense cover, the hunter suddenly hears a scramble, a couple of crashing bounds through the twigs and dead limbs, and gets a momentary glimpse of a dark outline vanishing into the thicket as the sole reward of his labor. Almost the only way to successfully still-hunt a deer in the middle of the day, is to find its trail and follow it up to the resting-places, and such a feat needs an expert tracker and a noiseless and most skilful stalker.

The black-tail prefers to live in the neighborhood of water, where he can get it every twenty-four hours; but he is perfectly willing to drink only every other day, if, as is often the case, he happens to be in a very dry locality. Nor does he stay long in the water or near it, like the white-tail, but moves off as soon as he is no longer thirsty. On moonlight nights he feeds a good deal of the time, and before dawn he is always on foot for his breakfast; the hours around daybreak are those in which most of his grazing is done. By the time the sun has been up an hour he is on his way homeward, grazing as he goes; and he will often stay for some little time longer, if there has been no disturbance from man or other foes, feeding, among the scattered scrub cedars skirting the thicket in which he intends to make his bed for the day. Having once made his bed he crouches very close in it, and is difficult to put up during the heat of the day; but as the afternoon wears on he becomes more restless, and will break from his bed and bound off at much smaller provocation, while if the place is lonely he will wander out into the open hours before sunset. If, however, he is in much danger of being molested, he will keep close to his hiding-place until nearly nightfall, when he ventures out to feed. Owing to the lateness of his evening appearance in localities where there is much hunting, it is a safer plan to follow him in the early morning, being on the ground and ready to start out by the time the first streak of dawn appears. Often I have lost deer when riding home in the evening, because the dusk had deepened so that it was impossible to distinguish clearly enough to shoot.

One day one of my cowboys and myself were returning from an unsuccessful hunt, about nightfall, and were still several miles from the river, when a couple of yearling black-tails jumped up in the bed of the dry creek down which we were riding. Our horses though stout and swift were not well trained; and the instant we were off their backs they trotted off. No sooner were we on the ground and trying to sight the deer, one of which was cantering slowly off among the bushes, than we found we could not catch the bead sights of our rifles, the outlines of the animals seeming vague, and shadowy, and confounding themselves with the banks and dull green sage bushes behind them. Certainly six or eight shots were fired, we doing our best to aim, but without any effect; and when we gave it up and turned to look for our horses we were annoyed to see the latter trotting off down the valley half a mile away. We went after at a round pace; but darkness closed in before we had gained at all on them. There was nothing left to do but to walk on down the valley to the bottoms, and then to wade the river; as the latter was quite high, we had to take off our clothes, and it is very uncomfortable to feel one's way across a a river at night, in bare feet, with the gun and bundle of clothes held high over head. However, when across the river and half a mile from home, we ran into our horses—a piece of good luck, as otherwise we should have had to spend the next day in looking for them.

Almost the only way in which it is possible to aim after dark is to get the object against the horizon, toward the light. One of the finest bucks I ever killed was shot in this way. It was some little time after the sun had set, and I was hurrying home, riding down along a winding creek at a gallop. The middle of the bottom was covered with brush, while the steep, grassy, rounded hills on each side sent off spurs into the valley, the part between every two spurs making a deep pocket. The horse's feet were unshod and he made very little noise, coming down against the wind. While passing a deep pocket I heard from within it a snort and stamping of feet, the well-known sounds made by a startled deer. Pulling up short I jumped off the horse—it was Manitou,—who instantly began feeding with perfect indifference to what he probably regarded as an irrational freak of his master; and, aiming as well as I could in the gathering dusk, held the rifle well ahead of a shadowy gray object which was scudding along the base of the hill towards the mouth of the pocket. The ball struck in front of and turned the deer, which then started obliquely up the hill. A second shot missed it; and I then (here comes in the good of having a repeater) knelt down and pointed the rifle against the sky line, at the place where the deer seemed likely to top the bluff. Immediately afterwards the buck appeared, making the last jump with a great effort which landed him square on the edge, as sharply outlined as a silhouette against the fading western light. My rifle bead was just above him; pulling it down I fired, as the buck paused for a second to recover himself from his last great bound, and with a crash the mighty antlered beast came rolling down the hill, the bullet having broken his back behind the shoulders, afterwards going out through his chest.

At times a little caution must be used in approaching a wounded buck, for if it is not disabled it may be a rather formidable antagonist. In my own experience I have never known a wounded buck to do more than make a pass with his horns, or, in plunging when the knife enters his throat, to strike with his forefeet. But one of my men was regularly charged by a great buck, which he had wounded, and which was brought to bay on the ice by a dog. It seemed to realize that the dog was not the main antagonist, and knocking him over charged straight past him at the man, and as the latter had in his haste not reloaded his rifle, he might have been seriously injured had it not been for the dog, a very strong and plucky one, which caught the buck by the hock and threw him. The buck got up and again came straight at his foe, uttering a kind of grunting bleat, and it was not till after quite a scuffle that the man, by the help of the dog, got him down and thrust the knife in his throat. Twice I have known hounds to be killed by bucks which they had brought to bay in the rutting season. One of these bucks was a savage old fellow with great thick neck and sharp-pointed antlers. He came to bay in a stream, under a bank thickly matted with willows which grew down into the water, guarding his rear and flanks, while there was a small pool in his front across which the hounds had to swim. Backing in among the willows he rushed out at every dog that came near, striking it under water with his forefeet, and then again retreating to his fortress. In this way he kept the whole pack off, and so injured one hound that he had to be killed. Indeed, a full-grown buck with antlers would be a match for a wolf, unless surprised, and could not improbably beat off a cougar if he received the latter's spring fairly on his prong points.

Bucks fight fiercely among themselves during the rutting season. At that time the black-tail, unlike the white-tail, is found in bands, somewhat like those of the elk, but much smaller, and the bucks of each band keep up an incessant warfare. A weak buck promptly gets out of the way if charged by a large one; but when two of equal strength come together the battle is well fought. Instances occasionally occur, of a pair of these duellists getting their horns firmly interlocked and thus perishing; but these instances are much rarer, owing to the shape of the antlers, than with the white-tail, of which species I have in my own experience come across two or three sets of skulls held together by their interlacing antlers, the bearers of which had doubtless died owing to their inability to break away from each other.

A black-tail buck is one of the most noble-looking of all deer. His branching and symmetrically curved antlers are set on a small head, carried with beautiful poise by the proud, massive neck. The body seems almost too heavy for the slender legs, and yet the latter bear it as if they were rods of springing steel. Every movement is full of alert, fiery life and grace, and he steps as lightly as though he hardly trod the earth. The large, sensitive ears are thrown forward to catch the slightest sound; and in the buck they are not too conspicuous, though they are the only parts of his frame which to any eye can be said to take away from his beauty. They give the doe a somewhat mulish look; at a distance, the head of a doe peering out from among twigs looks like a great black V. To me, however, even in the case of the doe, they seem to set off and strengthen by contrast the delicate, finely-moulded look of the head. Owing to these ears the species is called in the books the Mule Deer, and every now and then a plainsman will speak of it by this title. But all plainsmen know it generally, and ninety-nine out of a hundred know it only, as the Black-tail Deer; and as this is the title by which it is known among all who hunt it or live near it, it should certainly be called by the same name in the books.

But though so grand and striking an object when startled, or when excited, whether by curiosity or fear, love or hate, a black-tail is nevertheless often very hard to make out when standing motionless among the trees and brushwood, or when lying down among the boulders. A raw hand at hunting has no idea how hard it is to see a deer when at rest. The color of the hair is gray, almost the same tint as that of the leafless branches and tree trunks; for of course the hunting season is at its height only when the leaves have fallen. A deer standing motionless looks black or gray, according as the sunlight strikes it; but always looks exactly the same color as the trees around it. It generally stands or lies near some tree trunks; and the eye may pass over it once or twice without recognizing its real nature. In the brush it is still more difficult, and there a deer's form is often absolutely indistinguishable from the surroundings, as one peers through the mass of interlacing limbs and twigs. Once an old hunter and myself in walking along the ridge of a scoria butte passed by without seeing them, three black-tail lying among the scattered boulders of volcanic rock on the hillside, not fifty yards from us. After a little practical experience a would-be hunter learns not to expect deer always, or even generally, to appear as they do when near by or suddenly startled; but on the contrary to keep a sharp look-out on every dull-looking red or yellow patch he sees in a thicket, and to closely examine any grayish-looking object observed on the hillsides, for it is just such small patches or obscure-looking objects which are apt, if incautiously approached, to suddenly take to themselves legs, and go bounding off at a rate which takes them out of danger before the astonished tyro has really waked up to the fact that they are deer. The first lesson to be learned in still-hunting is the knowledge of how to tell what objects are and what are not deer; and to learn it is by no means as easy a task as those who have never tried it would think.

When he has learned to see a deer, the novice then has to learn to hit it, and this again is not the easy feat it seems. That he can do well with a shot-gun proves very little as to a man's skill with the rifle, for the latter carries but one bullet, and can therefore hit in but one place, while with a shot-gun, if you hold a foot off your mark you will be nearly as apt to hit as if you held plumb centre. Nor does *mere* practice at a mark avail, though excellent in its way; for a deer is never seen at a fixed and ascertained distance, nor is its outline often clearly and sharply defined as with a target. Even if a man keeps cool—and for the first shot or two he will probably be flurried—he may miss an absurdly easy shot by not taking pains. I remember on one occasion missing two shots in succession where it seemed really impossible for a man to help hitting. I was out hunting on horseback with one of my men, and on loping round the corner of a brushy valley came suddenly in sight of a buck with certainly more than a dozen points on his great spreading antlers. I jumped off my horse instantly, and fired as he stood facing me not over forty yards off; fired, as I supposed, perfectly coolly, though without dropping on my knee as I should have done. The shot must have gone high, for the buck bounded away unharmed, heedless of a second ball; and immediately his place was taken by another, somewhat smaller, who sprang out of a thicket into almost the identical place where the big buck had stood. Again I fired and missed; again the buck ran off, and was shot at and missed while running—all four shots being taken within fifty yards. I clambered on to the horse without looking at my companion, but too conscious of his smothered disfavor; after riding a few hundred yards, he said with forced politeness and a vague desire to offer some cheap consolation, that he supposed I had done my best; to which I responded with asperity that I'd be damned if I had; and we finished our journey homeward in silence. A man is likely to overshoot at any distance; but at from twenty-five to seventy-five yards he is certain to do so if he is at all careless.

Moreover, besides not missing, a man must learn to hit his deer in the right place; the first two or three times he shoots he will probably see the whole deer in the rifle sights, instead of just the particular spot he wishes to strike; that is, he will aim in a general way at the deer's whole body—which will probably result in a wound not disabling the animal in the least for the time, although ensuring its finally dying a lingering and painful death. The most instantaneously fatal places are the brain and any part of the spinal column; these offer such small marks that it is usually only by accident they are hit. The mark at any part of which one can fire with safety is a patch about eight inches or a foot square, including the shoulder-blades, lungs, and heart. A kidney-shot is very fatal; but a black-tail will go all day with a bullet through its entrails, and in cold weather I have known one to run several miles with a portion of its entrails sticking out of a wound and frozen solid. To break both shoulders by a shot as the deer stands sideways to the hunter, brings the buck down in its tracks; but perhaps the best place at which to aim is the point in the body right behind the shoulder-blade. On receiving a bullet in this spot the deer will plunge forward for a jump or two, and then go some fifty yards in a labored gallop; will then stop, sway unsteadily on its legs for a second, and pitch forward on its side. When the hunter comes up he will find his quarry stone dead. If the deer stands facing the hunter it offers only a narrow mark, but either a throat or chest shot will be fatal.

Good shooting is especially necessary after black-tail, because it is so very tenacious of life; much more so than the white-tail, or, in proportion to its bulk, than the elk. For this reason it is of the utmost importance to give an immediately fatal or disabling wound or the game will almost certainly be lost. It is wonderful to see how far and how fast a seemingly crippled deer will go. Of course, a properly trained dog would be of the greatest use in tracking and bringing to bay wounded black-tail; but, unless properly trained to come in to heel, a dog is worse than useless; and, anyhow, it will be hard to keep one, as long as the wolf-hunters strew the ground so plentifully with poisoned bait. We have had several hunting dogs on our ranch at different times; generally wirehaired deer-hounds, fox-hounds, or greyhounds, but no means absolutely pure in blood; but they all, sooner or later, succumbed to the effects of eating poisoned meat. Some of them were quite good hunting dogs, the rough deer-hounds being perhaps the best at following and tackling a wounded buck. They were all very eager for the sport, and when in the morning we started out on a hunt the dogs were apparently more interested than the men; but their judgement did not equal their zeal, and lack of training made them on the whole more bother than advantage.

But much more than good shooting is necessary before a man can be called a good hunter. Indians, for example, get a great deal of game, but they are in most cases very bad shots. Once, while going up the Clear Fork of the Powder, in Northern Wyoming, one of my men, an excellent hunter, and myself rode into a large camp of Cheyennes; and after a while started a shooting-match with some of them. We had several trials of skill with the rifle, and, a good deal to my astonishment, I found that most of the Indians (quite successful hunters, to judge by the quantity of smoked venison lying round) were very bad shots indeed. None of them came anywhere near the hunter who was with me; nor, indeed, to myself. An Indian gets his game by his patience, his stealth, and his tireless perseverance; and a white to be really successful in still-hunting must learn to copy some of the Indian's traits.

While the game butchers, the skin hunters, and their like, work such brutal slaughter among the plains animals that these will soon be either totally extinct or so thinned out as to cease being prominent features of plains life yet, on the other hand, the nature of the country debars them from following certain murderous and unsportsman-like forms of hunting much in vogue in other quarters of our land. There is no deep water into which a deer can be driven by hounds, and then shot at arm's-length from a boat, as is the fashion with some of the city sportsmen who infest the Adirondack forests during the hunting season; nor is the winter snow ever deep enough to form a crust over which a man can go on snowshoes, and after running down a deer, which plunges as if in a quagmire, knock the poor, worn-out brute on the head with an axe. Fire-hunting is never tried in the cattle country; it would be far more likely to result in the death of a steer or pony than in the death of a deer, if attempted on foot with a torch, as is done in some of the Southern States; while the streams are not suited to the floating or jacking with a lantern in the bow of the canoe, as practised in the Adirondacks. Floating and fire-hunting, though by no means to be classed among the nobler kinds of sport, yet have a certain fascination of their own, no so much for the sake of the actual hunting, as for the novelty of being out in the wilderness at night; and the noiselessness absolutely necessary to insure success often enables the sportsman to catch curious glimpses of the night life of the different kinds of wild animals.

If it were not for the wolf poison, the plains country would be peculiarly fitted for hunting with hounds; and, if properly carried on, there is no manlier form of sport. It does not imply in the man who follows it the skill that distinguishes the successful still-hunter, but it has a dash and excitement all its own, if the hunter follows the hounds on horseback. But, as carried on in the Adirondacks and in the Eastern and Southern mountains generally, hounding deer is not worthy of much regard. There the hunter is stationed at a runaway over which deer will probably pass, and has nothing to do but sit still for a number of weary hours and perhaps put a charge of buckshot into a deer running by but a few yards off.

If a rifle instead of a shotgun is used, a certain amount of skill is necessary, for then it is hard to hit a deer running, no matter how close up; but even with this weapon all the sportsman has to do is to shoot well; he need not show knowledge of a single detail of hunting craft, nor need he have any trait of mind or body such as he must possess to follow most other kinds of the chase.

Deer-hunting on horseback is something widely different. Even if the hunters carry rifles and themselves kill the deer, using the dogs merely to drive it out of the brush, they must be bold and skilful horsemen, and must show good judgement in riding to cut off the quarry, so as to be able to get a shot at it. This is the common American method of hunting the deer in those places where it is followed with horse and hound; but it is also coursed with greyhounds in certain spots where the lay of the land permits this form of sport, and in many districts, even where ordinary hounds are used, the riders go unarmed and merely follow the pack till the deer is bayed and pulled down. All kinds of hunting on horseback—and most hunting on horseback is done with hounds—tend to bring out the best and manliest qualities in the men who follow them, and they should be encouraged in every way. Long after the rifleman, as well as the game he hunts, shall have vanished from the plains, the cattle country will afford fine sport in coursing hares; and both wolves and deer could be followed and killed with packs of properly-trained hounds, and such sport would be even more exciting than still-hunting with the rifle. It is on the great plains lying west of the Missouri that riding to hounds will in the end receive its fullest development as a national pastime.

But at present, for the reasons already stated, it is almost unknown in the cattle country; and the ranchman who loves sport must try still-hunting—and by still-hunting is meant pretty much every kind of chase where a single man, unaided by a dog, and almost always on foot, outgenerals a deer and kills it with the rifle. To do this successfully, unless deer are very plenty and tame, implies a certain knowledge of the country, and a good knowledge of the habits of the game. The hunter must keep a sharp look-out for deer sign; for, though a man soon gets to have a general knowledge of the kind of places in which deer are likely to be, yet he will also find that they are either very capricious, or else that no man has more than a partial understanding of their tastes and likings; for many spots apparently just suited to them will be almost uninhabited, while in others they will be found where it would hardly occur to any one to suspect their presence. Any cause may temporarily drive deer out of a given locality. Still-hunting, especially, is sure to send many away, while rendering the others extremely wild and shy, and where deer have become used to being pursued in only one way, it is often an excellent plan to try some entirely different method.

A certain knowledge of how to track deer is very useful. To become a really skilful tracker is most difficult; and there are some kinds of ground, where, for instance, it is very hard and dry, or frozen solid, on which almost any man will be at fault. But any one with a little practice can learn to do a certain amount of tracking. On snow, of course, it is very easy; but on the other hand it is also peculiarly difficult to avoid being seen by the deer when the ground is white. After deer have been frightened once or twice, or have even merely been disturbed by man, they get the habit of keeping a watch back on their trail; and when snow has fallen, a man is such a conspicuous object deer see him a long way off, and even the tamest become wild. A deer will often, before lying down, take a half circle back to one side and make its bed a few yards from its trail, where it can, itself unseen, watch any person tracing it up. A man tracking in snow needs to pay very little heed to the footprints, which can be followed without effort, but requires to keep up the closest scrutiny over the ground ahead of him, and on either side of the trail.

In the early morning when there is a heavy dew the footprints will be as plain as possible in the grass, and can then be followed readily; and in any place where the ground is at all damp they will usually be plain enough to be made out without difficulty. When the ground is hard or dry the work is very much less easy, and soon becomes so difficult as not to be worth while following up. Indeed, at all times, even in the snow, tracks are chiefly of use to show the probable locality in which a deer may be found; and the still-hunter instead of laboriously walking along a trail will do far better to merely follow it until, from its freshness and direction, he feels confident that the deer is in some particular space of ground, and then hunt through it, guiding himself by his knowledge of the deer's habits and by the character of the land. Tracks are of most use in showing whether deer are plenty or scarce, whether they have been in the place recently or not. Generally, signs of deer are infinitely more plentiful than the animals themselves—although in regions where tracking is especially difficult deer are often jumped without any sign having been seen at all. Usually, however, the rule is the reverse, and as deer are likely to make any quantity of tracks the beginner is apt, judging purely from the sign, greatly to over-estimate their number. Another mistake of the beginner is to look for the deer during the daytime in the places where their tracks were made in the morning, when their day beds will probably be a long distance off. In the night-time deer will lie down almost anywhere, but during the day they go some distance from their feeding- or watering-place, as already explained.

If deer are at all plenty—and if scarce only a master in the art can succeed at still-hunting—it is best not to try to follow the tracks at all, but merely to hunt carefully through any ground which from its looks seems likely to contain the animals. Of course the hunting must be done either against or across the wind, and the greatest care must be taken to avoid making a noise. Moccasins should be worn, and not a twig should be trodden on, nor should the dress be allowed to catch in a brush. Especial caution should be used in going over a ridge or crest; no man should ever let his whole body appear at once, but should first carefully peep over, not letting his rifle barrel come into view, and closely inspect every

place in sight in which a deer could possibly stand or lie, always re-
membering that a deer is when still a most difficult animal to see,
and that it will be completely hidden in cover which would apparently hardly hold a rabbit. The rifle should be carried habitually so
that the sun will not glance upon it. Advantage must be taken, in
walking, of all cover, so that the hunter will not be a conspicuous
object at any distance. The heads of a series of brushy ravines
should always be crossed; and a narrow, winding valley, with
patches of bushes and young trees down through the middle, is always a likely place. Caution should never for a moment be forgot-
ten, especially in the morning or evening, the times when a hunter
will get nine tenths of his shots; for it is just then, when moving
and feeding, that deer are most watchful. One will never browse
for more than a minute or two without raising its head and peering
about for any possible foe, the great, sensitive ears thrown forward
to catch the slightest sound. But while using such caution it is also
well to remember that as much ground should be crossed as pos-
.sible; other things being equal, the number of shots obtained will
correspond to the amount of country covered. And of course a man
should be on the hunting ground—not starting for the hunting
ground—by the time there is enough light by which to shoot.

Deer are in season for hunting from August first to January
first. August is really too early to get full enjoyment out of the
sport. The bucks, though fat and good eating, are still in the velvet;
and neither does nor fawns should be killed, as many of the latter
are in the spotted coat. Besides it is very hot in the middle of the
day, though pleasant walking in the early morning and late
evening, and with cool nights. December is apt to be too cold, although with many fine days. The true time for the chase of the
black-tail is in the three fall months. Then the air is fresh and bracing, and a man feels as if he could walk or ride all day long without
tiring. In the bright fall weather the country no longer keeps its ordinary look of parched desolation, and the landscape loses its
sameness at the touch of the frost. Where every thing before had

been gray or dull green there are now patches of russet red and bright yellow. The clumps of ash, wild plum-trees, and rose-bushes in the heads and bottoms of the sloping valleys become spots of color that glow among the stretches of brown and withered grass; the young cotton-woods, growing on the points of land round which flow the rivers and streams, change to a delicate green or yellow, in which the eye rests with pleasure after having so long seen only the dull drab of the prairies. Often there will be days of bitter cold, when a man who sleeps out in the open feels the need of warm furs; but still more often there will be days and days of sunny weather, no cold enough to bring discomfort, but yet so cool that the blood leaps briskly through a man's veins and makes him feel that to be out and walking over the hills is a pleasure in itself, even where he not in hopes of any moment seeing the sun glint on the horns and hide of some mighty buck, as it rises to face the intruder. On days such as these, mere life is enjoyment; and on days such as these, the life of a hunter is at its pleasantest and best.

Many black-tail are sometimes killed in a day. I have never made big bags myself, for I rarely hunt except for a fine head or when we need meat, and if it can be avoided do not shoot at fawns or does; so the greatest number I have ever killed in a day was three. This was late one November, on an occasion when our larder was running low. My foreman and I, upon discovering this fact, determined to make a trip next day back in the broken country, away from the river, where black-tail were almost sure to be found.

We breakfasted hours before sunrise, and then mounted our horses and rode up the river bottom. The bright prairie moon was at the full, and was sunk in the west till it hung like a globe of white fire over the long row of jagged bluffs that rose from across the river, while its beams brought into fantastic relief the peaks and crests of the buttes upon our left. The valley of the river itself was in partial darkness, and the stiff, twisted branches of the sage-brush seemed to take on uncanny shapes as they stood in the hollows. The cold was stinging, and we let our willing horses gallop with loose reins, their hoofs ringing on the frozen ground. After going up a mile or two along the course of the river we turned off to follow the bed of a large dry creek. At its mouth was a great space of ground much cut up by the hoofs of the cattle, which was in summer overflowed and almost a morass; but now the frost-bound earth was like wrinkled iron beneath the horses' feet. Behind us the westering moon sank down out of sight; and with no light but that of the stars, we let our horses thread their own way up the creek bottom. When we had gone a couple of miles from the river the sky in front of our faces took on a faint grayish tinge, the fore-runner of dawn. Every now and then we passed by bunches of cattle, lying down or standing huddled together in the patches of brush or under the lee of some shelving bank or other wind-break; and as the eastern heavens grew brighter, a dark form suddenly appeared against the sky-line, on the crest of a bluff directly ahead of us. Another and another came up beside it. A glance told us that it was a troop of ponies, which stood motionless, like so many silhouettes, their outstretched necks and long tails vividly outlined against the light behind them. All in the valley was yet dark when we reached the place where the creek began to split up and branch out into the various arms and ravines from which it headed. We galloped smartly over the divide into a set of coulies and valleys which ran into a different creek, and selected a grassy place where there was good feed to leave the horses. My companion picketed his; Manitou needed no picketing.

The tops of the hills were growing rosy, but the sun was not yet above the horizon when we started off, with our rifles on our shoulders, walking in cautious silence, for we were in good ground and might any moment see a deer. Above us was a plateau of some size, breaking off sharply at the rim into a surrounding stretch of very rough and rugged country. It sent off low spurs with notched crests into the valleys round about, and its edges were indented with steep ravines and half-circular basins, their sides covered with clusters of gnarled and wind-beaten cedars, often gathered into groves of some size. The ground was so broken as to give excellent cover under which a man could approach game unseen; there were plenty of fresh signs of deer; and we were confident we should soon get a shot. Keeping at the bottom of the gullies, so as to be ourselves inconspicuous, we walked noiselessly on, cautiously examining every pocket or turn before we rounded the corner, and looking with special care along the edges of the patches of brush.

At last, just as the sun had risen, we came out by the mouth of a deep ravine or hollow, cut in the flank of the plateau, with steep, cedar-clad sides; and on the crest of a jutting spur, not more than thirty yards from where I stood, was a black-tail doe, half facing me. I was in the shadow, and for a moment she could not make me out, and stood motionless with her head turned toward me and her great ears thrown forward. Dropping on my knee, I held the rifle a little back of her shoulder—too far back, as it proved, as she stood quartering and not broadside to me. No fairer chance could ever fall to the lot of a hunter; but to my intense chagrin, she bounded off at the report as if unhurt, disappearing instantly. My companion had now come up, and we ran up a rise of ground, and crouched down beside a great block of sandstone, in a position from which we overlooked the whole ravine or hollow. After some minutes of quiet watchfulness, we heard a twig snap—the air was so still we could hear any thing—some rods up the ravine, but below us; and immediately afterward a buck stole out of the cedars. Both of us fired at once, and with a convulsive spring he rolled over backward, one bullet having gone through his neck, and the other—probably mine—having broken a hind leg. Immediately afterward, another buck broke from the upper edge of the cover, near the top of the plateau, and, though I took a hurried shot at him, bounded over the crest, and was lost to sight.

We now determined to go down into the ravine and look for the doe, and as there was a good deal of snow in the bottom and under the trees, we knew we could soon tell if she were wounded. After a little search we found her track, and walking along it a few yards, came upon some drops and then a splash of blood. There being no need to hurry, we first dressed the dead buck,—a fine, fat fellow, but with small, misshapen horns,—and then took up the trail of the wounded doe. Here, however, I again committed an error, and paid too much heed to the trail and too little to the country round about; and while following it with my eyes down on the ground in a place where it was faint, the doe got up some distance ahead and to one side of me, and bounded off round a corner of the ravine. The bed where she had lain was not very bloody, but from the fact of her having stopped so soon, I was sure she was badly wounded. However, after she got out of the snow the ground was as hard as flint, and it was impossible to track her; the valley soon took a turn, and branched into a tangle of coulies and ravines. I deemed it probable that she would not go up hill, but would run down the course of the main valley; but as it was so uncertain, we thought it would pay us best to look for a new deer.

Our luck, however, seemed—very deservedly—to have ended. We tramped on, as swiftly as was compatible with quiet, for hour after hour; beating through the valleys against the wind, and crossing the brushy heads of the ravines, sometimes close together, sometimes keeping about a hundred yards apart, according to the nature of the ground. When we had searched all through the country round the head of the creek, into which we had come down, we walked over to the next, and went over it with equal care and patience. The next morning was now well advanced, and we had to change our method of hunting. It was no longer likely that we should find the deer feeding or in the open, and instead we looked for places where they might be expected to bed, following any trails that led into thick patches of brush or young trees, one of us then hunting through the patch while the other kept watch without. Doubtless we must have passed close to more than one deer, and doubtless others heard us and skulked off through the thick cover; but, although we saw plenty of signs, we saw neither hoof nor hair of living thing. It is under such circumstances that a still-hunter needs to show resolution, and to persevere until his luck turns—this being a euphemistic way of saying until he ceases to commit the various blunders which alarm the deer and make them get out of the way. Plenty of good shots become disgusted if they do not see a deer early in the morning, and go home; still more, if they do not see one in two or three days. Others will go on hunting, but become careless, stumble and step on dried sticks, and let their eyes fall to the ground. It is a good test of a man's resolution to see if, at the end of a long and unsuccessful tramp after deer, he moves just as carefully, and keeps just as sharp a lookout as he did at the beginning. If he does this, and exercises a little common-sense—in still-hunting, as in everything else, common-sense is the most necessary of qualities,—he may be sure that his reward will come some day; and when it does come, he feels a gratification that only his fellow-sportsmen can understand.

We lunched at the foot of a great clay butte, where there was a bed of snow. Fall or winter hunting in the Bad Lands has one great advantage: the hunter is not annoyed by thirst as he is almost sure to be if walking for long hours under the blazing summer sun. If he gets very thirsty, a mouthful or two of snow from some hollow will moisten his lips and throat; and anyhow thirstiness is largely a mere matter of habit. For lunch, the best thing a hunter can carry is dried or smoked venison, with not too much salt in it. It is much better than bread, and not nearly so dry; and it is easier to carry, as a couple of pieces can be thrust into the bosom of the hunting-shirt or the pocket, or in fact anywhere; and for keeping up a man's strength there is nothing that comes up to it.

After lunch we hunted until the shadows began to lengthen out, when we went back to our horses. The buck was packed behind good old Manitou, who can carry any amount of weight at a smart pace, and does not care at all if a strap breaks and he finds his load dangling about his feet, an event that reduces most horses to a state of frantic terror. As soon as loaded we rode down the valley into which the doe had disappeared in the morning, one taking each side and looking into every possible lurking place. The odds were all against our finding any trace of her; but a hunter soon learns that he must take advantage of every chance, however slight. This time we were rewarded for our care; for after riding about a mile our attention was attracted by a white patch in a clump of low briars. On getting off and looking in it proved to be the white rump of the doe, which lay stretched out inside, stark and stiff. The ball had gone in too far aft and had come out on the opposite side near her hip, making a mortal wound, but one which allowed her to run over a mile before dying. It was little more than an accident that we in the end got her; and my so nearly missing at such short range was due purely to carelessness and bad judgement. I had killed too many deer to be at all nervous over them, and was as cool with a buck as with a rabbit; but as she was so close I made the common mistake of being too much in a hurry, and did not wait to see that she was standing quartering to me and that consequently I should aim at the point of the shoulder. As a result the deer was nearly lost.

Neither of my shots had so far done me much credit; but at any rate I had learned where the error lay, and this is going a long way toward correcting it. I kept wishing that I could get another chance to see if I had not profited by my lessons; and before we reached home my wish was gratified. We were loping down a grassy valley, dotted with clumps of brush, the wind blowing strong in our faces, and deadening the noise made by the hoofs on the grass. As we passed by a piece of broken ground a yearling black-tail buck jumped into view and cantered away. I was off Manitou's back in an instant. The buck was moving slowly and was evidently soon gong to stop and look round, so I dropped on one knee, with my rifle half raised, and waited. When about sixty yards off he halted and turned sideways to me, offering a beautiful broadside shot. I aimed at the spot just behind the shoulder and felt I had him. At the report he went off, but with short, weak, bounds, and I knew he would not go far; nor did he, but stopped short, swayed unsteadily about, and went over on his side, dead, the bullet clean through his body.

Each of us already had a deer behind his saddle, so we could not take the last buck along with us. Accordingly we dressed him and hung him up by the heels to a branch of a tree, piling the brush around as if building a slight pen or trap, to keep off the coyotes; who, anyhow, are not apt to harm game that is hanging up, their caution seeming to make them fear that it will not be safe to do so. In such cold weather a deer hung up in this way will keep an indefinite length of time; and the carcass was all right when a week or two afterwards we sent out the buck-board to bring it back.

A stout buck-board is very useful on a ranch, where men are continually taking short trips on which they do not wish to be encumbered by the heavy ranch wagon. Pack ponies are always a nuisance, though of course an inevitable one in making journeys through mountains or forests. But on the plains a buck-board is far more handy. The blankets and provisions can be loaded upon it, and it can then be given a definite course to travel or point to reach; and meanwhile the hunters without having their horses tired by carrying heavy packs, can strike off and hunt wherever they wish. There is little or no difficulty in going over the prairie; but it needs a skilful plainsman, as well as a good teamster, to take a wagon through the Bad Lands. There are but two courses to follow. One is to go along the bottoms of the valleys; the other is to go along the tops of the divides. The latter is generally the best; for each valley usually has at its bottom a deep winding ditch with perpendicular banks, which wanders first to one side and then to the other, and has to be crossed again and again, while a little way from it begin the gullies and gulches which come down from the side hills. It is no easy matter to tell which is the main divide, as it curves and twists about, and is all the time splitting up into lesser ones, which merely separate two branches of the same creek. If the teamster does not know the lay of the land he will be likely to find himself in a *cul-de-sac*, from which he can only escape by going back a mile or two and striking out afresh. In very difficult country the horsemen must be on hand to help the team pull up the steep places. Many horses that will not pull a pound in harness will haul for all there is in them from the saddle; Manitou is a case in point. Often obstacles will be encountered across which it is simply impossible for any team to drag a loaded or even an empty wagon. Such are steep canyons, or muddy-bottomed streams with sheer banks, especially if the latter have rotten edges. The horses must then be crossed first and the wagon dragged over afterward by the aid of long ropes. Often it may be needful to build a kind of rude bridge or causeway on which to get the animals over; and if the canyon is very deep the wagon may have to be taken in pieces, let down one side, and hauled up the other. An immense amount of labor may be required to get over a very trifling distance. Pack animals, however, can go almost anywhere that a man can.

Although still-hunting on foot, as described above, is on the whole the best way to get deer, yet there are many places where from the nature of the land the sport can be followed quite as well on horseback, than which there is no more pleasant kind of hunting. The best shot I ever made in my life—a shot into which, however, I am afraid the element of chance entered much more largely than the element of skill—was made while hunting black-tail on horseback.

We were at that time making quite a long trip with the wagon, and were going up the fork of a plains river in Western Montana. As we were out of food, those two of our number who usually undertook to keep the camp supplied with game determined to make a hunt off back of the river after black-tail; for though there were some white-tail in the more densely timbered river bottoms, we had been unable to get any. It was arranged that the wagon should go on a few miles, and then halt for the night, as it was already the middle of the afternoon when we started out. The country resembled in character other parts of the cattle plains, but it was absolutely bare of trees except along the bed of the river. The rolling hills sloped steeply off into long valleys and deep ravines. They were sparsely covered with coarse grass, and also with an irregular growth of tall sage-brush, which in some places gathered into dense thickets. A beginner would have thought the country entirely too barren of cover to hold deer, but a very little experience teaches one that deer will be found in thickets of such short and sparse growth that it seems as if they could hide nothing; and, what is more, that they will often skulk round in such thickets without being discovered. And a black-tail is a bold, free animal, liking to go out in comparatively open country, where he must trust to his own powers, and not to any concealment, to protect him from danger.

Where the hilly country joined the alluvial river bottom, it broke short off into steep bluffs, up which none but a Western pony could have climbed. It is really wonderful to see what places a pony can get over, and the indifference with which it regards tumbles. In getting up from the bottom we went into a wash-out, and then led our ponies along a clay ledge, from which we turned off and went straight up a very steep sandy bluff. My companion was ahead; just as he turned off the ledge, and as I was right underneath him, his horse, in plunging to try to get up the sand bluff, overbalanced itself, and, after standing erect on its hind legs for a second, came over backward. The second's pause while it stood bolt upright, gave me time to make a frantic leap out of the way with my pony, which scrambled after me, and we both clung with hands and hoofs to the side of the bank, while the other horse took two as complete somersaults as I ever saw, and landed with a crash at the bottom of the wash-out, feet uppermost. I thought it was done for, but not a bit. After a moment or two it struggled to its legs, shook itself, and looked round in rather a shamefaced way, apparently not in the least the worse for the fall. We now got my pony up to the top by vigorous pulling, and then went down for the other, which at first strongly objected to making another trial, but, after much coaxing and a good deal of abuse, took a start and went up without trouble.

For some time after reaching the top of the bluffs we rode along without seeing any thing. When it was possible, we kept one on each side of a creek, avoiding the tops of the ridges, because while on them a horseman can be seen at a very long distance, and going with particular caution whenever we went round a spur or came up over a crest. The country stretched away like an endless, billowy sea of dull-brown soil and barren sage-brush, the valleys making long parallel furrows, and every thing having a look of dreary sameness. At length, as we came out on a rounded ridge, three black-tail bucks started up from a lot of sage-brush some two hundred yards away and below us, and made off down hill. It was a very long shot, especially to try running, but, as game seemed scarce and cartridges were plenty, I leaped off the horse, and, kneeling, fired. The bullet went low striking in line at the feet of the hindmost. I held very high next time, making a wild shot above and ahead of them, which had the effect of turning them, and they went off round a shoulder of a bluff, being by this time down in the valley. Having plenty of time I elevated the sights (a thing I hardly ever do) to four hundred yards and waited for their reappearance. Meanwhile they had evidently gotten over their fright, for pretty soon one walked out from the other side of the bluff, and came to a standstill, broadside toward me. He was too far off for me to see his horns. As I was raising the rifle another stepped out and began to walk towards the first. I thought I might as well have as much of a target as possible to shoot at, and waited for the second buck to come out farther, which he did immediately and stood still just alongside of the first. I aimed above his shoulders and pulled the trigger. Over went the two bucks! And when I rushed down to where they lay I found I had pulled a little to one side, and the bullet had broken the backs of both. While my companion was dressing them I went back and paced off the distance. It was just four hundred and thirty-one long paces; over four hundred yards. Both were large bucks and very fat, with the velvet hanging in shreds from their antlers, for it was late in August. The day was waning and we had a long ride back to the wagon, each with a buck behind his saddle. When we came back to the river valley it was pitch dark, and it was rather ticklish work for our heavily laden horses to pick their way down the steep bluffs and over the rapid stream; nor were we sorry when we saw ahead under a bluff the gleam of the camp fire, as it was reflected back from the canvas-topped prairie schooner, that for the time being represented home to us.

This was much the best shot I ever made; and it is just such a shot as any one will occasionally make if he takes a good many chances and fires often at ranges where the odds are greatly against his hitting. I suppose I had fired a dozen times at animals four or five hundred yards off, and now, by the doctrine of chances, I happened to hit, but I would have been very foolish if I had thought for a moment that I had learned how to hit at over four hundred yards. I have yet to see the hunter who can hit with any regularity at that distance, when he has to judge it for himself; though I have seen plenty who could make such a long range hit now and then. And I have noticed that such a hunter, in talking over his experience, was certain soon to forget the numerous misses he made, and to say, and even to actually think, that his occasional hits represented his average shooting.

One of the finest black-tail bucks I ever shot was killed while lying out in a rather unusual place. I was hunting mountain-sheep, in a stretch of very high and broken country, and about mid-day, crept cautiously up to the edge of a great gorge, whose sheer walls went straight down several hundred feet. Peeping over the brink of the chasm I saw a buck, lying out on a ledge so narrow as to barely hold him, right on the face of the cliff wall opposite, some distance below, and about seventy yards diagonally across from me. He lay with his legs half stretched out, and his head turned so as to give me an exact centre-shot at his forehead; the bullet going in between his eyes, so that his legs hardly so much as twitched when he received it. It was toilsome and almost dangerous work climbing out to where he lay; I have never known any other individual, even of this bold and adventurous species of deer, to take its noonday siesta in a place so barren of all cover and so difficult of access even to the most surefooted climber. This buck was as fat as a prize sheep, and heavier than any other I have ever killed; while his antlers also were, with two exceptions, the best I ever got.

The Prong-Buck: A Trip on the Prairie
(From *Hunting Trips of a Ranchman*)

No antelope are found, except rarely, immediately round my ranch-house, where the ground is much too broken to suit them; but on the great prairies, ten or fifteen miles off, they are plentiful, though far from as abundant as they were a few years ago when the cattle were first driven into the land. By plainsmen they are called either prong-horn or antelope, but are most often known by the latter and much less descriptive title. Where they are found they are always very conspicuous figures in the landscape; for, far from attempting to conceal itself, an antelope really seems anxious to take up a prominent position, caring only to be able to itself see its foes. It is the smallest in size of the plains game, even smaller than a white-tail deer; and its hide is valueless, being thin and porous, and making very poor buckskin. In its whole appearance and structure it is a most singular creature. Unlike all other hollow-horned animals, it sheds its horns annually, exactly as the deer shed their solid antlers; but the shedding process in the prong-horn occupies but a

135

very few days, so short a time, indeed, that many hunters stoutly deny that it takes place at all. The hair is of remarkable texture, very long, coarse and brittle; in the spring it comes off in handfuls. In strong contrast to the reddish yellow of the other parts of the body, the rump is pure white, and when alarmed or irritated every hair in the white patch bristles up on end, greatly increasing the apparent area of the color. The flesh, unlike that of any other plains animal, is equally good all through the year. In the fall it is hardly so juicy as deer venison, but in the spring, when no other kind of game is worth eating, it is perfectly good; and at that time of the year, if we have to get fresh meat, we would rather kill antelope than any thing else; and as the bucks are always to be instantly distinguished from the does by their large horns, we confine ourselves to them, and so work no harm to the species.

The antelope is a queer-looking rather than a beautiful animal. The curious pronged horns, great bulging eyes, and strange bridle-like marks and bands on the face and throat are more striking, but less handsome, than the delicate head and branching antlers of a deer; and it entirely lacks the latter animal's grace of movement. In its form and look, when standing still, it is rather angular and goat-like, and its movements merely have the charm that comes from lightness, speed, and agility. Its gait is singularly regular and even, without any of the bounding, rolling movement of a deer; and it is, consequently, very easy to hit running, compared with other kinds of game.

Antelope possess a most morbid curiosity. The appearance of any thing out of the way, or to which they are not accustomed, often seems to drive them nearly beside themselves with mingled fright and desire to know what it is, a combination of feelings that throws them into a perfect panic, during whose continuance they will at times seem utterly unable to take care of themselves. In very remote, wild places, to which no white man often penetrates, the appearance of a white-topped wagon will be enough to excite this feeling in the prong-horn, and in such cases it is not unusual for a herd to come up and circle round the strange object heedless of rifle-shots. This curiosity is particularly strong in the bucks during rutting-time, and one method of hunting them is to take advantage of it, and "flag" them up to the hunters by waving a red handkerchief or some other object to and fro in the air. In very wild places they can sometimes be flagged up, even after they have seen the man; but, elsewhere, the latter must keep himself carefully concealed behind a ridge or hillock, or in tall grass, and keep cautiously waving the handkerchief overhead. The antelope will look fixedly at it, stamp, snort, start away, come nearer by fits and starts, and run from one side to the other, the better to see it. Sometimes a wary old buck will keep this up for half an hour, and at the end make off; but, again, the attraction may prove too strong, and the antelope comes slowly on until within rifle-shot. This method of hunting, however, is not so much practised now as formerly, as the antelope are getting continually shyer and more difficult to flag. I have never myself shot one in this manner, though I have often seen the feat performed, and have several times tried it myself, but always with the result that after I had made my arm really weak with waving the handkerchief to and fro, the antelope, which had been shifting about just out of range, suddenly took to its heels and made off.

No other kind of plains game, except the big-horn, is as shy and sharp-sighted as the antelope; and both its own habits and the open nature of the ground on which it is found render it peculiarly difficult to stalk. There is no cover, and if a man is once seen by the game the latter will not let him get out of sight again, unless it decides to go off at a gait that soon puts half a dozen miles between them. It shifts its position, so as to keep the hunter continually in sight. Thus, if it is standing on a ridge, and the hunter disappears into a ravine up which he intends to crawl, the antelope promptly gallops off to some other place of observation from which its foe is again visible; and this is repeated until the animal at last makes up its mind to start for good. It keeps up an incessant watch, being ever on the look-out for danger, far or near; and as it can see an immense distance, and has its home on ground so level that a horseman can be made out a mile off, its attention is apt to be attracted when still four or five rifle-shots beyond range, and after it has once caught a glimpse of the foe, the latter might as well give up all hopes of getting the game.

But while so much more wary than deer, it is also at times much more foolish, and has certain habits—some of which, such as its inordinate curiosity and liability to panic, have already been alluded to—that tend to its destruction. Ordinarily, it is a far more difficult feat to kill an antelope than it is to kill a deer, but there are times when the former can be slaughtered in such numbers that it becomes mere butchery.

The prong-horn is pre-eminently a gregarious animal. It is found in bands almost all the year through. During the two or three days after he has shed his horns and while the new ones are growing the buck retires to some out-of-the-way spot, and while bringing forth her fawns the doe stays by herself. But as soon as possible each again rejoins the band; and the fawns become members of it at a remarkably early age. In the late fall, when the bitter cold has begun, a large number of these bands collect together, and immense herds are formed which last throughout the winter. Thus at this season a man may travel for days through regions where antelope are most plentiful during the hot months and never see one; but if he does come across any they will be apt to be in great numbers, most probably along the edge of the Bad Lands, where the ground is rolling rather than broken, but where there is some shelter from the furious winter gales. Often they will even come down to the river bottom or find their way up to some plateau. They now always hang closely about the places they have chosen for their winter haunts, and seem very reluctant to leave them. They go in dense herds, and when starved and weak with cold are less shy;

and can often be killed in great numbers by any one who has found out where they are—though a true sportsman will not molest them at this season.

Sometimes a small number of individuals will at this time get separated from the main herd and take up their abode in some place by themselves; and when they have once done so it is almost impossible to drive them away. Last winter a solitary prong-horn strayed into the river bottom at the mouth of a wide creek-valley, half a mile from my ranch, and stayed there for three months, keeping with the cattle, and always being found within a mile of the same spot. A little band at the same time established itself on a large plateau, about five miles long by two miles wide, some distance up the river above me, and afforded fine sport to a couple of ranchmen who lived not far from its base. The antelope, twenty or thirty in number, would not leave the plateau, which lies in the midst of broken ground; for it is a peculiarity of these animals, which will be spoken of further on, that they will try to keep in the open ground at any cost or hazard. The two ranchmen agreed never to shoot at the antelope on foot, but only to try to kill them from horseback, either with their revolvers or their Winchesters. They thus hunted them for the sake of the sport purely; and certainly they got plenty of fun out of them. Very few horses indeed are as fast as a prong-horn; and these few did not include any owned by either of my two friends. But the antelope were always being obliged to break back from the edge of the plateau, and so were forced constantly to offer opportunities for cutting them off; and these opportunities were still further increased by the two hunters separating. One of them would go to the upper end of the plateau and start the band, riding after them at full speed. They would distance him, but would be checked in their career by coming to the brink of the cliff; then they would turn at an angle and give their pursuers a chance to cut them off; and if they kept straight up the middle the other hunter would head them. When a favorable moment came the hunters would dash in as close as possible and empty their revolvers or repeaters into the herd; but it is astonishing how hard it is, when riding a horse at full speed, to hit any object, unless it is directly under the muzzle of the weapon. The number of cartridges spent compared to the number of prong-horn killed was enormous; but the fun and excitement of the chase were the main objects with my friends, to whom the actual killing of the game was of entirely secondary importance. They went out after them about a dozen times during the winter, and killed in all ten or fifteen prong-horns.

A prong-horn is by far the fleetest animal on the plains; one can outrun and outlast a deer with the greatest ease. Very swift grey-hounds can overtake them, if hunted in leashes or couples; but only a remarkably good dog can run one down single-handed. Be-sides prong-horn are most plucky little creatures, and will make a most resolute fight against a dog or wolf, striking with their forefeet and punching with their not very formidable horns, and are so quick and wiry as to be really rather hard to master.

Antelope have the greatest objection to going on any thing but open ground, and seem to be absolutely unable to make a high jump. If a band is caught feeding in the bottom of a valley leading into a plain they invariably make a rush straight to the mouth, even if the foe is stationed there, and will run heedlessly by him, no matter how narrow the mouth is, rather than not try to reach the open country. It is almost impossible to force them into even a small patch of brush, and they will face almost certain death rather than try to leap a really very trifling obstacle. If caught in a glade surrounded by a slight growth of brushwood, they make no effort whatever to get through or over this growth, but dash frantically out through the way by which they got in. Often the deer, espe-cially the black-tail, will wander out on the edge of the plain fre-quented by antelope; and it is curious to see the two animals separate the second there is an alarm, the deer making for the bro-ken country, while the antelope scud for the level plains. Once two of my men nearly caught a couple of antelope in their hands. They were out driving in the buck-board, and saw two antelope, a long distance ahead, enter the mouth of a wash-out (a canyon *in petto*); they had strayed away from the prairie to the river bottom, and were evidently feeling lost. My two men did not think much of the matter but when opposite the mouth of the wash-out, which was only thirty feet or so wide, they saw the two antelope starting to come out, having found that it was a blind passage, with no outlet at the other end. Both men jumped out of the buck-board and ran to the entrance; the two antelope dashed frantically to and fro in-side the wash-out. The sides were steep, but a deer would have scaled them at once; yet the antelope seemed utterly unable to do this, and finally broke out past the two men and got away. They came so close that the men were able to touch each of them, but their movements were too quick to permit of their being caught.

However, though unable to leap any height, an antelope can skim across a level jump like a bird, and will go over water-courses and wash-outs that very few horses indeed will face. A mountain-sheep, on the other hand, is a marvellous vertical leaper; the black-tail deer comes next; the white-tail is pretty good, and the elk is at any rate better than the antelope; but when it comes to horizontal jumping the latter can beat them all.

In May or early June the doe brings forth her fawns, usually two in number, for she is very prolific. She makes her bed in some valley or hollow, and keeps with the rest of the band, only return-ing to the fawns to feed them. They lie out in the grass or under some slight bush, but are marvellously hard to find. By instinct they at once know how to crouch down so as to be as inconspicuous as possible. Once we scared away a female prong-horn from an ap-parently perfectly level hill-side; and in riding along passed over the spot she had left and came upon two little fawns that could have been but a few hours old. They lay flat in the grass, with their legs doubled under them and their necks and heads stretched out on the ground. When we took them up and handled them, they soon got used to us and moved awkwardly round, but at any sudden noise or motion they would immediately squat flat down again. But at a very early age the fawns learn how to shift for themselves, and can then run almost as fast as their parents, even when no larger than a jack-rabbit. Once, while we were haying, a couple of my cowboys spent half an hour in trying to run down and capture a little fawn, but they were unable to catch it, it ran so fast and ducked about so quickly. Antelope fawns are very easily tamed and make most amusing pets. We have had two or three, but have never succeeded in rearing any of them; but some of the adjoining ranchmen have been more fortunate. They are not nearly so pretty as deer fawns, having long, gangling legs and angular bodies, but they are much more familiar and interesting. One of my neighbors has three live prong-horns, as well as two little spotted white-tail deer. The deer fawns are always skulking about, and are by no means such bold inquisitive little creatures as the small antelope are. The latter have a nurse in the shape of a fat old ewe; and it is funny to see her, when alarmed, running off at a waddling gait, while her ungainly little foster-children skip round and round her, cutting the most extraordinary antics. There are a couple of very large dogs, mastiffs, on the place, whose natural solemnity is completely disconcerted by the importunities and fearlessness of the little antelope fawns. Where one goes the other two always follow; and so one of the mastiffs, while solemnly blinking in the sun, will suddenly find himself charged at full speed by the three queer little creatures, who will often fairly butt up against him. The uneasy look of the dog, and his efforts to get out of the way without compromising his dignity, are really very comical.

Young fawns seem to give out no scent, and thus many of them escape from the numerous carnivorous beasts that are ever prowling about at night over the prairie, and which, during the spring months, are always fat from feeding on the bodies of the innocents they have murdered. If discovered by a fox or coyote during its first few days of existence a little fawn has no chance of life, although the mother, if present, will fight desperately for it; but after it has acquired the use of its legs it has no more to fear than have any of the older ones.

Sometimes the fawns fall victims to the great Golden Eagle. This grand bird, the War Eagle of the Sioux, is not very common in the Bad Lands, but is sometimes still seen with us; and, as everywhere else, its mere presence adds a certain grandeur to its lonely haunts. Two or three years ago a nest was found by one of my men on the face of an almost inaccessible cliff, and a young bird was taken out from it and reared in a roughly extemporized cage. Wherever the eagle exists it holds undisputed sway over every thing whose size does not protect it from the great bird's beak and talons; not only does it feed on hares, grouse, and ducks, but it will also attack the young fawns of the deer and antelope. Still, the eagle is but an occasional foe, and aside from man, the only formidable enemies the antelope has to fear are the wolves and coyotes. These are very destructive to the young, and are always lounging about the band to pick up any wounded straggler; in winter, when the ground is slippery and the antelope numbed and weak, they will often commit great havoc even among those that are grown up.

The voice of the antelope is not at all like that of the deer. Instead of bleating it utters a quick, harsh noise, a kind of bark; a little like the sound "kau," sharply and clearly repeated. It can be heard a long distance off; and is usually uttered when the animal is a little startled or surprised by the presence of something it does not understand.

The prong-horn cannot go without water any longer than a deer can, and will go great distances to get it; for space is nothing to a traveller with such speed and such last. No matter how dry and barren may be the desert in which antelope are found, it may be taken for granted that they are always within reaching distance of some spring or pool of water, and that they visit it once a day. Once or twice I have camped out by some pool, which was the only one for miles around, and in every such case have been surprised at night by the visits of the antelope, who, on finding that their drinking-place was tenanted, would hover round at a short distance, returning again and again and continually uttering the barking "kau, kau," until they became convinced that there was no hope of their getting in, when they would set off at a run for some other place.

Prong-horn perhaps prefer the rolling prairies of short grass as their home, but seem to do almost equally well on the desolate and monotonous wastes where the sage-brush and prickly pear and a few blades of coarse grass are the only signs of plant life to be seen. In such places, the prong-horn, the sage cock, the rattlesnake, and the horned frog alone are able to make out a livelihood.

The horned frog is not a frog at all, but a lizard,—a queer, stumpy little fellow with spikes all over the top of its head and back, and given to moving in the most leisurely manner imaginable. Nothing will make it hurry. If taken home it becomes a very tame and quaint but also very uninteresting little pet.

Rattlesnakes are only too plentiful every where; along the river bottoms, in the broken, hilly ground, and on the prairies and the great desert wastes alike. Every cowboy kills dozens each season. To a man wearing top-boots there is little or no danger where he is merely walking about, for the fangs cannot get through the leather, and the snake does not strike as high as the knee. Indeed the rattlesnake is not nearly as dangerous as are most poisonous serpents, for it always gives fair warning before striking, and is both sluggish and timid. If it can it will get out of the way, and only coils up in its attitude of defence when it believes that it is actually menaced. It is, of course, however, both a dangerous and a disagreeable neighbor, and one of its annoying traits is the fondness it displays for crawling into a hut or taking refuge among the blankets left out on the ground. Except in such cases men are rarely in danger from it, unless they happen to be stooping over, as was the case with one of my cowboys who had leaned over to pick up a log, and was almost bitten by a snake which was underneath it; or unless the snake is encountered while stalking an animal. Once I was creeping up to an antelope under cover of some very low sage-brush—so low that I had to lie flat on my face and push myself along with my hands and feet. While cautiously moving on in this way I was electrified by hearing almost by my ears the well-known, ominous "whir-r-r" of a rattlesnake, and on hastily glancing up there was the reptile, not ten feet away from me, all coiled up and waiting. I backed off and crawled to one side, the rattler turning its head round to keep watch over my movements; when the stalk was over (the antelope took alarm and ran off before I was within rifle-shot) I came back, hunted up the snake, and killed it. Although I have known of several men being bitten, I know of but one case where the bite caused the death of a human being. This was a girl who had been out milking, and was returning, in bare feet; the snake struck her just above the ankle, and in her fright she fell and was struck again in the neck. The double wound was too much for her, and the poison killed her in the course of a couple of hours.

Occasionally one meets a rattlesnake whose rattle has been lost or injured; and such a one is always dangerous, because it strikes without warning. I once nearly lost a horse by the bite of one of these snakes without rattles. I was riding along a path when my horse gave a tremendous start and jump; looking back I saw that it had been struck at by a rattlesnake with an injured tail, which had been lying hid in a bunch of grass, directly beside the path. Luck-ily it had merely hit the hard hoof, breaking one of its fangs.

Horses differ very much in their conduct toward snakes. Some show great fright at sight of them or on hearing their rattles, plunging and rearing and refusing to go anywhere near the spot; while others have no fear of them at all, being really perfectly stu-pid about them. Manitou does not lose his wits at all over them, but at the same time takes very good care not to come within striking distance.

Ranchmen often suffer some loss among their stock owing to snake-bites; both horned cattle and horses, in grazing, frequently

145

coming on snakes and having their noses or cheeks bitten. Generally, these wounds are not fatal, though very uncomfortable; it is not uncommon to see a woe-begone looking mule with its head double the natural size, in consequence of having incautiously browsed over a snake. A neighbor lost a weak pony in this way; and one of our best steers also perished from the same cause. But in the latter case, the animal, like the poor girl spoken of above, had received two wounds with the poison fangs; apparently it had, while grazing with its head down, been first struck in the nose, and been again struck in the foreleg as it started away.

Of all kinds of hunting, the chase of the antelope is preeminently that requiring skill in the use of the rifle at long range. The distance at which shots have to be taken in antelope hunting is at least double the ordinary distance at which deer are fired at. In pursuing most other kinds of game, a hunter who is not a good shot may still do excellent work; but in prong-horn hunting, no man can make even a fairly good record unless he is a skilful marksman. I have myself done but little hunting after antelopes, and have not, as a rule, been very successful in the pursuit.

Ordinary hounds are rarely, or never, used to chase this game; but coursing it with greyhounds is as manly and exhilarating a form of sport as can be imagined,—a much better way of hunting it than is shooting it with the rifle, which latter, though needing more skill in the actual use of the weapon, is in every other respect greatly inferior as a sport to still-hunting the black-tail or big-horn.

I never but once took a trip of any length with antelope hunting for its chief object. This was one June, when all the men were away on the round-up. As is usual during the busy half of the ranchman's year, the spring and summer, when men have no time to hunt and game is out of condition, we had been living on salt pork, beans, potatoes, and bread; and I had hardly had a rifle in my hand for months; so, finding I had a few days to spare, I thought I should take a short trip on the prairie, in the beautiful June

weather, and get a little sport and a little fresh meat out of the
bands of prong-horn bucks, which I was sure to encounter. Intending to be gone but a couple of days, it was not necessary to take
many articles. Behind my saddle I carried a blanket for bedding,
and an oil-skin coat to ward off the wet; a large metal cup with the
hand riveted, not soldered on, so that water could be boiled in it; a
little tea and salt, and some biscuits; and a small water-proof bag
containing my half dozen personal necessaries—not forgetting a
book. The whole formed a small, light pack, very little encum-
brance to stout old Manitou. In June, fair weather can generally be
counted on in the dry plains country.

I started in the very earliest morning, when the intense brilliancy of the stars had just begun to pale before the first streak of
dawn. By the time I left the river bottom and struck off up the valley of a winding creek, which led through the Bad Lands, the eastern sky was growing rosy; and soon the buttes and cliffs were lit up
by the level rays of the cloudless summer sun. The air was fresh
and sweet, and odorous with the sweet scents of the spring-time
that was but barely passed; the dew lay heavy, in glittering drops
on the leaves and the blades of grass, whose vivid green, at this season, for a short time brightens the desolate and sterile-looking
wastes of the lonely western plains. The rose-bushes were all in
bloom and their pink blossoms clustered in every point and bend
of the stream; and the sweet, sad songs of the hermit thrushes rose
from the thickets, while the meadow larks perched boldly in sight
as they uttered their louder and more cheerful music. The round-
up had passed by our ranch, and all the cattle with our brands, the
maltese cross and cut dewlap, or the elk-horn and triangle, had
been turned loose; they had not yet worked away from the river,
and I rode by long strings of them, walking in single file off to the
hills, or standing in groups to look at me as I passed.

Leaving the creek I struck off among a region of scoria buttes,
the ground rising into rounded hills through whose grassy covering

the red volcanic rock showed in places, while boulder-like fragments of it were scattered all through the valleys between. There were a few clumps of bushes here and there, and near one of them were two magpies, who lit on an old buffalo skull, bleached white by sun and snow. Magpies are birds that catch the eye at once from their bold black and white plumage and long tails; and they are very saucy and at the same time very cunning and shy. In spring we do not often see them; but in the late fall and winter they will come close round the huts and out-buildings on the look-out for any thing to eat. If a deer is hung up and they can get at it they will pick it to pieces with their sharp bills; and their carnivorous tastes and their habit of coming round hunters' camps after the game that is left out, call to mind their kinsman, the whiskey-jack or moose-bird of the northern forests.

After passing the last line of low, rounded scoria buttes, the horse stepped out on the border of the great, seemingly endless stretches of rolling or nearly level prairie, over which I had planned to travel and hunt for the next two or three days. At intervals of ten or a dozen miles this prairie was crossed by dry creeks, with, in places in their beds, pools or springs of water, and alongside a spindling growth of trees and bushes; and my intention was to hunt across these creeks, and camp by some waterhole in one of them at night.

I rode over the land in a general southerly course, bending to the right or left according to the nature of the ground and the likelihood of finding game. Most of the time the horse kept on a steady single-foot, but this was varied by a sharp lope every now and then, to ease the muscles of both steed and rider. The sun was well up, and its beams beat fiercely down on our heads from out of the cloudless sky; for at this season, though the nights and the early morning and late evening are cool and pleasant, the hours around noon are very hot. My glass was slung alongside the saddle, and from every one of the scattered hillocks the country was scanned carefully far and near; and the greatest caution was used in riding up over any divide, to be sure that no game on the opposite side was scared by the sudden appearance of my horse or myself.

Nowhere, not even at sea, does a man feel more lonely than when riding over the far-reaching, seemingly never-ending plains; and, after a man has lived a little while on or near them, their very vastness and loneliness and their melancholy monotony have a strong fascination for him. The landscape seems always the same, and after the traveller has plodded on for miles and miles he gets to feel as if the distance was indeed boundless. As far as the eye can see there is no break; either the prairie stretches out into perfectly level flats, or else there are gentle, rolling slopes, whose crests mark the divides between the drainage systems of the different creeks, and when one of these is ascended, immediately another precisely like it takes is place in the distance, and so roll succeeds roll in a succession as interminable as that of the waves of the ocean. Nowhere else does one seem so far off from all mankind; the plains stretch out in death-like and measure-less expanse, and as he journeys over them they will for many miles be lacking in all signs of life. Although he can see so far, yet all objects on the outer-most verge of the horizon, even though within the ken of his vision, look unreal and strange; for there is no shade to take away from the bright glare, and at a little distance things seem to shimmer and dance in the hot rays of the sun. The ground is scorched to a dull brown, and against its monotonous expanse any objects stand out with a prominence that makes it difficult to judge of the distance at which they are. A mile off one can see, through the strange shimmering haze, the shadowy white outlines of something which looms vaguely up till it looks as large as the canvas-top of a prairies wagon; but as the horseman comes nearer it shrinks and dwindles and takes clearer form, until at last it changes into the ghastly staring skull of some mighty buffalo, long dead and gone to join the rest of his vanished race.

When the grassy prairies are left and the traveller enters a region of alkali desert and sage-brush, the look of the country becomes even more grim and forbidding. In places the alkali forms a white frost on the ground that glances in the sunlight like the surface of a frozen lake, the dusty little sage-brush, stunted and dried up, sprawls over the parched ground, from which it can hardly extract the small amount of nourishment necessary for even its weazened life; the spiny cactus alone seems to be really in its true home. Yet even in such places antelope will be found, as alert and as abounding with vivacious life as elsewhere. Owing to the magnifying and distorting power of the clear, dry plains air, every object, no matter what its shape or color or apparent distance, needs the closest examination. A magpie sitting on a white skull, or a couple of ravens, will look, a quarter of a mile off, like some curious beast; and time and again a raw hunter will try to stalk a lump of clay or a burnt stick; and after being once or twice disappointed he is apt to rush to the other extreme, and conclude too hastily that a given object is not an antelope, when it very possibly is.

During the morning I came in sight of several small bands or pairs of antelope. Most of them saw me as soon as or before I saw them, and after watching me with intense curiosity as long as I was in sight and at a distance, made off at once as soon as I went into a hollow or appeared to be approaching too near. Twice, in scanning the country narrowly with the glasses, from behind a sheltering divide, bands of prong-horn were seen that had not discovered me. In each case the horse was at once left to graze, while I started off after the game, nearly a mile distant. For the first half mile I could walk upright or go along half stooping; then, as the distance grew closer, I had to crawl on all fours and keep behind any little broken bank, or take advantage of a small, dry watercourse; and toward the end work my way flat on my face, wriggling like a serpent, using every stunted sage-brush or patch of cactus as a cover, bare-headed under the blazing sun. In each case, after nearly an hour's irksome, thirsty work, the stalk failed. One band simply ran off without a second's warning, alarmed at some awkward movement on my part, and without giving a chance for a shot. In the other instance, while still at very long and uncertain range, I heard the sharp barking alarm-note of one of the prong-horn; the whole band instantly raising their heads and gazing intently at their would-be destroyer. They were a very long way off; but, seeing it was hopeless to try to get nearer I rested my rifle over a little mound of earth and fired. The dust came up in a puff to one side of the nearest antelope; the whole band took a few jumps and turned again; the second shot struck at their feet, and they went off like so many race-horses, being missed again as they ran. I sat up by a sage-brush thinking they would of course not come back, when to my surprise I saw them wheel round with the precision of a cavalry squadron, all in line and fronting me, the white and brown markings on their heads and throats showing like the facings on soldiers' uniforms; and then back they came charging up till again within long range, when they wheeled their line as if on a pivot and once more made off, this time for good, not heeding an ineffectual fusillade from the Winchester. Antelope often go through a series of regular evolutions, like so many trained horsemen, wheeling, turning, halting, and running as if under command; and their coming back to again run the (as it proved very harmless) gauntlet of my fire was due either to curiosity or to one of those panicky freaks which occasionally seize those ordinarily wary animals, and cause them to run into danger easily avoided by creatures commonly much more readily approached than they are. I had fired half a dozen shots without effect; but while no one ever gets over his feeling of self-indignation at missing an easy shot at close quarters, any one who hunts antelope and is not of a disposition so timid as never to take chances, soon learns that he has to expect to expend a good deal of powder and lead before bagging his game.

By mid-day we reached a dry creek and followed up its course for a mile or so, till a small spot of green in the side of a bank showed the presence of water, a little pool of which lay underneath. The ground was so rotten that it was with difficulty I could get Manitou down where he could drink; but at last both of us satisfied our thirst, and he was turned loose to graze, with his saddle off, so as to cool his back, and I after eating a biscuit, lay on my face on the ground—there was no shade of any sort near—and dozed until a couple of hours' rest and feed had put the horse in good trim for the afternoon ride. When it came to crossing over the dry creek on whose bank we had rested, we almost went down in a quicksand, and it was only by frantic struggles and flounderings that we managed to get over.

On account of these quicksands and mud-holes, crossing the creeks on the prairie is often very disagreeable work. Even when apparently perfectly dry the bottom may have merely a thin crust of hard mud and underneath a fathomless bed of slime. If the grass appears wet and with here and there a few tussocks of taller blades in it, it is well to avoid it. Often a man may have to go along a creek nearly a mile before he can find a safe crossing, or else run the risk of seeing his horse mired hard and fast. When a horse is once in a mud-hole it will perhaps so exhaust itself by its first desperate and fruitless struggle that is it almost impossible to get it out. Its bridle and saddle have to be taken off; if another horse is along the lariat is drawn from the pommel of the latter's saddle to the neck of the one that is in, and it is hauled out by main force. Otherwise a man may have to work half a day fixing the horse's legs in the right position and then taking it by the forelock and endeavoring to get it to make a plunge; each plunge bring it perhaps a few inches nearer the firm ground. Quicksands are even more dangerous than these mud-holes, as, if at all deep, a creature that cannot get out immediately is sure to be speedily engulfed. Many parts of the Little Missouri are impassable on account of these quicksands. Always in crossing unknown ground that looks dangerous it is best to feel your way very cautiously along, and, if possible, to find out some cattle trail or even game trail which can be followed.

For some time after leaving the creek nothing was seen; until, on coming over the crest of the next great divide, I came in sight of a band of six or eight prong-horn about a quarter of a mile off to my right hand. There was a slight breeze from the southeast, which blew diagonally across my path towards the antelopes. The latter, after staring at me a minute, as I rode slowly on, suddenly started at full speed to run directly up wind, and therefore in a direction that would cut the line of my course less than half a mile ahead of where I was. Knowing that when antelope begin running in a straight line they are very hard to turn, and seeing that they would have to run a longer distance than my horse would to intercept them, I clapped spurs into Manitou, and the game old fellow, a very fleet runner, stretched himself down to the ground and seemed to go almost as fast as the quarry. As I had expected, the latter, when they saw me running, merely straightened themselves out and went on, possibly even faster than before, without changing the line of their flight, keeping right up wind. Both horse and antelope fairly flew over the ground, their courses being at an angle that would certainly bring them together. Two of the antelope led, by some fifty yards or so, the others, who were all bunched together. Nearer and nearer we came, Manitou, in spite of carrying myself and the pack behind the saddle, gamely holding his own, while the antelope, with outstretched necks, went at an even, regular gait that offered a strong contrast to the springing bounds with which a deer runs. At last the two leading animals crossed the line of my flight ahead of me; when I pulled short up, leaped from Manitou's back, and blazed into the band as they went by not forty yards off, aiming well ahead of a fine buck who was on the side nearest me. An antelope's gait is so even that it offers a good running mark; and as the smoke blew off I saw the buck roll over like a rabbit, with both shoulders broken. I then emptied the Winchester at the rest of the band, breaking one hind leg of a young buck. Hastily cutting the throat of, and opening, the dead buck, I again mounted and started off after the wounded one. But, though only on three legs, it went astonishingly fast, having had a good start; and after following it over a mile I gave up the pursuit, though I had gained a good deal; for the heat was very great, and I did not deem it well to tire the horse at the beginning of the trip. Returning to the carcass, I cut off the hams and strung them beside the saddle; an antelope is so spare that there is very little more meat on the body.

This trick of running in a straight line is another of the antelope's peculiar characteristics which frequently lead it into danger. Although with so much sharper eyes than a deer, antelope are in many ways far stupider animals, more like sheep, and they especially resemble the latter in their habit of following a leader, and in their foolish obstinacy in keeping to a course they have once adopted. If a horseman starts to head off a deer the latter will always turn long before he has come within range, but quite often an antelope will merely increase his speed and try to pass ahead of his foe. Almost always, however, one if alone will keep out of gunshot, owing to the speed at which he goes, but if there are several in a band which is well strung out, the leader only cares for his own safety and passes well ahead himself. The others follow like sheep, without turning in the least from the line the first followed, and thus may pass within close range. If the leader bounds into the air, those following will often go through exactly the same motions, and if he turns, the others are very apt to each in succession run up and turn in the same place, unless the whole band are maneuvering together, like a squadron of cavalry under orders, as has already been spoken of.

After securing the buck's hams and head (the latter for the sake of the horns, which were unusually long and fine), I pushed readily on without stopping to hunt, to reach some large creek which would contain both wood and water, for even in summer a fire adds greatly to the comfort and cosiness of a night camp. When the sun had nearly set we went over a divide and came in sight of a creek fulfilling the required conditions. It wound its way through a valley of rich bottom land, cotton-wood trees of no great height or size growing in thick groves along its banks, while its bed contained many deep pools of water, some of it fresh and good. I rode into a great bend, with a grove of trees on its right and containing excellent feed. Manitou was loosed, with the lariat round his neck, to feed where he wished until I went to bed, when he was to be taken to a place where the grass was thick and succulent, and tethered out for the night. There was any amount of wood with which a fire was started for cheerfulness, and some of the coals were soon raked off apart to cook over. The horse blanket was spread on the ground, with the oil-skin over it as a bed, underneath a spreading cotton-wood tree, while the regular blanket served as covering. The metal cup was soon filled with water and simmering over the coals to make tea, while an antelope steak was roasting on a forked stick. It is wonderful how cosy a camp, in clear weather, becomes if there is a good fire and enough to eat, and how sound the sleep is afterwards in the cool air, with the brilliant stars glimmering through the branches overhead. In the country where I was there was absolutely no danger from Indian horse-thieves, and practically none from white ones, for I felt pretty sure no one was anywhere within a good many miles of me, and none could have seen me come into the valley. Besides, in the cattle country stealing horses is a hazardous profession, as any man who is found engaged in it is at once, and very properly, strung up to the nearest tree, or shot if no trees are handy; so very few people follow it, at least for any length of time, and a man's horses are generally safe.

Near where we had halted for the night camp was a large prairie-dog town. Prairie-dogs are abundant all over the cattle country; they are in shape like little woodchucks, and are the most noisy and inquisitive animals imaginable. They are never found singly, but always in towns of several hundred inhabitants; and these towns are found in all kinds of places where the country is flat and treeless. Sometimes they will be placed on the bottoms of the creeks or rivers, and again far out on the prairie or among the Bad Lands, a long distance from any water. Indeed, so dry are some of the localities in which they exist, that it is a marvel how they can live at all; yet they seem invariably plump and in good condition. They are exceedingly destructive to grass, eating away every thing round their burrows, and thus each town is always extending at the borders, while the holes in the middle are deserted; in many districts they have become a perfect bane to the cattle-men, for the incoming of man has been the means of causing a great falling off in the ranks of their four-footed foes, and this main check to their increase being gone, they multiply at a rate that threatens to make them a serious pest in the future. They are among the few plains animals who are benefited instead of being injured by the presence of man; and it is most difficult to exterminate them or to keep their number in any way under, as they are prolific to a most extraordinary degree; and the quantity of good feed they destroy is very great, and as they eat up the roots of the grass it is a long time before it grows again. Already in many districts the stockmen are seriously considering the best way in which to take steps against them. Prairie-dogs wherever they exist are sure to attract attention, all the more so because, unlike most other rodents, they are diurnal and not nocturnal, offering therein a curious case of parallelism to their fellow denizen of the dry plains, the antelope, which is also a creature loving to be up and stirring in the bright daylight, unlike its relatives, the dusk-loving deer. They are very noisy, their shrill yelping resounding on all sides whenever a man rides through a town. None go far from their homes, always keeping close enough to be able to skulk into them at once; and as soon as a foe appears they take refuge on the hillocks beside their burrows, yelping continuously, and accompanying each yelp by a spasmodic jerking of the tail and body. When the man comes a little nearer they disappear inside and then thrust their heads out, for they are most inquisitive. Their burrows form one of the chief dangers to riding at full speed over the plains country; hardly any man can do much riding on the prairie for more than a year or two without coming to grief on more than one occasion by his horse putting its foot in a prairie-dog hole. A badger hole is even worse. When a horse gets his foot in such a hole, while going at full speed, he turns a complete somersault, and is lucky if he escape without a broken leg, while I have time and again known the rider to be severely injured. There are other smaller animals whose burrows sometimes cause a horseman to receive a sharp tumble. These are the pocket-gophers, queer creatures, shaped like moles and having the same subterranean habits, but with teeth like a rat's, and great pouches on the outside of their jaws, whose long, rambling tunnels cover the ground in certain places, though the animals themselves are very rarely seen; and the little striped gophers and gray gophers, entirely different animals, more like ground squirrels. But the prairie-dog is always the main source of danger to the horseman, as well as of mischief to the cattle-herder.

Around the prairie-dog towns it is always well to keep a look-out for the smaller carnivora, especially coyotes and badgers, as they are very fond of such neighborhoods, and almost always it is also a favorite resort for the larger kinds of hawks, which are so numerous through the cattle country. Rattlesnakes are quite plenty, living in the deserted holes, and the latter are also the homes of the little burrowing owls, which will often be seen standing at the opening, ready to run in as quick as any of the prairie-dogs if danger threatens. They have a funny habit of gravely bowing or posturing at the passer-by, and stand up very erect on their legs. With the exception of this species, owls are rare in the cattle country.

A prairie-dog is rather a difficult animal to get, as it stands so close to its burrow that a spasmodic kick, even if at the last gasp, sends the body inside, where it cannot be recovered. The cowboys are always practising at them with their revolvers, and as they are pretty good shots, mortally wound a good many, but unless the force of the blow fairly knocks the prairie-dog away from the mouth of the burrow, it almost always manages to escape inside. But a good shot with the rifle can kill any number by lying down quietly and waiting a few minutes until the dogs get a little distance from the mouths of their homes.

Badgers are more commonly found round prairie-dog towns than anywhere else; and they get their chief food by digging up the prairie-dogs and gophers with their strong forearms and long, stout claws. They are not often found wandering away from their homes in the daytime, but if so caught are easily run down and killed. A badger is a most desperate fighter, and an overmatch for a coyote, his hide being very thick and his form so squat and strong that it is hard to break his back or legs, while his sharp teeth grip like a steel trap. A very few seconds allow him to dig a hole in the ground, into which he can back all except his head; and when placed thus, with his rear and flanks protected, he can beat off a dog many times his own size. A young badger one night came up round the ranch-house, and began gnawing at some bones that had been left near the door. Hearing the noise one of my men took a lantern and went outside. The glare of the light seemed to make the badger stupid, for after looking at the lantern a few moments, it coolly turned and went on eating the scraps of flesh on the bones, and was knocked on the head without attempting to escape.

To come back to my trip. Early in the morning I was awakened by the shrill yelping of the prairie-dogs whose town was near me. The sun had not yet risen, and the air had the peculiar chill it always takes on toward morning, while little wreathes of light mist rose from the pools. Getting up and loosing Manitou to let him feed round where he wished and slake his thirst, I took the rifle, strolled up the creek valley a short distance, and turned off out on the prairie. Nothing was in sight in the way of game; but overhead a skylark was singing, soaring up above me so high that I could not make out his form in the gray morning light. I listened for some time, and the music never ceased for a moment, coming down clear, sweet, and tender from the air above. Soon the strains of another answered from a little distance off, and the two kept soaring and singing as long as I stayed to listen; and when I walked away I could still hear their notes behind me. In some ways the skylark is the sweetest singer we have; only certain of the thrushes rival it, but though the songs of the latter have perhaps even more melody, they are far from being as uninterrupted and well sustained, being rather a succession of broken bursts of music.

The sun was just appearing when I walked back to the creek bottom. Coming slowly out of a patch of brushwood, was a doe, going down to drink; her great, sensitive ears thrown forward as she peered anxiously and timidly round. She was very watchful, lifting her head and gazing about between every few mouthfuls. When she had drunk her fill she snatched a hasty mouthful or two of the wet grass, and then cantered back to the edge of the brush, when a little spotted fawn came out and joined her. The two stood together for a few moments and then walked off into the cover. The little pond at which they had drunk was within fifty yards of my night bed; and it had other tenants in the shape of a mallard duck, with a brood of little ducklings, balls of fuzzy yellow down, that bobbed off into the reeds like little corks as I walked by.

Breaking camp is a simple operation for one man; and but a few minutes after breakfast Manitou and I were off; the embers of the fire having been extinguished with the care that comes to be almost second nature with the cattleman, one of whose chief dreads is the prairie fire, that sometimes robs his stock of such an immense amount of feed. Very little game was seen during the morning, as I rode in an almost straight line over the hot, parched plains, the ground cracked and seamed by the heat, and the dull brown blades bending over as if the sun was too much even for them. The sweat drenched the horse even when we were walking; and long before noon we halted for rest by a bitter alkaline pool with border so steep and rotten that I had to bring water up to the horse in my hat; having taken some along in a canteen for my own use. But there was a steep bank near, overgrown with young trees, and thus giving good shade; and it was this that induced me to stop. When leaving this halting-place, I spied three figures in the distance, loping towards me; they turned out to be cowboys, who had been out a couple of days looking up a band of strayed ponies, and as they had exhausted their supply of food, I gave them the antelope hams, trusting to shoot another for my own use.

Nor was I disappointed. After leaving the cowboys I headed the horse towards the more rolling country where the prairies begin to break off into the edges of the Bad Lands. Several bands of antelope were seen, and I tried one unsuccessful stalk, not being able to come within rifle range; but towards evening, when only about a mile from a wooded creek on whose banks I intended to sleep, I came across a solitary buck, just as I was topping the ridge of the last divide. As I was keeping a sharp lookout at the time, I reined in the horse the instant the head of the antelope came in sight, and jumping off crept up till I could see his whole body, when I dropped on my knee and took steady aim. He was a long way off (three hundred yards by actual pacing), and not having made out exactly what we were he stood still, looking intently in our direction and broadside to us. I held well over his shoulder, and at the report he dropped like a shot, the ball having broken his neck. It was a very good shot; the best I ever made at antelope, of which game, as already said, I have killed but very few individuals. Taking the hams and saddle I rode on down to the creek and again went into camp among timber. Thus on this trip I was never successful in outwitting antelope on the several occasions when I pitted my craft and skill against their wariness and keen sense, always either failing to get within range or else missing them; but nevertheless I got two by taking advantage of the stupidity and curiosity which they occasionally show.

The middle part of the days having proved so very hot, and as my store of biscuits was nearly gone, and as I knew, moreover, that the antelope meat would not keep over twenty-four hours, I decided to push back home next day; and accordingly I broke camp at the first streak of dawn, and took Manitou back to the ranch at a smart lope.

A solitary trip such as this was, through a comparatively wild region in which game is still plentiful, always has great attraction for any man who cares for sport and for nature, and who is able to be his own companion, but the pleasure after all depends a good deal on the weather. To be sure, after a little experience in roughing it, the hardships seem a good deal less formidable than they formerly did, and a man becomes able to roll up in a wet blanket and sleep all night in a pelting rain without hurting himself—though he will shiver a good deal, and feel pretty numb and stiff in those chill and dreary hours just before dawn. But when a man's clothes and bedding and rifle are all wet, no matter how philosophically he may bear it, it may be taken for granted that he does not enjoy it. So fair weather is a very vital and important element among those that go to make up the pleasure and success of such a trip. Luckily fair weather can be counted on with a good deal of certainty in late spring and throughout most of the summer and fall on the northern cattle plains. The storms that do take place, though very violent, do not last long.

Every now and then, however, there will be in the fall a three-days' storm in which it is almost impossible to travel, and then the best thing to be done is to lie up under any shelter that is at hand until it blows over. I remember one such camp which was made in the midst of the most singular and picturesque surroundings. It was toward the end of a long wagon trip that we had been taking, and all of the horses were tired by incessant work. We had come through country which was entirely new to us, passing nearly all day in a long flat prairie through which flowed a stream that we supposed to be either the Box Alder or the Little Beaver. In leaving this we had struck some heavy sand-hills, and while pulling the loaded wagon up them one of the team played out completely, and we had to take her out and put in one of the spare saddle-ponies, a tough little fellow. Night came on fast, and the sun was just setting when we crossed the final ridge and came in sight of as singular a bit of country as I have ever seen. The cowboys, as we afterward found, had christened the place "Medicine Buttes." In plains dialect, I may explain, "Medicine" has been adopted from the Indians, among whom it means any thing supernatural or very unusual. It is used in the sense of "magic," or "out of the common."

Over an irregular tract of gently rolling sandy hills, perhaps about three quarters of a mile square, were scattered several hundred detached and isolated buttes or cliffs of sandstone, each butte from fifteen to fifty feet high, and from thirty to a couple of hundred feet across. Some of them rose as sharp peaks or ridges, or as connected chains, but much the greater number had flat tops like little table-lands. The sides were perfectly perpendicular, and were cut and channelled by the weather into the most extraordinary forms; caves, columns, battlements, spires, and flying buttresses were mingled in the strangest confusion. Many of the caves were worn clear through the buttes, and they were at every height in the sides, while ledges ran across the faces, and shoulders and columns jutted out from the corners. On the tops and at the bases of most of the cliffs grew pine trees, some of considerable height, and the sand gave every thing a clean, white look.

Altogether it was as fantastically beautiful a place as I have ever seen: it seemed impossible that the hand of man should not have had something to do with its formation. There was a spring of clear cold water a few hundred yards off, with good feed for the horses round it; and we made our camp at the foot of one of the largest buttes, building a roaring pine-log fire in an angle in the face of the cliff, while our beds were under the pine trees. It was the time of the full moon, and the early part of the night was clear. The flame of the fire leaped up the side of the cliff, the red light bringing out into lurid and ghastly relief the bold corners and strange-looking escarpments of the rock, while against it the stiff limbs of the pines stood out like rigid bars of iron. Walking off out of sight of the circle of firelight, among the tall crags, the place seemed almost as unreal as if we had been in fairy-land. The flood of clear moonlight turned the white faces of the cliffs and the grounds between them into shining silver, against which the pines showed dark and sombre, while the intensely black shadows of the buttes took on forms that were grimly fantastic. Every cave or cranny in the crags looked so black that it seemed almost to be thrown out from the surface, and when the branches of the trees moved, the bright moonlight danced on the ground as if it were a sheet of molten metal. Neither in shape nor in color did our surroundings seem to belong to the dull gray world though which we had been travelling all day.

But by next morning every thing had changed. A furious gale of wind was blowing, and we were shrouded in a dense, drizzling mist, through which at times the rain drove in level sheets. Now and then the fog would blow away, and then would come on thicker than ever; and when it began to clear off a steady rain took its place, and the wind increased to a regular hurricane. With its canvas top on, the wagon would certain have been blown over if on open ground, and it was impossible to start or keep a fire except under the sheltered lee of the cliff. Moreover, the wind kept shifting, and we had to shift too, as fast as ever it started to blow from a new quarter; and thus in the course of the twenty-four hours we made a complete circle of the cliff at whose base we were. Our blankets got wet during the night; and they got no drier during the day; and the second night, as we slept on them they got steadily damper. Our provisions were pretty nearly out, and so, with little to eat and less to do, wet and uncomfortable, we cowered over the sputtering fire, and whiled the long day away as best we might with our own thoughts; fortunately we had all learned that no matter how bad things are, grumbling and bad temper can always be depended upon to make them worse, and so bore our ill-fortune, if not with stoical indifference, at least in perfect quiet. Next day the storm still continued, but the fog was gone and the wind somewhat easier; and we spent the whole day looking up the horses, which had drifted a long distance before the storm, nor was it till the morning of the third day that we left our beautiful but, as events had made it, uncomfortable camping-ground.

In midsummer the storms are rarely of long duration, but are very severe while they last. I remember well one day when I was caught in such a storm. I had gone some twenty-five miles from the ranch to see the round-up, which had reached what is known as the Oxbow of the Little Missouri, where the river makes a great loop round a flat grassy bottom, on which the cattle herd was gathered. I stayed, seeing the cattle cut out and the calves branded, until after dinner; for it was at the time of the year when the days were longest.

At last the work was ended, and I started home in the twilight. The horse splashed across the shallow ford, and then spent half an hour in climbing up through the rugged side hills, till we reached the top of the first great plateau that had to be crossed. As soon as I got on it I put in the spurs and started off at a gallop. In the dusk the brown level land stretched out in formless expanse ahead of me, unrelieved, except by the bleached white of a buffalo's skull, whose outlines glimmered indistinctly to one side of the course I was riding. On my left the sun had set behind a row of jagged buttes, that loomed up in sharp relief against the western sky; above them it had left a bar of yellow light, which only made more intense the darkness of the surrounding heavens. In the quarter towards which I was heading there had gathered a lowering mass of black storm-clouds, lit up by the incessant play of the lightning. The wind had totally died away, and the death-like stillness was only broken by the continuous, measured beat of the horse's hoofs

164

as he galloped over the plain, and at times by the muttered roll of the distant thunder.

Without slacking pace I crossed the plateau, and as I came to the other edge the storm burst in sheets and torrents of water. In five minutes I was drenched though, and to guide myself had to take advantage of the continual flashes of lightning; and I was right glad, half an hour afterward, to stop and take shelter in the log hut of a couple of cowboys, where I could get dry and warm.

Still-Hunting Elk on the Mountains
(From *Hunting Trips of a Ranchman*)

After the buffalo the elk are the first animals to disappear from a country when it is settled. This arises from their size and consequent conspicuousness, and the eagerness with which they are followed by hunters; and also because of their gregariousness and their occasional fits of stupid panic during whose continuance hunters can now and then work great slaughter in a herd. Five years ago elk were abundant in the valley of the Little Missouri, and in fall were found wandering in great bands of over a hundred individuals each. But they have now vanished completely, except that one or two may still lurk in some of the most remote and broken places, where there are deep, wooded ravines.

Formerly the elk were plentiful all over the plains, coming down into them in great bands during the fall months and traversing their entire extent. But the incoming of hunters and cattle-men has driven them off the ground as completely as the buffalo; unlike the latter, however, they are still very common in the dense woods that cover the Rocky Mountains and the other great western chains. In the old days running elk on horseback was a highly esteemed form of plains sport; but now that it has become a beast of the timber and the craggy ground, instead of a beast of the open, level prairie, it is followed almost solely on foot and with the rifle. Its sense of smell is very acute, and it has good eyes and quick ears; and its wariness makes it under ordinary circumstances very difficult to approach. But it is subject to fits of panic folly, and during their continuance great numbers can be destroyed. A band places almost as much reliance upon the leaders as does a flock of sheep; and if the leaders are shot down, the others will huddle together in a terrified mass, seemly unable to make up their minds in which direction to flee. When one, more bold than the rest, does at last step out, the hidden hunter's at once shooting it down will produce a fresh panic; I have known of twenty elk (or wapiti, as they are occasionally called) being thus procured out of one band. And at times they show a curious indifference to danger, running up on a hunter who is in plain sight, or standing still for a few fatal seconds to gaze at one that unexpectedly appears.

In spite of its size and strength and great branching antlers, the elk is but little more dangerous to the hunter than is an ordinary buck. Once, in coming up to a wounded one, I had it strike at me with its forefeet, bristling up the hair on the neck, and making a harsh, grating noise with its teeth; as its back was broken it could not get at me, but the savage glare in its eyes left me no doubt as to its intentions. Only in a single instance have I ever known of a hunter being regularly charged by one of these great deer. He had struck a band of elk and wounded an old bull, which, after going a couple of miles, received another ball and then separated from the rest of the herd and took refuge in a dense patch of small timber. The hunter went in on its trail and came upon it lying down; it jumped to its feet and, with hair all bristling, made a regular charge upon its pursuer, who leaped out of the way behind a tree just in time to avoid it. It crashed past through the undergrowth without turning, and he killed it with a third and last shot. But this was a very exceptional case, and in most instances the elk submits to death with hardly an effort at resistance; it is by no means as dangerous an antagonist as is a bull moose.

The elk is unfortunately one of those animals seemingly doomed to total destruction at no distant date. Already its range has shrunk to far less than one half its former size. Originally it was found as far as the Atlantic sea-board; I have myself known of several sets of antlers preserved in the house of a Long Island gentleman, whose ancestors had killed the bearers shortly after the first settlement of New York. Even so late as the first years of this century elk were found in many mountainous and densely wooded places east of the Mississippi, in New York, Pennsylvania, Virginia, Kentucky, Tennessee, and all of what were then the Northwestern States and Territories. The last individual of the race was killed in the Adirondacks in 1834; in Pennsylvania not till nearly thirty years later; while a very few are still to be found in Northern Michigan. Elsewhere they must now be sought far to the west of the Mississippi; and even there they are almost gone from the great plains, and are only numerous in the deep mountain forests. Wherever it exists the skin hunters and meat butchers wage the most relentless and unceasing war upon it for the sake of its hide and flesh, and their unremitting persecution is thinning out the herds with terrible rapidity.

The gradual extermination of this, the most stately and beautiful animal of the chase to be found in America, can be looked upon only with unmixed regret by every sportsman and lover of nature. Excepting the moose, it is the largest and, without exception, it is the noblest of the deer tribe. No other species of true deer, in either the Old or the New World, comes up to it in size and in the shape, length, and weight of its mighty antlers; while the grand, proud carriage and lordly bearing of an old bull make it perhaps the most majestic-looking of all the animal creation. The open plains have already lost one of their great attractions, now that we no more see the long lines of elk trotting across them; and it will be a sad day when the lordly, antlered beasts are no longer found in the wild rocky glens and among the lonely woods of towering pines that cover the great western mountain chains.

The elk has other foes besides man. The grizzly will always make a meal of one if he gets a chance; and against his ponderous weight and savage prowess hoofs and antlers avail but little. Still he is too clumsy and easily avoided ever to do very much damage in the herds. Cougars, where they exist, work more havoc. A bull elk in rutting season, if on his guard, would with ease beat off a cougar, but the sly, cunning cat takes its quarry unawares, and once the cruel fangs are fastened in the game's throat or neck, no plunging or struggling can shake it off. The gray timber wolves also join in twos and threes to hunt down and hamstring the elk, if other game is scarce. But these great deer can hold their own and make head against all their brute foes; it is only when pitted against Man the Destroyer, that they succumb in the struggle for life.

I have never shot any elk in the immediate neighborhood of where my cattle range; but I have had very good sport with them in a still wilder and more western region; and this I will now describe.

During last summer we found it necessary to leave my ranch on the Little Missouri and take quite a long trip through the cattle country of Southeastern Montana and Northern Wyoming; and, having come to the foot of the Bighorn Mountains, we took a fortnight's hunt through them after elk and bear.

We went into the mountains with a pack train, leaving the ranch wagon at the place where we began to go up the first steep rise. There were two others, besides myself, in the party; one of them, the teamster, a weather-beaten old plainsman, who possessed a most extraordinary stock of miscellaneous misinformation upon every conceivable subject, and the other my ranch foreman, Merrifield. None of us had ever been within two hundred miles of the Bighorn range before; so that our hunting trip had the added zest of being also an exploring expedition.

Each of us rode one pony, and the packs were carried on four others. We were not burdened by much baggage. Having no tent we took the canvas wagon sheet instead; our bedding, plenty of spare cartridges, some flour, bacon, coffee, sugar and salt, and a few very primitive cooking utensils, completed the outfit.

The Bighorn range is a chain of bare, rocky peaks stretching lengthwise along the middle of a table-land which is about thirty miles wide. At its edges this table-land falls sheer off into the rolling plains country. From the rocky peaks flow rapid brooks of clear, icy water, which take their way through deep gorges that they have channelled out in the surface of the plateau; a few miles from the heads of the streams these gorges become regular canyons, with sides so steep as to be almost perpendicular; in travelling, therefore, the trail has to keep well up toward timber line, as lower down horses find it difficult or impossible to get across the valleys. In strong contrast to the treeless cattle plains extending to its foot, the sides of the table-land are densely wooded with tall pines. Its top forms what is called a park country, that is, it is covered with alternating groves of trees and open glades, each grove or glade varying in size from half a dozen to many hundred acres.

We went in with the pack train two days' journey before pitching camp in what we intended to be our hunting grounds, following an old Indian trail. No one who has not tried it can understand the work and worry that it is to drive a pack train over rough ground and through timber. We were none of us very skilful at packing, and the loads were all the time slipping; sometimes the ponies would stampede with the pack half tied, or they would get caught among the fallen logs, or in a ticklish place would suddenly decline to follow the trail, or would commit some one of the thousand other tricks which seem to be all a pack-pony knows. Then at night they were a bother; if picketed out they fed badly and got thin, and if they were not picketed they sometimes strayed away. The most valuable one of the lot was also the hardest to catch. Accordingly we used to let him loose with a long lariat tied round his neck, and one night this lariat twisted up in a sagebrush, and in struggling to free himself the pony got a half hitch round his hind leg, threw himself, and fell over a bank into a creek on a large stone. We found him in the morning very much the worse for wear, and his hind legs swelled up so that his chief method of progression was by a series of awkward hops. Of course no load could be put upon him, but he managed to limp along behind the other horses, and actually in the end reached the ranch on the Little Missouri three hundred miles off. No sooner had he got there and been turned loose to rest than he fell down a big wash-out and broke his neck. Another time one of the mares—a homely beast with a head like a camel's—managed to flounder into the very centre of a mud-hole, and we spent the better part of a morning in fishing her out.

It was on the second day of our journey into the mountains, while leading the pack-ponies down the precipitous side of a steep valley, that I obtained my first sight of elk. The trail wound through a forest of tall, slender pines, standing very close together, and with dead trees lying in every direction. The narrow trunks or overhanging limbs threatened to scrape off the packs at every moment, as the ponies hopped and scrambled over the fallen trunks; and it was difficult work, and most trying to the temper, to keep them going along straight and prevent them from wandering off to one side or the other. At last we got out into a succession of small, open glades with boggy spots in them; the lowest glade was of some size, and as we reached it we saw a small band of cow elk disappearing into the woods on its other edge. I was riding a restive horse, and when I tried to jump off to shoot, it reared and turned round, before I could get my left foot out of the stirrup; when I at last got free I could get a glimpse of but one elk, vanishing behind a dead trunk, and my hasty shot missed. I was a good deal annoyed at this, my opening experience with mountain game, feeling that it was an omen of misfortune; but it did not prove so, for during the rest of my two weeks' stay, I with one exception got every animal I fired at.

A beautiful, clear mountain brook ran through the bottom of the valley, and in an open space by its side we pitched camp. We were entirely out of fresh meat, and after lunch all three of us separated to hunt, each for his own hand. The teamster went up stream, Merrifield went down, while I followed the tracks of the band of cows and calves that we had started in the morning; their trail led along the wooded hill-crests parallel to the stream, and therefore to Merrifield's course. The crests of the hills formed a wavy-topped but continuous ridge between two canyon-like valleys, and the sides fell off steeper and steeper the farther down stream I went, until at last they were broken in places by sheer precipices and cliffs; the groves of trees too, though with here and there open glades, formed a continuous forest of tall pines. There was a small growth of young spruce and other evergreen, thick enough to give cover, but not to interfere with seeing and shooting to some distance. The pine trunks rose like straight columns, standing quite close together; and at their bases the ground was carpeted with the sweet-scented needles, over which, in my moccasined feet, I trod without any noise. It was but a little past noon, and the sun in the open was very hot; yet underneath the great archways of the pine woods the air though still was cool, and the sunbeams that struggled down here and there through the interlacing branches, and glinted on the rough trunks only made bright spots in what was elsewhere the uniform, grayish half-light of the mountain forest. Game trails threaded the woods in all directions, made for the most part by the elk. These animals, when not disturbed, travel strung out in single file, each one stepping very nearly in the tracks of the one before; they are great wanderers, going over an immense amount of country during the course of a day, and so they soon wear regular, well-beaten paths in any place where they are at all plentiful.

The band I was following had, as is their custom, all run together into a wedge-shaped mass when I fired, and crashed off through the woods in a bunch during the first moments of alarm. The footprints in the soil showed that they had in the beginning taken a plunging gallop, but after a few strides had settled into the swinging, ground-covering trot that is the elk's most natural and characteristic gait. A band of elk when alarmed is likely to go twenty miles without halting; but these had probably been very little molested, and there was a chance that they would not go far without stopping. After getting through the first grove, the huddled herd had straightened itself out into single file, and trotted off in a nearly straight line. A mile or two of ground having been passed over in this way, the animals had slackened their pace into a walk, evidently making up their minds that they were out of danger. Soon afterwards they had begun to go slower, and to scatter out on each side, browsing or grazing.

It was not difficult work to follow up the band at first. While trotting their sharp hoofs came down with sufficient force to leave very distinct footprints, and, moreover, the trail was the more readily made out as all the animals trod nearly in each other's steps. But when the band spread out the tracking was much harder, as each single one, walking slowly along, merely made here and there a slight scrape in the soil or a faint indentation in the bed of pine needles. Besides, I had to advance with the greatest caution, keeping the sharpest look-out in front and on all sides of me. Even as it was, though I got very close up to my game, they were on foot before I saw them, and I did not get a standing shot. While carefully looking to my footsteps I paid too little heed to the rifle which I held in my right hand, and let the barrel tap smartly on a tree trunk. Instantly there was a stamp and movement among the bushes ahead and to one side of me; the elk had heard but had neither seen nor smelt me; and a second afterward I saw the indistinct, shadowy outlines of the band as they trotted down hill, from where their beds had been made on the very summit of the crest, taking a course diagonal to mine. I raced forward and also down hill, behind some large mossy boulders, and cut them fairly off, the band passing directly ahead of me and not twenty yards away, at a slashing trot, which a few of them changed for a wild gallop, as I opened fire. I was so hemmed in by the thick tree trunks and it was so difficult to catch more than a fleeting glimpse of each animal, that though I fired four shots I only brought down one elk, a full-grown cow, with a broken neck, dead in its tracks; but I also broke the hind leg of a bull calf. Elk offer easy marks when in motion, much easier than deer, because of their trotting gait, and their regular, deliberate movements. They look very handsome as they trot through a wood, stepping lightly and easily over the dead trunks and crashing through the underbrush, with the head held up and nose pointing forward. In galloping, however, the neck is thrust straight out in front and the animal moves with labored bounds, which carry it along rapidly but soon tire it out.

After thrusting the hunting-knife into the throat of the cow, I followed the trail of the band; and in an open glade, filled with tall sage-brush, came across and finished the wounded calf. Meanwhile the others ran directly across Merrifield's path, and he shot two. This gave us much more meat than we wished; nor would we have shot as many but neither of us could reckon upon the other's getting as much game, and flesh was a necessity. Leaving Merrifield to skin and cut up the dead animals, I walked back to camp where I found the teamster, who had brought in the hams and tongues of two deer he had shot, and sent him back with a pack-pony for the hides and meat of the elk. Elk tongues are most delicious eating, being juicy, tender, and well flavored; they are excellent to take out as a lunch on a long hunting trip.

We now had more than enough meat in camp, and did not shoot at another cow or calf elk while on the mountains, though we saw quite a number; the last day of my stay I was within fifty yards of two that were walking quietly through a very dense, swampy wood. But it took me some time longer before I got any fine heads.

The day after killing the cow and calf I went out in the morning by myself and hunted through the woods up toward the rocky peaks, going above timber line, and not reaching camp until after nightfall. In hunting through a wild and unknown country a man must always take great care not to get lost. In the first place he should never, under any conceivable circumstances, stir fifty yards from camp without a compass, plenty of matches, and his rifle; then he need never feel nervous, even if he is lost, for he can keep himself from cold and hunger, and can steer a straight course until he reaches some settlement. But he should not get lost at all. Old plainsmen or backwoodsmen get to have almost an instinct for finding their way, and are able to tell where they are and the way home in almost any place; probably they keep in their head an accurate idea of their course and of the general lay of the land. But most men cannot do this. In hunting through a new country a man should if possible, choose some prominent landmarks, and then should learn how they look from different sides—for they will with difficulty be recognized as the same objects, if seen from different points of view. If he gets out of sight of these, he should choose another to work back to, as a kind of half-way point; and so on. He should keep looking back; it is wonderful how different a country looks when following back on one's trail. If possible, he should locate his camp, in his mind, with reference to a line, and not a point; he should take a river or a long ridge, for example, then at any time he can strike back to this line and follow it up or down till he gets home.

If possible, I always spend the first day, when on new ground, in hunting up-stream. Then, so long as I am sure I do not wander off into the valleys or creeks of another water-course, I am safe, for, no matter on what remote branch, all I have to do is to follow down-stream until I reach camp; if I was below camp, it would be difficult to tell which fork to follow up every time the stream branched. A man should always notice the position of the sun, the direction from which the wind blows, the slope of the water-courses, prominent features in the landscape, and so forth, and should keep in mind his own general course; and he had better err on the side of caution rather than on that of boldness. Getting lost is very uncomfortable, both for the man himself and for those who have to break up their work and hunt for him. Deep woods or perfectly flat, open country are almost equally easy places in which to get lost; while if the country is moderately open and level, with only here and there a prominent and easily recognized hill or butte, a man can safely go where he wishes hardly paying any heed to his course. But even here he should know his general direction from camp, so as to be able to steer for it with a compass if a fog comes up. And if he leaves his horse hidden in a gully or pocket while he goes off to hunt on foot, he must recollect to keep the place well in his mind; on one occasion, when I feared that somebody might meddle with my horse, I hid him so successfully that I spent the better part of a day in finding him.

Keeping in mind the above given rules, when I left camp the morning after the breaking up of the band of cows and calves, I hunted up-stream, and across and through the wooded spurs dividing the little brooks that formed its head waters. No game was encountered, except some blue grouse, which I saw when near camp on my return, and shot for the pot. These blue grouse are the largest species found in America, except the sage fowl. They are exclusively birds of the deep mountain forests, and in their manners remind one of the spruce grouse of the Northeastern woods, being almost equally tame. When alarmed, they fly at once into a tree, and several can often be shot before the remainder take fright and are off. On this trip we killed a good many shooting off their heads with our rifles. They formed a most welcome addition to our bill of fare, the meat being white and excellent. A curious peculiarity in their flesh is that the breast meat has in it a layer of much darker color. They are very handsome birds, and furnish dainty food to men wearied of venison; but, unless their heads are knocked off with a rifle, they do not furnish much sport, as they will not fly off when flushed, but simply rise into a fairly tall tree, and there sit, motionless, except that the head is twisted and bobbed round to observe the acts of the foe.

All of the sights and sounds in these pine woods that clothed the Bighorn Mountains reminded me of the similar ones seen and heard in the great, sombre forests of Maine and the Adirondacks. The animals and birds were much the same. As in the East, there were red squirrels, chipmunks, red hares, and woodchucks, all of them differing but slightly from our common kinds; woodpeckers, chickadees, nuthatches, and whisky jacks came about camp; ravens and eagles flew over the rocky cliffs. There were some new forms, however. The nutcracker, a large noisy, crow-like bird, with many of the habits of a woodpecker, was common, and in the rocks above timber line, we came upon the Little Chief hare, a wee animal, with a shrill, timorous squeak.

During our stay upon the mountains the weather was generally clear, but always cold, thin ice covering the dark waters of the small mountain tarns, and there were slight snow-falls every two or three days; but we were only kept in camp one day, when it sleeted, snowed, and rained from dawn till nightfall. We passed this day very comfortably, however. I had far too much forethought to go into the woods without a small supply of books for just such occasions. We had rigged the canvas wagon sheet into a tent, at the bottom of the ravine, near the willow-covered brink of the brook that ran through it. The steep hill-sides bounding the valley, which a little below us became sheer cliffs, were partly covered with great pines and spruces, and partly open ground grown up with tall grass and sage-brush. We were thus well sheltered from the wind; and when one morning we looked out and saw the wet snow lying on the ground, and with its weight bending down the willow bushes and loading the tall evergreens, while the freezing sleet rattled against the canvas, we simply started a roaring fire of pine logs in front of the tent, and passed a cosy day inside, cleaning guns, reading, and playing cards. Blue grouse, elk hams, and deer saddles hung from the trees around, so we had no fear of starvation. Still, towards evening we got a little tired, and I could not resist taking a couple of hours' brisk ride in the mist, through a chain of open glades that sloped off from our camp.

Later on we made a camp at the head of a great natural meadow, where two streams joined together, and in times long gone by had been dammed by the beaver. This had at first choked up the passage and made a small lake; then dams were built higher and higher up, making chains of little ponds. By degrees these filled up, and the whole valley became a broad marshy meadow, through which the brook wound between rows of willows and alders. These beaver meadows are very common; but are not usually of such large size. Around this camp there was very little game; but we got a fine mess of spotted trout by taking a long and most toilsome walk up to a little lake lying very near timber line. Our rods and lines were most primitive, consisting of two clumsy dead cedars (the only trees within reach), about six feet of string tied to one and a piece of catgut to the other, with preposterous hooks; yet the trout were so ravenous that we caught them at the rate of about one a minute; and they formed another welcome change in our camp fare. This lake lay in a valley whose sides were so steep and boulder-covered as to need hard climbing to get into and out of it. Every day in the cold, clear weather we tramped miles and miles through the woods and mountains, which, after a snow-storm took on a really wintry look; while in the moonlight the snow-laden forests shone and sparkled like crystal. The dweller in cities has but a faint idea of the way we ate and slept.

One day Merrifield and I went out together and had a rather exciting chase after some bull elk. The previous evening, toward sunset, I had seen three bulls trotting off across an open glade toward a great stretch of forest and broken ground, up near the foot of the rocky peaks. Next morning early we started off to hunt through this country. The walking was hard work, especially up and down the steep cliffs, covered with slippery pine needles; or among the windfalls, where the rows of dead trees lay piled up across one another in the wildest confusion. We saw nothing until we came to a large patch of burnt ground, where we at once found the soft, black soil marked up by elk hoofs; nor had we penetrated into it more than a few hundred yards before we came to tracks made but a few minutes before, and almost instantly afterward saw three bull elk, probably those I had seen on the preceding day. We had been running briskly up-hill through the soft, heavy loam, in which our feet made no noise but slipped and sank deeply; as a consequence, I was all out of breath and my hand so unsteady that I missed my first shot. Elk, however, do not vanish with the instantaneous rapidity of frightened deer, and these three trotted off in a direction quartering to us. I doubt if I ever went through more violent exertion than in the next ten minutes. We raced after them at full speed, opening fire; I wounded all three but none of the wounds were immediately disabling. They trotted on and we panted afterwards, slipping on the wet earth, pitching headlong over charred stumps, leaping on dead logs that broke beneath our weight, more than once measuring our full-length on the ground, halting and firing whenever we got the chance. At last one bull fell; we passed him by after the others which were still running up-hill. The sweat streamed into my eyes and made furrows in the sooty mud that covered my face, from having fallen full length down on the burnt earth; I sobbed for breath as I toiled at a shambling trot after them, as nearly done out as could well be. At this moment they turned down-hill. It was a great relief; a man who is too done up to go a step up-hill can still run fast enough down; with a last spurt I closed in near enough to fire again; one elk fell; the other went off at a walk. We passed the second elk and I kept on along after the third, not able to go at more than a slow trot myself, and too much winded to dare risk a shot at any distance. He got out of the burnt patch, going into some thick timber in a deep ravine; I closed pretty well and rushed after him into a thicket of young evergreens. Hardly was I in when there was a scramble and bounce among them and I caught a glimpse of a yellow body moving out to one side; I ran out toward the edge and fired through the twigs at the moving beast. Down it went, but when I ran up, to my disgust I found that I had jumped and killed, in my haste, a black-tail deer, which must have been already roused by the passage of the wounded elk. I at once took up the trail of the latter again, but after a little while the blood grew less, and ceased, and I lost the track; nor could I find it, hunt as hard as I might. The poor beast could not have gone five hundred yards; yet we never found the carcass.

Then I walked slowly back past the deer I had slain by so curious a mischance, to the elk. The first one shot down was already dead. The second was only wounded, though it could not rise. When it saw us coming it sought to hide from us by laying its neck flat on the ground, but when we came up close it raised its head and looked proudly at us, the heavy mane bristling up on the neck, while its eyes glared and its teeth grated together. I felt really sorry to kill it. Those were both well-grown elks, their antlers, of ten points, were small, twisted, and ill-shaped; in fact hardly worth preserving, except to call to mind a chase in which during a few minutes I did as much downright hard work as it has often fallen to my lot to do. The burnt earth had blackened our faces and hands till we looked like negroes.

The bull elk had at this time begun calling, and several times they were heard right round camp at night, challenging one another or calling to the cows. Their calling is known to hunters as "whistling"; but this is a most inappropriate name for it. It is a most singular and beautiful sound, and is very much the most musical cry uttered by any four-footed beast. When heard for the first time it is almost impossible to believe that it is the call of an animal; it sounds far more as if made by an Aeolian harp or some strange wind instrument. It consists of quite a series of notes uttered continuously, in a most soft, musical, vibrant tone, so clearly that they can be heard half a mile off. Heard in the clear, frosty moonlight from the depths of the rugged and forest-clad mountains the effect is most beautiful; for its charm is heightened by the wild and desolate surroundings. It has the sustained, varied melody of some bird songs, with, of course, a hundred-fold greater power. Now and then, however, the performance is marred by the elk's apparently getting out of breath towards the close, and winding up with two or three gasping notes which have an unpleasantly mule-like sound.

The great pine-clad mountains, their forests studded with open glades, were the best of places for the still-hunter's craft. Going noiselessly through them in our dun-colored buckskin and noiseless moccasins, we kept getting glimpses, as it were, of the inner life of the mountains. Each animal that we saw had its own individuality. Aside from the thrill and tingle that a hunter experiences at the sight of his game, I by degrees grew to feel as if I had a personal interest in the different traits and habits of the wild creatures. The characters of the animals differed widely, and the differences were typified by their actions; and it was pleasant to watch them in their own homes, myself unseen, when after stealthy, silent progress through the sombre and soundless depths of the woods I came upon them going about the ordinary business of their lives. The lumbering, self-confident gait of the bears, their burly strength, and their half-humorous, half-ferocious look, gave me a real insight into their character; and I never was more impressed by the exhibition of vast, physical power, then when watching from an ambush a grizzly burying or covering up an elk carcass. His motions looked awkward, but it was marvellous to see the ease and absence of effort with which he would scoop out great holes in the earth, or twitch the heavy carcass from side to side. And the proud, graceful, half-timid, half-defiant bearing of the elk was in its own way quite as noteworthy; they seemed to glory in their own power and beauty, and yet to be ever on the watch for foes against whom they knew they might not dare to contend. The true still-hunter should be a lover of nature as well as of sport, or he will miss half the pleasure of being in the wood.

The finest bull, with the best head that I got, was killed in the midst of very beautiful and grand surroundings. We had been hunting through a great pine wood which ran up to the edge of a broad canyon-like valley, bounded by sheer walls of rock. There were fresh tracks of elk about, and we had been advancing upwind with even more than our usual caution when, on stepping out into a patch of open ground, near the edge of the cliff, we came upon a great bull, beating and thrashing his antlers against a young tree, about eighty yards off. He stopped and faced us for a second, his mighty antlers thrown in the air, as he held his head aloft. Behind him towered the tall and sombre pines, while at his feet the jutting crags overhung the deep chasm below, that stretched off between high walls of barren and snow-streaked rocks, the evergreens clinging to their sides, while along the bottom the rapid torrent gathered in places into black and sullen mountain lakes. As the bull turned to run I struck him just behind the shoulder; he reeled to the death-blow, but staggered gamely on a few rods into the forest before sinking to the ground, with my second bullet through his lungs.

Two or three days later than this I killed another bull, nearly as large, in the same patch of woods in which I had slain the first. A bear had been feeding on the carcass of the latter, and, after a vain effort to find his den, we determined to beat through the woods and try to start him up. Accordingly Merrifield, the teamster, and myself took parallel courses some three hundred yards apart, and started at one end to walk through to the other. I doubt if the teamster much wished to meet a bear alone (while nothing would have given Merrifield more hearty and unaffected enjoyment than to have encountered an entire family), and he gradually edged in pretty close to me. Where the woods became pretty open I saw him suddenly lift his rifle and fire, and immediately afterwards a splendid bull elk trotted past in front of me, evidently untouched, the teamster having missed. The elk ran to the other side of two trees that stood close together some seventy yards off, and stopped for a moment to look round. Kneeling down I fired at the only part of his body I could see between the two trees, and sent a bullet into his flank. Away he went, and I after, running in my moccasins over the moss and pine needles for all there was in me. If a wounded elk gets fairly started he will go at a measured trot for many hours, and even if mortally hurt may run twenty miles before falling; while at the same time he does not start off at full speed, and will often give an active hunter a chance for another shot as he turns and changes his course preparatory to taking a straight line. So I raced along after the elk at my very best speed for a few hundred feet, and then got another shot as he went across a little glade, injuring his hip somewhat. This made it all right for me, and another hundred yards' burst took me up to where I was able to put a ball in a fatal spot, and the grand old fellow sank down and fell over on his side.

No sportsman can ever feel much keener pleasure and self-satisfaction than when, after a successful stalk and good shot, he walks up to a grand elk lying dead in the cool shade of the great evergreens, and looks at the massive and yet finely moulded form, and at the mighty antlers which are to serve in the future as the trophy and proof of his successful skill. Still-hunting the elk on the mountains is as noble a kind of sport as can well be imagined; there is nothing more pleasant and enjoyable, and at the same time it demands that the hunter shall bring into play many manly qualities. There have been few days of my hunting life that were so full of unalloyed happiness as were those spent on the Bighorn range. From morning till night I was on foot, in cool, bracing air, now moving silently through the vast, melancholy pine forests, now treading the brink of high, rocky precipices, always amid the most grand and beautiful scenery; and always after as noble and lordly game as is to be found in the Western world.

Since writing the above I killed an elk near my ranch; probably the last of his race that will ever be found in our neighborhood. It was just before the fall round-up. An old hunter, who was under some obligation to me, told me that he had shot a cow elk and had seen the tracks of one or two others not more than twenty-five miles off, in a place where the cattle rarely wandered. Such a chance was not to be neglected; and, on the first free day, one of my Elk-horn foremen, Will Dow by name, and myself, took our hunting horses and started off, accompanied by the ranch wagon, in the direction of the probable haunts of the doomed deer. Towards nightfall we struck a deep spring pool, near by the remains of an old Indian encampment. It was at the head of a great basin, several miles across, in which we believed the game to lie. The wagon was halted and we pitched camp; there was plenty of dead wood, and soon the venison steaks were broiling over the coals raked from beneath the cracking cottonwood logs, while in the narrow valley the ponies grazed almost within the circle of the flickering fire-light. It was in the cool and pleasant month of September; and long after going to bed we lay awake under the blankets watching the stars that on clear nights always shine with such intense brightness over the lonely Western plains.

We were up and off by the gray of the morning. It was a beautiful hunting day; the sundogs hung in the red dawn; the wind hardly stirred over the crisp grass; and though the sky was cloudless yet the weather had that queer, smoky, hazy look that it is most apt to take on during the time of the Indian summer. From a high spur of the table-land we looked out far and wide over a great stretch of broken country, the brown of whose hills and valleys was varied everywhere by patches of dull red and vivid yellow, tokens that the trees were already putting on the dress with which they greet the mortal ripening of the year. The deep and narrow but smooth ravines running up towards the edges of the plateaus were heavily wooded, the bright green tree-tops rising to a height they rarely reach in the barren plains-country; and the rocky sides of the sheer gorges were clad with a thick growth of dwarfed cedars, while here and there the trailing Virginia creepers burned crimson among their sombre masses.

We hunted stealthily up-wind, across the line of the heavily timbered coulies. We soon saw traces of our quarry; old tracks at first, and then the fresh footprints of a single elk—a bull, judging by the size—which had come down to drink at a mirey alkali pool, its feet slipping so as to leave the marks of the false hoofs in the soft soil. We hunted with painstaking and noiseless care for many hours; at last as I led old Manitou up to look over the edge of a narrow ravine, there was a crash and movement in the timber below me, and immediately afterwards I caught a glimpse of a great bull elk trotting up through the young trees as he gallantly breasted the steep hill-side opposite. When clear of the woods, and directly across the valley from me, he stopped and turned half round, throwing his head in the air to gaze for a moment at the intruder. My bullet struck too far back, but, nevertheless, made a deadly wound, and the elk went over the crest of the hill at a wild, plunging gallop. We followed the bloody trail for a quarter of a mile, and found him dead in a thicket. Though of large size, he yet had but small antlers, with few points.

A Trip After Mountain Sheep
(From *Hunting Trips of a Ranchman*)

Late one fall a spell of bitter weather set in, and lasted on through the early part of the winter. For many days together the cold was fierce in its intensity; and the wheels of the ranch-wagon, when we drove out for a load of fire-wood, creaked and sang as they ground through the powdery snow that lay light on the ground. At night in the clear sky the stars seemed to snap and glitter; and for weeks of cloudless white weather the sun shone down on a land from which his beams glanced and glistened as if it had been the surface of a mirror, till the glare hurt the eyes that looked upon it. In the still nights we could hear the trees crack and jar from the strain of the biting frost; and in its winding bed the river lay fixed like a huge bent bar of blue steel.

We had been told that a small band of big-horn was hanging around some very steep and broken country about twenty-five miles from the ranch-house. I had been out after them once alone, but had failed to find even their tracks, and had made up my mind that in order to hunt them it would be necessary to make a three- or four-days' trip, taking along the buck-board with our bedding and eatables. The trip had been delayed owing to two of my men, who had been sent out to buy ponies, coming in with a bunch of fifty, for the most part hardly broken. Some of them were meant for the use of the lower ranch, and the men from the latter had come up to get them. At night the ponies were let loose, and each day were gathered into the horse corral and broken as well as we could break them in such weather. It was my intention not to start on the hunt until the ponies were separated into the two bands, and the men from the lower ranch (the Elkhorn) had gone off with theirs. Then one of the cowboys was to take the buck-board up to a deserted hunter's hut, which lay on a great bend of the river near by the ground over which the big-horn were said to wander, while my foreman, Merrifield, and myself would take saddle-horses, and each day ride to the country through which we intended to hunt, returning at night to the buck-board and hut. But we started a little sooner than we had intended, owing to a funny mistake made by one of the cowboys.

The sun did not rise until nearly eight, but each morning we breakfasted at five, and the men were then sent out on the horses which had been kept in overnight, to find and drive home the pony band; of course they started in perfect darkness, except for the starlight. On the last day of our proposed stay the men had come in with the ponies before sunrise; and, leaving the latter in the corral, they entered the house and crowded round the fire, stamping and beating their numbed hands together. In the midst of the confusion word was brought by one of the cowboys, that while hunting for the horses he had seen two bears go down into a wash-out; and he told us that he could bring us right to the place where he had seen them, for as soon as he left it he had come in at speed on his swift, iron-gray horse—a vicious, clean-limbed devil, with muscles like bundles of tense wire; the cold had made the brute savage, and it had been punished with the cruel curb bit until long, bloody icicles hung from his lips.

At once Merrifield and I mounted in hot haste, and rode off with the bringer of good tidings, leaving hasty instructions where we were to be joined by the buck-board. The sun was still just below the horizon as we started, wrapped warmly in our fur coats and with our caps drawn down over our ears to keep out the cold. The cattle were standing in the thickets and sheltered ravines, huddled together with their heads down, the frost lying on their backs and the icicles hanging from their muzzles; they stared at us as we rode along, but were too cold to move a hand's breadth out of our way; indeed it is a marvel how they survive the winter at all. Our course at first lay up a long valley, cut up by cattle trails; then we came out, just as the sun had risen, upon the rounded, gently-sloping highland, thickly clad with the short, nutritious grass, which curls on the stalk into good hay, and on which the cattle feed during winter. We galloped rapidly over the hills, our blood gradually warming up from the motion; and soon came to the long wash-out, cutting down like a miniature canyon for a space of two or three miles through the bottom of a valley, into which the cowboy said he had seen the bears go. One of us took one side and one the other, and we rode along up wind, but neither the bears nor any traces of them could we see; at last, half a mile ahead of us, two dark objects suddenly emerged from the wash-out and came out on the plain. For a second we thought they were the quarry; then we saw that they were merely couple of dark-colored ponies. The cowboy's chapfallen face was a study; he had seen, in the dim light, the two ponies going down with their heads held near the ground, and had mistaken them for bears (by no means the unnatural mistake that it seems; I have known an experienced hunter fire twice at a black calf in the late evening, thinking it was a bear). He knew only too well the merciless chaff to which he would be henceforth exposed; and a foretaste of which he at once received from my companion. The ponies had strayed from the main herd, and the cowboy was sent back to drive them to the home corral, while Merrifield and myself continued our hunt.

We had all day before us, and but twenty miles or so to cover before reaching the hut where the buck-board was to meet us; but the course we intended to take was through country so rough that no Eastern horse could cross it, and even the hardy Western hunting-ponies, who climb like goats, would have difficulty in keeping their feet. Our route lay through the heart of the Bad Lands, but of course the country was not equally rough in all parts. There were tracts of varying size, each covered with a tangled mass of chains and peaks, the buttes in places reaching a height that would in the East entitle them to be called mountains. Every such tract was riven in all directions by deep chasms and narrow ravines, whose sides sometimes rolled off in gentle slopes, but far more often rose as sheer cliffs, with narrow ledges along their fronts. A sparse growth of grass covered certain portions of these lands, and on some of the steep hillsides, or in the canyons, were scanty groves of coniferous evergreens, so stunted by the thin soil and bleak weather that many of them were bushes rather than trees. Most of the peaks and ridges, and many of the valleys, were entirely bare of vegetation, and these had been cut by wind and water into the strangest and most fantastic shapes. Indeed it is difficult, in looking at such formations, to get rid of the feeling that their curiously twisted and contorted forms are due to some vast volcanic upheavals or other subterranean forces; yet they are merely caused by the action of the various weathering forces of the dry climate on the different strata of sandstones, clays, and marls. Isolated columns shoot up into the air, bearing on their summits flat rocks like tables; square buttes tower high above surrounding depressions, which are so cut up by twisting gullies and low ridges as to be almost impassable; shelving masses of sandstone jut out over the sides of the cliffs; some of the ridges, with perfectly perpendicular sides, are so worn away that they stand up like gigantic knife blades; and gulches, wash-outs, and canyons dig out the sides of each butte, while between them are thrust out long spurs, with sharp ragged tops. All such patches of barren, broken ground, where the feed seems too scant to support any large animal, are the favorite haunts of the big-horn, though it also wanders far into the somewhat gentler and more fertile, but still very rugged, domain of the black-tail deer.

Between all such masses of rough country lay wide, grassy plateaus or long stretches of bare plain, covered with pebbly shingle. We loped across all these open places; and when we came to a reach of broken country would leave our horse and hunt through it on foot. Except where the wind had blown it off, there was a thin coat of snow over every thing, and the icy edges and sides of the cliffs gave only slippery and uncertain foothold, so as to render the climbing doubly toilsome. Hunting the big-horn is at all times the hardest and most difficult kind of sport, and is equally trying to both wind and muscle; and for that very reason the big-horn ranks highest among all the species of game that are killed by still-hunting where the quarry is itself dangerous to attack. Climbing kept us warm in spite of the bitter weather; we only wore our fur coats and shaps while on horseback, leaving them where we left the horses, and doing our still-hunting in buckskin shirts, fur caps, and stout shoes.

Big-horn, more commonly known as mountain sheep, are extremely wary and cautious animals, and are plentiful in but few places. This is rather surprising, for they seem to be fairly prolific (although not as much so as deer and antelope), and comparatively few are killed by the hunters; indeed, much fewer are shot than of any other kind of western game in proportion to their numbers. They hold out in a place long after the elk and buffalo have been exterminated, and for many years after both of these have become things of the past the big-horn will still exist to afford sport to the man who is a hardy mountaineer and skilful with the rifle. For it is the only kind of game on whose haunts cattle do not trespass.

191

Good buffalo or elk pasture is sure to be also good pasture for steers and cows; and in summer the herds of the ranchman wander far into the prairies of the antelope, while in winter their chosen and favorite resorts are those of which the black-tail is equally fond. Thus, the cattle-men are almost as much foes of these kinds of game as are the hunters, but neither cattle nor cowboys penetrate into the sterile and rocky wastes where the big-horn is found. And it is too wary game, and the labor of following it is too great, for it ever to be much persecuted by the skin or market hunters.

In size the big-horn comes next to buffalo and elk, averaging larger than the black-tail deer, while an old ram will sometimes be almost as heavy as a small cow elk. In his movements he is not light and graceful like the prong-horn and other antelopes, his marvellous agility seeming rather to proceed from sturdy strength and wonderful command over iron sinews and muscles. The huge horns are carried proudly erect by the massive neck; every motion of the body is made with perfect poise; and there seems to be no ground so difficult that the big-horn cannot cross it. There is probably no animal in the world his superior in climbing; and his only equals are the other species of mountain sheep and the ibexes. No matter how sheer the cliff, if there are ever so tiny cracks or breaks in the surface, the big-horn will bound up or down it with wonderful ease and seeming absence of effort. The perpendicular bounds it can make are truly startling—in strong contrast with its distant relative the prong-horn which can leap almost any level jump but seems unable to clear the smallest height. In descending a sheer wall of rock the big-horn holds all four feet together and goes down in long jumps, bounding off the surface almost like a rubber ball every time he strikes it. The way that one will vanish over the roughest and most broken ground is a perpetual surprise to any one that has hunted them; and the ewes are quite as skilful as the rams, while even the very young lambs seem almost as well able to climb, and certainly follow wherever their elders lead. Time and again one will rush over a cliff to what appeared certain death, and will gallop away from the bottom unharmed. Their perfect self-confidence seems to be justified, however, for they never slip or make a misstep, even on the narrowest ledges when covered with ice and snow. And all their marvelous jumping and climbing is done with an apparent ease that renders it the more wonderful. Rapid though the movements of one are they made without any of the nervous hurry so characteristic of the antelopes and smaller deer; the on-looker is really as much impressed with the animal's sinewy power and self-command as with his ability. His strength and his self-reliance seem to fit him above all other kinds of game to battle with the elements and with his brute foes; he does not care to have the rough ways of his life made smooth; were his choice free his bode would still be the vast and lonely wilderness in which he is found. To him the barren wastes of the Bad Lands offer a most attractive home; yet to other living creatures they are at all times as grimly desolate and forbidding as any spot on earth can be; at all seasons they seem hostile to every form of life. In the raging heat of summer the dry earth cracks and crumbles, and the sultry, lifeless air sways and trembles as if above a furnace. Through the high, clear atmosphere, the intense sunlight casts unnaturally deep shadows; and where there are no shadows, brings out in glaring re-lief the weird, fantastic shapes and bizarre coloring of the buttes. In winter snow and ice coat the thin crests and sharp sides of the cliffs, and increase their look of savage wildness; the cold turns the ground into ringing iron; and the icy blasts sweep through the clefts and over the ridges with an angry fury even more terrible than is the intense, death-like, silent heat of midsummer. But the mountain ram is alike proudly indifferent to the hottest summer sun and to the wildest winter storm.

The lambs are brought forth late in May or early in June. Like the antelope, the dam soon leads her kids to join the herd, which may range in size from a dozen to four or five times as many individuals, generally approaching nearer the former number. The ewes, lambs and yearling or two-year-old rams go together. The young but full-gown rams keep in small parties of three or four, while the old fellows, with monstrous heads, keep by themselves, except when they join the ewes in the rutting season. At this time they wage savage war with each other. The horns of the old rams are always battered and scarred from these butting contests— which appearance, by the way, has given rise to the ridiculous idea that they were in the habit of jumping over precipices and landing on their heads.

Occasionally the big-horn come down into the valleys or along the grassy slopes to feed, but this is not often, and in such cases every member of the band is always keeping the sharpest look-out, and at the slightest alarm they beat a retreat to their broken fast-nesses. At night-time or in the early morning they come down to drink at the small pools or springs, but move off the instant they have satisfied their thirst. As a rule, they spend their time among the rocks and rough ground, and it is in these places that they must be hunted. They cover a good deal of ground when feeding, for the feed is scanty in their haunts, and they walk quite rapidly along the ledges or peaks, by preference high up, as they graze or browse. When through feeding they always choose as a resting-place some point from which they can command a view over all the surround-ing territory. An old ram is peculiarly wary. The crest of a ridge or the top of a peak is a favorite resting-bed; but even more often they choose some ledge, high up, but just below the crest, or lie on a shelf of rock that juts out from where a ridge ends, and thus en-ables them to view the country on three sides of them. In color they harmonize curiously with the grayish or yellowish brown of the ground on which they are found, and it is often very difficult to make them out when lying motionless on a ledge of rock. Time and again they will be mistaken for boulders, and, on the other hand, I have more than once stalked up to masses of sandstone that I have mistaken for sheep.

When lying down the big-horn can thus scan every thing below it; and both while feeding and resting it invariably keeps the sharpest possible look-out for all danger from beneath, and this trait makes it needful for the hunter to always keep on the highest ground and try to come on it from above. For protection against danger it relies on ears, eyes, and nose alike. The slightest sound startles it and puts it on its guard, while if it sees or smells any thing which it deems may bode danger it is off like a flash. It is as wary and quick-sighted as the antelope, and its senses are as keen as are those of the elk, while it is not afflicted by the occasional stupidity nor heedless recklessness of these two animals, nor by the intense curiosity of the black-tail, and it has all the white-tail's sound common-sense, coupled with a much shyer nature and much sharper faculties, so that it is more difficult to kill then are any of these creatures. And the climbing is rendered all the more tiresome by the traits above spoken of, which make it necessary for the hunter to keep above it. The first thing to do is to clamber up to the top of a ridge, and after that to keep on the highest crests.

At all times, and with all game, the still-hunger should be quiet, and should observe caution, but when after mountain sheep he must be absolutely noiseless and must not neglect a single chance. He must be careful not to step on a loose stone or to start any crumbing earth; he must always hunt up or across wind, and he must take advantage of every crag or boulder to shelter himself from the gaze of his watchful quarry. While keeping up as high as possible, he should not go on the very summit, as that brings him out in too sharp relief against the sky. And all the while he will be crossing land where he will need to pay good heed to his own footing or else run the risk of breaking his neck.

As far as lay in us, on our first day's hunt we paid proper heed to all the rules of hunting-craft; but without success. Up the slippery, ice-covered buttes we clambered, clinging to the rocks, and slowly working our way across the faces of the cliffs, or cautiously creeping along the narrow ledges, peering over every crest long and carefully, and from the peaks scanning the ground all about with the field-glasses. But we saw no sheep, and but little sign of them. Still we did see some sign, and lost a shot, either through bad luck or bad management. This was while going through a cluster of broken buttes, whose peaks rose up like sharp cones. On reaching the top of one at the leeward end, we worked cautiously up the side, seeing nothing, to the other end, and then down along the middle. When about half-way back we came across the fresh footprints of a ewe or yearling ram in a little patch of snow. On tracing them back we found that it had been lying down on the other side of a small bluff, within a hundred yards of where we had passed, and must have either got our wind, or else have heard us make some noise. At any rate it had gone off, and though we followed its tracks a little in the snow, they soon got on the bare, frozen ground and we lost them.

After that we saw nothing. The cold, as the day wore on, seemed gradually to chill us through and through; our hands and feet became numb, and our ears tingled under our fur caps. We hunted carefully through two or three masses of jagged buttes which seemed most likely places for the game we were after, taking a couple of hours to each place; and then, as the afternoon was beginning to wane, mounted our shivering horses for good, and pushed toward the bend of the river where we were to meet the buck-board. Our course lay across a succession of bleak, wind-swept plateaus, broke by deep and narrow pine-clad gorges. We galloped swiftly over the plateaus, where the footing was good and the going easy, for the gales had driven the feathery snow off the withered brown grass; but getting on and off these table-lands was often a real labor, their sides were so sheer. The horses plunged and scrambled after us as we led them up; while in descending they would sit back on their haunches and half-walk, half-slide, down the steep inclines. Indeed, one or two of the latter were so very straight that the horses would not face them, and we had to turn them round and back them over the edge, and then all go down with a rush. At any rate it warmed our blood to keep out of the way of the hoofs. On one of the plateaus I got a very long shot at a black-tail, which I missed.

Finally we struck the head of a long, winding valley with a smooth bottom, and after cantering down it four or five miles, came to the river, just after the cold, pale-red sun had sunk behind the line of hills ahead of us. Our horses were sharp shod, and crossed the ice without difficulty; and in a grove of leafless cotton-woods, on the opposite side, we found the hut for which we had been making, the cowboy already inside with the fire started. Throughout the night the temperature sank lower and lower, and it was impossible to keep the crazy old hut anywhere near freezing-point; the wind whistled through the chinks and crannies of the logs, and, after a short and by no means elaborate supper, we were glad to cower down with our great fur coats still on, under the pile of buffalo robes and bear-skins. My sleeping-bag came in very handily, and kept me as warm as possible, in spite of the bitter frost.

We were up and had taken breakfast next morning by the time the first streak of dawn had dimmed the brilliancy of the stars, and immediately afterwards strode off on foot, as we had been hampered by the horses on the day before. We walked briskly across the plain until, by the time it was light enough to see to shoot, we came to the foot of a great hill, known as Middle Butte, a huge, isolated mass of rock, several miles in length, and with high sides, very steep towards the nearly level summit; it would be deemed a mountain of no inconsiderable size in the East. We hunted carefully through the outlying foothills and projecting spurs around its base, without result, finding but a few tracks, and those very old ones, and then toiled up to the top, which, though narrow in parts, in others widened out into plateaus half a mile square. Having made a complete circuit of the top, peering over the edge and closely examining the flanks of the butte with the field-glass, without having seen any thing, we slid down the other side and took off through a streak of very rugged but low country. This day, though the weather had grown even colder, we did not feel it, for we walked all the while with a quick pace, and the climbing was very hard work. The shoulders and ledges of the cliffs had become round and slippery with the ice, and it was no easy task to move up and along them, clutching the gun in one hand, and grasping each little projection with the other. Climbing through the Bad Lands is just like any other kind of mountaineering, except that the precipices and chasms are much lower; but this really makes very little difference when the ground is frozen as solid as iron, for it would be almost as unpleasant to fall fifty feet as to fall two hundred, and the result to the person who tried it would be very much the same in each case.

Hunting for a day or two without finding game where the work is severe and toilsome, is a good test of the sportsman's staying qualities; the man who at the end of the time is proceeding with as much caution and determination as at the beginning, has got the right stuff in him. On this day I got rather tired, and committed one of the blunders of which no hunter ought ever to be guilty; that is, I fired at small game while on ground where I might expect large. We had seen two or three jack-rabbits scudding off like noiseless white shadows, and finally came upon some sharp-tail prairie fowl in a hollow. One was quite near me, perched on a bush, and with its neck stretched up offered a beautiful mark; I could not resist it, so knelt and fired. At the report of the rifle (it was a miss, by the by) a head suddenly appeared over a ridge some six hundred yards in front—too far off for us to make out what kind of animal it belonged to,—looked fixedly at us, and then disappeared. We feared it might be a mountain sheep, and that my unlucky shot had deprived us of the chance of a try at it; but on hurrying up to the place where it had been were relieved to find that the tracks were only those of a black-tail. After this lesson we proceeded in silence, making a long circle though the roughest kind of country. When on the way back to camp, where the buttes rose highest and steepest, we came upon fresh tracks, but as it was then late in the afternoon, did not try to follow them that day. When near the hut I killed a sharp-tail for supper, making rather a neat shot, the bird being eighty yards off. The night was even colder than the preceding one, and all signs told us that we would soon have a change for the worse in the weather, which made me doubly anxious to get a sheep before the storm struck us. We determined that next morning we would take the horses and made a quick push for the chain of high buttes where we had seen the fresh tracks, and hunt them through with thorough care.

We started in the cold gray of the next morning and pricked rapidly off over the frozen plain, columns of white steam rising from the nostrils of the galloping horses. When we reached the foot of the hills where we intended to hunt, and had tethered the horses, the sun had already risen, but it was evident that the clear weather of a fortnight past was over. The air was thick and hazy, and away off in the northwest a towering mass of grayish white clouds looked like a weather-breeder; every thing boded a storm at no distant date. The country over which we now hunted was wilder and more mountainous than any we had yet struck. High, sharp peaks and ridges broke off abruptly into narrow gorges and deep ravines; they were bare of all but the scantiest vegetation, save on some of the sheltered sides where grew groves of dark pines, now laden down with feathery snow. The climbing was as hard as ever. At first we went straight up the side of the tallest peak, and then along the knife-like ridge which joined it with the next. The ice made the footing very slippery as we stepped along the ledges or crawled round the jutting shoulders, and we had to look carefully for our footholds; while in the cold, thin air every quick burst we made up a steep hill caused us to pant for breath. We had gone but a little way before we saw fresh signs of the animals we were after, but it was some time before we came upon the quarry itself.

We left the high ground and descending into a narrow chasm walked along its bottom, which was but a couple of feet wide, while the sides rose up from it at an acute angle. After following this for a few hundred yards, we turned a sharp corner, and shortly afterward our eyes were caught by some grains of fresh earth lying on the snow in front of our feet. On the side, some feet above our heads, were marks in the snow made by a couple of mountain sheep that had come down one side of the gorge and had leaped across to the other, their sharp toes going through the thin snow and displacing the earth that had fallen to the bottom. The tracks had evidently been made just before we rounded the corner, and as we had been advancing noiselessly on the snow with the wind in our favor, we knew that the animal could have no suspicion of our presence. They had gone up the cliff on our right, but as that on our left was much lower, and running for some distance parallel to the other, we concluded that by running along its top we would be most certain to get a good shot. Clambering instantly up the steep side, digging my hands and feet into the loose snow, and grasping at every little rock or frozen projection, I reached the top; and then ran forward along the ridge a few paces, crouching behind the masses of queerly-shaped sandstone; and saw, about ninety yards off across the ravine, a couple of mountain rams. The one with the largest horns was broadside toward me, his sturdy, massive form outlined clearly against the sky, as he stood on the crest of the ridge. I dropped on my knee, raising the rifle as I did so; for a second he did not quite make me out, turning his head half round to look. I held the sight fairly on the point just behind his shoulder and pulled the trigger. At the report he staggered and pitched forward, but recovered himself and crossed over the ridge out of sight. We jumped and slid down into the ravine again, and clambered up the opposite side as fast as our lungs and the slippery ice would let us; then taking the trail of the wounded ram we trotted along it. We had not far to go; for, as I expected, we found him lying on his side a couple of hundred yards beyond the ridge, his eyes already glazed in death. The bullet had gone in behind the shoulder and ranged clean through his body crosswise, going a little forward; no animal less tough than a mountain ram could have gone any distance at all with such a wound. He had most obligingly run round to a part of the hill where we could bring up one of the horses without very much difficulty. Accordingly I brought up old Manitou, who can carry any thing and has no fear, and the big-horn was soon strapped across his back. It was a fine ram, with perfectly-shaped but not very large horns.

The other ram, two years old, with small horns, had bounded over the ridge before I could get a shot at him; we followed his trail for half a mile, but as he showed no signs of halting, and we were anxious to get home, we then gave up the pursuit.

It was still early in the day, and we made up our minds to push back for the home ranch, as we did not wish to be caught out in a long storm. The lowering sky was already overcast by a mass of leaden-gray clouds; and it was evident that we had no time to lose. In a little over an hour we were back at the log camp, where the ram was shifted from Manitou's back to the buck-board. A very few minutes sufficed to pack up our bedding and provisions, and we started home. Merrifield and I rode on ahead, not sparing the horses; but before we got home the storm had burst, and a furious blizzard blew in our teeth as we galloped along the last mile of the river bottom, before coming to the home ranch house; and as we warmed our stiffened limbs before the log fire, I congratulated myself upon the successful outcome of what I knew would be the last hunting trip I should take during that season.

The death of this ram was accomplished without calling for any very good shooting on our part. He was standing still, less than a hundred yards off, when the shot was fired; and we came across him so close merely by accident. Still, we fairly deserved our luck, for we had hunted with the most patient and painstaking care from dawn till nightfall for the better part of three days, spending most of the time in climbing at a smart rate of speed up sheer cliffs and over rough and slippery ground. Still-hunting the big-horn is always a toilsome and laborious task, and the very bitter weather during which we had been out had not lessened the difficulty of the work, though in the cold it was much less exhausting than it would have been to have hunted across the same ground in summer. No other kind of hunting does as much to bring out the good qualities, both moral and physical, of the sportsmen who follow it. If a man keeps at it, it is bound to make him both hardy and resolute; to strengthen his muscles and fill out his lungs.

Mountain mutton is in the fall the most delicious eating furnished by any game animal. Nothing else compares with it for juiciness, tenderness, and flavor; but at all other times of the year it is tough, stringy, and worthless.

The Black Bear
(From *The Wilderness Hunter*)

Next to the whitetail deer the black bear is the commonest and most widely distributed of American big game. It is still found quite plentifully in northern New England, in the Adirondacks, Catskills, and along the entire length of the Alleghenies, as well as in the swamps and canebrakes of the southern States. It is also common in the great forests of northern Michigan, Wisconsin, and Minnesota, and throughout the Rocky Mountains and the timbered ranges of the Pacific coast. In the East it has always ranked second only to the deer among the beasts of chase. The bear and the buck were the staple objects of pursuit of all the old hunters. They were more plentiful than the bison and elk even in the long vanished days when these two great monarchs of the forest still ranged eastward to Virginia and Pennsylvania. The wolf and the cougar were always too scarce and too shy to yield much profit to the hunter. The black bear is a timid, cowardly animal, and usually a vegetarian, though it sometimes preys on the sheep, hogs, and even cattle of the settler, and is very fond of raiding his corn and melons. Its meat is good and its fur often valuable, and in its chase there is much excitement, and occasionally a slight spice of danger, just enough to render it attractive; so it has always been eagerly followed. Yet it still holds it own, though in greatly diminished numbers, in the more thinly settled portions of the country. One of the standing riddles of American zoölogy is the fact that the black bear, which is easier killed and less prolific than the wolf, should hold its own in the land better than the latter, this being directly the reverse of what occurs in Europe, where the brown bear is generally exterminated before the wolf.

In a few wild spots in the East, in northern Maine for instance, here and there in the neighborhood of the upper Great Lakes, in the east Tennessee and Kentucky mountains and the swamps of Florida and Mississippi, there still lingers an occasional representative of the old wilderness hunters. These men live in log-cabins in the wilderness. They do their hunting on foot, occasionally with the help of a single trailing dog. In Maine they are as apt to kill moose and caribou as bear and deer; but elsewhere the two last, with an occasional cougar or wolf, are the beasts of chase which they follow. Nowadays as these old hunters die there is no one to take their places, though there are still plenty of backwoods settlers in all of the regions named who do a great deal of hunting and trapping. Such an old hunter rarely makes his appearance at the settlements except to dispose of his peltry and hides in exchange for cartridges and provisions, and he leads a life of such lonely isolation as to insure his individual characteristics developing into peculiarities. Most of the wilder districts in the eastern States still preserve memories of some such old hunter who lived his long life alone, waging ceaseless warfare on the vanishing game, whose oddities, as well as his courage, hardihood, and woodcraft, are laughingly remembered by the older settlers, and who is usually best known as having killed the last wolf or bear or cougar ever seen in the locality.

Generally the weapon mainly relied on by these old hunters is the rifle; and occasionally some old hunter will be found even to this day who uses a muzzle loader, such as Kit Carson carried in the middle of the century. There are exceptions to this rule of the rifle however. In the years after the Civil War one of the many noted hunters of southwest Virginia and east Tennessee was Wilbur Waters, sometimes called The Hunter of White Top. He often killed black bear with a knife and dogs. He spent all his life in hunting and was very successful, killing the last gang of wolves to be found in his neighborhood; and he slew innumerable bears, with no worse results to himself than an occasional bite or scratch.

In the southern States the planters living in the wilder regions have always been in the habit of following the black bear with horse and hound, many of them keeping regular packs of bear hounds. Such a pack includes not only pure-bred hounds, but also cross-bred animals, and some sharp, agile, hard-biting fierce dogs and terriers. They follow the bear and bring him to bay but do not try to kill him, although there are dogs of the big fighting breeds which can readily master a black bear if loosed at him three or four at a time; but the dogs of these southern bear-hound packs are not fitted for such work, and if they try to close with the bear he is certain to play havoc with them, disembowelling them with blows of his paws or seizing them in his arms and biting through their spines or legs. The riders follow the hounds through the cane-brakes, and also try to make cutoffs and station themselves at open points where they think the bear will pass, so that they may get a shot at him. The weapons used are rifles, shotguns, and occasionally revolvers.

Sometimes, however, the hunter uses the knife. General Wade Hampton, who has probably killed more black bears then any other man living in the United States, frequently used the knife, slaying thirty or forty with his weapon. His plan was, when he found that the dogs had the bear at bay, to walk up close and cheer them on. They would instantly seize the bear in a body, and he would then rush in and stab it behind the shoulder, reaching over so as to inflict the wound on the opposite side from that where he stood. He escaped scathless from all these encounters save one, in which he was rather severely torn in the forearm. Many other hunters have used the knife, but perhaps none so frequently as he; for he was always fond of steel, as witness his feats with the "white arm" during the Civil War.

General Hampton always hunted with large packs of hounds, managed sometimes by himself and sometimes by his negro hunters. He occasionally took out forty dogs at a time. He found that all his dogs together could not kill a big fat bear, but they occasionally killed three-year-olds, or lean and poor bears. During the course of his life he has himself killed, or been in at the death of, five hundred bears, at least two thirds of them falling by his own hand. In the years just before the war he had on one occasion, in Mississippi, killed sixty-eight bears in five months. Once he killed four bears in a day; at another time three, and frequently two. The two largest bears he himself killed weighed, respectively, 408 and 410 pounds. They were both shot in Mississippi. But he saw at least one bear killed which was much larger than either of these. These figures were taken down at the time, when the animals were actually weighed on the scales. Most of his hunting for bear was done in northern Mississippi, where one of his plantations was situated, near Greenville. During the half century that he hunted, on and off, in this neighborhood, he knew of two instances where hunters were fatally wounded in the chase of the black bear. Both of the men were inexperienced, one being a raftsman who came down the river, and the other a man from Vicksburg. He was not able to learn the particulars in the last case, but the raftsman came too close to a bear that was at bay, and it broke through the dogs, rushed at and overthrew him, then lying on him, it bit him deeply in the thigh, through the femoral artery, so that he speedily bled to death.

The Black Bear

But a black bear is not usually a formidable opponent, and though he will sometimes charge home he is much more apt to bluster and bully than actually to come to close quarters. I myself have but once seen a man who had been hurt by one of these bears. This was an Indian. He had come on the beast close up in a thick wood, and had mortally wounded it with his gun; it had then closed with him, knocking the gun out of his hand, so that he was forced to use his knife. It charged him on all fours, but in the grapple, when it had failed to throw him down, it raised itself on its hind legs, clasping him across the shoulders with its fore-paws. Apparently it had no intention of hugging, but merely sought to draw him within reach of his jaws. He fought desperately against this, using the knife freely, and striving to keep its head back; and the flow of blood weakened the animal, so that it finally fell exhausted, before being able dangerously to injure him. But it had bitten his left arm very severely, and its claws had made long gashes on his shoulders.

Black bears, like grislies, vary greatly in their modes of attack. Sometimes they rush in and bite; and again they strike with their fore-paws. Two of my cowboys were originally from Maine, where I knew them well. There they were fond of trapping bears, and caught a good many. The huge steel gins, attached by chains to heavy clogs, prevented the trapped beasts from gong far, and when found they were always tied tight round some tree or bush, and usually nearly exhausted. The men killed them either with a little 32-calibre pistol or a hatchet. But once did they meet with any difficulty. On this occasion one of them incautiously approached a captured bear to knock it on the head with his hatchet, but the animal managed to partially untwist itself, and with its free fore-arm made a rapid sweep at him; he jumped back just in time, the bear's claws tearing his clothes—after which he shot it. Bears are shy and have very keen noses; they are therefore hard to kill by fair hunting, living, as they generally do, in dense forests or thick brush. They are easy enough to trap, however. Thus, these two men, though they trapped so many, never but once killed them in any other way. On this occasion one of them, in the winter, found in a great hollow log a den where a she and two well-grown cubs had taken up their abode, and shot all three with his rile as they burst out.

Where they are much hunted, bear become purely nocturnal; but in the wilder forests I have seen them abroad at all hours, though they do not much relish the intense heat of noon. They are rather comical animals to watch feeding and going about the ordinary business of their lives. Once I spent half an hour lying at the edge of a wood and looking at a black bear some three hundred yards off across an open glade. It was in good stalking country, but the wind was unfavorable and I waited for it to shift—waited too long as it proved, for something frightened the beast and he made off before I could get a shot at him. When I first saw him he was shuffling along and rooting in the ground, so that he looked like a great pig. Then he began to turn over the stones and logs to hunt for insects, small reptiles, and the like. A moderate-sized stone he would turn over with a single clap of his paw, and then plunge his nose down into the hollow to gobble up the small creatures beneath while still dazed by the light. The big logs and rocks he would tug and worry at with both paws; once, over-exerting his clumsy strength, he lost his grip and rolled clean on his back. Under some of the logs he evidently found mice and chipmunks; then, as soon as the log was overturned, he would be seen jumping about with grotesque agility, and making quick dabs here and there, as the little scurrying rodent turned and twisted, until at last he put his paw on it and scooped it up into his mouth. Sometimes, probably when he smelt the mice underneath, he would cautiously turn the log over with one paw, holding the other lifted and ready to strike. Now and then he would halt and sniff the air in every direction, and it was after one of these halts that he suddenly shuffled off into the woods.

The Black Bear

Black bear generally feed on berries, nuts, insects, carrion, and the like; but at times they take to killing very large animals. In fact, they are curiously irregular in their food. They will kill deer if they can get at them; but generally the deer are too quick. Sheep and hogs are their favorite prey, especially the latter, for bears seem to have a special relish for pork. Twice I have known a black bear kill cattle. Once the victim was a bull which had got mired, and which the bear deliberately proceeded to eat alive, heedless of the bellows of the unfortunate beast. On the other occasion, a cow was surprised and slain among some bushes at the edge of a remote pasture. In the spring, soon after the long winter sleep, they are very hungry, and are especially apt to attack large beasts at this time; although during the very first days of their appearance, when they are just breaking their fast, they eat rather sparingly, and by preference the tender shoots of green grass and other herbs, or frogs and crayfish; it is not for a week or two that they seem to be overcome by lean, ravenous hunger. They will even attack and master that formidable fighter the moose, springing at it from an ambush as it passes—for a bull moose would surely be an over-match for one of them if fronted fairly in the open. An old hunter, whom I could trust, told me that he had seen in the snow in early spring the place where a bear had sprung at two moose, which were trotting together; he missed his spring, and the moose got off, their strides after they settled down into their pace being tremendous, and showing how thoroughly they were frightened. Another time he saw a bear chase a moose into a lake, where it waded out a little distance, and then turned to bay, bidding defiance to his pursuer, the latter not daring to approach in the water. I have been told—but cannot vouch for it—that instances have been known where the bear, maddened by hunger, has gone in on a moose thus standing at bay, only to be beaten down under the water by the terrible fore-hoofs of the quarry, and to yield its life in the contest. A lumberman told me that he once saw a moose, evidently much startled, trot through a swamp, and immediately afterwards a bear came up following the tracks. He almost ran into the man, and was evidently not in a good temper, for he growled and blustered, and two or three times made feints of charging, before he finally concluded to go off.

Bears will occasionally visit hunters' or lumbermen's camps, in the absence of the owners, and play sad havoc with all there therein is, devouring everything eatable, especially if sweet, and trampling into a dirty mess whatever they do not eat. The black bear does not average more than a third the size of the grisly; but, like all its kind, it varies greatly in weight. The largest I myself ever saw weighed was in Maine, and tipped the scale at 346 pounds; but I have a perfectly authentic record of one in Maine that weighed 397, and my friend, Dr. Hart Merriam, tells me that he has seen several in the Adirondacks that when killed weighed about 350.

I myself shot but one or two black bears, and these were obtained under circumstances of no special interest, as I merely stumbled on them while after other game, and killed them before they had a chance either to run or show fight.

Mountain Game; The White Goat
(From *The Wilderness Hunter*)

Late one August I started on a trip to the Big Hole Basin, in Western Montana, to hunt white goats. With me went a friend of many hunts, John Willis, a tried mountain man.

We left the railroad at the squalid little hamlet of Divide, where we hired a team and wagon from a "busted" granger, suspected of being a Mormon, who had failed, even with the help of irrigation, in raising a crop. The wagon was in fairly good order; the harness was rotten, and needed patching with ropes; while the team consisted of two spoiled horses, overworked and thin, but full of the devil the minute they began to pick up condition. However, on the frontier one soon grows to accept little facts of this kind with bland indifference; and Willis was not only an expert teamster, but possessed that inexhaustible fertility of resource and unfailing readiness in an emergency so characteristic of the veteran of the border. Through hard experience he had become master of plainscraft and woodcraft, skilled in all frontier lore.

For a couple of days we jogged up the valley of the Big Hole River, along the mail road. At night we camped under our wagon. At the mouth of the stream the valley was a mere gorge, but it broadened steadily the farther up we went, till the rapid river wound through a wide expanse of hilly, treeless prairie. On each side the mountains rose, their lower flanks and the foot-hills covered with the evergreen forest. We got milk and bread at the scattered log-houses of the few settlers; and for meat we shot sage fowl, which abounded. They were feeding on grasshoppers at this time, and the flesh, especially of the young birds, was as tender and well tasting as possible; whereas, when we again passed through the valley in September, we found the birds almost uneatable, being fairly bitter with sage. Like all grouse they are far tamer earlier in the season than later, being very wild in winter; and, of course, they are boldest where they are least hunted; but for some unexplained reason they are always tamer than the sharp-tail prairie fowl which are to be found in the same locality.

Finally we reached the neighborhood of the Battle Ground, where a rude stone monument commemorates the bloody drawn fight between General Gibbons' soldiers and the Nez Percés warriors of Chief Joseph. Here, on the third day of our journey, we left the beaten road and turned towards the mountains, following an indistinct trail made by wood-choppers. We met with our full share of the usual mishaps incident to prairie travel; and towards evening our team got mired in crossing a slough. We attempted the crossing with some misgivings, which were warranted by the result; for the second plunge of the horses brought them up to their bellies in the morass, where they stuck. It was freezing cold, with a bitter wind blowing, and the bog holes were skimmed with ice; so that we passed a thoroughly wretched two hours while freeing the horses and unloading the wagon. However, we eventually got across; my companion preserving an absolutely unruffled temper throughout, perseveringly whistling the "Arkansas Traveller." At one period, when we were up to our waists in the icy mud, it began to sleet and hail, and I muttered that I would "rather it didn't storm"; whereat he stopped whistling for a moment to make the laconic rejoinder, "We're not having our rathers this trip."

At nightfall we camped among the willow bushes by a little brook. For firewood we had only dead willow sticks; they made a hot blaze which soon died out; and as the cold grew intense, we rolled up in our blankets as soon as we had eaten our supper. The climate of the Big Hole Basin is alpine; that night, though it was the 20th of August, the thermometer sank to 10° F.

Early next morning we struck camp, shivering with cold as we threw the stiff, frozen harness on the horses. We soon got among the foot-hills, where the forest was open and broken by large glades, forming what is called a park country. The higher we went the smaller grew the glades and the denser the woodland; and it began to be very difficult to get the wagon forward. In many places one man had to go ahead to pick out the way, and if necessary do a little chopping and lopping with the axe, while the other followed driving the team. At last we were bought to a standstill, and pitched camp beside a rapid, alder-choked brook in the uppermost of a series of rolling glades, hemmed in by mountains and the dense coniferous forest. Our tent stood under a grove of pines, close to the brook; at night we built in front of it a big fire of crackling, resinous logs. Our goods were sheltered by the wagon, or covered with a tarpaulin; we threw down sprays of odorous evergreens to make a resting-place for our bedding; we built small scaffolds on which to dry the flesh of elk and deer. In an hour or two we had round us all the many real comforts of such a little wilderness home.

Whoever has long roamed and hunted in the wilderness always cherishes with wistful pleasure the memory of some among the countless camps he has made. The camp by the margin of the clear, mountain-hemmed lake; the camp in the dark and melancholy forest, where the gusty wind booms through the tall pine tops; the camp under gnarled cottonwoods, on the bank of a shrunken river, in the midst of endless grassy prairies,—of these, and many like them, each has had its own charm. Of course in hunting one must expect much hardship and repeated disappointment; and in many a camp, bad weather, lack of shelter, hunger, thirst, or ill success with game, renders the days and nights irksome and trying. Yet the hunter worthy of the name always willingly takes the bitter if by so doing he can get the sweet, and gladly balances failure and success, spurning the poorer souls who know neither.

We turned our horses loose, hobbling one; and as we did not look after them for several days, nothing but my companion's skill as a tracker enabled us to find them again. There was a spell of warm weather which brought out a few of the big bull-dog flies, which drive a horse—or indeed a man—nearly frantic; we were in the haunts of these dreaded and terrible scourges, which up to the beginning of August render it impossible to keep stock of any description unprotected where they abound, but which are never formidable after the first frost. In many parts of the wilderness these pests, or else the incredible swarms of mosquitoes, blackflies, and buffalo gnats, render life not worth living during the last weeks of spring and the early months of summer.

There were elk and deer in the neighborhood; also ruffed, blue, and spruce grouse; so that our camp was soon stocked with meat. Early one morning while Willis was washing in the brook, a little black bear thrust its sharp nose through the alders a few feet from him, and then hastily withdrew and was seen no more. The smaller wild-folk were more familiar. As usual in the northern mountains, the gray moose-birds and voluble, nervous little chipmunks made themselves at home in the camp. Parties of chickadees visited us occasionally. A family of flying squirrels lived overhead in the grove; and at nightfall they swept noiselessly from tree to tree, in long graceful curves. There were sparrows of several kinds moping about in the alders; and now and then one of them would sing a few sweet, rather mournful bars.

After several days' preliminary exploration we started on foot for white goat. We took no packs with us, each carrying merely his jacket, with a load of bread and a paper of salt thrust into the pockets. Our aim was to get well to one side of a cluster of high, bare peaks, and then to cross them and come back to camp; we reckoned that the trip would take three days.

All the first day we tramped through dense woods and across and around steep mountain spurs. We caught glimpses of two or three deer and a couple of elk, all does or fawns, however, which we made no effort to molest. Late in the afternoon we stumbled across a family of spruce grouse, which furnished us material for both supper and breakfast. The mountain men call this bird the fool-hen; and most certainly it deserves the name. The members of this particular flock, consisting of a hen and her three-parts grown chickens, acted with a stupidity unwonted even for their kind. They were feeding on the ground among some young spruce, and on our approach flew up and perched in the branches four or five feet above our heads. There they stayed, uttering a low, complaining whistle, and showed not the slightest suspicion when we came underneath them with long sticks and knocked four off their perches—for we did not wish to alarm any large game that might be in the neighborhood by firing. One particular bird was partially saved from my first blow by the intervening twigs; however, it merely flew a few yards, and then sat with its bill open,—having evidently been a little hurt,—until I came up and knocked it over with a better directed stroke.

Spruce grouse are plentiful in the mountain forests of the northern Rockies, and, owing to the ease with which they are killed, they have furnished me my usual provender when off on trips of this kind, where I carried no pack. They are marvellously tame and stupid. The young birds are the only ones I have ever killed in this manner with a stick; but even a full plumaged old cock in September is easily slain with a stone by any one who is at all a good thrower. A man who has played much base-ball need never use a gun when after spruce grouse. They are the smallest of the grouse kind; the cock is very handsome, with red eyebrows and dark, glossy plumage. Moreover, he is as brave as he is stupid and good-looking, and in the love season becomes fairly crazy: at such time he will occasionally make a feint of attacking a man, strutting, fluttering, and ruffling his feathers. The flesh of the spruce grouse is not so good as that of his ruffed and blue kins-folk; and in winter, when he feeds on spruce buds, it is ill tasting. I have never been able to understand why closely allied species, under apparently the same surroundings, should differ so radically in such important traits are wariness and capacity to escape from foes. Yet the spruce grouse in this respect shows the most marked contrast to the blue grouse and the ruffed grouse. Of course all three kinds vary greatly in their behavior accordingly as they do or do not live in localities where they have been free from man's per-secutions. The ruffed grouse, a very wary game bird in all old-settled regions, is often absurdly tame in the wilderness; and under persecution, even the spruce grouse gains some little wisdom; but the latter never becomes as wary as the former, and under no circumstances is it possible to outwit the ruffed grouse by such clumsy means as serve for his simple-minded brother. There is a similar difference between the sage fowl and prairie fowl, in favor of the latter. It is odd that the largest and the small-est kinds of grouse found in the United States should be the tamest; and also the least savory.

After tramping all day through the forest, at nightfall we camped in its upper edge, just at the foot of the steep rock walls of the mountain. We chose a sheltered spot, where the small spruce grew thick, and there was much dead timber; and as the logs, though long, were of little girth, we speedily dragged together a number sufficient to keep the fire blazing all night. Having drunk our full at a brook we cut two forked willow sticks, and then each plucked a grouse, split it, thrust the willow-fork into it, and roasted it before the fire. Besides this we had salt, and bread; moreover we were hungry and healthily tired; so the supper seemed, and was, delicious. Then we turned up the collars of our jackets, and lay down, to pass the night in broken slumber; each time the fire died down the chill waked us, and we rose to feed it with fresh logs.

At dawn we rose, and cooked and ate the two remaining grouse. Then we turned our faces upwards, and passed a day of severe toil in climbing over the crags. Mountaineering is very hard work; and when we got high among the peaks, where snow filled the rifts, the thinness of the air forced me to stop for breath every few hundred yards of the ascent. We found much sign of white goats, but in spite of steady work and incessant careful scanning of the rocks, we did not see our quarry until early in the afternoon.

We had clambered up one side of a steep saddle of naked rock, some of the scarped ledges being difficult, and indeed dangerous, of ascent. From the top of the saddle a careful scrutiny of the neighboring peaks failed to reveal any game, and we began to go down the other side. The mountain fell away in a succession of low cliffs, and we had to move with the utmost caution. In letting ourselves down from ledge to ledge one would hold the guns until the other got safe footing, and then pass them down to him. In many places we had to work our way along the cracks in the faces of the frost-riven rocks. At last, just as we reached a little smooth shoulder, my companion said, pointing down beneath us, "Look at the white goat!"

A moment or two passed before I got my eyes on it. We were looking down into a basin-like valley, surrounded by high mountain chains. At one end of the basin was a low pass, where the ridge was cut up with the zigzag trails made by the countless herds of game which had travelled it for many generations. At the other end was a dark gorge, through which a stream foamed. The floor of the basin was bright emerald green, dotted with darker bands where belts of fir trees grew; and in its middle lay a little lake.

At last I caught sight of the goat, feeding on a terrace rather over a hundred and twenty-five yards below me. I promptly fired, but overshot. The goat merely gave a few jumps and stopped. My second bullet went through its lungs; but fearful lest it might escape to some inaccessible cleft or ledge I fired again, missing; and yet again, breaking its back. Down it went, and the next moment began to roll over and over, from ledge to ledge. I greatly feared it would break its horns; an annoying and oft-recurring incident of white-goat shooting, where the nature of the ground is such that the dead quarry often falls hundreds of feet, its body being torn to ribbons by the sharp crags. However in this case the goat speedily lodged unharmed in a little dwarf evergreen.

Hardly had I fired my fourth shot when my companion again exclaimed, "Look at the white goats! look at the white goats!" Glancing in the direction in which he pointed I speedily made out four more goats standing in a bunch rather less than a hundred yards off, to one side of my former line of fire. They were all looking up at me. They stood on a slab of white rock, with which the color of their fleece harmonized well; and their black horns, muzzles, eyes, and hoofs looked like dark dots on a light-colored surface, so that it took me more than one glance to determine what they were. White goat invariably run up-hill when alarmed, their one idea seeming to be to escape danger by getting above it; for their brute foes are able to overmatch them on anything like level ground, but are helpless against them among the crags. Almost as soon as I saw them these four started up the mountain, nearly in my direction, while I clambered down and across to meet them. They halted at the foot of a cliff, and I at the top, being unable to see them; but in another moment they came bounding and cantering up the sheer rocks, not moving quickly, but traversing the most seemingly impossible places by main strength and sure-footedness. As they broke by me, some thirty yards off, I fired two shots at the rearmost, an old buck, somewhat smaller than the one I had just killed; and he rolled down the mountain dead. Two of the others, a yearling and a kid, showed more alarm than their elders, and ran off at a brisk pace. The remaining one, an old she, went off a hundred yards, and then deliberately stopped and turned round to gaze at us for a couple of minutes! Verily the white goat is the fool-hen among beasts of the chase.

Having skinned and cut off the heads we walked rapidly onwards, slanting down the mountain side, and then over and down the pass of the game trails; for it was growing late and we wished to get well down among the timber before nightfall. On the way an eagle came soaring over head, and I shot at it twice without success. Having once killed an eagle on the wing with a rifle, I always have a lurking hope that sometime I may be able to repeat the feat. I revenged myself for the miss by knocking a large blue goshawk out of the top of a blasted spruce, where it was sitting in lazy confidence, its crop stuffed with rabbit and grouse.

A couple of hours' hard walking brought us down to timber; just before dusk we reached a favorable camping spot in the forest, beside a brook, with plenty of dead trees for the night fire. Moreover, the spot fortunately yielded us our supper too, in the shape of a flock of young spruce grouse, of which we shot off the heads of a couple. Immediately afterwards I ought to have procured our breakfast, for a cock of the same kind suddenly flew down nearby; but it was getting dark, I missed with the first shot, and with the second must have merely creased the neck, for though the tough old bird dropped, it fluttered and ran off among the underbrush and escaped.

We broiled our two grouse before our fire, dragged plenty of logs into a heap beside it, and then lay down to sleep fitfully, an hour or so at a time, throughout the night. We were continually wakened by the cold, when we had to rise and feed the flames. In the early morning we again started, walking for some time along the fresh trail made by a large band of elk, cows and calves. We thought we knew exactly the trend and outlet of the valley in which we were, and that therefore we could tell where the camp was; but, as so often happens in the wilderness, we had not reckoned aright, having passed over one mountain spur too many, and entered the ravines of an entirely different watercourse-system. In consequence, we became entangled in a network of hills and valleys, making circle after circle to find our bearings; and we only reached camp after twelve hours' tiresome tramp without food.

On another occasion I shot a white goat while it was in a very curious and characteristic attitude. I was hunting, again with an old mountain man as my sole companion, among the high mountains of the Kootenai country, near the border of Montana and British Columbia. We had left our main camp, pitched by the brink of the river, and were struggling wearily on foot through the tangled forest and over the precipitous mountains, carrying on our backs light packs, consisting of a little food and two or three indispensable utensils, wrapped in our blankets. One day we came to the foot of a great chain of bare rocks, and climbed laboriously to its crest, up cliff after cliff, some of which were almost perpendicular. Swarming round certain of the rock shoulders, crossing an occasional sheer chasm, and in many places clinging to steep, smooth walls by but slight holds, we reached the top. The climbing at such a height was excessively fatiguing; moreover, it was in places difficult and even dangerous. Of course it was not to be compared to the ascent of towering, glacier-bearing peaks, such as those of the Selkirks and Alaska, where climbers must be roped to one another and carry ice axes.

Once at the top we walked very cautiously, being careful not to show ourselves against the sky-line, and scanning the mountain sides through our glasses. At last we made out three goats, grazing unconcernedly on a narrow grassy terrace, which sloped abruptly to the brink of a high precipice. They were not very far off, and there was a little rock spur above them which offered good cover for a stalk; but we had to crawl so slowly, partly to avoid falling, and partly to avoid detaching loose rocks, that it was nearly an hour before we got in a favorable position above them, and some seventy yards off. The frost-disintegrated mountains in which they live are always sending down showers of detached stones, so that the goats are not very sensitive to this noise; still, they sometimes pay instantaneous heed to it, especially if the sound is repeated.

When I peeped over the little ridge of rock, shoving my rifle carefully ahead of me, I found that the goats had finished feeding and were preparing to leave the slope. The old billy saw me at once, but evidently could not quite make me out. Thereupon, gazing intently at me, he rose gravely on his haunches, sitting up almost in the attitude of a dog when begging. I know no other horned animal that ever takes this position.

As I fired he rolled backwards, slipped down the grassy slope, and tumbled over the brink of the cliff, while the other two, a she and a kid, after a moment's panic-struck pause, and a bewildered rush in the wrong direction, made off up a little rocky gully, and were out of sight in a moment. To my chagrin when I finally reached the carcass, after a tedious and circuitous climb to the foot of the cliff, I found both horns broken off.

It was late in the afternoon, and we clambered down to the border of a little marshy alpine lake, which we reached in an hour or so. Here we made our camp about sunset, in a grove of stunted spruces, which furnished plenty of dead timber for the fire. There were many white-goat trails leading to this lake, and from the slide rock roundabout we heard the shrill whistling of hoary rock-woodchucks, and the querulous note of the little conies—two of the sounds most familiar to the white-goat hunter. These conies had gathered heaps of dried plants, and had stowed them carefully away for winter use in the cracks between the rocks.

While descending the mountain we came on a little pack of snow grouse or mountain ptarmigan, birds which, save in winter, are always found above timber line. They were tame and fearless, though hard to make out as they ran among the rocks, cackling noisily, with their tails cocked aloft; and we had no difficulty in killing four, which gave us a good breakfast and supper. Old white goats are intolerably musky in flavor, there being a very large musk-pod between the horn and ear. The kids are eatable, but of course are rarely killed; the shot being usually taken at the animal with best horns—and the shes and young of any game should only be killed when there is a real necessity.

These two hunts may be taken as samples of most expeditions after white goat. There are places where the goats live in mountains close to bodies of water, either ocean fiords or large lakes, and in such places canoes can be used, to the greatly increased comfort and lessened labor of the hunters. In other places, where the mountains are low and the goats spend all the year in the timber, a pack-train can be taken right up to the hunting grounds. But generally one must go on foot, carrying everything on one's back, and at night lying out in the open or under a brush lean-to; meanwhile living on spruce grouse and ptarmigan, with an occasional meal of trout, and in times of scarcity squirrels, or anything else. Such a trip entails severe fatigue and not a little hardship. The actual hunting, also, implies difficult and laborious climbing, for the goats live by choice among the highest and most inaccessible mountains; though where they are found, as they sometimes are, in comparatively low forest-clad ranges, I have occasionally killed them with little trouble by lying in wait beside the well-trodden game trails they make in the timber.

In any event the hard work is to get up to the grounds where the game is found. Once the animals are spied there is but little call for the craft of the still-hunter in approaching them. Of all American game the white goat is the least wary and most stupid. In places where it is much hunted it of course gradually grows wilder and becomes difficult to approach and kill; and much of its silly tameness is doubtless due to the inaccessible nature of its haunts, which renders it ordinarily free from molestation; but aside from this it certainly seems as if it was naturally less wary than either deer or mountain sheep. The great point is to get above it. All its foes live in the valleys, and while it is in the mountains, if they strive to approach it at all, they must do so from below. It is in consequence always on the watch for danger from beneath; but it is easily approached from above, and then, as it generally tries to escape by running up hill, the hunter is very apt to get a shot.

Its chase is thus laborious rather than exciting; and to my mind it is less attractive than is the pursuit of most of our other game. Yet it has an attraction of its own after all; while the grandeur of the scenery amid which it must be carried, the freedom and hardihood of the life and the pleasure of watching the queer habits of the game, all combine to add to the hunter's enjoyment.

White goats are self-confident, pugnacious beings. An old billy, if he discovers the presence of a foe without being quite sure what it is, often refuses to take flight, but walks around, stamping, and shaking his head. The needle-pointed black horns are alike in both sexes, save that the males' are a trifle thicker; and they are most effective weapons when wielded by the muscular neck of a resolute and wicked old goat. They wound like stilettos and their bearer is in consequence a much more formidable foe in a hand-to-hand struggle than either a branching-antlered deer or a mountain ram, with his great battering head. The goat does not butt; he thrusts. If he can cover his back by a tree trunk or boulder he can stand off most carnivorous animals, no larger than he is.

Though awkward in movement, and lacking all semblance of lightness or agility, goats are excellent climbers. One of their queer traits is their way of getting their fore-hoofs on a slight ledge, and then drawing or lifting their bodies up by simple muscular exertion, stretching out their elbows, much as a man would. They do a good deal of their climbing by strength and command over their muscles; although they are also capable of making astonishing bounds. If a cliff surface has the least slope, and shows any inequalities or roughness whatever, goats can go up and down it with ease. With their short, stout legs, and large, sharp-edged hoofs they clamber well over ice, passing and repassing the mountains at a time when no man would so much as crawl over them. They bear extreme cold with indifference, but are intolerant of much heat; even when the weather is cool they are apt to take their noontide rest in caves; I have seen them solemnly retiring for this purpose, to great rents in the rocks, at a time when my own teeth chattered because of the icy wind.

They go in small flocks; sometimes in pairs or little family parties. After the rut the bucks often herd by themselves, or go off alone, while the young and the shes keep together throughout the winter and the spring. The young are generally brought forth above timber line, or at its uppermost edge, save of course in those places where the goats live among mountains wooded to the top. Throughout the summer they graze on the short mountain plants which in many places form regular mats above timber line; the deep winter snows drive them low down in the wooded valleys and force them to subsist by browsing. They are so strong that they plough their way readily through deep drifts; and a flock of goats at this season, when their white coat is very long and thick, if seen waddling off through the snow, have a comical likeness to so many diminutive polar bears. Of course they could easily be run down in the snow by a man on snowshoes, in the plain; but on a mountain side there are always bare rocks and cliff shoulders, glassy with winter ice, which give either goats or sheep an advantage over their snowshoe-bearing foes that deer and elk lack. Whenever the goats pass the winter in woodland they leave plenty of sign in the shape of patches of wool clinging to all the sharp twigs and branches against which they have brushed. In the spring they often form the habit of drinking at certain low pools, to which they beat deep paths; and at this season, and to a less extent in the summer and fall, they are very fond of frequenting mineral licks. At any such lick the ground is tramped bare of vegetation, and is filled with pits and hollows, actually dug by the tongues of innumerable generations of animals; while the game paths lead from them in a dozen directions.

In spite of the white goat's pugnacity, its clumsiness renders it no very difficult prey when taken unawares by either wolf or cougar, its two chief enemies. They cannot often catch it when it is above timber line; but it is always in sore peril from them when it ventures into the forest. Bears, also, prey upon it in the early spring; and one mid-winter my friend Willis found a wolverine eating a goat which it had killed in a snowdrift at the foot of a cliff. The savage little beast growled and showed fight when he came near the body. Eagles are great enemies of the young kids, as they are of the young lambs of the bighorn.

The white goat is the only game beast of America which has not decreased in numbers since the arrival of the white man. Although in certain localities it is now decreasing, yet, taken as a whole, it is probably quite as plentiful now as it was fifty years back; for in the early part of the present century there were Indian tribes who hunted it perseveringly to make the skins into robes, whereas now they get blankets from the traders and no longer persecute the goats. The early trappers and mountain-men knew but little of the animal. Whether they were after beaver, or were hunting big game, or were merely exploring, they kept to the valleys; there was no inducement for them to climb to the tops of the mountains; so it resulted that there was no animal with which the old hunters were so unfamiliar as with the white goat. The professional hunters of to-day likewise bother it but little; they do not care to undergo severe toil for an animal with worthless flesh and a hide of little value—for it is only in the late fall and winter that the long hair and fine wool give the robe any beauty.

So the quaint, sturdy, musky beasts, with their queer and awkward ways, their boldness and their stupidity, with their white coats and big black hoofs, black muzzles, and sharp, gently-curved span-long black horns, have held their own well among the high mountains that they love. In the Rockies and the Coast ranges they abound from Alaska south to Montana, Idaho, and Washington; and here and there isolated colonies are found among the high mountains to the southward, in Wyoming, Colorado, even in New Mexico, and, strangest of all, in one or two spots among the barren coast mountains of southern California. Long after the elk has followed the buffalo to the happy hunting grounds the white goat will flourish among the towering and glacier-riven peaks, and, grown wary with succeeding generations, will furnish splendid sport to those hunters who are both good riflemen and hardy cragsmen.

The Moose; The Beast of the Woodland

(From *The Wilderness Hunter*)

The moose is the giant of all deer; and many hunters esteem it the noblest of American game. Beyond question there are few trophies more prized than the huge shovel horns of this strange dweller in the cold northland forests.

I shot my first moose after making several fruitless hunting trips with this special game in view. The season I finally succeeded it was only after having hunted two or three weeks in vain, among the Bitter Root Mountains, and the ranges lying southeast of them.

I began about the first of September by making a trail with my old hunting friend Willis. We speedily found a country where there were moose, but of the animals themselves we never caught a glimpse. We tried to kill them by hunting in the same manner that we hunted elk; that is, by choosing a place where there was sign, and going carefully through it against or across the wind. However, this plan failed; though at that very time we succeeded in killing

227

elk in this way, devoting one or two days to their pursuit. There were both elk and moose in the country, but they were usually found in different kinds of ground, though often close alongside one another. The former went in herds, the cows, calves, and yearlings by themselves, and they roamed through the higher and more open forests, well up towards timber line. The moose, on the contrary, were found singly or in small parties composed at the outside of a bull, a cow, and her young of two years; for the moose is practically monogamous, in strong contrast to the highly polygamous wapiti and caribou.

The moose did not seem to care much whether they lived among the summits of the mountains or not, so long as they got the right kind of country; for they were much more local in their distribution, and at this season less given to wandering than their kin with round horns. What they wished was a cool, swampy region of very dense growth; in the main chains of the northern Rockies even the valleys are high enough to be cold. Of course many of the moose lived on the wooded summits of the lower ranges; and most of them came down lower in winter than in summer, following about a fortnight after the elk; but if in a large tract of woods the cover was dense and the ground marshy, though it was in a valley no higher than the herds of the ranchmen grazed, or perchance even in the immediate neighborhood of a small frontier hamlet, then it might be chosen by some old bull who wished to lie in seclusion till his horns were grown, or by some cow with a calf to raise. Before settlers came to this high mountain region of western Montana, a moose would often thus live in an isolated marshy tract surrounded by open country. They grazed throughout the summer on marsh plants, notably lily stems, and nibbled at the tops of the very tall natural hay of the meadows. The legs of the beast are too long and the neck too short to allow it to graze habitually on the short grass; yet in the early spring when greedy for the tender blades of young, green marsh grass, the moose will often shuffle down on its knees to get at them, and it will occasionally perform the same feat to get a mouthful or two of snow in winter.

The moose which lived in isolated, exposed localities were speedily killed or driven away after the incoming of settlers; and at the time that we hunted we found no sign of them until we reached the region of continuous forest. Here, in a fortnight's hunting, we found as much sign as we wished, and plenty of it fresh; but the animals themselves we not only never saw but we never so much as heard. Often after hours of careful still-hunting or cautious tracking, we found the footprints deep in the soft earth, showing where our quarry had winded or heard us, and had noiselessly slipped away from the danger. It is astonishing how quietly a moose can steal through the woods if it wishes: and it has what is to the hunter a very provoking habit of making a half or three quarters circle before lying down, and then crouching with its head so turned that it can surely perceive any pursuer who may follow its trail. We tried every method to outwit the beasts. We attempted to track them; we beat through likely spots; sometimes we merely "sat on a log" and awaited events, by a drinking hole, meadow, mud wallow or other such place (a course of procedure which often works well in still-hunting); but all in vain.

Our main difficulty lay in the character of the woods which the moose haunted. They were choked and tangled to the last degree, consisting of a mass of thick-growing conifers, with dead timber strewn in every direction, and young growth filling the spaces between the trunks. We could not see twenty yards ahead of us, and it was almost impossible to walk without making a noise. Elk were occasionally found in these same places; but usually they frequented more open timber, where the hunting was beyond comparison easier. Perhaps more experienced hunters would have killed their game; though in such cover the best tracker and still-hunter alive cannot always reckon on success with really wary animals. But, be this as it may, we, at any rate, were completely baffled, and I began to think that this moose-hunt, like all my former ones, was doomed to end in failure.

However, a few days later I met a crabbed old trapper named Hank Griffin, who was going after beaver in the mountains, and who told me that if I would come with him he would show me moose. I jumped at the chance, and he proved as good as his word; though for the first two trials my ill luck did not change.

At the time that it finally did change we had at last reached a place where the moose were on favorable ground. A high, marshy valley stretched for several miles between two rows of stony mountains, clad with a forest of rather small fir-trees. This valley was covered with reeds, alders, and rank grass, and studded with little willow-bordered ponds and island-like clumps of spruce and graceful tamaracks.

Having surveyed the ground and found moose sign the preceding afternoon, we were up betimes in the cool morning to begin our hunt. Before sunrise we were posted on a rocky spur of the foot-hills, behind a mask of evergreens; ourselves unseen we overlooked all the valley, and we knew we could see any animal which might be either feeding away from cover or on its journey homeward from its feeding ground to its day-bed.

As it grew lighter we scanned the valley with increasing care and eagerness. The sun rose behind us; and almost as soon as it was up we made out some large beast moving among the dwarf willows beside a little lake half a mile in our front. In a few minutes the thing walked out where the bushes were thinner, and we saw that it was a young bull moose browsing on the willow tops. He had evidently nearly finished his breakfast, and he stood idly for some moments, now and then lazily cropping a mouthful of twig tips. Then he walked off with great strides in a straight line across the marsh, splashing among the wet water-plants, and ploughing through boggy spaces with the indifference begotten of vast strength and legs longer than those of any other animals on this continent. At times he entered beds of reeds which hid him from view, though their surging and bending showed the wake of his passage; at other times he walked through meadows of tall grass, the withered yellow stalks rising to his flanks, while his body loomed above them, glistening black and wet in the level sunbeams. Once he stopped for a few moments on a rise of dry ground, seemingly to enjoy the heat of the young sun; he stood motionless, save that his ears were continually pricked, and his head sometimes slightly turned, showing that even in this remote land he was on the alert. Once, with a somewhat awkward motion, he reached his hind leg forward to scratch his neck. Then he walked forward again into the marsh; where the water was quite deep he broke into the long, stretching, springy trot, which forms the characteristic gait of his kind, churning the marsh water into foam. He held his head straight forwards, the antlers resting on his shoulders.

After a while he reached a spruce island, through which he walked to and fro; but evidently could find therein no resting place quite to his mind, for he soon left and went on to another. Here after a little wandering he chose a point where there was some thick young growth, which hid him from view when he lay down, though not when he stood. After some turning he settled himself in his bed just as a steer would.

He could not have chosen a spot better suited for us. He was nearly at the edge of the morass, the open space between the spruce clump where he was lying and the rocky foot-hills being comparatively dry and not much over couple of hundred yards broad; while some sixty yards from it, and between it and the hills, was a little hummock, tufted with firs, so as to afford us just the cover we needed. Keeping back from the edge of the morass we were able to walk upright through the forest, until we got to the point where he was lying in a line with this little hummock. We then dropped on our hands and knees, and crept over the soft, wet sward, where there was nothing to make a noise. Wherever the ground rose at all we crawled flat on our bellies. The air was still, for it was a very calm morning.

At last we reached the hummock, and I got into position for a shot, taking a final look at my faithful 45–90 Winchester to see that all was in order. Peering cautiously through the shielding evergreens, I at first could not make out where the moose was lying, until my eye was caught by the motion of his big ears, as he occasionally flapped them lazily forward. Even then I could not see his outline; but I knew where he was, and having pushed my rifle forward on the moss, I snapped a dry twig to make him rise. My veins where thrilling and my heart beating with that eager, fierce excitement, known only to the hunter of big game, and forming one of the keenest and strongest of the many pleasures which with him go to make up "the wild joy of living."

As the sound of the snapping twig smote his ears the moose rose nimbly to his feet, with a lightness on which one would not have reckoned in a beast so heavy of body. He stood broadside to me for a moment, his ungainly head slightly turned, while his ears twitched and his nostrils snuffed the air. Drawing a fine bead against his black hide, behind his shoulder and two thirds of his body's depth below his shaggy withers, I pressed the trigger. He neither flinched nor reeled, but started with his regular ground-covering trot through the spruces; yet I knew he was mine, for the light blood sprang from both of his nostrils, and he fell dying on his side before he had gone thirty rods.

Later in the fall I was again hunting among the lofty ranges which continue towards the southeast the chain of the Bitter Root, between Idaho and Montana. There were but two of us, and we were travelling very light, each having but one pack-pony and the saddle animal he bestrode. We were high among the mountains, and followed no regular trail. Hence our course was often one of extreme difficulty. Occasionally we took our animals through the forest near timber line, where the slopes were not too steep; again we threaded our way through a line of glades, or skirted the foothills, in an open, park country; and now and then we had to cross stretches of tangled mountain forest, making but a few miles a day, at the cost of incredible toil, and accomplishing even this solely by virtue of the wonderful docility and sure-footedness of the ponies, and of my companion's skill with the axe and thorough knowledge of woodcraft.

Late one cold afternoon we came out in a high alpine valley in which there was no sign of any man's having ever been before us. Down its middle ran a clear brook. On each side was a belt of thick spruce forest, covering the lower flanks of the mountains. The trees came down in points and isolated clumps to the brook, the banks of which were thus bordered with open glades, rendering the travelling easy and rapid.

Soon after starting up this valley we entered a beaver meadow of considerable size. It was covered with lush, rank grass, and the stream wound through it rather sluggishly in long curves, which were fringed by a thick growth of dwarfed willows. In one or two places it broadened into small ponds, bearing a few lily-pads. This meadow had been all tramped up by moose. Trails led hither and thither through the grass, the willow twigs were cropped off, and the muddy banks of the little black ponds were indented by hoof-marks. Evidently most of the lilies had been plucked. The foot-prints were unmistakable; a moose's foot is longer and slimmer than a caribou's, while on the other hand it is much larger than an elk's, and a longer oval in shape.

Most of the sign was old, this high alpine meadow, surrounded by snow mountains, having clearly been a favorite resort for moose in the summer; but some enormous, fresh tracks told that one or more old bulls were still frequenting the place.

The light was already fading, and, of course, we did not wish to camp where we were, because we would then certainly scare the moose. Accordingly we pushed up the valley for another mile, through an open forest, the ground being quite free from under-brush and dead timber, and covered with a carpet of thick moss, in which the feet sank noiselessly. Then we came to another beaver-meadow, which offered fine feed for the ponies. On its edge we hastily pitched camp, just at dusk. We tossed down the packs in a dry grove, close to the brook, and turned the tired ponies loose in the meadow, hobbling the little mare that carried the bell. The ground was smooth. We threw a cross-pole from one to the other of two young spruces, which happened to stand handily, and from it stretched and pegged out a piece of canvas, which we were using as a shelter tent. Beneath this we spread our bedding, laying under it the canvas sheets in which it has been wrapped. There was still bread left over from yesterday's baking, and in a few moments the kettle was boiling and the frying-pan sizzling, while one of us skinned and cut into suitable pieces two grouse we had knocked over on our march. For fear of frightening the moose we built but a small fire, and went to bed soon after supper, being both tired and cold. Fortunately, what little breeze there was blew up the valley.

At dawn I was awake, and crawled out of my buffalo bag, shivering and yawning. My companion still slumbered heavily. White frost covered whatever had been left outside. The cold was sharp, and I hurriedly slipped a pair of stout moccasins on my feet, drew on my gloves and cap, and started through the ghostly woods for the meadow where we had seen the moose sign. The tufts of grass were stiff with frost, black ice skimmed the edges and quiet places of the little brook.

I walked slowly, it being difficult not to make a noise by cracking sticks or brushing against trees, in the gloom; but the forest was so open that it favored me. When I reached the edge of the beaver-meadow, where the brook broadened into small willow-bordered pools, I knew at once that a moose was in one of these pools, wading about and pulling up the water-lilies by seizing their slippery stems in his lips, plunging his head deep under water to do so. The moose love to feed in this way in the hot months, when they spend all the time they can in the water, feeding or lying down; nor do they altogether abandon the habit even when the weather is so cold that icicles form in their shaggy coats.

Crouching, I stole noiselessly along the edge of the willow thicket. The stream twisted through it from side to side in zigzags, so that every few rods I got a glimpse down a lane of black water. In a minute I heard a slight splashing near me; and on passing the next point of bushes, I saw the shadowy outline of the moose's hindquarters, standing in a bend of the water. In a moment he walked onwards, disappearing. I ran forward a couple of rods, and then turned in among the willows, to reach the brook where it again bent back towards me. The splashing in the water, and the rustling of the moose's body against the frozen twigs, drowned the little noise made by my moccasined feet.

I strode out on the bank at the lower end of a long narrow pool of water, dark and half frozen. In this pool, half way down and facing me, but a score of yards off, stood the mighty marsh beast, strange and uncouth in look as some monster surviving over from the Pliocene. His vast bulk loomed black and vague in the dim gray dawn; his huge antlers stood out sharply; columns of steam rose from his nostrils. For several seconds he fronted me motionless; then he began to turn, slowly, and as if he had a stiff neck. When quarter way round I fired into his shoulder; whereat he reared and bounded on the bank with a great leap, vanishing in the willows. Through these I heard him crash like a whirlwind for a dozen rods; then down he fell, and when I reached the spot he had ceased to struggle. The ball had gone through his heart.

When a moose is thus surprised at close quarters, it will often stand at gaze for a moment or two, and then turn stiffly around until headed in the right direction; once thus headed aright it starts off with extraordinary speed.

The flesh of the moose is very good; though some deem it coarse. Old hunters, who always like rich, greasy food, rank a moose's nose with a beaver's tail, as the chief of backwood delicacies; personally I never liked either. The hide of the moose, like the hide of the elk, is of very poor quality, much inferior to ordinary buckskin; caribou hide is the best of all, especially when used as webbing for snow-shoes.

The moose is very fond of frequenting swampy woods throughout the summer, and indeed late into the fall. These swampy woods are not necessarily in the lower valleys, some being found very high among the mountains. By preference it haunts those containing lakes, where it can find the long lily-roots of which it is so fond, and where it can escape the torment of the mosquitoes and deer-flies by lying completely submerged save for its nostrils. It is a bold and good swimmer, readily crossing lakes of large size; but it is of course easily slain if discovered by canoe-men while in the water. It travels well through bogs, but not as well as the caribou; and it will not venture on ice at all if it can possibly avoid it.

After the rut begins the animals roam everywhere through the woods; and where there are hardwood forests the winter-yard is usually made among them, on high ground, away from the swamps. In the mountains the deep snows drive the moose, like all other game, down to the lower valleys, in hard winters. In the summer it occasionally climbs to the very summits of the wooded ranges, to escape the flies; and it is said that in certain places where wolves are plenty the cows retire to the tops of the mountains to calve. More often, however, they select some patch of very dense cover, in a swamp or by a lake, for this purpose. Their ways of life of course vary with the nature of the country they frequent. In the towering chains of the Rockies, clad in sombre and unbroken evergreen forests, their habits, in regard to winter- and summer-homes, and choice of places of seclusion for cows with young calves and bulls growing their antlers, differ from those of their kind which haunt the comparatively low, hilly, lake-studded country of Maine and Nova Scotia, where the forests are of birch, beech, and maple, mixed with the pine, spruce, and hemlock.

The moose being usually monogamous is never found in great herds like the wapiti and caribou. Occasionally a troop of fifteen or twenty individuals may be seen, but this is rare; more often it is found singly, in pairs, or in family parties, composed of a bull, a cow, and two or more calves and yearlings. In yarding, two or more such families may unite to spend the winter together in an unusually attractive locality; and during the rut many bulls are sometimes found together, perhaps following the trail of a cow in single file.

In the fall, winter, and early spring, and in certain places during summer, the moose feeds principally by browsing, though always willing to vary its diet by mosses, lichens, fungi, and ferns. In the eastern forests, with their abundance of hardwood, the birch, maple, and moose-wood form its favorite food. In the Rocky Mountains, where the forests are almost purely evergreen, it feeds on such willows, alders, and aspens as it can find, and also, when pressed by necessity, on balsam, fir, spruce, and very young pine. It peels the bark between its hard palate and sharp lower teeth, to a height of seven or eight feet; these "peelings" form conspicuous moose signs. It crops the juicy, budding twigs and stem tops to the same height; and if the tree is too tall it "rides" it, that is, straddles the slender trunk with its fore legs, pushing it over and walking up it until the desired branches are within reach. No beast is more destructive to the young growth of a forest than the moose. Where much persecuted it feeds in the late evening, early morning, and by moonlight. Where rarely disturbed it passes the day much as cattle do, alternately resting and feeding for two or three hours at a time.

Young moose, when caught, are easily tamed, and are very playful, delighting to gallop to and fro, kicking, striking, butting, and occasionally making grotesque faces. As they grow old they are apt to become dangerous, and even their play takes the form of a mock fight. Some lumbermen I knew on the Aroostook, in Maine, once captured a young moose and put it in a pen of logs. A few days later they captured another, somewhat smaller, and put it in the same pen, thinking the first would be grateful at having a companion. But if it was it dissembled its feelings, for it promptly fell on the unfortunate new-comer and killed it before it could be rescued.

During the rut the bulls seek the cows far and wide, uttering continually throughout the night a short, loud roar, which can be heard at a distance of four or five miles; the cows now and then respond with low, plaintive bellows. The bulls also thrash the tree trunks with their horns, and paw big holes in soft ground; and when two rivals come together at this season they fight with the most desperate fury. It is chiefly in these battles with one another that the huge antlers are used; in contending with other foes they strike terrible blows with their fore hoofs and also sometimes lash out behind like a horse. The bear occasionally makes a prey of the moose; the cougar is a more dangerous enemy in the few districts where both animals are found at all plentifully; but next to man its most dreaded foe is the big timber wolf, that veritable scourge of all animals of the deer kind. Against all of these the moose defends itself valiantly; a cow with a calf and a rutting bull being especially dangerous opponents. In deep snows through which the great deer flounders while its adversary runs lightly on the crust, a single wolf may overcome and slaughter a big bull moose; but with a fair chance no one or two wolves would be a match for it. Desperate combats take place before a small pack of wolves can master the shovel-horned quarry, unless it is taken at a hopeless disadvantage; and in these battles the prowess of the moose is shown by the fact that it is no unusual thing for it to kill one or more of the ravenous throng; generally by a terrific blow of the foreleg, smashing a wolf's skull or breaking its back. I have known of several instances of wolves being found dead, having perished in this manner. Still the battle usually ends the other way, the wolves being careful to make the attack with the odds in their favor; and even a small pack of the ferocious brutes will in a single winter often drive the moose completely out of a given district. Both cougar and bear generally reckon on taking the moose unawares, when they jump on it. In one case that came to my knowledge a black bear was killed by a cow moose whose calf he had attacked.

In the northeast a favorite method of hunting the moose is by "calling" the bulls in the rutting season, at dawn or nightfall; the caller imitating their cries through a birch-bark trumpet. If the animals are at all wary, this kind of sport can only be carried on in still weather, as the approaching bull always tries to get the wind of the caller. It is also sometimes slain by fire-hunting, from a canoe, as the deer are killed in the Adirondacks. This, however, is but an ignoble sport; and to kill the animal while it is swimming in a lake is worse. However, there is sometimes a spice of excitement even in these unworthy methods of the chase; for a truculent moose will do its best, with hoofs and horns, to upset the boat.

The true way to kill the noble beast, however, is by fair still-hunting. There is no grander sport than still-hunting the moose, whether in the vast pine and birch forests of the northeast, or among the stupendous mountain masses of the Rockies. The moose has wonderfully keen nose and ears, though its eyesight is not remarkable. Most hunters assert that he is the wariest of all game, and the most difficult to kill. I have never been quite satisfied that this was so; it seems to me that the nature of the ground wherein it dwells helps it even more than do its own sharp senses. It is true that I made many trips in vain before killing my first moose; but then I had to hunt through tangled timber, where I could hardly move a step without noise, and could never see thirty yards ahead. If moose were found in open park-like forests like those where I first killed elk, on the Bighorn Mountains, or among brushy coulies and bare hills, like the Little Missouri Bad Lands, where I first killed blacktail deer, I doubt whether they would prove especially difficult animals to bag. My own experience is much too limited to allow me to speak with any certainty on the point; but it is borne out by what more skilled hunters have told me. In the Big Hole Basin, in southwest Montana, moose were quite plentiful in the late 'seventies. Two or three of the old set-tlers, whom I know as veteran hunters and trustworthy men, have told me that in those times the moose were often found in very ac-cessible localities; and that when such was the case they were quite as easily killed as elk. In fact, when run across by accident they fre-quently showed a certain clumsy slowness of apprehension which amounted to downright stupidity. One of the most successful moose-hunters I know is Col. Cecil Clay, of the Department of Law, in Washington; he it was who killed the moose composing the fine group mounted by Mr. Hornaday, in the National Museum. Col. Clay lost his right arm in the Civil War; but is an expert rifle-shot nevertheless, using a short, light forty-four calibre old style Winchester carbine. With this weapon he has killed over a score of moose, by fair still-hunting; and he tells me that on similar ground he considers it if anything rather less easy to still-hunt and kill a whitetail deer than it is to kill a moose.

My friend Col. James Jones killed two moose in a day in north-western Wyoming, not far from the Tetons; he was alone when he shot them and did not find them especially wary. Ordinarily, moose are shot at fairly close range; but another friend of mine, Mr. E. P. Rogers, once dropped one with a single bullet, at a distance of nearly three hundred yards. This happened by Bridger's Lake, near Two-Ocean Pass.

The moose has a fast walk, and its ordinary gait when going at any speed is a slashing trot. Its long legs give it a wonderful stride, enabling it to clear down-timber and high obstacles of all sorts without altering its pace. It also leaps well. If much pressed or startled it breaks into an awkward gallop, which is quite fast for a few hundred yards, but which speedily tires it out. After being disturbed by the hunter a moose usually trots a long distance be-fore halting.

One thing which renders the chase of the moose particularly interesting is the fact that there is in it on rare occasions a spice of peril. Under certain circumstances it may be called dangerous quarry, being, properly speaking, the only animal of the deer kind which ever fairly deserves the title. In a hand to hand grapple an elk or caribou, or even under exceptional circumstances a blacktail or a whitetail, may show itself an ugly antagonist; and indeed a maddened elk may for a moment take the offensive; but the moose is the only one of the tribe with which this attitude is at all common. In bodily strength and capacity to do harm it surpasses the elk; and in temper it is far more savage and more apt to show fight when assailed by man; exactly as the elk in these respects surpasses the common deer. Two hunters with whom I was well acquainted once wintered between the Wind River Mountains and the Three Tetons, many years ago, in the days of the buffalo. They lived on game, killing it on snowshoes; for the most part wapiti and deer, but also bison, and one moose, though they saw others. The wapiti bulls kept their antlers two months longer than the moose; nevertheless, when chased they rarely made an effort to use them, while the hornless moose displayed far more pugnacity, and also ran better through the deep snow. The winter was very severe, the snows were heavy and the crusts hard; so that the hunters had little trouble in overtaking their game, although—being old mountain-men, and not hide-hunters—they killed only what was needed. Of course in such hunting they came very close to the harried game, usually after a chase of from twenty minutes to three hours. They found that the ordinary deer would scarcely charge under any circumstances; that among the wapiti it was only now and then that individuals would turn upon their pursuers—though they sometimes charged boldly; but that both the bison and especially the moose when worried and approached too near, would often turn to bay and make charge after charge in the most resolute manner, so that they had to be approached with some caution.

Under ordinary conditions, however, there is very little danger, indeed, of a moose charging. A charge does not take place once in a hundred times when the moose is killed by fair still-hunting; and it is altogether exceptional for those who assail them from boats or canoes to be put in jeopardy. Even a cow moose, with her calf, will run if she has the chance; and a rutting bull will do the same. Such a bull when wounded may walk slowly forward, grunting savagely, stamping with his forefeet, and slashing the bushes with his antlers; but, if his antagonist is any distance off, he rarely actually runs at him. Yet there are now and then found moose prone to attack on slight provocation; for these great deer differ as widely as men in courage and ferocity. Occasionally a hunter is charged in the fall when he has lured the game to him by calling, or when he has wounded it after a stalk. In one well-authenticated instance which was brought to my attention, a settler on the left bank of the St. Johns, in New Brunswick, was trampled to death by a moose which he had called to him and wounded. A New Yorker of my acquaintance, Dr. Merrill, was charged under rather peculiar circumstances. He stalked and mortally wounded a bull which promptly ran towards him. Between them was a gully in which it disappeared. Immediately afterwards, as he thought, it reappeared on his side of the gully, and with a second shot he dropped it. Walking forward he found to his astonishment that with his second bullet he had killed a cow moose; the bull lay dying in the gully, out of which he had scared the cow by his last rush.

However, speaking broadly, the danger to the still-hunter engaged in one of the legitimate methods of the chase is so small that it may be disregarded; for he usually kills his game at some little distance, while the moose, as a rule, only attacks if it has been greatly worried and angered, and if its pursuer is close at hand. When a moose is surprised and shot at by a hunter some way off, its one thought is of flight. Hence, the hunters who are charged by moose are generally those who follow them during the late winter and early spring, when the animals have yarded and can be killed on snow-shoes—by "crusting," as it is termed, a very destructive, and often a very unsportsmanlike species of chase.

If the snow-fall is very light, moose do not yard at all; but in a hard winter they begin to make their yards in December. A "yard" is not, as some people seem to suppose, a trampled-down space, with definite boundaries; the term merely denotes the spot which a moose has chosen for its winter home, choosing it because it contains plenty of browse in the shape of young trees and saplings, and perhaps also because it is sheltered to some extent from the fiercest winds and heaviest snowdrifts. The animal travels to and fro across this space in straight lines and irregular circles after food, treading in its own footsteps, where practicable. As the snow steadily deepens, these lines of travel become beaten paths. There results finally a space half a mile square—sometimes more, sometimes very much less, according to the lay of the land, and the number of moose yarding together—where the deep snow is seamed in every direction by a network of narrow paths along which a moose can travel at speed, its back level with the snow round about. Sometimes, when moose are very plenty many of these yards lie so close together that the beasts can readily make their way from one to another. When such is the case, the most expert snow-shoer, under the most favorable conditions, cannot overtake them, for they can then travel very fast through the paths, keeping their gait all day. In the early decades of the present century, the first settlers in Aroostook County, Maine, while moose-hunting in winter, were frequently baffled in this manner.

When hunters approach an isolated yard the moose immediately leave it and run off through the snow. If there is no crust, and if their long legs can reach the ground, the snow itself impedes them but little, because of their vast strength and endurance. Snowdrifts which render an ordinary deer absolutely helpless, and bring even an elk to a standstill, offer no impediment whatever to a moose. If, as happens very rarely, the loose snow is of such depth that even the silt-like legs of the moose cannot touch solid earth, it flounders and struggles forward for a little time, and then sinks exhausted; for a caribou is the only large animal which can travel under such conditions. If there be a crust, even though the snow is not remarkably deep, the labor of the moose is vastly increased, as it breaks through it at every step, cutting its legs and exhausting itself. A caribou, on the other hand, will go across a crust as well as a man on snow-shoes, and can never be caught by the latter, save under altogether exceptional conditions of snow fall and thaw.

"Crusting," or following game on snow-shoes, is, as the name implies, almost always practised after the middle of February, when thaws begin, and the snow crusts on top. The conditions for success in crusting moose and deer are very different. A crust through which a moose would break at every stride may carry a running deer without mishap; while the former animal would trot at ease through drifts in which the latter would be caught as if in a quicksand.

Hunting moose on snow, therefore, may be, and very often is, mere butchery; and because of this possibility or probability, and also because of the fact that it is by far the most destructive kind of hunting, and is carried on at a season when the bulls are hornless and the cows heavy with calf, it is rigidly and properly forbidden wherever there are good game-laws. Yet this kind of hunting may also be carried on under circumstances which render it if not a legitimate, yet a most exciting and manly sport, only to be followed by men of tried courage, hardihood, and skill. This is not because it ever necessitates any skill whatever in the use of the rifle, or any particular knowledge of hunting-craft; but because under the conditions spoken of the hunter must show great endurance and resolution, and must be an adept in the use of snow-shoes.

It all depends upon the depth of the snow and the state of the crust. If when the snow is very deep there comes a thaw, and if it then freezes hard, the moose are overtaken and killed with ease; for the crust cuts their legs, they sink to their bellies at every plunge, and speedily become so worn out that they can no longer keep ahead of any man who is even moderately skilful in the use of snow-shoes; though they do not, as deer so often do, sink exhausted after going a few rods from their yard. Under such circumstances a few hardy hunters or settlers, who are perfectly reckless in slaughtering game, may readily kill all the moose in a district. It is a kind of hunting which just suits the ordinary settler, who is hardy and enduring, but knows little of hunting-craft proper.

If the snow is less deep, or the crust not so heavy, the moose may travel for scores of miles before it is overtaken; and this even though the crust be strong enough to bear a man wearing show-shoes without breaking. The chase then involves the most exhausting fatigue. Moreover, it can be carried on only by those who are very skilful in the use of snow-shoes. These show-shoes are of two kinds. In the northeast, and in the most tangled forests of the northwest, the webbed snow-shoes are used; on the bare mountain-sides, and in the open forests of the Rockies, the long narrow wooden skees, or Norwegian snow-skates are preferred, as upon them men can travel much faster, though they are less handy in thick timber. Having donned his snow-shoes and struck the trail of a moose, the hunter may have to follow it three days if the snow is of only ordinary depth, with a moderate crust. He shuffles across the snow without halt while daylight lasts, and lies down wherever he happens to be when night strikes him, probably with a little frozen bread as his only food. The hunter thus goes through inordinate labor, and suffers from exposure; not infrequently his feet are terribly cut by the thongs of the snow-shoes, and become sore and swollen, causing great pain. When overtaken after such a severe chase, the moose is usually so exhausted as to be unable to make any resistance; in all likelihood it has run itself to a standstill. Accordingly, the quality of the fire-arms makes but little difference in this kind of hunting. Many of the most famous old moose-hunters of Maine, in the long past days, before the Civil War, when moose were plenty there, used what were known as "three dollar" guns; light, single-barrelled smooth-bores. One whom I knew used a flint-lock musket, a relic of the War of 1812. Another in the course of an exhausting three days' chase lost the lock off his cheap, percussion-cap gun, and when he overtook the moose he had to explode the cap by hammering it with a stone.

It is in "crusting," when the chase has lasted but a comparatively short time, that moose most frequently show fight; for they are not cast into a state of wild panic by a sudden and unlooked-for attack by a man who is a long distance from them, but on the contrary, after being worried and irritated, are approached very near by foes from whom they have been fleeing for hours. Nevertheless, in the majority of cases even crusted moose make not the slightest attempt at retaliation. If the chase has been very long, or if the depth of the snow and character of the crust are exceptionally disadvantageous to them, they are so utterly done out, when overtaken, that they cannot make a struggle, and may even be killed with an axe. I know of at least five men who have thus killed crusted moose with an axe; one in the Rocky Mountains, one in Minnesota, three in Maine.

But in ordinary snow a man who should thus attempt to kill a moose would merely jeopardize his own life; and it is not an uncommon thing for chased moose, when closely approached by their pursuers, even when the latter carry guns and are expert snowshoers, to charge them with such ferocity as to put them in much peril. A brother of one of my cow-hands, a man from Maine, was once nearly killed by a cow moose. She had been in a yard with her last year's calf when started. After two or three hours' chase he overtook them. They were travelling in single file, the cow breaking her path through the snow, while the calf followed close behind, and in his nervousness sometimes literally ran up on her. The man trotted close alongside; but, before he could fire, the old cow spun round and charged him, her mane bristling and her green eyes snapping with rage. It happened that just there the snow became shallow, and the moose gained so rapidly that the man, to save his life, sprang up a tree. As he did so the cow reared and struck at him, one forefoot catching in his snow-shoe and tearing it clear off, giving his ankle a bad wrench. After watching him a minute or two she turned and continued her flight; whereupon he climbed down the tree, patched up his torn snow-shoe and limped after the moose, which he finally killed.

An old hunter named Purvis told me of an adventure of the kind, which terminated fatally. He was hunting near the Coeur d'Alene Mountains with a mining prospector named Pingree; both were originally from New Hampshire. Late in November there came a heavy fall of snow, deep enough to soon bring a deer to a standstill, although not so deep as to hamper a moose's movement. The men bound on their skees and started to the borders of a lake, to kill some blacktail. In a thicket close to the lake's brink they suddenly came across a bull moose; a lean old fellow, still savage from the rut. Pingree, who was nearest, fired at and wounded him; whereupon he rushed straight at the man, knocked him down before he could turn round in his skees, and began to pound him with his terrible forefeet. Summoned by his comrade's despairing cries, Purvis rushed round the thickets, and shot the squealing trampling monster through the body, and immediately after had to swing himself up a small tree to avoid its furious rush. The moose did not turn after this charge, but kept straight on, and was not seen again. The wounded man was past all help, for his chest was beaten in, and he died in a couple of hours.

Hunting Lore
(From *The Wilderness Hunter*)

It has been my good-luck to kill every kind of game properly belonging to the United States: though one beast which I never had a
chance to slay, the jaguar, from the torrid South, sometimes comes
just across the Rio Grande; nor have I ever hunted the musk-ox
and polar bear in the boreal wastes where they dwell, surrounded
by the frozen desolation of the uttermost North.

I have never sought to make large bags, for a hunter should not
be a game butcher. It is always lawful to kill dangerous or noxious
animals, like the bear, cougar, and wolf; but other game should
only be shot when there is need of the meat, or for the sake of an
unusually fine trophy. Killing a reasonable number of bulls, bucks,
or rams does no harm whatever to the species; to slay half the males
of any kind of game would not stop the natural increase, and they
yield the best sport, and are the legitimate objects of the chase.
Cows, does, and ewes, on the contrary, should only be killed (unless barren) in case of necessity; during my last five years' hunting I

have killed but five—one by a mischance, and the other four for the table.

From its very nature, the life of the hunter is in most places evanescent; and when it has vanished there can be no real substitute in old settled countries. Shooting in a private game preserve is but a dismal parody; the manliest and healthiest features of the sport are lost with the change of conditions. We need, in the interest of the community at large, a rigid system of game laws rigidly enforced, and it is not only admissible, but one may almost say necessary, to establish, under the control of the State, great national forest reserves, which shall also be breeding grounds and nurseries for wild game; but I should much regret to see grow up in this country a system of large private game preserves, kept for the enjoyment of the very rich. One of the chief attractions of the life of the wilderness is its rugged and stalwart democracy; there every man stands for what he actually is, and can show himself to be.

There are, in different parts of our country, chances to try so many various kinds of hunting, with rifle, or with horse and hound, that it is nearly impossible for one man to have experience of them all. There are many hunts I long hoped to take, but never did and never shall; they must be left for men with more time, or for those whose homes are nearer to the hunting grounds. I have never seen a grisly roped by the riders of the plains, nor a black bear killed with the knife and hounds in the southern canebrakes; though at one time I had for many years a standing invitation to witness this last feat on a plantation in Arkansas. The friend who gave it, an old backwoods planter, at one time lost almost all his hogs by the numerous bears who infested his neighborhood. He took a grimly humorous revenge each fall by doing his winter killing among the bears instead of among the hogs they had slain; for as the cold weather approached he regularly proceeded to lay in a stock of bear-bacon, scouring the canebrakes in a series of systematic hunts, bringing the quarry to bay with the help of a big pack of hard-fighting mongrels, and then killing it with his long, broad-bladed bowie.

Again, I should like to make a trial at killing peccaries with the spear, whether on foot or on horseback, and with or without dogs. I should like much to repeat the experience of a friend who cruised northward through Bearing Sea, shooting walrus and polar bear; and that of two other friends who travelled with dog-sleds to the Barren Grounds, in chase of the caribou, and of that last survivor of the Ice Age, the strange musk-ox. Once in a while it must be good sport to shoot alligators by torchlight in the everglades of Florida or the bayous of Louisiana.

If the big-game hunter, the lover of the rifle, has a taste for kindred field sports with rod and shotgun, many are his chances for pleasure, though perhaps of a less intense kind. The wild turkey really deserves a place beside the deer; to kill a wary old gobbler with the small-bore rifle, by fair still-hunting, is a triumph for the best sportsman. Swans, geese, and sandhill cranes likewise may sometimes be killed with the rifle; but more often all three, save perhaps the swan, must be shot over decoys. Then there is prairie-chicken shooting on the fertile grain prairies of the middle West, from Minnesota to Texas; and killing canvas-backs from behind blinds, with the help of that fearless swimmer, the Chesapeake Bay dog. In Californian mountains and valleys live the beautiful plumed quails, and who does not know their cousin bob-white, the bird of the farm, with his cheery voice and friendly ways? For pure fun, nothing can surpass a night scramble through the woods after coon and possum.

The salmon, whether near Puget sound or the St. Lawrence, is the royal fish; his only rival is the giant of the warm Gulf waters, the silver-mailed tarpon; while along the Atlantic coast the great striped bass likewise yields fine sport to the men of rod and reel. Every hunter of the mountains and the northern woods knows the many kinds of spotted trout; for the black bass he cares less; and least of all for the sluggish pickerel, and his big brother of the Great Lakes, the muscallonge.

Yet the sport yielded by rod and smooth-bore is really less closely kin to the strong pleasures so beloved by the hunter who trusts in horse and rifle than are certain other outdoor pastimes, of the rougher and hardier kind. Such a pastime is snow-shoeing, whether with webbed rackets, in the vast northern forests, or with skees, in the bare slopes of the Rockies. Such is mountaineering, especially when joined with bold exploration of the unknown. Most of our mountains are of rounded shape, and though climbing them is often hard work, it is rarely difficult or dangerous, save in bad weather, or after a snowfall. But there are many of which this is not true; the Tetons, for instance, and various glacier-bearing peaks in the Northwest; while the lofty, snow-clad ranges of British Columbia and Alaska offer one of the finest fields in the world for the daring cragsman. Mountaineering is among the manliest of sports, and it is to be hoped that some of our young men with a taste for hard work and adventure among the high hills will attempt the conquest of these great untrodden mountains of their own continent. As with all pioneer work, there would be far more discomfort and danger, far more need to display resolution, hardihood, and wisdom in such an attempt than in any expedition on well known and historic ground like the Swiss Alps; but the victory would be a hundred-fold better worth winning.

The dweller or sojourner in the wilderness who most keenly loves and appreciates his wild surroundings, and all their sights and sounds, is the man who also loves and appreciates the books which tell of them.

Foremost of all American writers on outdoor life is John Burroughs; and I can scarcely suppose that any man who cares for existence outside the cities would willingly be without anything that he has ever written. To the naturalist, to the observer and lover of nature, he is of course worth many times more than any closet systematist; and though he has not been very much in really wild regions, his pages so thrill with the sights and sounds of outdoor life that nothing by any writer who is a mere professional scientist or a mere professional hunter can take their place, or do more than supplement them—for scientist and hunter alike would do well to remember that before a book can take the highest rank in any particular line it must also rank high in literature proper. Of course, for us Americans, Burroughs has a peculiar charm that he cannot have for others, no matter how much they, too, may like him; for what he writes of is our own, and he calls to our minds memories and associations that are very dear. His books make us homesick when we read them in foreign lands; for they spring from our soil as truly as *Snowbound* or *The Biglow Papers*.[1]

As a woodland writer, Thoreau comes second only to Burroughs.

For natural history in the narrower sense there are still no better books than Audubon and Bachman's Mammals and Audubon's Birds. There are also good works by men like Coues and Bendire; and if Hart Merriam, of the Smithsonian, will only do for the mammals of the United States what he has already done for those of the Adirondacks, we shall have the best book of its kind in existence. Nor, among less technical writings, should one overlook such essays as those of Maurice Thompson and Olive Thorne Miller.

There have been many American hunting-books; but too often they have been very worthless, even when the writers possessed the necessary first-hand knowledge, and the rare capacity of seeing

---

[1] I am under many obligations to the writing of Mr. Burroughs (though there are one or two of his theories from which I should dissent); and there is a piece of indebtedness in this very volume of which I have only just become aware. In my chapter on the prong-buck there is a paragraph which will at once suggest to any lover of Burroughs some sentences in his essay on "Birds and Poets." I did not notice the resemblance until happening to reread the essay after my own chapter was written, and at the time I had no idea that I was borrowing from anybody, the more so as I was thinking purely of western wilderness life and western wilderness game, with which I knew Mr. Burroughs had never been familiar. I have concluded to leave the paragraph in with this acknowledgement.

the truth. Few of the old-time hunters ever tried to write of what they had seen and done; and of those who made the effort fewer still succeeded. Innate refinement and the literary faculty—that is, the faculty of writing a thoroughly interesting and readable book, full of valuable information—may exist in uneducated people; but if they do not, no amount of experience in the field can supply their lack. However, we have had some good works on the chase and habits of big game, such as Caton's *Deer and Antelope of America*, Van Dyke's *Still-Hunter*, Elliott's *Carolina Sports*, and Dodge's *Hunting Groups of the Great West*, besides the Century Company's *Sport with Rod and Gun*. Then there is Catlin's book, and the journals of the explorers from Lewis and Clarke down; and occasional volumes on outdoor life, such as Theodore Winthrop's *Canoe and Saddle*, and Clarence King's *Mountaineering in the Sierra Nevada*.

Two or three of the great writers of American literature, notably Parkman in his *Oregon Trail*, and, with less interest, Irving in his *Trip on the Prairies* have written with power and charm of life in the American wilderness; but no one has risen to do for the far western plainsmen and Rocky Mountain trappers quite what Hermann Melville did for the South Sea whaling folk in *Omoo* and *Moby Dick*. The best description of these old-time dwellers among the mountains and on the plains is to be found in a couple of good volumes by the Englishman Ruxton. However, the backwoodsmen proper, both in their forest homes and when they first began to venture out on the prairie, have been portrayed by a master hand. In a succession of wonderfully drawn characters, ranging from "Aaron Thousandacres" to "Ishmael Bush," Fenimore Cooper has preserved for always the likenesses of these stark pioneer settlers and backwoods hunters; uncouth, narrow, hard, suspicious, but with all the virile virtues of a young and masterful race, a race of mighty breeders, mighty fighters, mighty commonwealth builders. As for Leatherstocking, he is one of the undying men of story; grand, simple, kindly, pure-minded, staunchly loyal, the type of the steel-thewed and iron-willed hunter-warrior.

Turning from the men of fiction to the men of real life, it is worth noting how many of the leaders among our statesmen and soldiers have sought strength and pleasure in the chase, or in kindred vigorous pastimes. Of course field sports, or at least the wilder kinds, which entail the exercise of daring and the endurance of toil and hardship, and which lead men afar into the forests and mountains, stand above athletic exercises; exactly as among the latter, rugged outdoor games, like football and lacrosse, are much superior to mere gymnastics and calisthenics.

With a few exceptions the men among us who have stood foremost in political leadership, like their fellows who have led our armies, have been of stalwart frame and sound bodily health. When they sprang from the frontier folk, as did Lincoln and Andrew Jackson, they hunted much in their youth, if only as an incident in the prolonged warfare waged by themselves and their kinsmen against the wild forces of nature. Old Israel Putnam's famous wolf-killing feat comes strictly under this head. Doubtless he greatly enjoyed the excitement of the adventure; but he went into it as a matter of business, not of sport. The wolf, the last of its kind in his neighborhood, had taken heavy toll of the flocks of himself and his friends; when they found the deep cave in which it had made its den it readily beat off the dogs sent in to assail it; and so Putnam crept in himself, with his torch and his flint-lock musket, and shot the beast where it lay.

When such men lived in long settled and thickly peopled regions, they needs had to accommodate themselves to the conditions and put up with humbler forms of sport. Webster, like his great rival for Whig leadership, Henry Clay, cared much for horses, dogs, and guns; but though an outdoor man he had no chance to develop a love for big-game hunting. He was, however, very fond of the rod and shotgun. Mr. Cabot Lodge recently handed me a letter written to his grandfather by Webster, and describing a day's trout fishing. It may be worth giving for the sake of the writer, and because of the fine heartiness and zest in enjoyment which it shows:

Sandwich, June 4,
Saturday mor'g
6 o'clock

Dear Sir:

I send you eight or nine trout, which I took yesterday, in that chief of all brooks, Mashpee. I made a long day of it, and with good success, for me. John was with me, full of good advice, but did not fish—nor carry a rod.

I took 26 trouts, all weighing	17 lb.	12 oz.
The largest (you have him)	2"	4"
weighed at Crokers		
The 5 largest	3"	5"
The eight largest	11"	8"

I got these by following your advice; that is, by *careful & thorough* fishing of the difficult places, which others do not fish. The brook is fished, nearly every day. I entered it, not so high up as we sometimes do, between 7 & 8 o'clock, & at 12 was hardly more than half way down to the meeting house path. You see I did not hurry. The day did not hold out to fish the whole brook properly. The largest trout I took at 3 P.M. (you see I am precise) below the meeting house, under a bush on the right bank, two or three rods below the large *beeches*. It is singular, that in the whole day, I did not take two trouts out of the same hole. I found both ends, or parts of the Brook about equally productive. Small fish not plenty, in either. So many hooks get everything which is not hid away in the manner large trouts take care of themselves. I hooked one, which I suppose to be larger than any which I took, as he broke my line, by fair pulling, after I had pulled him out of his den, & was playing him in fair open water.

Of what I send you, I pray you keep what you wish yourself, send three to Mr. Ticknor, & three to Dr. Warren; or two of the larger ones, to each will perhaps be enough—& if there be any left, there is Mr. Callender & Mr. Blake, & Mr. Davis, either of them not "averse to fish." Pray let Mr. Davis *see* them—especially the large one.—As he promised to come, & fell back, I desire to excite his regrets. I hope you will have the large one on your own table.

The day was fine—not another hook in the Brook. John steady as a judge—and every thing else exactly right. I never, on the whole, had so agreeable a day's fishing tho the result, in pounds or numbers, is not great;—nor ever expect such another.

Please preserve this letter; but rehearse not these particulars to the uninitiated.

I think the Limerick *not* the best hook. Whether it pricks too soon, or for what other reason, I found, or thought I found, the fish more likely to let go his hold, from this, than from the old fashioned hook.

Yrs.

H. Cabot, Esq.   D. Webster.

The greatest of Americans, Washington, was very fond of hunting both with rifle or fowling-piece, and especially with horse, horn, and hound. Essentially the representative of all that is best in our national life, standing high as a general, high as a statesman, and highest of all as a man, he could never have been what he was had he not taken delight in feats of hardihood, of daring, and of bodily prowess. He was strongly drawn to those field sports which demand in their follower the exercise of the manly virtues—courage, endurance, physical address. As a young man, clad in the distinctive garb of the backwoodsman, the fringed and tasselled hunting-shirt, he led the life of a frontier surveyor; and like his fellow adventurers in wilderness exploration and Indian campaigning, he was often forced to trust to the long rifle for keeping his party in food. When at his home, at Mount Vernon, he hunted from simple delight in the sport.

His manuscript diaries, preserved in the State Department at Washington, are full of entries concerning his feats in the chase; almost all of them naturally falling in the years between the ending of the French war and the opening of the Revolutionary struggle against the British, or else in the period separating his service as Commander-in-chief of the Continental armies from his term of office as President of the Republic. These entries are scattered through others dealing with his daily duties in overseeing his farm and mill, his attendance at the Virginia House of Burgesses, his journeys, the drill of the local militia, and all the various interests of his many-sided life. Fond though he was of hunting, he was wholly incapable of the career inanity led by those who make sport, not a manly pastime, but the one serious business of their lives.

The entries in the diaries are short, and are couched in the homey vigorous English, so familiar to the readers of Washington's journals and private letters. Sometimes they are brief jottings in reference to shooting trips; such as: "Rid out with my gun"; "went pheasant hunting"; "went ducking," and "went a gunning up the Creek." But far more often they are: "Rid out with my hounds," "went a fox hunting," or "went a hunting." In their perfect simplicity and good faith they are strongly characteristic of the man. He enters his blank days and failures as conscientiously as his red-letter days of success; recording with equal care on one day, "Fox hunting with Captain Posey—catch a Fox," and another, "Went a hunting with Lord Fairfax . . . catched nothing."

Occasionally he began as early as August and continued until April; and while he sometimes made but eight or ten hunts in a season, at others he made as many in a month. Often he hunted from Mt. Vernon, going out once or twice a week, either alone or with a party of his friends and neighbors; and again he would meet with these same neighbors at one of their houses, and devote several days solely to the chase. The country was still very wild, and now and then game was encountered with which the fox-hounds proved unable to cope; as witness entries like: "found both a Bear and a Fox, but got neither"; "went a hunting . . . started a Deer & then a Fox but got neither" and "Went a hunting and after trailing a fox a good while the Dogs Raized a Deer & ran out of the Neck with it & did not some of them at least come home till the next day." If it was a small animal, however, it was soon accounted for. "Went a Hunting . . . catched a Rakoon but never found a Fox."

The woods were so dense and continuous that it was often impossible for the riders to keep close to the hounds throughout the run; though in one or two of the best covers, as the journal records, Washington "directed paths to be cut for Fox Hunting." This thickness of the timber made it difficult to keep the hounds always under control; and there are frequent allusions to their going off on their own account, as "Joined some dogs that were self hunting." Sometimes the hounds got so far away that it was impossible to tell whether they had killed or not, the journal remarking "catched nothing that we know of," or "found a fox at the head of the blind Pocoson which we supposed was killed in an hour but could not find it."

Another result of this density and continuity of cover was the frequent recurrence of days of ill success. There are many such entries as: "Went Fox hunting, but started nothing"; "Went a hunting, but catched nothing"; "found nothing"; "found a Fox and lost it." Often a failure followed long and hard runs: "Started a Fox, run him four hours, took the Hounds off at night"; "found a Fox and run it 6 hours and then lost"; "Went a hunting above Darrells . . . found a fox by two Dogs but lost it upon joining the Pack." In the season of 1772–73 Washington hunted eighteen days and killed nine foxes; and though there were seasons when he was out much more often, this proportion of kills to runs was if anything above the average. At the beginning of 1768 he met with a a series of blank days which might well have daunted a less patient and persevering hunter. In January and the early part of February he was out nine times without getting a thing; but his diary does not contain a word of disappointment or surprise, each successive piece of ill-luck being entered without comment, even when one day he met some more fortunate friends "who had just catched 2 foxes." At last, on February 12th, he himself "catched two foxes"; the six or eight gentlemen of the neighborhood who made up the field all went home with him to Mt. Vernon, to dine and pass the night, and in the hunt of the following day they repeated the feat of a double score. In the next seven days' hunting he killed four times.

The runs of course varied greatly in length; on one day he "found a bitch fox at Piney Branch and killed it in an hour"; on another he "killed a Dog fox after having him on foot three hours & hard running an hour and a qr."; and on yet another he "catched a fox with a bobd Tail & cut ears after 7 hours chase in which most of the Dogs were worsted." Sometimes he caught his fox in thirty-five minutes, and again he might run it nearly the whole day in vain; the average run seems to have been from an hour and a half to three hours. Sometimes the entry records merely the barren fact of the run; at others a few particulars are given, with homespun, telling directness, as: "Went a hunting with Jacky Custis and catched a Bitch Fox after three hours chace—founded it on ye. ck. by I. Soals"; or "went a Fox hunting with Lund Washington—took the drag of a fox by Isaac Gates & carrd. it tolerably well to the old Glebe then touched now and then upon a cold scent till we came into Col. Fairfaxes Neck where we found about half after three upon the Hills just above Accotinck Creek—after running till quite Dark took off the Dogs and came home."

The foxes were doubtless mostly of the gray kind, and besides going to holes they treed readily. In January, 1770, he was out seven days, killing four foxes; and two of the entries in the journal relate to foxes which treed; one, on the 10th, being, "I went a hunting in the Neck and visited the plantn. there found and killed a bitch fox after treeing it 3 t. chasg. it abt. 3 hrs.," and the other, on the 23d: "Went a hunting after breakfast & found a Fox at muddy hole & killed her (it being a bitch) after a chase of better than two hours and after treeing her twice the last of which times she fell dead out of the Tree after being therein sevl. minutes apparently." In April, 1769, he hunted hour days, and on every occasion the fox treed. April 7th, "Dog fox killed, ran an hour & treed twice." April

11th, "Went a fox hunting and took a fox alive after running him to a Tree—brot him home." April 12th, "Chased the above fox an hour & 45 minutes when he treed again after which we lost him." April 13th, "Killed a dog fox after treeing him in 35 minutes."

Washington continued his fox-hunting until, in the spring of 1775, the guns of the minute-men in Massachusetts called him to the command of the Revolutionary soldiery. When the eight weary years of campaigning were over, he said good-by to the war-worn veterans whom he had led through defeat and disaster to ultimate triumph, and became once more a Virginia country gentleman. Then he took up his fox-hunting with as much zest as ever. The entries in his journal are now rather longer, and go more into detail than formerly. Thus, on December 12, 1786, he writes that after an early breakfast he went on a hunt and found a fox at half after ten, "being first plagued with the dogs running hogs," followed on his drag for some time, then ran him hard for an hour, when there came a fault; but when four dogs which had been thrown out rejoined the pack they put the fox up afresh, and after fifty minutes' run killed him in an open field, "every Rider & every Dog being present at the Death." With his usual alternations between days like this, and days of ill-luck, he hunted steadily every season until his term of private life again drew to a close and he was called to the headship of the nation he had so largely helped to found.

In a certain kind of fox-hunting lore there is much reference to a Warwickshire squire who, when the Parliamentary and Royalist armies were forming for the battle at Edgehill, was discovered between the hostile lines, unmovedly drawing the covers for a fox. Now, this placid sportsman should by rights have been slain off-hand by the first trooper who reached him, whether Cavalier or Roundhead. He had mistaken means for ends, he had confounded the healthful play which should fit a man for needful work with the work itself; and mistakes of this kind are sometimes criminal. Hardy sports of the field offer the best possible training for war;

but they become contemptible when indulged in while the nation is at death-grips with her enemies.

It was not in Washington's strong nature to make such an error. Nor yet, on the other hand, was he likely to undervalue either the pleasure, or the real worth of outdoor sports. The qualities of heart, mind, and body, which made him delight in the hunting-field, and which he there exercised and developed, stood him in good stead in many a long campaign and on many a stricken field; they helped to build that stern capacity for leadership in war which he showed alike through the bitter woe of the winter at Valley Forge, on the night when he ferried his men across the half-frozen Delaware to the overthrow of the German mercenaries at Trenton, and in the brilliant feat of arms whereof the outcome was the decisive victory of Yorktown.

Part Two

Safari

Selections from

African Game Trails

An Account of the African Wanderings

of an American Hunter-Naturalist

Foreword

"I speak of Africa and golden joys"; the joy of wandering through lonely lands; the joy of hunting the mighty and terrible lords of the wilderness, the cunning, the wary, and the grim.

In these greatest of the world's great hunting-grounds there are mountain peaks whose snows are dazzling under the equatorial sun; swamps where the slime oozes and bubbles and festers in the steaming heat; lakes like seas; skies that burn above deserts where the iron desolation is shrouded from view by the wavering mockery of the mirage; vast grassy plains where palms and thorn-trees fringe the dwindling streams; mighty rivers rushing out of the heart of the continent through the sadness of endless marshes; forests of gorgeous beauty, where death broods in the dark and silent depths.

There are regions as healthy as the northland; and other regions, radiant with bright-hued flowers, birds and butterflies, odorous with sweet and heavy scents, but, treacherous in their beauty, and sinister to human life. On the land and in the water there are dread brutes that feed on the flesh of man; and among the lower things, that crawl, and fly, and sting, and bite, he finds swarming foes far more evil and deadly than any beast or reptile; foes that kill his crops and his cattle, foes before which he himself perishes in his hundreds of thousands.

The dark-skinned races that live in the land vary widely. Some are warlike, cattle-owning nomads; some till the soil and live in thatched huts shaped like beehives; some are fisherfolk; some are ape-like naked savages, who dwell in the woods and prey on creatures not much wilder or lower than themselves.

The land teems with beasts of the chase, infinite in number and incredible in variety. It holds the fiercest beasts of ravin, and the fleetest and most timid of those beings that live in undying fear of talon and fang. It holds the largest and the smallest of hoofed animals. It holds the mightiest creatures that tread the earth or swim in its rivers; it also holds distant kinsfolk of these same creatures, no bigger than woodchucks, which dwell in crannies of the rocks and in the tree tops. There are antelope smaller than hares, and antelope larger than oxen. There are creatures which are the embodiment of grace; and others whose huge ungainliness is like that of a shape in a nightmare. The plains are alive with droves of strange and beautiful animals whose like is not known elsewhere; and with others even stranger that show both in form and temper something of the fantastic and the grotesque. It is a never-ending pleasure to gaze at the great herds of buck as they move to and fro in their myriads; as they stand for their noontide rest in the quivering heat haze; as the long files come down to drink at the watering-places; as they feed and fight and rest and make love.

The hunter who wanders through these lands sees sights which ever afterward remain fixed in his mind. He sees the monstrous river-horse snorting and plunging beside the boat; the giraffe looking over the tree tops at the nearing horseman; the ostrich fleeing at a speed that none may rival; the snarling leopard and coiled python, with their lethal beauty, the zebras, barking in the moonlight, as the laden caravan passes on its night march through a thirsty land. In after years there shall come to him memories of the lion's charge; of the gray bulk of the elephant, close at hand in the sombre woodland; of the buffalo, his sullen eyes lowering from under his helmet of horn; of the rhinoceros, truculent and stupid, standing in the bright sunlight on the empty plain.

These things can be told. But there are no words that can tell the hidden spirit of the wilderness, that can reveal its mystery, its melancholy, and its charm. There is delight in the hardy life of the open, in long rides rifle in hand, in the thrill of the fight with dangerous game. Apart from this, yet mingled with it, is the strong attraction of the silent places, of the large tropic moons, and the splendor of the new stars; where the wanderer sees the awful glory of sunrise and sunset in the wide waste spaces of the earth, unworn of man, and changed only by the slow change of the ages through time everlasting.

Theodore Roosevelt
Khartoum, March 15, 1910

A Railroad Through the Pleistocene

The great world movement which began with the voyages of Columbus and Vasco da Gama, and which has gone on with ever-increasing rapidity and complexity until our own time, has developed along myriad lines of interest. In no way has it been more interesting than in the way in which it has brought into sudden, violent, and intimate contact phases of the world's life history which would normally be separated by untold centuries of slow development. Again and again, in the continents new to peoples of European stock, we have seen the spectacle of a high civilization all at once thrust into and superimposed upon a wilderness of savage men and beasts. Nowhere, and at no time, has the contrast been more strange and more striking than in British East Africa during the last dozen years.

The country lies directly under the equator; and the hinterland, due west, contains the huge Nyanza lakes, vast inland seas which gather the head-waters of the White Nile. This hinterland, with its lakes and its marshes, its snow-capped mountains, its high, dry plateaus, and its forests of deadly luxuriance, was utterly

269

unknown to white men half a century ago. The map of Ptolemy in the second century of our era gave a more accurate view of the lakes, mountains, and head-waters of the Nile than the maps published at the beginning of the second half of the nineteenth century, just before Speke, Grant, and Baker made their great trips of exploration and adventure. Behind these explorers came others; and then adventurous missionaries, traders, and elephant hunters; and many men, whom risk did not daunt, who feared neither danger nor hardship, traversed the country hither and thither, now for one reason, now for another, now as naturalists, now as geographers, and again as government officials or as mere wanderers who loved the wild and strange life which had survived over from an elder age.

Most of the tribes were of pure savages; but here and there were intrusive races of higher type; and in Uganda, beyond the Victoria Nyanza, and on the head-waters of the Nile proper, lived a people which had advanced to the upper stages of barbarism, which might almost be said to have developed a very primitive kind of semi-civilization. Over this people—for its good fortune—Great Britain established a protectorate; and ultimately, in order to get easy access to this new outpost of civilization in the heart of the Dark Continent, the British Government built a railroad from the old Arab coast town of Mombasa westward to Victoria Nyanza.

This railroad, the embodiment of the eager, masterful, materialistic civilization of to-day, was pushed through a region in which nature, both as regards wild man and wild beast, did not and does not differ materially from what it was in Europe in the late Pleistocene. The comparison is not fanciful. The teeming multitudes of wild creatures, the stupendous size of some of them, the terrible nature of others, and the low culture of many of the savage tribes, especially of the hunting tribes, substantially reproduces the conditions of life in Europe as it was led by our ancestors ages before the dawn of anything that could be called civilization. The great beasts that now live in East Africa were in that by-gone age represented by close kinsfolk in Europe; and in many places, up to the present moment. African man, absolutely naked, and armed as our early paleolithic ancestors were armed, lives among, and on, and in constant dread of, these beasts, just as was true of the men to whom the cave lion was a nightmare of terror, and the mammoth and the woolly rhinoceros possible but most formidable prey.

This region, this great fragment out of the long-buried past of our race, is now accessible by railroad to all who care to go thither; and no field more inviting offers itself to hunter or naturalist, while even to the ordinary traveller it teems with interest. On March 23, 1909, I sailed thither from New York, in charge of a scientific expedition sent out by the Smithsonian, to collect birds, mammals, reptiles, and plants, but especially specimens of big game, for the National Museum at Washington. In addition to myself and my son Kermit (who had entered Harvard a few months previously), the party consisted of three naturalists: Surgeon-Lieut. Col. Edgar A. Mearns, U.S.A., retired; Mr. Edmund Heller, of California, and Mr. J. Alden Loring, of Owego, N.Y. My arrangements for the trip had been chiefly made through two valued English friends, Mr. Frederick Courteney Selous, the greatest of the world's big-game hunters, and Mr. Edward North Buxton, also a mighty hunter. On landing we were to be met by Messrs. R. J. Cuningham and Leslie Tarlton, both famous hunters; the latter an Australian, who served through the South African war; the former by birth a Scotchman, and a Cambridge man, but long a resident of Africa, and at one time a professional elephant hunter—in addition to having been a whaler in the Arctic Ocean, a hunter-naturalist in Lapland, a transport rider in South Africa, and a collector for the British Museum in various odd corners of the earth.

We sailed on the *Hamburg* from New York—what headway the Germans have made among those who go down to the sea in ships!—and at Naples trans-shipped to the *Admiral*, of another German line, the East African. On both ships we were as comfortable as possible, and the voyage was wholly devoid of incidents.

On the ship, at Naples, we found Selous, also bound for East Africa on a hunting trip; but he, a veteran whose first hunting in Africa was nearly forty years ago, cared only for exceptional trophies of a very few animals, while we, on the other hand, desired specimens of both sexes of all the species of big game that Kermit and I could shoot, as well as complete series of all the smaller mammals. We believed that our best work of a purely scientific character would be done with the mammals, both large and small.

No other hunter alive has had the experience of Selous; and so far as I now recall, no hunter of anything like his experience has ever also possessed his gift of penetrating observation joined to his power of vivid and accurate narration. He has killed scores of lion and rhinoceros and hundreds of elephant and buffalo; and these four animals are the most dangerous of the world's big game, when hunted as they are hunted in Africa. To hear him tell of what he has seen and done is no less interesting to a naturalist than to a hunter. There were on the ship many men who loved wild nature, and who were keen hunters of big game; and almost every day, as we steamed over the hot, smooth waters of the Red Sea and the Indian Ocean, we would gather on deck around Selous to listen to tales of those strange adventures that only come to the man who has lived long the lonely life of the wilderness.

On April 21 we steamed into the beautiful and picturesque harbor of Mombasa. Many centuries before the Christian era, dhows from Arabia, carrying seafarers of Semitic races whose very names have perished, rounded the Lion's Head at Guardafui and crept slowly southward along the barren African coast. Such dhows exist to-day almost unchanged, and bold indeed were the men who first steered them across the unknown oceans. They were men of iron heart and supple conscience, who fronted inconceivable danger and hardship; they established trading stations for gold and ivory and slaves; they turned these trading stations into little cities and sultanates, half Arab, half negro. Mombasa was among them. In her time of brief splendor Portugal seized the city; the Arabs won it back; and now England holds it. It lies just south of the equator, and when we saw it the brilliant green of the tropic foliage showed the town at its best.

We were welcomed to Government House in most cordial fashion by the acting governor, Lieutenant-Governor Jackson, who is not only a trained public official of long experience, but a first-class field naturalist and a renowned big-game hunter; indeed I could not too warmly express my appreciation of the hearty and generous courtesy with which we were received and treated alike by the official and the unofficial world throughout East Africa. We landed in the kind of torrential downpour that only comes in the tropics; it reminded me of Panama at certain moments in the rainy season. That night we were given a dinner by the Mombasa Club; and it was interesting to meet the merchants and planters of the town and the neighborhood as well as the officials.

The most thrilling book of true lion stories ever written is Colonel Patterson's "The Man-eaters of Tsavo." Colonel Patterson was one of the engineers engaged, some ten or twelve years back, in building the Uganda Railway; he was in charge of the work, at a place called Tsavo, when it was brought to a complete halt by the ravages of a couple of man-eating lions which, after many adventures, he finally killed. At the dinner at the Mombasa Club I met one of the actors in a blood-curdling tragedy which Colonel Patterson relates. He was a German, and, in company with an Italian friend, he went down in the special car of one of the English railroad officials to try to kill a man-eating lion which had carried away several people from a station on the line. They put the car on a siding; as it was hot the door was left open, and the Englishman sat by the open window to watch for the lion, while the Italian finally lay down on the floor and the German got into an upper bunk. Evidently the Englishman must have fallen asleep, and the lion, seeing him through the window, entered the carriage by the door to get at him. The Italian waked to find the lion standing on him with its hind feet, while its fore paws were on the seat as it killed the unfortunate Englishman, and the German, my informant, hearing the disturbance, leaped out of his bunk actually onto the back of the lion. The man-eater, however, was occupied only with his prey; holding the body in his mouth he forced his way out through the window sash, and made his meal undisturbed but a couple of hundred yards from the railway carriage.

The day after we landed we boarded the train to take what seems to me, as I think it would to most men fond of natural history, the most interesting railway journey in the world. It was Governor Jackson's special train, and in addition to his own party and ours there was only Selous; and we travelled with the utmost comfort through a naturalist's wonderland. All civilized governments are now realizing that it is their duty here and there to preserve, unharmed, tracts of wild nature, with thereon the wild things the destruction of which means the destruction of half the charm of wild nature. The English Government has made a large game reserve of much of the region on the way to Nairobi, stretching far to the south, and one mile to the north, of the track. The reserve swarms with game; it would be of little value except as a reserve; and the attraction it now offers to travellers renders it an asset of real consequence to the whole colony. The wise people of Maine, in our own country, have discovered that intelligent game preservation, carried out in good faith, and in a spirit of common sense as far removed from mushy sentimentality as from brutality, results in adding one more to the State's natural resources of value; and in consequence there are more moose and deer in Maine today than there were forty years ago; there is a better chance for every man in Maine, rich or poor, provided that he is not a game butcher, to enjoy his share of good hunting; and the number of sportsmen and tourists attracted to the State adds very appreciably to the means of livelihood of the citizen. Game reserves should not be established where they are detrimental to the interests of large bodies of settlers, nor yet should they be nominally established in regions so remote that the only men really interfered with are those who respect the law, while a premium is thereby put on the activity of the unscrupulous persons who are eager to break it. Similarly, game laws should be drawn primarily in the interest of the whole people, keeping steadily in mind certain facts that ought to be self-evident to every one above the intellectual level of those well-meaning persons who apparently think that all shooting is wrong and that man could continue to exist if all wild animals were allowed to increase unchecked. There must be recognition of the fact that almost any wild animal of the defenseless type, if its multiplication were unchecked while its natural enemies, the dangerous carnivores were killed, would by its simple increase crowd man off the plant, and of the further fact that, far short of such increase, a time speedily comes when the existence of too much game is incompatible with the interests, or indeed the existence, of the cultivator. As in most other matters, it is only the happy mean which is healthy and rational. There should be certain sanctuaries and nurseries where game can live and breed absolutely unmolested; and elsewhere the laws should so far as possible provide for the continued existence of the game in sufficient numbers to allow a reasonable amount of hunting on fair terms to any hardy and vigorous man fond of the sport, and yet not in sufficient numbers to jeopard the interests of the actual settler, the tiller of the soil, the man whose well-being should be the prime object to be kept in mind by every statesman. Game butchery is as objectionable as any other form of wanton cruelty or barbarity; but to protest against all hunting of game is a sign of softness of head, not of soundness of heart.

In the creation of the great game reserve through which the Uganda Railway runs the British government has conferred a boon upon mankind, and no less in the enactment and enforcement of the game laws in the African provinces generally. Of course experience will show where, from time to time, there must be changes.

In Uganda proper buffaloes and hippos throve so under protection as to become sources of grave danger not only to the crops but to the lives of the natives, and they had to be taken off the protected list and classed as vermin, to be shot in any numbers at any time; and only the great demand for ivory prevented the necessity of following the same course with regard to the elephant; while recently in British East Africa the increase of the zebras, and the harm they did to the crops of the settlers, rendered it necessary to remove a large measure of the protection formerly accorded them, and in some cases actually to encourage their slaughter; and increase in settlement may necessitate further changes. But, speaking generally, much wisdom and foresight, highly creditable to both government and people, have been shown in dealing with and preserving East African game while at the same time safeguarding the interests of the settlers.

On our train the locomotive was fitted with a comfortable seat across the cow-catcher, and on this, except at mealtime, I spent most of the hours of daylight, usually in company with Selous, and often with Governor Jackson, to whom the territory and the game were alike familiar. The first afternoon we did not see many wild animals, but birds abounded, and the scenery was both beautiful and interesting. A black-and-white hornbill, feeding on the track, rose so late that we nearly caught it with out hands; guinea-fowl and francolin, and occasionally bustard, rose near by; brilliant rollers, sun-birds, bee-eaters, and weaver-birds flew beside us, or sat unmoved among the trees as the train passed. In the dusk we nearly ran over a hyena; a year or two previously the train actually did run over a lioness one night, and the conductor brought in her head in triumph. In fact, there have been continual mishaps such as could only happen to a railroad in the Pleistocene! The very night we went up there was an interruption in the telegraph service due to giraffes having knocked down some of the wires and a pole in crossing the track; and elephants have more than once performed the same feat. Two or three times, at night, giraffes have been run into and killed; once a rhinoceros was killed, the engine being damaged in the encounter; and on other occasions the rhino has only just left the track in time, once the beast being struck and a good deal hurt, the engine again being somewhat crippled. But the lions now offer, and have always offered, the chief source of unpleasant excitement. Throughout East Africa the lions continually take to man eating at the expense of the native tribes, and white hunters are continually being killed or crippled by them. At the lonely stations on the railroad the two or three subordinate officials often live in terror of some fearsome brute that has taken to haunting the vicinity; and every few months, at some one of these stations, a man is killed, or badly hurt by, or narrowly escapes from, a prowling lion.

The stations at which the train stopped were neat and attractive; and besides the Indian officials there were usually natives from the neighborhood. Some of these might be dressed in the fez and shirt and trousers which indicate a coming under the white man's influence, or which, rather curiously may also indicate Mohammedanism. But most of the natives are still wild pagans, and many of them are unchanged in the slightest particular from what their forefathers were during the countless ages when they alone were the heirs of the land—a land which they were utterly powerless in any way to improve. Some of the savages we saw wore red blankets, and in deference to white prejudice draped them so as to hide their nakedness. But others appeared—men and women—with literally not one stitch of clothing, although they might have rather elaborate hairdresses, and masses of metal ornaments on their arms and legs. In the region where one tribe dwelt all the people had their front teeth filed to sharp points; it was strange to see a group of these savages, stark naked, with oddly shaved heads and filed teeth, armed with primitive bows and arrows, stand gravely gazing at the train as it rolled into some station; and none the less strange, by the way, because the locomotive was a Baldwin, brought to Africa across the great ocean from our own country. One group of women, nearly nude, had their upper arms so tightly bound with masses of bronze or copper wire that their muscles were completely malformed. So tightly was the wire wrapped round the upper third of the upper arm that it was reduced to about one-half of its normal size; and the muscles could only play, and that in deformed fashion, below this unyielding metal bondage. Why the arms did not mortify it was hard to say; and their freedom of use was so hampered as to make it difficult to understand how man or women whose whole lives are passed in one or another form of manual labor could inflict upon themselves such crippling and pointless punishment. Next morning we were in the game country, and as we sat on the seat over the cow-catcher it was literally like passing through a vast zoological garden. Indeed no such railway journey can be taken on any other line in any other land. At one time we passed a herd of a dozen or so of great giraffes, cows and calves, cantering along through the open woods a couple of hundred yards to the right of the train. Again, still closer, four water-buck cows, their big ears thrown forward, stared at us without moving until we had passed. Hartebeests were everywhere; one herd was on the track, and when the engine whistled they bucked and sprang with ungainly ability and galloped clear of the danger. A long-tailed straw-colored monkey ran from one tree to another. Huge black ostriches appeared from time to time. Once a troop of impalla, close by the track, took fright; and as the beautiful creatures fled we saw now one and now another bound clear over the high bushes. A herd of zebra clattered across a cutting of the line not a hundred yards ahead of the train; the whistle hurried their progress, but only for a moment, and as we passed they were already turning round to gaze. The wild creatures were in their sanctuary, and they knew it. Some of the settlers have at times grumbled at this game reserve being kept of such size; but surely it is one of the most valuable possessions the country could have. The lack of water in parts, the prevalence in other parts of diseases harmful to both civilized man and domestic cattle, render this great tract of country the home of all homes for the creatures of the waste. The protection given these wild creatures is genuine, not nominal; they are preserved, not for the pleasure of the few, but for the good of all who choose to see this strange and attractive spectacle; and from this nursery and breeding ground the overflow keeps up the stock of game in the adjacent land, to the benefit of the settler to whom the game gives fresh meat, and to the benefit of the whole country because of the attraction it furnishes to all who desire to visit a veritable happy hunting ground.

Soon after lunch we drew up at the little station of Kapiti Plains, where our safari was awaiting us; "safari" being the term employed throughout East Africa to denote both the caravan with which one makes an expedition and the expedition itself. Our aim being to cure and send home specimens of all the common big game—in addition to as large a series as possible of the small mammals and birds—it was necessary to carry an elaborate apparatus of naturalists' supplies; we had brought with us, for instance, four tons of fine salt, as to cure the skins of the big beasts is a herculean labor under the best conditions; we had hundreds of traps for the small creatures; many boxes of shot-gun cartridges in addition to the ordinary rifle cartridges which alone would be necessary on a hunting trip; and, in short, all the many impedimenta needed if scientific work is to be properly done under modern conditions. Few laymen have any idea of the expense and pains which must be undergone in order to provide groups of mounted big animals from far-off lands, such as we see in museums like the National Museum in Washington and the American Museum of Natural History in New York. The modern naturalist must realize that in some of its branches his profession, while more than ever a science, has also become an art. So our preparations were necessarily on a very large scale; and as we drew up at the station the array of porters and of tents looked as if some small military expedition was about to start.

As a compliment, which I much appreciated, a large American flag was floating over my own tent; and in the front line, flanking this tent on either hand, were other big tents for the members of the party, with a dining tent and skinning tent; while behind were the tents of the two hundred porters, the gun-bearers, the tent boys, the askaris or native soldiers, and the horse boys or saises. In front of the tents stood the men in two lines; the first containing the fifteen askaris, the second the porters with their head men. The askaris were uniformed, each in a red fez, a blue blouse, and white knickerbockers, and each carrying his rifle and belt. The porters were chosen from several different tribes of races to minimize the danger of combination in the event of mutiny.

Here and there in East Africa one can utilize ox wagons, or pack trains of donkeys; but for a considerable expedition it is still best to use a safari of native porters, of the type by which the commerce and exploration of the country have always been carried on. The backbone of such a safari is generally composed of Swahili, the coast men, negroes who have acquired the Moslem religion, together with a partially Arabicized tongue and a strain of Arab blood from the Arab warriors and traders who have been dominant in the coast towns for so many centuries. It was these Swahili trading caravans, under Arab leadership, which, in their quest for ivory and slaves, trod out the routes which the early white explorers followed. Without their work as a preliminary the work of the white explorers could not have been done; and it was the Swahili porters themselves who rendered this work itself possible. To this day every hunter, trader, missionary, or explorer must use either a Swahili safari or one modelled on the Swahili basis. The part played by the white-topped ox wagon in the history of South Africa, and by the camel caravan in North Africa, has long been played in middle Africa by the files of strong, patient, childlike savages, who have borne the burdens of so many masters and employers hither and thither, through and across, the dark heart of the continent.

Equatorial Africa is in most places none too healthy a place for the white man, and he must care for himself as he would scorn to do in the lands of pine and birch and frosty weather. Camping in the Rockies or the North Woods can with advantage be combined with "roughing it"; and the early pioneers of the West, the explorers, prospectors, and hunters, who always roughed it, were as hardy as bears, and lived to a hale old age, if Indians and accidents permitted. But in tropic Africa a lamentable proportion of the early explorers paid in health or life for the hardships they endured; and throughout most of the country no man can long rough it, in the Western and Northern sense, with impunity.

At Kapiti Plains our tents, our accommodations generally, seemed almost too comfortable for men who knew camp life only on the Great Plains, in the Rockies, and in the North Woods. My tent had a fly which was to protect it from the great heat; there was a little rear extension in which I bathed—a hot bath, never a cold bath, is almost a tropic necessity; there was a ground canvas, of vital moment in a land of ticks, jiggers, and scorpions; and a cot to sleep on, so as to be raised from the ground. Quite a contrast to life on the round-up! Then I had two tent boys to see after my belongings, and to wait at table as well as in the tent. Ali, a Mohammedan mulatto (Arab and negro), was the chief of the two, and spoke some English, while under him was "Bill," a speechless black boy; Ali being particularly faithful and efficient. Two other Mohammedan negroes, clad like the askaris, reported to me as my gun-bearers, Muhamed and Bakari; seemingly excellent men, loyal and enduring, no trackers, but with keen eyes for game, and the former speaking a little English. My two horse boys, or saises, were both pagans. One, Hamisi, must have had in his veins Galla or other non-negro blood; derived from the Hamitic, or bastard Semitic, or at least non-negro, tribes which, pushing slowly and fitfully southward and southwestward among the negro peoples, have created an intricate tangle of ethnic and linguistic types from the middle Nile to far south of the equator. Hamisi always wore a long feather

281

in one of his sandals, the only ornament he affected. The other sais was a silent, gentle-mannered black heathen; his name was Simba, a lion, and as I shall later show he was not unworthy of it. The two horses for which these men cared were stout, quiet little beasts; one, a sorrel, I named Tranquillity, and the other, a brown, had so much the coblike build of a zebra that we christened him Zebra-shape. One of Kermit's two horses, by the way, was more roman-tically named after Huandaw, the sharp-eared steed of the Mabinogion. Cuninghame, lean, sinewy, bearded, exactly the type of hunter and safari manager that one would wish for such an expe-dition as ours, had ridden up with us on the train, and at the station we met Tarlton, and also two settlers of the neighborhood, Sir Al-fred Pease and Mr. Clifford Hill. Hill was an Africander. He and his cousin, Harold Hill, after serving through the South African war, had come to the new country of British East Africa to settle, and they represented the ideal type of settler for taking the lead in the spread of empire. They were descended from the English colonists who came to South Africa in 1820; they had never been in Eng-land, and neither had Tarlton. It was exceedingly interesting to meet these Australians and Africanders, who typified in their lives and deeds the greatness of the English Empire, and yet had never seen England.

As for Sir Alfred, Kermit and I were to be his guests for the next fortnight, and we owe primarily to him, to his mastery of hunt-ing craft, and his unvarying and generous hospitality and kindness, the pleasure and success of our introduction to African hunting. His life had been one of such varied interest as has only been pos-sible in our own generation. He had served many years in Parlia-ment; he had for some years been a magistrate in a peculiarly responsible post in the Transvaal; he had journeyed and hunted and explored in the northern Sahara, in the Soudan, in Somaliland, in Abyssinia; and now he was ranching in East Africa. A singularly good rider and one of the best game shots I have ever seen, it would have been impossible to find a kinder host or a hunter better fitted to teach us how to begin our work with African big game.

At Kapiti Station there was little beyond the station buildings, a "compound" or square enclosure in which there were many natives, and an Indian store. The last was presided over by a turbaned Mussulman, the agent of other Indian traders who did business in Machakos-boma, a native village a dozen miles distant; the means of communication being two-wheeled carts, each drawn by four humped oxen, driven by a well-nigh naked savage.

For forty-eight hours we were busy arranging our outfit; and the naturalists took much longer. The provisions were those usually included in an African hunting or exploring trip, save that, in memory of my days in the West, I included in each provision box a few cans of Boston baked beans, California peaches, and tomatoes. We had plenty of warm bedding, for the nights are cold at high altitudes, even under the equator. While hunting I wore heavy shoes, with hobnails or rubber soles; khaki trousers, the knees faced with leather, and the legs buttoning tight from the knee to below the ankle, to avoid the need of leggings; a khaki-colored army shirt; and a sun helmet, which I wore in deference to local advice, instead of my beloved and far more convenient slouch hat. My rifles were an army Springfield, 30-calibre, stocked and sighted to suit myself; a Winchester 405; and a double-barrelled 500–450 Holland, a beautiful weapon presented to me by some English friends.[2]

Kermit's battery was of the same type, except that instead of a Springfield he had another Winchester shooting the army ammunition, and his double-barrel was a Rigby. In addition I had a Fox No. 12 shot-gun; no better gun was ever made.

There was one other bit of impedimenta, less usual for African travel, but perhaps almost as essential for real enjoyment even on a

---

[2]Mr. E. N. Buxton took the lead in the matter when he heard that I intended making a trip after big game in Africa.

hunting trip, if it is to be of any length. This was the "Pigskin Library," so called because most of the books were bound in pigskin. They were carried in a light aluminum and oil-cloth case, which, with its contents, weighted a little less than sixty pounds, making a load for one porter. Including a few volumes carried in the various bags, so that I might be sure always to have one with me, and Gregorovius, read on the voyage outward, the list was as printed in Appendix F. [Editor's Note: The Appendix is not included in this volume.]

It represents in part Kermit's taste, in part mine; and, I need hardly say, it also represents in no way all the books we most care for, but merely those which, for one reason or another, we thought we should like to take on this particular trip.

I used my Whitman tree army saddle and my army field-glasses; but, in addition, for studying the habits of the game, I carried a telescope given me on the boat by a fellow traveller and big-game hunter, an Irish hussar captain from India—and incidentally I am out in my guess if this same Irish hussar captain be not worth watching should his country ever again be engaged in war. I had a very ingenious beam or scale for weighing game, designed and presented to me by my friend, Mr. Thompson Seton. I had a slicker for wet weather, an army overcoat, and a mackinaw jacket for cold, if I had to stay out over night in the mountains. In my pockets I carried, of course, a knife, a compass, and a water-proof matchbox. Finally, just before leaving home, I had been sent, for good luck, a gold-mounted rabbit's foot, by Mr. John L. Sullivan, at one time ring champion of the world.

Our camp was on a bare, dry plain, covered with brown and withered grass. At most hours of the day we could see round about, perhaps a mile or so distant, or less, the game feeding. South of the track the reserve stretched for a long distance; north it went for but a mile, just enough to prevent thoughtless or cruel people from shooting as they went by in the train. There was very little water; what we drank, by the way, was carefully boiled. The drawback to the camp, and to all this plains regions, lay in the ticks, which swarmed, and were a scourge to man and beast. Every evening the saises picked them by hundreds off each horse; and some of our party were at times so bitten by the noisome little creatures that they could hardly sleep at night, and in one or two cases the man was actually laid up for a couple of days; and two of our horses ultimately got tick fever, but recovered.

In mid-afternoon of our third day in this camp we at last had matters in such shape that Kermit and I could begin our hunting; and forth we rode, he with Hill, I with Sir Alfred, each accompanied by his gun-bearers and sais, and by a few porters to carry in the game. For two or three miles our little horses shuffled steadily northward across the desolate flats of short grass until the ground began to rise here and there into low hills, or koppies, with rock-strewn tops. It should have been the rainy season, the season of "the big rains"; but the rains were late, as the parched desolation of the landscape bore witness; nevertheless there were two or three showers that afternoon. We soon began to see game, but the flatness of the country and the absence of all cover made stalking a matter of difficulty; the only bushes were a few sparsely scattered mimosas; stunted things, two or three feet high, scantily leaved, but abounding in bulbous swellings on the twigs, and in long, sharp spikes of thorns. There were herds of hartebeest and wildebeest, and smaller parties of beautiful gazelles. The last were of two kinds, named severally after their discoverers, the explorers Grant and Thomson; many of the creatures of this region commemorate the men—Schilling, Jackson, Neuman, Kirke, Chanler, Abbot—who first saw and hunted them and brought them to the notice of the scientific world. The Thomson's gazelles, or Tommies as they are always locally called, are pretty, alert little things, half the size of our prongbuck; their big brothers, the Grant's, are among the most beautiful of all antelopes, being rather larger than a whitetail deer, with singularly graceful carriage, while the old bucks carry long lyre-shaped horns.

Distances are deceptive on the bare plains under the African sunlight. I saw a fine Grant, and stalked him in a rain squall; but the bullets from the little Springfield fell short as he raced away to safety; I had underestimated the range. Then I shot, for the table, a good buck of the smaller gazelle, at two hundred and twenty-five yards; the bullet went a little high, breaking his back above the shoulders.

But what I really wanted were two good specimens, bull and cow, of the wildebeest. These powerful, ungainly beasts, a variety of the brindled gnu or blue wildebeest of South Africa, are interesting creatures of queer, eccentric habits. With their shaggy manes, heavy forequarters and generally bovine look, they remind one somewhat of our bison, at a distance, but of course they are much less bulky, a big old bull in prime condition rarely reaching a weight of seven hundred pounds. They are beasts of the open plains, ever alert and wary; the cows, with their calves, and one or more herd bulls, keep in parties of several score; the old bulls, single, or two or three together, keep by themselves, or with herds of zebra, hartebeest, or gazelle; for one of the interesting features of African wild life is the close association and companionship so often seen between totally different species of game. Wildebeest are as savage as they are suspicious; when wounded they do not hesitate to charge a man who comes close, although of course neither they nor any other antelopes can be called dangerous when in a wild state, any more than moose or other deer can be called dangerous; when tame, however, wildebeest are very dangerous indeed, more so than an ordinary domestic bull. The wild, queer-looking creatures prance and rollick and cut strange capers when a herd first makes up its mind to flee from a stranger's approach; and even a solitary bull will sometimes plunge and buck as it starts to gallop off; while a couple of bulls, when the herd is frightened, may relieve their feelings by a moment's furious battle, occasionally dropping to their knees before closing. At this time, the end of April, there were little calves with the herds of cows; but in many places in equatorial Africa the various species of antelope seem to have no settled rutting time or breeding time; at last we saw calves of all ages.

Our hunt after wildebeest this afternoon was successful; but though by veldt law each animal was mine, because I hit it first, yet in reality the credit was communistic, so to speak, and my share was properly less than that of others. I first tried to get up to a solitary old bull, and after a good deal of manoeuvring, and by taking advantage of a second rain squall, I got a standing shot at him at four hundred yards, and hit him, but too far back. Although keeping a good distance away, he tacked and veered so, as he ran, that by much running myself I got various other shots at him, at very long range, but missed them all, and he finally galloped over a distant ridge, his long tail switching, seemingly not much the worse. We followed on horseback; for I hate to let any wounded thing escape to suffer. But meanwhile he had run into view of Kermit; and Kermit—who is of an age and build which better fit him for successful breakneck galloping over unknown country dotted with holes and bits of rotten ground—took up the chase with enthusiasm. Yet it was sunset, after a run of six or eight miles, when he finally ran into and killed the tough old bull, which had turned to bay, snorting and tossing its horns.

Meanwhile I managed to get within three hundred and fifty yards of a herd, and picked out a large cow which was unaccompanied by a calf. Again my bullet went too far back; and I could not hit the animal at that distance as it ran. But after going half a mile it lay down, and would have been secured without difficulty if a wretched dog had not run forward and put it up; my horse was a long way back, but Pease, who had been looking on at a distance, was mounted, and sped after it. By the time I had reached my horse Pease was out of sight; but riding hard for some miles I overtook him, just before the sun went down, standing by the cow which he had ridden down and slain. It was long after nightfall before we reached camp, ready for a hot bath and a good supper. As always thereafter with anything we shot, we used the meat for food and preserved the skins for the national Museum. Both the cow and the bull were fat and in fine condition; but they were covered with ticks, especially wherever the skin was bare. Around the eyes the loathsome creatures swarmed so as to make complete rims, like spectacles; and in the armpits and the groin they were massed so that they looked like barnacles on an old boat. It is astonishing that the game should mind them so little; the wildebeest evidently dreaded far more the biting flies which hung around them; and the maggots of the bot-flies in their nostrils must have been a sore torment. Nature is merciless indeed.

The next day we rode some sixteen miles to the beautiful hills of Kitanga, and for over a fortnight were either Pease's guests at his farm—ranch, as we should call it in the West—or were on safari under his guidance.

Lion Hunting on the Kapiti Plains

The dangerous game of Africa are the lion, buffalo, elephant, rhinoceros, and leopard. The hunter who follows any of these animals always does so at a certain risk to life or limb; a risk which it is his business to minimize by coolness, caution, good judgement, and straight shooting. The leopard is in point of pluck and ferocity more than the equal of the other four; but his small size always renders it likely that he will merely maul, and not kill, a man. My friend, Carl Akeley, of Chicago, actually killed bare-handed a leopard which sprang on him. He had already wounded the beast twice, crippling it in one front and one hind paw; whereupon it charged, followed him as he tried to dodge the charge, and struck him full just as he turned. It bit him in one arm, biting again and again as it worked up the arm from the wrist to the elbow; but Akeley threw it, holding its throat with the other hand, and flinging its body to one side. It luckily fell on its side with its two wounded legs uppermost, so that it could not tear him. He fell forward with it and crushed in its chest with his knees until he distinctly felt one of its ribs crack; this, said Akeley, was the first moment when he felt he

289

might conquer. Redoubling his efforts, with knees and hand, he actually choked and crushed the life out of it, although his arm was badly bitten. A leopard will charge at least as readily as one of the big beasts, and is rather more apt to get his charge home, but the risk is less to life than to limb.

There are other animals often or occasionally dangerous to human life which are, nevertheless, not dangerous to the hunter. Crocodiles are far greater pests, and far more often man-eaters, than lions or leopards; but their shooting is not accompanied by the smallest element of risk. Poisonous snakes are fruitful sources of accident, but they are actuated only by fear, and the anger born of fear. The hippopotamus sometimes destroys boats and kills those in them; but again there is no risk in hunting him. Finally, the hyena, too cowardly ever to be a source of danger to the hunter, is sometimes a dreadful curse to the weak and helpless. The hyena is a beast of unusual strength, and of enormous power in his jaws and teeth, and thrice over would he be dreaded were fang and sinew driven by a heart of the leopard's cruel courage. But though the creature's foul and evil ferocity has no such backing as that yielded by the angry daring of the spotted cat, it is yet fraught with a terror all its own; for on occasion the hyena takes to man-eating after its own fashion. Carrion-feeder though it is, in certain places it will enter native huts and carry away children or even sleeping adults; and where famine or disease has worked havoc among a people, the hideous spotted beasts become bolder and prey on the survivors. For some years past Uganda has been scourged by the sleeping sickness, which has ravaged it as in the Middle Ages the Black Death ravaged Europe. Hundreds of thousands of natives have died. Every effort has been made by the Government officials to cope with the disease; and among other things sleeping-sickness camps have been established, where those stricken by the dread malady can be isolated and cease to be possible sources of infection to their fellows. Recovery among those stricken is so rare as to be almost unknown, but the disease is often slow, and months may elapse during which the diseased man is still able to live his life much as usual. In the big camps of doomed men and women thus established there were, therefore, many persons carrying on their avocations much as in an ordinary native village. But the hyenas speedily found that in many of the huts the inmates were a help-less prey. In 1908 and throughout the early part of 1909 they grew constantly bolder, haunting these sleeping-sickness camps, and each night entering them, bursting into the huts and carrying off and eating the dying people. To guard against them each little group of huts was inclosed by a thick hedge; but after a while the hyenas learned to break through the hedges, and continued their ravages; so that every night armed sentries had to patrol the camps, and every night they could be heard firing at the marauders.

The men thus preyed on were sick to death, and for the most part helpless. But occasionally men in full vigor are attacked. One of Pease's native hunters was seized by a hyena as he slept beside the camp-fire, and part of his face torn off. Selous informed me that a friend of his, Major R. T. Coryndon, then administrator of North-western Rhodesia, was attacked by a hyena but two or three years ago. At the time Major Coryndon was lying, wrapped in a blanket, beside his wagon. A hyena, stealthily approaching through the night, seized him by the hand, and dragged him out of bed; but as he struggled and called out, the beast left him and ran off into the darkness. In spite of his torn hand the major was determined to get his assailant, which he felt sure would soon return. Accordingly, he went back to his bed, drew his cocked rifle beside him, pointing to-ward his feet, and feigned sleep. When all was still once more, a dim form loomed up through the uncertain light, toward the foot of the bed; it was the ravenous beast returning for his prey; and the major shot and killed it where it stood.

A few months ago a hyena entered the outskirts of Nairobi, crept into a hut, and seized and killed a native man. At Nairobi the wild creatures are always at the threshold of the town, and often cross it. At Governor Jackson's table at Government House, I met Mr. and Mrs. Sandiford. Mr. Sandiford is managing the railroad. A few months previously, while he was sitting, with his family, in his own house in Nairobi, he happened to ask his daughter to look for something in one of the bedrooms. She returned in a minute, quietly remarking, "Father, there's a leopard under the bed." So there was; and it was then remembered that the house-cat had been showing a marked and alert distrust of the room in question—very probably the leopard had gotten into the house while trying to catch her or one of the dogs. A neighbor with a rifle was summoned, and shot the leopard.

Hyenas not infrequently kill mules and donkeys, tearing open their bellies, and eating them while they are still alive. Yet when themselves assailed they usually behave with abject cowardice. The Hills had a large Airedale terrier, an energetic dog of much courage. Not long before our visit this dog put up a hyena from a bushy ravine, in broad daylight, ran after it, overtook it, and flew at it. The hyena made no effective fight, although the dog—not a third its weight—bit it severely, and delayed its flight so that it was killed. During the first few weeks of our trip I not infrequently heard hyenas after nightfall, but saw none. Kermit, however, put one out of a ravine or dry creek-bed—a donga, as it is locally called—and though the brute had a long start he galloped after it and succeeded in running it down. The chase was a long one, for twice the hyena got in such rocky country that he almost distanced his pursuer; but at last, after covering nearly ten miles, Kermit ran into it in the open, shooting it from the saddle as it shambled along at a canter growling with rage and terror. I would not have recognized the cry of the hyenas from what I had read, and it was long before I heard them laugh. Pease said that he had only once heard them really laugh. On that occasion he was watching for lions outside a Somali zareba. Suddenly a leopard leaped clear over the zareba, close beside him and in a few seconds came flying back again, over the high thorn fence, with a sheep in its mouth; but no sooner had it landed than the hyenas rushed at it and took away the sheep; and then their cackling and shrieking sounded exactly like the most unpleasant kind of laughter. The normal death of very old lions, as they grow starved and feeble—unless they are previously killed in an encounter with dangerous game like buffalo—is to be killed and eaten by hyenas; but of course a lion in full vigor pays no heed to hyenas, unless it is to kill one if it gets in the way.

During the last few decades, in Africa, hundreds of white hunters, and thousands of native hunters, have been killed or wounded by lions, buffaloes, elephants, and rhinos. All are dangerous game; each species has to its grewsome credit a long list of mighty hunters slain or disabled. Among those competent to express judgment there is the widest difference of opinion as to the comparative danger in hunting the several kinds of animals. Probably no other hunter who has ever lived has combined Selous's experience with his skill as a hunter and his power of accurate observation and narration. He has killed between three and four hundred lions, elephants, buffaloes, and rhinos, and he ranks the lion as much the most dangerous, and the rhino as much the least, while he puts the buffalo and elephant in between, and practically on a par. Governor Jackson has killed between eighty and ninety of the four animals; and he puts the buffalo unquestionably first in point of formidable capacity as a foe, the elephant equally unquestionably second, the lion third, and the rhino last. Stigand puts them in the following order: lion, elephant, rhino, leopard, and buffalo. Drummond, who wrote a capital book on South African game, who was for years a professional hunter like Selous, and who had fine opportunities for observation, but who was a much less accurate observer than Selous, put the rhino as unquestionably the most dangerous, with the lion as second, and the buffalo and elephant nearly on a level. Samuel Baker, a mighty hunter and good observer, but with less experience of African game than any one of the above, put the elephant first, the rhino second, the buffalo

293

seemingly third, and the lion last. The experts of greatest experience thus absolutely disagree among themselves; and there is the same wide divergence of view among good hunters and trained observers whose opportunities have been less. Mr. Abel Chapman, for instance, regards both the elephant and the rhino as more dangerous than the lion; and many of the hunters I met in East Africa seemed inclined to rank the buffalo as more dangerous than any other animal. A man who has shot but a dozen or a score of these various animals, all put together, is not entitled to express any but the most tentative opinion as to their relative prowess and ferocity; yet on the whole it seems to me that the weight of opinion among those best fitted to judge is that the lion is the most formidable opponent of the hunter, under ordinary conditions. This is my own view. But we must ever keep in mind the fact that the surrounding conditions, the geographical locality, and the wide individual variation of temper within the ranks of each species, must all be taken into account. Under certain circumstances a lion may be easily killed, whereas a rhino would be a dangerous foe. Under other conditions the rhino could be attacked with impunity, and the lion only with the utmost hazard; and one bull buffalo might flee and one bull elephant charge, and yet the next couple met with might show an exact reversal of behavior.

At any rate, during the last three or four years, in German and British East Africa and Uganda, over fifty white men have been killed or mauled by lions, buffaloes, elephants, and rhinos; and the lions have much the largest list of victims to their credit. In Nairobi church-yard I was shown the graves of seven men who had been killed by lions, and of one who had been killed by a rhino. The first man to meet us on the African shore was Mr. Campbell, Governor Jackson's A.D.C., and only a year previously he had been badly mauled by a lion. We met one gentleman who had been crippled for life by a lioness. He had marked her into some patches of brush, and coming up, tried to put her out of one thick clump. Failing, he thought she might have gone into another thicket, and walked toward it; instantly that his back was turned, the lioness, who had really been in the first clump of brush, raced out after him, threw him down, and bit him again and again before she was driven off. One night we camped at the very spot where, a score of years before, a strange tragedy had happened. It was in the early days of the opening of the country, and an expedition was going toward Uganda; one of the officials in charge was sleeping in a tent with the flap open. There was an askari on duty; yet a lion crept up, entered the tent, and seized and dragged forth the man. He struggled and made outcry; there was a rush of people, and the lion dropped his prey and bounded off. The man's wounds were dressed, and he was put back to bed in his own tent; but an hour or two after the camp again grew still, the lion returned, bent on the victim of whom he had been robbed; he re-entered the tent, seized the unfortunate wounded man with his great fangs, and this time made off with him into the surrounding darkness, killed and ate him. Not far from the scene of this tragedy, another had occurred. An English officer named Stewart, while endeavoring to kill his first lion, was himself set on and slain. At yet another place we were shown where two settlers, Messrs. Lucas and Goldfinch, had been one killed and one crippled by a lion they had been hunting. They had been following the chase on horseback, and being men of bold nature, and having killed several lions, had become too daring. They hunted the lion into a small piece of brush and rode too near it. It came out at a run and was on them before their horses could get under way. Goldfinch was knocked over and badly bitten and clawed; Lucas went to his assistance, and was in his turn knocked over, and the lion then lay on him and bit him to death. Goldfinch, in spite of his own severe wounds, crawled over and shot the great beast as it lay on his friend.

Most of the settlers with whom I was hunting had met with various adventures in connection with lions. Sir Alfred had shot many in different parts of Africa; some had charged fiercely, but he always stopped them. Captain Slatter had killed a big male with a mane a few months previously. He was hunting it in company with Mr. Humphery, the District commissioner of whom I have already spoken, and it gave them some exciting moments, for when hit it charged savagely. Humphery had a shot-gun loaded with buckshot, Slatter his rifle. When wounded, the lion charged straight home, hit Slatter, knocking him flat and rolling him over and over in the sand, and then went after the native gun-bearer, who was running away—the worst possible course to follow with a charging lion. The mechanism of Slatter's rifle was choked by the sand, and as he rose to his feet he saw the lion overtake the fleeing man, rise on his hind legs like a rearing horse—not springing—and strike down the fugitive. Humphery fired into him with buckshot, which merely went through the skin; and some minutes elapsed before Slatter was able to get his rifle in shape to kill the lion, which, fortunately, had begun to feel the effect of his wounds, and was too sick to resume hostilities of its own accord. The gun-bearer was badly but not fatally injured. Before this, Slatter, while on a lion hunt, had been set afoot by one of the animals he was after, which had killed his horse. It was at night and the horse was tethered within six yards of his sleeping master. The latter was aroused by the horse galloping off, and he heard it staggering on for some sixty yards before it fell. He and his friend followed it with lanterns and drove off the lion, but the horse was dead. The tracks and the marks on the horse showed what had happened. The lion had sprung clean on the horse's back, his fore claws dug into the horse's shoulders, his hind claws cutting into its haunches, while the great fangs bit at the neck. The horse struggled off at a heavy run, carrying its fearsome burden. After going some sixty yards the lion's teeth went through the spinal cord, and the ride was over. Neither animal had made a sound, and the lion's feet did not touch the earth until the horse fell.

While a magistrate in the Transvaal, Pease had under him as game officer a white hunter, a fine fellow, who underwent an extraordinary experience. He had been off some distance with his Kaffir boys, to hunt a lion. On his way home the hunter was hunted. It was after nightfall. He had reached a region where lions had not been seen for a long time, and where an attack by them was unknown. He was riding along a trail in the darkness, his big boarhound trotting ahead, his native "boys" some distance behind. He heard a rustle in the bushes alongside the path, but paid no heed, thinking it was a reedbuck. Immediately afterward two lions came out in the path behind and raced after him. One sprang on him, tore him out of the saddle, and trotted off holding him in its mouth, while the other continued after the frightened horse. The lion had him by the right shoulder, and yet with his left hand he wrenched his knife out of his belt and twice stabbed it. The second stab went to the heart and the beast let go of him, stood a moment, and fell dead. Meanwhile, the dog had followed the other lion, which now, having abandoned the chase of the horse, and with the dog still at his heels, came trotting back to look for the man. Crippled though he was, the hunter managed to climb a small tree; and though the lion might have gotten him out of it, the dog interfered. Whenever the lion came toward the tree the dog worried him, and kept him off until, at the shouts and torches of the approaching Kaffir boys, he sullenly retired, and the hunter was rescued.

Percival had a narrow escape from a lion, which nearly got him, though probably under a misunderstanding. He was riding through a wet spot of ground, where the grass was four feet high, when his horse suddenly burst into a run and the next moment a lion had galloped almost alongside of him. Probably the lion thought it was a zebra, for when Percival, leaning over, yelled in his face, the lion stopped short. But he at once came on again, and nearly caught the horse. However, they were now out of the tall grass, and the lion gradually drew up when they reached the open country.

The two Hills, Clifford and Harold, were running an ostrich-farm. The lions sometimes killed their ostriches and stock; and the Hills in return had killed several lions. The Hills were fine fellows; Africanders, as their forefathers for three generations had been, and frontiersmen of the best kind. From the first moment they and I became fast friends, for we instinctively understood one another, and found that we felt alike on all the big questions, and looked at life, and especially the life of effort led by the pioneer settler, from the same stand-point. They reminded me, at every moment, of those Western ranchmen and homemakers with whom I have always felt a special sense of companionship and with whose ideas and aspirations I have always felt a special sympathy. A couple of months before my visit, Harold Hill had met with a rather unpleasant adventure. He was walking home across the lonely plains, in the broad daylight, never dreaming that lions might be abroad, and was unarmed. When still some miles from his house, while plodding along, he glanced up and saw three lions in the trail only fifty yards off, staring fixedly at him. It happened to be a place where the grass was rather tall, and lions are always bold where there is the slightest cover; whereas, unless angered, they are cautious on bare ground. He halted, and then walked slowly to one side; and then slowly forward toward his house. The lions followed him with their eyes, and when he had passed they rose and slouched after him. They were not pleasant followers, but to hurry would have been fatal; and he walked slowly on along the road, while for a mile he kept catching glimpses of the tawny bodies of the beasts as they trod stealthily forward through the sunburned grass, alongside or a little behind him. Then the grass grew short, and the lions halted and continued to gaze after him until he disappeared over a rise.

Everywhere throughout the country we were crossing were signs that the lion was lord and that his reign was cruel. There were many lions, for the game on which they feed was extraordinarily abundant. They occasionally took the ostriches or stock of the settlers, ravaged the herds and flocks of the natives, but not often; for their favorite food was yielded by the swarming herds of kongoni and zebras, on which they could prey at will. Later we found that in this region they rarely molested the buffalo, even where they lived in the same reed-beds; and this though elsewhere they habitually prey on the buffalo. But where zebras and hartebeests could be obtained without effort, it was evidently not worth their while to challenge such formidable quarry. Every "kill" I saw was a kongoni or a zebra; probably I came across fifty of each. One zebra kill, which was not more than eighteen hours old (after the lapse of that time the vultures and marabouts, not to speak of the hyenas and jackals, leave only the bare bones), showed just what had occurred. The bones were all in place, and the skin still on the lower legs and head. The animal was lying on its belly, the legs spread out, the neck vertebra crushed; evidently the lion had sprung clean on it, bearing it down by his weight while he bit through the back of the neck, and the zebra's legs had spread out as the body yielded under the lion. One fresh kongoni kill showed no marks on the haunches, but a broken neck and claw marks on the face and withers; in this case the lion's hind legs had remained on the ground, while with his fore paws he grasped the kongoni's head and shoulders, holding it until the teeth splintered the neck bone.

One or two of our efforts to get lions failed, or course; the ravines we beat did not contain them, or we failed to make them leave some particularly difficult hill or swamp—for lions lie close. But Sir Alfred knew just the right place to go to, and was bound to get us lions—and he did.

One day we started from the ranch house in good season for an all-day hunt. Besides Kermit and myself, there was a fellow guest, Medlicott, and not only our host, but our hostess and her daughter; and we were joined by Percival at lunch, which we took under a great fig-tree, at the foot of a high, rocky hill. Percival had with him a little mongrel bull-dog, and a Masai "boy," a fine, bold-looking savage, with a handsome head-dress and the usual formidable spear; master, man, and dog evidently all looked upon any form of encounter with lions simply in the light of a spree.

After lunch we began to beat down a long donga, or dry watercourse—a creek, as we should call it in the Western plains country. The watercourse, with low, steep banks, wound in curves, and here and there were patches of brush, which might contain anything in the shape of lion, cheetah, hyena, or wild dog. Soon we came upon lion spoor in the sandy bed; first the footprints of a big male, then those of a lioness. We walked cautiously along each side of the donga, the horses following close behind so that if the lion were missed we could gallop after him and round him up on the plain. The dogs—for besides the little bull, we had a large brindled mongrel named Ben, whose courage belied his looks—began to show signs of scenting the lion; and we beat out each patch of brush, the natives shouting and throwing in stones, while we stood with the rifles where we could best command any probable exit. After a couple of false alarms the dogs drew toward one patch, their hair bristling, and showing such eager excitement that it was evident something big was inside; and in a moment one of the boys called, "simba" (lion), and pointed with his finger. It was just across the little ravine, there about four yards wide and as many feet deep; and I shifted my position, peering eagerly into the bushes for some moments before I caught a glimpse of tawny hide; as it moved, there was a call to me to "shoot," for at that distance, if the lion charged, there would be scant time to stop it; and I fired into what I saw. There was a commotion in the bushes, and Kermit fired; and immediately afterward there broke out on the other side, not the hoped-for big lion, but two cubs the size of mastiffs. Each was badly wounded and we finished them off; even if unwounded they were too big to take alive.

This was a great disappointment, and as it was well on in the afternoon, and we had beaten the country most apt to harbor our game, it seemed unlikely that we would have another chance. Percival was on foot and a long way from his house, so he started for it; and the rest of us also began to jog homeward. But Sir Alfred, though he said nothing, intended to have another try. After going a mile or two he started off to the left at a brisk canter; and we, the other riders, followed, leaving behind our gun-bearers, saises, and porters. A couple of miles away was another donga, another shallow watercourse with occasional big brush patches along the winding bed; and toward this we cantered. Almost as soon as we reached it our leader found the spoor of two big lions, and with every sense acock, we dismounted and approached the first patch of tall bushes. We shouted and threw in stones, but nothing came out; and another small patch showed the same result. Then we mounted our horses again, and rode toward another patch a quarter of a mile off. I was mounted on Tranquillity, the stout and quiet sorrel.

This patch of tall, thick brush stood on the hither bank—that is, on our side of the watercourse. We rode up to it and shouted loudly. The response was immediate, in the shape of loud gruntings, and crashings through the thick brush. We were off our horses in an instant, I throwing the reins over the head of mine; and without delay the good old fellow began placidly grazing, quite unmoved by the ominous sounds immediately in front.

I sprang to one side; and for a second or two we waited, uncertain whether we should see the lions charging out ten yards distant or running away. Fortunately, they adopted the latter course. Right in front of me, thirty yards off, there appeared, from behind the bushes which had first screened him from my eyes, the tawny, galloping form of a big maneless lion. Crack! the Winchester spoke; and as the soft-nosed bullet ploughed forward through his flank the lion swerved so that I missed him with the second shot; but my third bullet went through the spine and forward into his chest. Down he came, sixty yards off, his hind quarters dragging, his head up, his ears back, his jaws open and lips drawn up in a prodigious snarl, as he endeavored to turn to face us. His back was broken; but of this we could not at the moment be sure, and it if had merely been grazed, he might have recovered, and then, even though dying, his charge might have done mischief. So Kermit, Sir Alfred, and I fired, almost together, into his chest. His head sank, and he died.

This lion had come out on the left of the bushes; the other, to the right of them, had not been hit, and we saw him galloping off across the plain, six or eight hundred yards away. A couple more shots missed, and we mounted our horses to try to ride him down. The plain sloped gently upward for three-quarters of a mile to a low crest or divide, and long before we got near him he disappeared over this. Sir Alfred and Kermit were tearing along in front and to the right, with Miss Pease close behind; while Tranquillity carried me, as fast as he could, on the left, with Medlicott near me. On topping the divide Sir Alfred and Kermit missed the lion, which had swung to the left, and they raced ahead too far to the right. Medlicott and I, however, saw the lion, loping along close behind some kongoni; and this enabled me to get up to him as quickly as the lighter men on the faster horses. The going was now slightly downhill, and the sorrel took me along very well, while Medlicott, whose horse was slow, bore to the right and joined the other two men. We gained rapidly, and, finding out this, the lion suddenly halted and came to bay in a slight hollow, where the grass was rather long. The plain seemed flat, and we could see the lion well from horseback; but, especially when he lay down, it was most difficult to make him out on foot, and impossible to do so when kneeling.

We were about a hundred and fifty yards from the lion, Sir Alfred, Kermit, Medlicott and Miss Pease off to one side, and slightly above him on the slope, while I was on the level, about equidistant from him and them. Kermit and I tried shooting from the horses; but at such a distance this was not effective. Then Kermit got off, but his horse would not let him shoot; and when I got off I could not make out the animal through the grass with sufficient distinctness to enable me to take aim. Old Ben the dog had arrived, and, barking loudly, was strolling about near the lion, which paid him not the slightest attention. At this moment my black sais, Simba, came running up to me and took hold of the bridle; he had seen the chase from the line of march and had cut across to join me. There was no other sais or gun-bearer anywhere near, and his action was plucky, for he was the only man afoot, with the lion at bay. Lady Pease had also ridden up and was an interested spectator only some fifty yards behind me.

Now, an elderly man with a varied past which includes rheumatism does not vault lightly into the saddle; as his sons, for instance, can; and I had already made up my mind that in the event of the lion's charging it would be wise for me to trust to straight powder rather than to try to scramble into the saddle and get under way in time. The arrival of my two companions settled matters. I was not sure of the speed of Lady Pease's horse; and Simba was on foot and it was of course out of the question for me to leave him. So I said, "Good, Simba, now we'll see this thing through," and gentle-mannered Simba smiled a shy appreciation of my tone, though he could not understand the words. I was still unable to see the lion when I knelt, but he was now standing up, looking first at one group of horses and then at the other, his tail lashing to and fro, his head held low, and his lips dropped over his mouth in peculiar fashion, while his harsh and savage growling rolled thunderously over the plain. Seeing Simba and me on foot, he turned toward us, his tail lashing quicker and quicker. Resting my elbow on Simba's bent shoulder, I took steady aim and pressed the trigger; the bullet went in between the neck and shoulder, and the lion fell over on his side, one foreleg in the air. He recovered in a moment and stood up, evidently very sick, and once more faced me, growling hoarsely. I think he was on the eve of charging. I fired again at once, and this bullet broke his back just behind the shoulders; and with the next I killed him outright, after we had gathered round him.

These were two good-sized maneless lions; and very proud of them I was. I think Sir Alfred was at least as proud, especially because we had performed the feat alone, without any professional hunters being present. "We were all amateurs, only gentlemen riders up," said Sir Alfred. It was late before we got the lions skinned. Then we set off toward the ranch, two porters carrying each lion skin, strapped to a pole; and two others carrying the cub skins. Night fell long before we were near the ranch; but the brilliant tropic moon lighted the trail. The stalwart savages who carried the bloody lion skins swung along at a faster walk as the sun went down and the moon rose higher; and they began to chant in unison, one uttering a single word or sentence, and the others joining in a deep-toned musical chorus. The men on a safari, and indeed African natives generally, are always excited over the death of a lion, and the hunting tribes then chant their rough hunting songs, or victory songs, until the monotonous, rhythmical repetitions make them grow almost frenzied. The ride home through the moonlight, the vast barren landscape shining like silver on either hand, was one to be remembered; and above all, the sight of our trophies and of their wild bearers.

Three days later we had another successful lion hunt. Our camp was pitched at a waterhole in a little stream called Potha, by a hill of the same name. Pease, Medlicott, and both the Hills were with us, and Heller came too; for he liked when possible to be with the hunters so that he could at once care for any beast that was shot. As the safari was stationary, we took fifty or sixty porters as beaters. It was thirteen hours before we got into camp that evening. The Hills had with them as beaters and water-carriers half a dozen of the Wakamba who were working on their farm. It was interesting to watch these naked savages, with their filed teeth, their heads shaved in curious patterns, and carrying for arms little bows and arrows.

Before lunch we beat a long, low hill. Harold Hill was with me; Medlicott and Kermit were together. We placed ourselves, one couple on each side of a narrow neck, two-thirds of the way along the crest of the hill; and soon after we were in position we heard the distant shouts of the beaters as they came toward us, covering the crest and the tops of the slopes on both sides. It was rather disconcerting to find how much better Hill's eyes were than mine. He saw everything first, and it usually took some time before he could make me see it. In this first drive nothing came my way except some mountain reedbuck does, at which I did not shoot. But a fine male cheetah came to Kermit, and he bowled it over in good style as it ran.

Then the beaters halted, and waited before resuming their march until the guns had gone clear round and established themselves at the base of the farther end of the hill. This time Kermit, who was a couple of hundred yards from me, killed a reedbuck and a steinbuck. Suddenly Hill said "Lion," and endeavored to point it out to me, as it crept cautiously among the rocks on the steep hillside, a hundred and fifty yards away. At first I could not see it; finally I thought I did and fired, but, as it proved, at a place just above him. However, it made him start up, and I immediately put the next bullet behind his shoulders; it was a fatal shot; but growling, he struggled down the hill, and I fired again and killed him. It was not much of a trophy, however, turning out to be a half-grown male.

We lunched under a tree, and then arranged for another beat. There was a long, wide valley, or rather a slight depression in the ground—for it was only three or four feet below the general level—in which the grass grew tall, as the soil was quite wet. It was the scene of Percival's adventure with the lion that chased him. Hill and I stationed ourselves on one side of this valley or depression, toward the upper end; Pease took Kermit to the opposite side; and we waited, our horses some distance behind us. The beaters were put in at the lower end, formed a line across the valley, and beat slowly toward us, making a great noise.

They were still some distance away when Hill saw three lions, which had slunk stealthily off ahead of them thorough the grass. I have called the grass tall, but this was only by comparison with the short grass of the dry plains. In the depression or valley it was some three feet high. In such grass, a lion, which is marvellously adept at hiding, can easily conceal itself, not merely when lying down, but when advancing at a crouching gait. It if stands erect, however, it can be seen.

There were two lions near us, one directly in our front, a hundred and ten yards off. Some seconds passed before Hill could make me realize that the dim yellow smear in the yellow-brown grass was a lion; and then I found such difficulty in getting a bead on him that I overshot. However, the bullet must have passed very close—indeed, I think it just grazed him—for he jumped up and faced us, growling savagely. Then, his head lowered, he threw his tail straight into the air and began to charge. The first few steps he took at a trot, and before he could start into a gallop I put the soft-nosed Winchester bullet in between the neck and shoulder. Down he went with a roar; the wound was fatal, but I was taking no chances, and I put two more bullets in him. Then we walked toward where Hill had already seen another lion—the lioness, as it proved. Again he had some difficulty in making me see her; but he succeeded and I walked toward her through the long grass, repressing the zeal of my two gun-bearers, who were stanch, but who showed a tendency to walk a little ahead of me on each side, instead of a little behind. I walked toward her because I could not kneel to shoot in grass so tall; and when shooting off-hand I like to be fairly close, so as to be sure that my bullets go in the right place. At sixty yards I could make her out clearly, snarling at me as she faced me; and I shot her full in the chest. She at once performed a series of extraordinary antics, tumbling about on her head, just as if she were throwing somersaults, first to one side and then to the other. I fired again, but managed to shoot between the somersaults, so to speak, and missed her. The shot seemed to bring her to herself, and away she tore; but instead of charging us she charged the line of beaters. She was dying fast, however, and in her weakness failed to catch any one; and she sank down into the long grass. Hill and I advanced to look her up, our rifles at full cock, and the gun-bearers close behind. It is ticklish work to follow a wounded lion in tall grass, and we walked carefully, every sense on the alert. We passed Heller, who had been with the beaters. He spoke to us with an amused smile. His only weapon was a pair of field-glasses, but he always took things as they came, with entire coolness, and to be close to a wounded lioness when she charged merely interested him. A beater came running up and pointed toward where he had seen her, and we walked toward the place. At thirty yards' distance Hill pointed and, eagerly peering, I made out the form of the lioness showing indistinctly through the grass. She was half crouching, half sitting, her head bent down; but she still had strength to do mischief. She saw us, but before she could turn I sent a bullet through her shoulders; down she went, and was dead when we walked up. A cub had been seen, and another full-grown lion, but they had slunk off and we got neither.

This was a full-grown, but young, lioness of average size; her cubs must have been several months old. We took her to camp to weigh; she weighed two hundred and eighty-three pounds. The first lion, which we had difficulty in finding, as there were no identifying marks in the plain of tall grass, was a good-sized male, weighing about four hundred pounds, but not yet full grown; although he was probably the father of the cubs.

We were a long way from camp, and, after beating in vain for the other lion, we started back; it was after nightfall before we saw the camp-fires. It was two hours later before the porters appeared, bearing on poles the skin of the dead lion, and the lioness entire. The moon was nearly full, and it was interesting to see them come swinging down the trail in the bright silver light, chanting in deep tones, over and over again, a line or phrase that sounded like:

"Zou-zou-boulé ma ja guntai; zou-zou-boulé ma ja guntai."

Occasionally they would interrupt it by the repetition in unison, at short intervals, of a guttural ejaculation, sounding like "huzlem." They marched into camp, then up and down the lines, before the rows of small fires; then, accompanied by all the rest of the porters, they paraded up to the big fire where I was standing. Here they stopped and ended the ceremony by a minute or two's vigorous dancing amid singing and wild shouting. The firelight gleamed and flickered across the grim dead beasts, and the shining eyes and black features of the excited savages, while all around the moon flooded the landscape with her white light.

On Safari: Rhino and Giraffe

When we killed the last lions we were already on safari, and the camp was pitched by a waterhole on the Potha, a half-dried stream, little more than a string of pools and reed-beds, winding down through the sun-scorched plain. Next morning we started for another waterhole at the rocky hill of Bondoni, about eight miles distant.

Safari life is very pleasant, and also very picturesque. The porters are strong, patient, good-humored savages, with something childlike about them that makes one really fond of them. Of course, like all savages and most children, they have their limitations, and in dealing with them firmness is even more necessary than kindness; but the man is a poor creature who does not treat them with kindness also, and I am rather sorry for him if he does not grow to feel for them, and to make them in return feel for him, a real and friendly liking. They are subject to gusts of passion, and they are now and then guilty of grave misdeeds and short-comings; sometimes for no conceivable reason, at least from the white man's stand-point. But they are generally cheerful, and when cheerful are always amusing; and they work hard, if the white man is able to combine tact and consideration with that insistence on the performance of duty the lack of which they despise as weakness. Any little change or excitement is a source of pleasure to them. When the march is over they sing; and after two or three days in camp they will not only sing, but dance when another march is to begin. Of course at times they suffer greatly from thirst and hunger and fatigue, and at times they will suddenly grow sullen or rebel without what seems to us any adequate cause; and they have an inconsequent type of mind which now and then leads them to commit follies all the more exasperating because they are against their own interest no less than against the interest of their employer. But they do well on the whole, and safari life is attractive to them. They are fed well; the government requires that they be fitted with suitable clothes and given small tents, so that they are better clad and sheltered than they would be otherwise; and their wages represent money which they could get in no other way. The safari represents a great advantage to the porter; who in his turn alone makes the safari possible.

When we were to march, camp was broken as early in the day as possible. Each man had his allotted task, and the tents, bedding, provisions, and all else were expeditiously made into suitable packages. Each porter is supposed to carry from fifty-five to sixty pounds, which may all be in one bundle or in two or three. The American flag, which flew over my tent, was a matter of much pride to the porters, and was always carried at the head or near the head of the line of march; and after it in single file came the long line of burden bearers. As they started, some of them would blow on horns or whistles and others beat little tomtoms; and at intervals this would be renewed again and again throughout the march; or the men might suddenly began to chant, or merely to keep repeating in unison some one word or one phrase which, when we asked to have it translated, might or might not prove to be entirely meaningless. The headmen carried no burdens, and the tent boys hardly anything, while the saises walked with the spare horses. In addition to the canonical and required costume of blouse or jersey and drawers, each porter wore a blanket, and usually something else to which his soul inclined. It might be an exceedingly shabby coat; it might be, of all things in the world; an umbrella, an article for which they had a special attachment. Often I would see a porter, who thought nothing whatever of walking for hours at midday under the equatorial sun with his head bare, trudging along with solemn pride either under an open umbrella, or carrying the umbrella (tied much like Mrs. Gamp's) in one hand, as a wand of dignity. Then their head-gear varied according to the fancy of the individual. Normally it was a red fez, a kind of cap only used in hot climates, and exquisitely designed to be useless therein because it gives absolutely no protection from the sun. But one would wear a skin cap; another would suddenly put one or more long feathers in his fez; and another, discarding the fez, would revert to some purely savage head-dress which he would wear with equal gravity whether it were, in our eyes, really decorative or merely comic. One such head-dress, for instance, consisted of the skin of the top of a zebra's head, with the two ears. Another was made of the skins of squirrels, with the tails both sticking up and hanging down. Another consisted of a bunch of feathers woven in the hair, which itself was pulled out into strings that were stiffened with clay. Another was really too intricate for description because it included the man's natural hair, some strips of skin, and an empty tin can.

If it were a long journey and we broke it by a noonday halt, or if it were a short journey and we reached camp ahead of the safari, it was interesting to see the long file of men approach. Here and there, leading the porters, scattered through the line, or walking alongside, were the askaris, the rifle-bearing soldiers. They were not marksmen, to put it mildly, and I should not have regarded them as particularly efficient allies in a serious fight; but they were excellent for police duty in camp, and were also of use in preventing collisions with the natives. After the leading askaris might come one of the headmen; one of whom, by the way, looked exactly like a Semitic negro, and always travelled with a large dirty-white umbrella in one hand; while another, a tall, powerful fellow, was a mission boy who spoke good English; I mention his being a mission boy because it is so frequently asserted that mission boys never turn out well. Then would come the man with the flag, followed by another blowing on an antelope horn, or perhaps beating an empty can as a drum; and then the long line of men, some carrying their loads on their heads, others on their shoulders, others, in a very few cases, on their backs. As they approached the halting place their spirits rose, the whistles and horns were blown, and the improvised drums beaten, and perhaps the whole line would burst into a chant.

On reaching the camping ground each man at once set about his allotted task, and the tents were quickly pitched and the camp put in order, while water and firewood were fetched. The tents were pitched in long lines, in the first of which stood my tent, flanked by those of the other white men and by the dining tent. In the next line were the cook tent, the provision tent, the store tent, the skinning tent, and the like; and then came the lines of small white tents for the porters. Between each row of tents was a broad street. In front of our own tents in the first line an askari was always pacing to and fro; and when night fell we would kindle a campfire and sit around it under the stars. Before each of the porters' tents was a little fire, and beside it stood the pots and pans in which the porters did their cooking. Here and there were larger fires, around which the gun-bearers or a group of askaris or of saises might gather. After nightfall the multitude of fires lit up the darkness and showed the tents in shadowy outline; and around them squatted the porters, their faces flickering from dusk to ruddy light, as they chatted together or suddenly started some snatch of wild African melody in which all their neighbors might join. After a while the talk and laughter and singing would gradually die away, and as we white men sat around our fire, the silence would be unbroken except by the queer cry of a hyena, or much more rarely by a sound that always demanded attention—the yawning grunt of a questing lion.

If we wished to make an early start we would breakfast by dawn and then we often returned to camp for lunch. Otherwise we would usually be absent all day, carrying our lunch with us. We might get in before sunset or we might be out till long after nightfall; and then the gleam of the lit fires was a welcome sight as we stumbled toward them through the darkness. Once in, each went to his tent to take a hot bath; and then, clean and refreshed, we sat down to a comfortable dinner, with game of some sort as the principal dish.

On the first march after leaving our lion camp at Potha I shot a wart-hog. It was a good-sized sow, which, in company with several of her half-grown offspring, was grazing near our line of march; there were some thorn-trees which gave a little cover, and I killed her at a hundred and eighty yards, using the Springfield, the lightest and handiest of all my rifles. Her flesh was good to eat, and the skin, as with all our specimens, was saved for the National Museum. I did not again have to shoot a sow, although I killed half-grown pigs for the table, and boars for specimens. This sow and her porkers were not rooting, but were grazing as if they had been antelope; her stomach contained nothing but chopped green grass. Wart-hogs are common throughout the country over which we hunted. They are hideous beasts, with strange protuberances on their cheeks; and when alarmed they trot or gallop away, holding the tail perfectly erect with the tassel bent forward. Usually they are seen in family parties, but a big boar will often be alone. They often root up the ground, but the stomachs of those we shot were commonly filled with nothing but grass. If the weather is cloudy or wet they may be out all day long, but in hot, dry weather we generally found them abroad only in the morning and evening. A pig is always a comical animal; even more so than is the case with a bear, which also impresses one with a sense of grotesque humor—and this notwithstanding the fact that both boar and bear may be very formidable creatures. A wart-hog standing alertly at gaze, head and tail up, legs straddled out, and ears cocked forward, is rather a figure of fun; and not the less so when with characteristic suddenness he bounces round with a grunt and scuttles madly off to safety. Wart-hogs are beasts of the bare plain or open forest, and though they will often lie up in patches of brush they do not care for thick timber.

After shooting the wart-hog we marched on to our camp at Bondoni, the gun-bearers were Mohammedans, and the dead pig was of no service to them; and at their request I walked out while camp was being pitched and shot them a buck; this I had to do now and then, but I always shot males, so as not the damage the species.

Next day we marched to the foot of Kilimakiu Mountain, near Captain Slatter's ostrich-farm. Our route lay across bare plains thickly covered with withered short grass. All around us as we marched were the game herds, zebras and hartebeests, gazelles of the two kinds, and now and then wildebeests. Hither and thither over the plain, crossing and recrossing, ran the dusty game trails, each with its myriad hoof-marks; the round hoof-prints of the zebra, the heart-shaped marks that showed where the hartebeest herd had trod, and the delicate etching that betrayed where the smaller antelope had passed. Occasionally we crossed the trails of the natives, worn deep in the hard soil by the countless thousands of bare or sandalled feet that had trodden them. Africa is a country of trails. Across the high veldt, in every direction, run the tangled trails of the multitudes of game that have lived thereon from time immemorial. The great beasts of the marsh and the forest made therein broad and muddy trails which often offer the only pathway by which a man can enter the sombre depths. In wet ground and dry alike are also found the trails of savage man. They lead from village to village, and in places they stretch for hundreds of miles, where trading parties have worn them in the search for ivory, or in the old days when raiding or purchasing slaves. The trails made by the men are made much as the beasts make theirs. They are generally longer and better defined, although I have seen hippo tracks more deeply marked than any made by savage man. But they are made simply by men following in one another's footsteps, and they are never quite straight. They bend now a little to one side, now a little to the other, and sudden loops mark the spot where some vanished obstacle once stood; around it the first trail makers went, and their successors have ever trodden in their footsteps, even though the need for so doing has long passed away.

Our camp at Kilimakiu was by a grove of shady trees, and from it at sunset we looked across the vast plain and saw the far-off mountains grow umber and purple as the light waned. Back of the camp, and of the farm-house near which we were, rose Kilimakiu Mountain, beautifully studded with groves of trees of many kinds. On its farther side lived a tribe of the Wakamba. Their chief with all the leading men of his village came in state to call upon me, and presented me with a fat hairy sheep, of the ordinary kind found in this part of Africa, where the sheep very wisely do not grow wool. The headman was dressed in khaki, and showed me with pride an official document which confirmed him in his position by direction of the government, and required him to perform various acts, chiefly in the way of preventing his tribes-people from committing robbery or murder, and of helping to stamp out cattle disease. Like all the Wakamba they had flocks of goats and sheep, and herds of humped cattle; but they were much in need of meat and hailed my advent. They were wild savages with filed teeth, many of them stark naked, though some of them carried a blanket. Their heads were curiously shaved so that the hair tufts stood out in odd patterns, and they carried small bows, and arrows with poisoned heads.

The following morning I rode out with Captain Slatter. We kept among the hills. The long drought was still unbroken. The little pools were dry and their bottoms baked like iron and there was not a drop in the watercourses. Part of the land was open and part covered with a thin forest or bush of scattered mimosa trees. In the open country were many zebras and hartebeests, and the latter were found even in the thin bush. In the morning we found a small herd of eland at which, after some stalking, I got a long shot and missed. The eland is the largest of all the horned creatures that are called antelope, being quite as heavy as a fattened ox. The herd I approached consisted of a dozen individuals, two of them huge bulls, their coats having turned a slaty blue, their great dewlaps hanging down, and the legs looking almost too small for the massive bodies. The reddish-colored cows were of far lighter build. Eland are beautiful creatures and ought to be domesticated. As I crept toward them I was struck by their likeness to great, clean, handsome cattle. They were grazing or resting, switching their long tails at the flies that hung in attendance upon them and lit on their flanks, just as if they were Jerseys in a field at home. My bullet fell short, their size causing me to underestimate the distance, and away they went at a run, one or two of the cows in the first hurry and confusion skipping clean over the backs of others that got in their way—a most unexpected example of agility in such large and ponderous animals. After a few hundred yards they settled down to the slashing trot which is their natural gait, and disappeared over the brow of a hill.

The morning was a blank, but early in the afternoon we saw the eland herd again. They were around a tree in an open space, and we could not get near them. But instead of going straight away they struck off to the right and described almost a semicircle, and though they were over four hundred yards distant, they were such big creatures and their gait was so steady that I felt warranted in shooting. On the dry plain I could mark where my bullets fell, and though I could not get a good chance at the bull I finally downed a fine cow; and by pacing I found it to be a little over a quarter of a mile from where I stood when shooting.

It was about nine miles from camp, and I dared not leave the eland alone, so I stationed one of the gun-bearers by the great carcass and sent a messenger in to Heller, on whom we depended for preserving the skins of the big game. Hardly had this been done when a Wakamba man came running up to tell us that there was a rhinoceros on the hillside three-quarters of a mile away, and that he had left a companion to watch it while he carried us the news. Slater and I immediately rode in the direction given, following our wild-looking guide; the other gun-bearer trotting after us. In five minutes we had reached the opposite hillcrest, where the watcher stood, and he at once pointed out the rhino. The huge beast was standing in entirely open country, although there were a few scattered trees of no great size at some little distance from him. We left our horses in a dip of the ground and began the approach; I cannot say that we stalked him, for the approach was too easy. The wind blew from him to us, and a rhino's eyesight is dull. Thirty yards from where he stood was a bush four or five feet high, and though it was so thin that we could distinctly see him through the leaves, it shielded us from the vision of his small, piglike eyes as we advanced toward it, stooping and in single file, I leading. The big beast stood like an uncouth statue, his hide black in the sunlight; he seemed what he was, a monster surviving over from the world's past, from the days when the beasts of the prime ran riot in their strength, before man grew so cunning of brain and hand as to master them. So little did he dream of our presence that when we were a hundred yards off he actually lay down.

Walking lightly, and with every sense keyed up, we at last reached the bush, and I pushed forward the safety of the double-barrelled Holland rifle which I was now to use for the first time on big game. As I stepped to one side of the bush so as to get a clear aim, with Slatter following, the rhino saw me and jumped to his feet with the agility of a polo pony. As he rose I put in the right barrel, the bullet going through both lungs. At the same moment he wheeled, the blood spouting from his nostrils, and galloped full on us. Before he could get quite all the way round in his headlong rush to reach us, I struck him with my left-hand barrel, the bullet entering between the neck and shoulder and piercing his heart. At the same instant Captain Slatter fired, his bullet entering the neck vertebrae. Ploughing up the ground with horn and feet, the great bull rhino, still head toward us, dropped just thirteen paces from where we stood.

This was a wicked charge, for the rhino meant mischief and came on with the utmost determination. It is not safe to generalize from a few instances. Judging from what I have since seen, I am declined to believe that both lion and buffalo are more dangerous game than rhino; yet the first two rhinos I met both charged, whereas we killed our first four lions and first four buffaloes without any of them charging, though two of each were stopped as they were on the point of charging. Moreover, our experience with this bull rhino illustrates what I have already said as to one animal being more dangerous under certain conditions, and another more dangerous under different conditions. If it had been a lion instead of a rhino, my first bullet would, I believe, have knocked all the charge out of it; but the vitality of the huge pachyderm was so great, its mere bulk counted for so much, that even such a hard-hitting rifle as my double Holland—than which I do not believe there exists a better weapon for heavy game—could not stop it outright, although either of the wounds inflicted would have been fatal in a few seconds.

Leaving a couple of men with the dead rhino, to protect it from the Wakamba by day and the lions by night, we rode straight to camp, which we reached at sunset. It was necessary to get to work on the two dead beasts as soon as possible in order to be sure of preserving their skins. Heller was the man to be counted on for this task. He it was who handled all the skins, who, in other words, was making the expedition of permanent value so far as big game was concerned; and no work at any hour of the day or night ever came amiss to him. He had already trained eight Wakamba porters to act as skinners under his supervision. On hearing of our success, he at once said that we ought to march out to the game that night so as to get to work by daylight. Moreover, we were not comfortable at leaving only two men with each carcass, for lions were both bold and plentiful.

The moon rose at eight and we started as soon as she was above the horizon. We did not take the horses, because there was no water where we were going, and furthermore, we did not like to expose them to a possible attack by lions. The march out by moonlight was good fun, for though I had been out all day, I had been riding, not walking, and so was not tired. A hundred porters went with us so as to enable us to do the work quickly and bring back to camp the skins and all the meat needed, and these porters carried water, food for breakfast, and what little was necessary for a one-night camp. We tramped along in single file under the moonlight, up and down the hills, and through the scattered thorn forest. Kermit and Medlicott went first, and struck such a pace that after an hour we had to halt them so as to let the tail end of the file of porters catch up. Then Captain Slatter and I set a more decorous pace, keeping the porters close up in line behind us. In another hour we began to go down a long slope toward a pin-point of light in the distance which we knew was the fire by the rhinoceros. The porters, like the big children they were, felt in high feather, and began to chant to an accompaniment of whistling and horn-blowing as we tramped through the dry grass which was flooded with silver by the moon, now high in the heavens.

As soon as we reached the rhino, Heller with his Wakamba skinners pushed forward the three-quarters of a mile to the eland, returning after midnight with the skin and all the best parts of the meat.

Around the dead rhino the scene was lit up both by the moon and by the flicker of the fires. The porters made their camp under a small tree a dozen rods to one side of the carcass, building a low circular fence of branches on which they hung their bright colored blankets, two or three big fires blazing to keep off possible lions. Half as far on the other side of the rhino a party of naked savages had established their camp, if camp it could be called, for really all they did was to squat down round a couple of fires with a few small bushes disposed round about. The rhino had been opened, and they had already taken out of the carcass what they regarded as tit-bits and what we certainly did not grudge them. Between the two camps lay the huge dead beast, his hide glistening in the moon-light. In each camp the men squatted around the fires chatting and laughing as they roasted strips of meat on long sticks, the fitful blaze playing over them, now leaving them in darkness, now bring-ing them out into a red relief. Our own tent was pitched under an-other tree a hundred yards off, and when I went to sleep, I would still hear the drumming and chanting of our feasting porters; the savages were less at ease, and their revel was quiet.

Early next morning I went back to camp, and soon after reach-ing there again started out for a hunt. In the afternoon I came on gi-raffes and got up near enough to shoot at them. But they are such enormous beasts that I thought them far nearer than they were. My bullet fell short, and they disappeared among the mimosas, at their strange leisurely looking gallop. Of all the beasts in an African land-scape none is more striking than the giraffe. Usually it is found in small parties or in herds of fifteen or twenty or more individuals. Al-though it will drink regularly if occasion offers, it is able to get along without water for months at a time, and frequents by choice the dry plains or else the stretches of open forest where the trees are scat-tered and ordinarily somewhat stunted. Like the rhinoceros—the ordinary or prehensile-lipped rhinoceros—the giraffe is a browsing and not a grazing animal. The leaves, buds, and twigs of the mi-mosas or thorn-trees form its customary food. Its extra-ordinary height enables it to bring into play to the best possible advantage its noteworthy powers of vision, and no animal is harder to approach unseen. Again and again I have made it out a mile off or rather have seen it a mile off when it was pointed out to me, and looking at it through my glasses, would see that it was gazing steadily at us. It is a striking-looking animal and handsome in its way, but its length of leg and neck and sloping back make it appear awkward even at rest. When alarmed it may go off at a long swinging pace or walk, but if really frightened it strikes into a peculiar gallop or canter. The tail is cocked and twisted, and the huge hind legs are thrown forward well to the outside of the forelegs. The movements seem deliberate and the giraffe does not appear to be going at a fast pace, but if it has any start a horse must gallop hard to overtake it. When it starts on this gait, the neck may be dropped forward at a sharp angle with the straight line of the deep chest, and the big head is thrust in advance. They are defenseless things and, though they may kick at a man who incautiously comes within reach, they are in no way dangerous.

The following day I again rode out with Captain Slatter. During the morning we saw nothing except the ordinary game, and we lunched on a hilltop, ten miles distance from camp, under a huge fig-tree with spreading branches and thick, deep green foliage. Throughout the time we were taking lunch a herd of zebras watched us from near by, standing motionless with their ears pricked forward, their beautifully striped bodies showing finely in the sunlight. We scanned the country round about with our glasses, and made out first a herd of elands, a mile in our rear, and then three giraffes a mile and a half in our front. I wanted a bull eland, but I wanted a giraffe still more, and we mounted our horses and rode toward where the three tall beasts stood, on an open hillside with trees thinly scattered over it. Half a mile from them we left the horses in a thick belt of timber beside a dry watercourse, and went forward on foot.

There was no use in trying a stalk for that would merely have aroused the giraffe's suspicion. But we knew they were accustomed to the passing and repassing of Wakamba men and women, whom they did not fear if they kept at a reasonable distance, so we walked in single file diagonally in their direction; that is, toward a tree which I judged to be about three hundred yards from them. I was carrying the Winchester loaded with full metal-patched bullets. I wished to get for the museum both a bull and a cow. One of the three giraffes was much larger than the other two, and as he was evidently a bull I thought the two others were cows.

As we reached the tree the giraffes showed symptoms of uneasiness. One of the smaller ones began to make off, and both the others shifted their positions slightly, curling their tails. I instantly dropped on my knee, and getting the bead just behind the big bull's shoulder, I fired with the three-hundred-yard sight. I heard the "pack" of the bullet as it struck just where I aimed; and away went all three giraffes at their queer rocking-horse canter. Running forward I emptied my magazine, firing at the big bull and also at one of his smaller companions, and then, slipping into the barrel what proved to be a soft-nosed bullet, I fired at the latter again. The giraffe was going straightaway and it was a long shot, at four or five hundred yards; but by good luck the bullet broke its back and down it came. The others were now getting over the crest of the hill, but the big one was evidently sick, and we called and beckoned to the two saises to hurry up with the horses. The moment they arrived we jumped on, and Captain Slatter cantered up a neighboring hill so as to mark the direction in which the giraffes went if I lost sight of them. Meanwhile I rode full speed after the giant quarry. I was on the tranquil sorrel, the horse I much preferred in riding down game of any kind, because he had a fair turn of speed, and yet was good about letting me get on and off. As soon as I reached the hill-crest I saw the giraffes ahead of me, not as far off as I had feared, and I raced toward them without regard to rotten ground and wart-hog holes. The wounded one lagged behind, but when I got near he put on a spurt and as I thought I was close enough I leaped off, throwing the reins over the sorrel's head, and opened fire. Down went the big bull, and I thought my task was done. But as I went back to mount the sorrel he struggled to his feet again and disappeared after his companion among the trees, which were thicker here, as we had reached the bottom of the valley. So I tore after him again, and in a minute came to a dry watercourse. Scrambling into and out of this I saw the giraffes ahead of me just beginning the ascent of the opposite slope; and touching the horse with the spur we flew after the wounded bull. This time I made up my mind I would get up close enough; but Tranquillity did not quite like the look of the thing ahead of him. He did not refuse to come up to the giraffe, but he evidently felt that, with such an object close by and evident in the landscape, it behooved him to be careful as to what might be hidden therein, and he shied so at each bush we passed that we progressed in a series of loops. So off I jumped, throwing the reins over his head, and opened fire once more; this time the great bull went down for good.

Tranquillity recovered his nerve at once and grazed contentedly while I admired the huge proportions and beautiful coloring of my prize. In a few minutes Captain Slatter loped up, and the gun-bearers and saises followed. As if my magic, three or four Wakamba turned up immediately afterward, their eyes glistening at the thought of the feast ahead for the whole tribe. It was mid-afternoon, and there was no time to waste. My sais, Simba, an excellent long-distance runner, was sent straight to camp to get Heller and pilot him back to the dead giraffes. Beside each of the latter, for they had fallen a mile apart, we left a couple of men to build fires. Then we rode toward camp. To my regret, the smaller giraffe turned out to be a young bull and not a cow.

At this very time, and utterly without our knowledge, there was another giraffe hunt going on. Sir Alfred had taken out Kermit and Medlicott, and they came across a herd of a dozen giraffes right out in the open plains. Medlicott's horse was worn out and he could not keep up, but both the others were fairly well mounted. Both were light men and hard riders, and although the giraffes had three-quarters of a mile the start, it was not long before both were at the heels of the herd. They singled out the big bull, which by the way turned out to be an even bigger bull than mine, and fired at him as they galloped. In such a headlong, helter-skelter chase, however, it is no easy matter to score a hit from horseback unless one is very close up; and Sir Alfred made up his mind to try to drive out the bull from the rest of the herd. He succeeded; but at this moment his horse put a forefoot into a hole and turned a complete somersault, almost wrenching out his shoulder. Sir Alfred was hurled off head over heels, but even as he rolled over, clutching his rifle, he twisted himself round to his knees, and took one last shot at the flying giraffe. This left Kermit alone and he galloped hard on the giraffe's heels, firing again and again with his Winchester. Finally his horse became completely done out and fell behind; whereupon Kermit jumped off, and being an excellent long-distance runner, ran after the giraffe on foot for more than a mile. But he did not need to shoot again. The great beast had been mortally wounded and it suddenly slowed down, halted, and fell over dead. As a matter of curiosity we kept the Winchester bullets both from Kermit's giraffe and from mine. I made a point of keeping as many as possible of the bullets with which the different animals were slain so as to see just what was done by the different types of rifles we had with us.

When I reached camp I found that Heller had already started. Next morning I rode down to see him and found him hard at work with the skins; but as it would take him two or three days to finish them and put them in condition for transport, we decided that the safari should march back to the Potha camp, and that from thence we would send Percival's ox wagon to bring back to the camp all the skins, Heller and his men accompanying him. The plan was carried out, and the following morning we shifted the big camp as proposed.

Heller, thus left behind, came near having an unpleasant adventure. He slept in his own tent, and his Wakamba skinners slept under the fly not far off. One night they let the fires die down and were roused at midnight by hearing the grunting of a hungry lion apparently not a dozen yards off in the darkness. Heller quickly lit his lantern and sat up with his shot-gun loaded with bird shot, the only weapon he had with him. The lion walked round and round the tent, grunting at intervals, then, after some minutes of suspense, he drew off. While the grunting had been audible, not a sound came from the tent of the Wakambas, who all cowered under their blankets in perfect silence. But once he had gone there was a great chattering, and in a few minutes the fires were roaring, nor were they again suffered to die down.

Heller's skinners had grown to work very well when under his eye. He had encountered much difficulty in getting men who would do the work, and had tried the representatives of various tribes, but without success until he struck the Wakamba. These were real savages who filed their teeth and delighted in raw flesh, and Heller's explanation of their doing well was that their taste for the raw flesh kept them thoroughly interested in their job, so that they learned without difficulty. The porters speedily christened each of the white men by some title of their own, using the ordinary Swahili title of Bwana (master) as a prefix. Heller was the Bwana Who Skinned; Loring, who collected the small mammals, was named, merely descriptively, the Mouse Master, Bwana Pania. I was always called Bwana Makuba, the chief or Great Master; Kermit was first called Bwana Medogo, the young master, and afterward was christened "the Dandy," Bwana Merodadi.

From Potha the safari went in two days to McMillan's place, Juja Farm, on the other side of the Athi. I stayed behind, as I desired to visit the American Mission Station at Machakos. Accordingly, Sir Alfred and I rode thither. Machakos has long been a native town, for it was on the route formerly taken by the Arab caravans that went from the coast to the interior after slaves and ivory. Riding toward it we passed herd after herd of cattle, sheep, and goats, each guarded by two or three savage herdsmen. The little town itself was both interesting and attractive. Besides the natives there were a number of Indian traders and the English Commissioner and Assistant Commissioner, with a small body of native soldiers. The latter not a long time before had been just such savages as those round about them, and the change for the better wrought in their physique and morale by the ordered discipline to which they had submitted themselves could hardly be exaggerated. When we arrived, the Commissioner and his assistant were engaged in cross-examining some neighboring chiefs as to the cattle sickness. The English rule in Africa has been of incalculable benefit to Africans themselves, and indeed this is true of the rule of most European nations. Mistakes have been made, of course, but they have proceeded at least as often from an unwise effort to accomplish too much in the way of beneficence, as from a desire to exploit the natives. Each of the civilized nations that has taken possession of any part of Africa has had its own peculiar good qualities and its own peculiar defects. Some of them have done too much in supervising and ordering the lives of the natives, and in interfering with their practices and customs. The English error, like our own under similar conditions, has, if anything, been in the other direction. The effort has been to avoid wherever possible all interference with tribal customs, even when of an immoral and repulsive character, and to do no more than what is obviously necessary, such as insistence upon keeping the peace and preventing the spread of cattle disease. Excellent reasons can be advanced in favor of this policy, and it must always be remembered that a fussy and ill-considered benevolence is more sure to awaken a resentment than cruelty itself; while the natives are apt to resent deeply even things that are obviously for their ultimate welfare. Yet I cannot help thinking that with caution and wisdom it would be possible to proceed somewhat farther than has yet been the case in the direction of pushing upward some at least of the East African tribes; and this though I recognize fully that many of these tribes are of a low and brutalized type. Having said this much in the way of criticism, I wish to add my tribute of unstinted admiration for the disinter-

ested and efficient work being done, alike in the interest of the
white man and the black, by the government officials whom I met
in East Africa. They are men in whom their country has every reason to feel a just pride.

We lunched with the American missionaries. Mission work
among savages offers many difficulties, and often the wisest and
most earnest effort meets with dishearteningly little reward; while
lack of common-sense, and of course, above all, lack of a firm and
resolute disinterestedness, insures the worst kind of failure. There
are missionaries who do not do well, just as there are men in every
conceivable walk of life who do not do well; and excellent men
who are not missionaries, including both government officials and
settlers, are only too apt to jump at the chance of criticizing a missionary for every alleged sin of either omission or commission. Finally, zealous missionaries, fervent in the faith, do not always find
it easy to remember that savages can only be raised by slow steps,
that an empty adherence to forms and ceremonies amount to nothing, that industrial training is an essential in any permanent upward movement, and that the gradual elevation of mind and
character is a prerequisite to the achievement of any kind of Chris-
tianity which is worth calling such. Nevertheless, after all this has
been said, it remains true that the good done by missionary effort
in Africa has been incalculable. There are parts of the great continent, and among them I include many sections of East Africa,
which can be made a white man's country; and in these parts every
effort should be made to favor the growth of a large and prosperous
white population. But over most of Africa the problem for the
white man is to govern, with wisdom and firmness, and when necessary with severity, but always with an eye single to their own interests and development, the black and brown races. To do this
needs sympathy and devotion no less than strength and wisdom,
and in the task the part to be played by the missionary and the part
to be played by the official are alike great, and the two should work
hand in hand.

After returning from Machakos, I spent the night at Sir Alfred's and next morning said good-by with most genuine regret to my host and his family. Then, followed by my gun-bearers and sais, I rode off across the Athi Plains. Through the bright white air the sun beat down mercilessly, and the heat haze wavered above the endless flats of scorched grass. Hour and hour we went slowly forward, through the morning, and through the burning heat of the equatorial noon, until in mid-afternoon we came to the tangled tree growth which fringed the half-dried bed of the Athi. Here I off-saddled for an hour; then, mounting, I crossed the river bed where it was waterless, and before evening fell I rode up to Juja Farm.

Hunting in the Sotik

Next day we shifted camp to a rush-fringed pool by a grove of tall, flat-topped acacias at the foot of a range of low, steep mountains. Before us the plain stretched, and in front of our tents it was dotted by huge candelabra euphorbias. I shot a buck for the table just as we pitched camp. There were Masai kraals and cattle herds near by, and tall warriors, pleasant and friendly, strolled among our tents, their huge razor-edges spears tipped with furry caps to protect the points. Kermit was off all day with Tarlton, and killed a magnificent lioness. In the morning, on some high hills, he obtained a good impalla ram, after persevering hours of climbing and running—for only one of the gun-bearers and none of the whites could keep up with him on foot when he went hard. In the afternoon at four he and Tarlton saw the lioness. She was followed by three three-parts grown young lions, doubtless her cubs, and, without any concealment, was walking across the open plain toward a pool by which lay the body of a wildebeest bull she had killed the preceding night. The smaller lions saw the hunters and shrank back, but the old lioness never noticed them until they

329

were within a hundred and fifty yards. Then she ran back, but Kermit crumpled her up with his first bullet. He then put another bullet in her, and as she seemed disabled walked up within fifty yards, and took some photos. By this time she was recovering, and, switching her tail she gathered her hind quarters under her for a charge; but he stopped her with another bullet, and killed her out-right with a fourth.

We heard that Mearns and Loring, whom we had left ten days before, had also killed a lioness. A Masai brought in word to them that he had marked her down taking her noonday rest near a kon-goni she had killed; and they rode out, and Loring shot her. She charged him savagely; he shot her straight through the heart, and she fell literally at his feet. The three naturalists were all good shots, and were used to all the mishaps and adventures of life in the wilderness. Not only would it have been indeed difficult to find three better men for their particular work—Heller's work, for instance, with Cuninghame's help gave the chief point to our big-game shooting—but it would have been equally difficult to find three better men for any emergency. I could not speak too highly of them; nor indeed of our two other companions, Cuninghame and Tarlton, whose mastery of their own field was as noteworthy as the pre-eminence of the naturalists in their field.

The following morning the headmen asked that we get the porters some meat; Tarlton, Kermit, and I sallied forth accordingly. The country was very dry, and the game in our immediate neighborhood was not plentiful and was rather shy. I killed three kongoni out of a herd, at from two hundred and fifty to three hun-dred and ninety paces; one topi at three hundred and thirty paces, and a Roberts' gazelle at two hundred and seventy. Meanwhile the other two had killed a kongoni and five of the big gazelles; wher-ever possible the game being hallalled in orthodox fashion by the Mahometans among our attendants, so as to fit it for use by their coreligionists among the porters. Then we saw some giraffes, and galloped them to see if there was a really big bull in the lot. They had a long start, but Kermit and Tarlton overtook them after a couple of miles, while I pounded along in the rear. However, there was no really good bull, Kermit and Tarlton pulled up, and we jogged along toward the koppies where two days before I had shot the lioness. I killed a big bustard, a very handsome, striking-looking bird, larger than a turkey, by a rather good shot at two hundred and thirty yards.

It was now mid-day, and the heat waves quivered above the brown plain. The mirage hung in the middle distance, and beyond it the bold hills rose like mountains from a lake. In mid-afternoon we stopped at a little pool, to give the men and horses water; and here Kermit's horse suddenly went dead lame, and we started it back to camp with a couple of men, while Kermit went forward with us on foot, as we rode round the base of the first koppies. After we had gone a mile loud shouts called our attention to one of the men who had left with the lame horse. He was running back to tell us that they had just seen a big maned lion walking along in the open plain toward the body of a zebra he had killed the night before. Immediately Tarlton and I galloped in the direction indicated, while the heart-broken Kermit ran after us on foot, so as not to miss the fun; the gun-bearers and saises stringing out behind him. In a few minutes Tarlton pointed out the lion, a splendid old fellow, a heavy male with a yellow and black mane; and after him we went. There was no need to go fast; he was too burly and too savage to run hard, and we were anxious that our hands should be reasonably steady when we shot; all told, the horses, galloping and cantering, did not take us two miles.

The lion stopped and lay down behind a bush; jumping off I took a shot at him at two hundred yards, but only wounded him slightly in one paw; and after a moment's sullen hesitation off he went, lashing his tail. We mounted our horses and went after him; Tarlton lost sight of him, but I marked him lying down behind a low grassy ant-hill. Again we dismounted at a distance of two hundred yards; Tarlton telling me that now he was sure to charge. In all East Africa there is no man, not even Cuninghame himself, whom I would rather have by me than Tarlton, if in difficulties with a charging lion; on this occasion, however, I am glad to say that his rifle was badly sighted, and shot altogether too low.

Again I knelt and fired; but the mass of hair on the lion made me think he was nearer than he was, and I undershot, inflicting a flesh wound that was neither crippling nor fatal. He was already grunting savagely and tossing his tail erect, with his head held low; and at the shot the great sinewy beast came toward us with the speed of a greyhound. Tarlton then, very properly, fired, for lion hunting is no child's play, and it is not good to run risks. Ordinarily it is a very mean thing to experience joy at a friend's miss; but this was not an ordinary case, and I felt keen delight when the bullet from the badly sighted rifle missed, striking the ground many yards short. I was sighting carefully, from my knee, and I knew I had the lion all right; for though he galloped at a great pace, he came on steadily—ears laid back, and uttering terrific coughing grunts— and there was now no question of making allowance for distance, nor, as he was out in the open, for the fact that he had not before been distinctly visible. The bead of my foresight was exactly on the centre of his chest as I pressed the trigger, and the bullet went as true as if the place had been plotted with dividers. The blow brought him up all standing, and he fell forward on his head. The soft-nosed Winchester bullet had gone straight through the chest cavity, smashing the lungs and the big blood-vessels of the heart. Painfully he recovered his feet, and tried to come on, his ferocious courage holding out to the last; but he staggered, and turned from side to side, unable to stand firmly, still less to advance at a faster pace then a walk. He had not ten seconds to live; but it is a sound principle to take no chances with lions. Tarlton hit him with his second bullet, probably in the shoulder; and with my next shot I broke his neck. I had stopped him when he was still a hundred yards away; and certainly no finer sight could be imagined than that of this great maned lion as he charged. Kermit gleefully joined us as we walked up to the body; only one of our followers had been able to keep up with him on his two-miles run. He had had a fine view of the charge, from one side, as he ran up still three hundred yards distant; he could see all the muscles play as the lion galloped in, and then everything relax as he fell to the shock of my bullet.

The lion was a big old male, still in his prime. Between up-rights his length was nine feet four inches, and his weight four hundred and ten pounds, for he was not fat. We skinned him and started for camp, which we reached after dark. There was a thunder-storm in the south-west, and in the red sunset that burned behind us the rain clouds turned to many gorgeous hues. Then daylight failed, the clouds cleared, and, as we made our way across the formless plain, the half-moon hung high overhead, strange stars shone in the brilliant heavens, and the Southern Cross lay radiant above the sky-line.

Our next camp was pitched on a stony plain, by a winding stream-bed still containing an occasional rush-fringed pool of muddy water, fouled by the herds and flocks of the numerous Masai. Game was plentiful around this camp. We killed what we needed of the common kinds, and in addition each of us killed a big rhino. The two rhinos were almost exactly alike, and their horns were of the so-called "Keitloa" type; the fore-horn twenty-two inches long, the rear over seventeen. The day I killed mine I used all three of my rifles. We all went out together, as Kermit was desirous of taking photos of my rhino, if I shot one; he had not been able to get good ones of his on the previous day. We also took the small ox wagon, so as to bring into camp bodily the rhino—if we got it—and one or two zebras, of which we wanted the flesh for the safari, the skeletons for the Museum. The night had been cool, but the day was sunny and hot. At first we rode through a broad valley, bounded by high, scrub-covered hills. The banks of the dry stream were fringed with deep green acacias, and here and there in relief against their dark foliage flamed the orange-red flowers of the tall aloe clumps. With the Springfield I shot a steinbuck and a lesser bustard. Then we came out on the vast rolling brown plains. With the Winchester I shot two zebra stallions, missing each standing, at long range, and then killing them as they ran; one after a two-miles hard gallop, on my brown pony, which had a good turn of speed. I killed a third zebra stallion with my Springfield, again missing it standing and killing it running. In mid-afternoon we spied our rhino, and getting near saw that it had good horns. It was in the middle of the absolutely bare plain, and we walked straight up to the dull-sighted, dull-witted beast; Kermit with his camera, I with the Holland double-barrel. The tick-birds warned it, but it did not make us out until we were well within a hundred yards, when it trotted toward us, head and tail up. At sixty yards I put the heavy bullet straight into its chest, and knocked it flat, with the left-hand barrel; but it needed two more bullets before it died, screaming like an engine whistle. Before I fired my last shot I had walked up directly beside the rhino; and just then Tarlton pointed me out a great bustard, stalking along with unmoved composure at a distance of a hundred and fifty yards; I took the Springfield, and kneeling down beside the rhino's hind quarters I knocked over the bustard, and then killed the rhino. We rode into camp by moonlight. Both these rhinos had their stomachs filled with the closely chewed leaves and twig tips of short brush mixed with grass—rather thick-stemmed grass—and in one case with the pulpy, spiny leaves of a low, ground-creeping euphorbia.

At this camp we killed five poisonous snakes: a light-colored tree snake, two puff adders, and two seven-foot cobras. One of the latter three times "spat" or ejected its poison at us, the poison coming out from the fangs like white films or threads, to a distance of several feet. A few years ago the singular power of this snake, and perhaps of certain other African species, thus to eject the poison at the face of an assailant was denied by scientists; but it is now well known. Selous had already told me of an instance which came under his own observation; and Tarlton had once been struck in the eyes and for the moment nearly blinded by the poison. He found that to wash the eyes with milk was of much relief. On the bigger puff adder, some four feet long, were a dozen ticks, some swollen to the size of cherries; apparently they were disregarded by their sluggish and deadly host. Heller trapped some jackals, of two species; and two striped hyenas, the first we had seen; apparently more timid and less noisy beasts than their bigger spotted brothers.

One day Kermit had our first characteristic experience with a honey bird; a smallish bird, with its beak like a grosbeak's and its toes like a woodpecker's, whose extraordinary habits as a honey guide are known to all the natives of Africa throughout its range. Kermit had killed an eland bull, and while he was resting, his gun-bearers drew his attention to the calling of the honey bird in a tree near by. He got up, and as he approached the bird, it flew into another tree in front and again began its twitter. This was re- peated again and again as Kermit walked after it. Finally the bird darted round behind his followers, in the direction from which they had come; and for a moment they thought it had played them false. But immediately afterward they saw that it had merely overshot its mark, and had now flown back a few rods to the honey tree, round which it was flitting, occasionally twitter- ing. When they came toward the tree it perched silent and mo- tionless in another, and thus continued while they took some honey—a risky business, as the bees were vicious. They did not observe what the bird then did; but Cuninghame told me that in one instance where a honey bird led him to honey he carefully watched it and saw it picking up either bits of honey and comb, or else, more probably, the bee grubs out of the comb, he could not be certain which.

To my mind no more interesting incident occurred at this camp.

335

Elephant Hunting on Mount Kenia

On July 24th, in order to ship our fresh accumulations of specimens and trophies, we once more went into Nairobi. It was a pleasure again to see its tree-bordered streets and charming houses bowered in vines and bushes, and to meet once more the men and women who dwelt in the houses. I wish it were in my power to thank individually the members of the many East African households of which I shall always cherish warm memories of friendship and regard.

At Nairobi I saw Selous, who had just returned from a two months' safari with McMillan, Williams, and Judd. Their experience shows how large the element of luck is in lion hunting. Selous was particularly anxious to kill a good lion; there is nowhere to be found a more skilful or more hardworking hunter; yet he never even got a shot. Williams, on the other hand, came across three. Two he killed easily. The third charged him. He was carrying a double-barrelled .450, but failed to stop the beast; it seized him by the leg, and his life was saved by his Swahili gun-bearer, who gave the lion a fatal shot as it stood over him. He came within an ace of dying; but when I saw him, at the hospital, he was well on the road to recovery. One day Selous while on horseback saw a couple of lionesses, and galloped after them, followed by Judd, seventy or eighty yards behind. One lioness stopped and crouched under a bush, let Selous pass, and then charged Judd. She was right alongside him, and he fired from the hip; the bullet went into her eye; his horse jumped and swerved at the shot, throwing him off, and he found himself sitting on the ground, not three yards from the dead lioness. Nothing more was seen of the other.

Continually I met men with experiences in their past lives which showed how close the country was to those primitive conditions in which warfare with wild beasts was one of the main features of man's existence. At one dinner my host and two of my fellow-guests had been within a year or eighteen months severely mauled by lions. All three, by the way, informed me that the actual biting caused them at the moment no pain whatever; the pain came later. On meeting Harold Hill, my companion on one of my Kapiti Plains lion hunts, I found that since I had seen him he had been roughly handled by a dying leopard. The government had just been obliged to close one of the trade routes to native caravans because of the ravages of a man-eating lion, which carried men away from the camps. A safari which had come in from the north had been charged by a rhino, and one of the porters tossed and killed, the horn being driven clear through his loins. At Heatley's farm three buffalo (belonging to the same herd from which we had shot five) rushed out of the papyrus one afternoon at a passing buggy, which just managed to escape by a breakneck run across the level plain, the beasts chasing it for a mile. One afternoon, at Government House, I met a government official who had once succeeded in driving into a corral seventy zebras, including more stallions than mares; their misfortune in no way abated their savagery toward one another, and as the limited space forbade the escape of the weaker, the stallions fought to the death with teeth and hoofs during the first night, and no less then twenty were killed outright or died of their wounds.

Most of the time in Nairobi we were the guests of ever-hospitable McMillan, in his low, cool house, with its broad, vine-shaded veranda, running around all four sides, and its garden, fragrant and brilliant with innumerable flowers. Birds abounded, singing beautifully; the bulbuls were the most noticeable singers, but there were many others. The dark ant-eating chats haunted the dusky roads on the outskirts of the town, and were interesting birds; they were usually found in parties, flirted their tails up and down as they sat on bushes or roofs or wire, sang freely in chorus until after dusk, and then retired to holes in the ground for the night. A tiny owl with a queer little voice called continually not only after nightfall, but in the bright afternoons. Shrikes spitted insects on the spines of the imported cactus in the gardens.

It was race week, and the races, in some of which Kermit rode, were capital fun. The white people—army officers, government officials, farmers from the country roundabout, and their wives—rode to the races on ponies or even on camels, or drove up in rickshaws, in gharries, in bullock tongas, occasionally in automobiles, most often in two-wheel carts or rickety hacks drawn by mules and driven by a turbaned Indian or a native in a cotton shirt. There were Parsees, and Goanese dressed just like the Europeans. There were many other Indians, their picturesque womenkind gaudy in crimson, blue, and saffron. The constabulary, Indian and native, were in neat uniforms and well set up, though often bare-footed. Straight, slender Somalis with clear-cut features were in attendance on the horses. Native negroes, of many different tribes, flocked to the race-course and its neighborhood. The Swahilis, and those among the others who aspired toward civilization, were well clad, the men in half European costume, the women in flowing, parti-colored robes. But most of them were clad, or unclad, just as they always had been. Wakamba, with filed teeth, crouched in circles on the ground. Kikuyu passed, the men each with a blanket hung round the shoulders, and girdles of chains, and armlets and anklets of solid metal; the older women bent under burdens they carried on the back, half of them in addition with babies slung somewhere round them, while now and then an unmarried girl would have her face painted with ochre and vermilion. A small party of Masai warriors kept close together, each clutching his shining, long-bladed war spear, their hair daubed red and twisted into strings. A large band of Kavirondo, stark naked, with shield and spear and head-dress of nodding plumes, held a dance near the race-track. As for the races themselves, they were carried on in the most sporting spirit, and only the Australian poet Patterson could adequately write of them.

On August 4th I returned to Lake Naivasha, stopping on the way at Kijabe to lay the corner-stone of the new mission building. Mearns and Loring had stayed at Naivasha and had collected many birds and small mammals. That night they took me out on a spring-haas hunt. Thanks to Kermit we had discovered that the way to get this curious and purely nocturnal animal was by "shining" it with a lantern at night, just as in our own country deer, coons, owls, and other creatures can be killed. Springhaas live in big burrows, a number of them dwelling together in one community, the holes close to one another, and making what in the West we would call a "town" in speaking of prairie dogs. At night they come out to feed on the grass. They are as heavy as a big jack-rabbit, with short forelegs, and long hind legs and tail, so that they look and on occasion move like miniature kangaroos, although in addition to making long hops or jumps, they often run almost like an ordinary rat or rabbit. They are pretty creatures, fawn-colored above, and white beneath, with the terminal half of the tail very dark. In hunting them we simply walked over the flats for a couple of hours, flashing the bull's eye lantern on all sides, until we saw the light reflected back by a springhaas's eyes. Then I would approach to within range, and hold the lantern in my left hand so as to shine both on the sight and on the eyes in front, resting my gun on my left wrist. The number 3 shot, in the Fox double-barrel, would always do the business, if I held straight enough. There was nothing but the gleam of the eyes to shoot at; and this might suddenly be raised or lowered as the intently watching animal crouched on all-fours or raised itself on its hind legs. I shot half a dozen, all that the naturalists wanted. Then I tried to shoot a fox; but the moon had risen from behind a cloud bank; I had to take a long shot and missed; but my companions killed several, and found that they were a new species of the peculiar African long-eared fox.

While waiting for the safari to get ready, Kermit went off on a camping trip and shot two bushbuck, while I spent a couple of days trying for singsing waterbuck on the edge of the papyrus. I missed a bull, and wounded another which I did not get. This was all the more exasperating because interspersed with the misses were some good shots: I killed a fine waterbuck cow at a hundred yards, and a buck tommy for the table at two hundred and fifty; and, after missing a handsome black and white, red-billed and red-legged jabiru, or saddle-billed stork, at a hundred and fifty yards, as he stalked through the meadow after frogs, I cut him down on the wing at a hundred and eighty, with the little Springfield rifle. The waterbuck spent the daytime outside, but near the edge of, the papyrus; I found them grazing or resting, in the open, at all times between early morning and late afternoon. Some of them spent most of the day in the papyrus, keeping to the watery trails made by the hippos and by themselves; but this was not the general habit, unless they had been persecuted. When frightened they often ran into the papyrus, smashing the dead reeds and splashing the water in their rush. They are noble-looking antelope, with long, shaggy hair, and their chosen haunts beside the lake were very attractive. Clumps of thorn-trees and flowering bushes grew at the edge of the tall papyrus here and there, and often formed a matted jungle, the trees laced together by creepers, many of them brilliant in their bloom. The climbing morning-glories sometimes completely covered a tree with their pale-purple flowers; and other blossoming vines spangled the green over which their sprays were flung with masses of bright yellow.

Four days' march from Naivasha, where we again left Mearns and Loring, took us to Neri. Our line of march lay across the high plateaus and mountain chains of the Aberdare range. The steep, twisting trail was slippery with mud. Our last camp, at an altitude of about ten thousand feet, was so cold that the water froze in the basins and the shivering porters slept in numbed discomfort. There was constant fog and rain, and on the highest plateau the bleak landscape, shrouded in driving mist, was northern to all the senses. The ground was rolling, and through the deep valleys ran brawling brooks of clear water; one little foaming stream, suddenly tearing down a hill-side, might have been that which Childe Roland crossed before he came to the dark tower.

There was not much game, and it generally moved abroad by night. One frosty evening we killed a duiker by shining its eyes. We saw old elephant tracks. The high, wet levels swarmed with mice and shrews, just as our arctic and alpine meadows swarm with them. The species were really widely different from ours, but many of them showed curious analogies in form and habits; there was a short-tailed shrew much like our mole shrew, and a long-haired, short-tailed rat like a very big meadow mouse. They were so plentiful that we frequently saw them, and the grass was cut up by their runways. They were abroad during the day, probably finding the nights too cold, and in an hour Heller trapped a dozen or two individuals belonging to seven species and five different genera. There were not many birds so high up. There were deer ferns; and Spanish moss hung from the trees and even from the bamboos. The flowers included utterly strange forms, as for instance giant lobelias ten feet high. Others we know in our gardens; geraniums and red-hot-pokers, which in places turned the glades to a fire color. Yet others either were like, or looked like, our own wild flowers: orange lady-slippers, red gladiolas on stalks six feet high, pansy-like violets, and blackberries and yellow raspberries. There were stretches of bushes bearing masses of small red or large white flowers shaped somewhat like columbines, or like the garden balsam; the red flower bushes were under the bamboos, the white at lower level. The crests and upper slopes of the mountains were clothed in the green uniformity of the bamboo forest, the trail winding dim under its dark archway of tall, close-growing stems. Lower down were junipers and yews, and then many other trees, with among them tree ferns and strange dragon trees with lily-like frondage. Zone succeeded zone from top to bottom, each marked by a different plant life.

In this part of Africa, where flowers bloom and birds sing all the year round, there is no such burst of bloom and song as in the northern spring and early summer. There is nothing like the mass of blossoms which carpet the meadows of the high mountain valleys and far northern meadows, during their brief high tide of life, when one short joyous burst of teeming and vital beauty atones for the long death of the iron fall and winter. So it is with the bird songs. Many of them are beautiful, though to my ears none quite as beautiful as the best of our own bird songs. At any rate there is nothing that quite corresponds to the chorus that during May and June moves northward from the Gulf States and southern California to Maine, Minnesota, and Oregon, to Ontario and Saskatchewan; when there comes the great vernal burst of bloom and song; when the mayflower, bloodroot, wake-robin, anemone, adder's tongue, liverwort, shadblow, dogwood, redbud, gladden the woods; when mocking-birds and cardinals sing in the magnolia groves of the South, and hermit thrushes, winter wrens and sweetheart sparrows in the spruce and hemlock forests of the North; when bobolinks in the East and meadowlarks East and West sing in the fields; and water ousels by the cold streams of the Rockies, and canyon wrens in their sheer gorges; when from the Atlantic seaboard to the Pacific wood thrushes, veeries, rufous-backed thrushes, robins, bluebirds, orioles, thrashers, cat-birds, house finches, song sparrows—some in the East, some in the West, some both East and West—and many, many other singers thrill the gardens at sunrise; until the long days begin to shorten, and tawny lilies burn by the roadside, and the indigo buntings trill from the tops of little trees throughout the hot afternoons.

We were in the Kikuyu country. On our march we met several parties of natives. I had been much inclined to pity the porters, who had but one blanket apiece; but when I saw the Kikuyus, each with nothing but a smaller blanket, and without the other clothing and the tents of the porters, I realized how much better off the latter were simply because they were on a white man's safari. At Neri boma we were greeted with the warmest hospitality by the District Commissioner, Mr. Browne. Among other things, he arranged a great Kikuyu dance in our honor. Two thousand warriors, and many women, came in; as well as a small party of Masai moran. The warriors were naked, or half-naked; some carried gaudy blankets, others girdles of leopard skin; their ox-hide shields were colored in bold patterns, their long-bladed spears quivered and gleamed. Their faces and legs were painted red and yellow; the faces of the young men who were about to undergo the rite of circumcision were stained a ghastly white, and their bodies fantastically painted. The warriors wore bead necklaces and waist belts and armlets of brass and steel, and spurred anklets of monkey skin. Some wore head-dresses made out of a lion's mane or from the long black and white fur of the Colobus monkey; others had plumes stuck in their red-daubed hair. They chanted in unison a deep-toned chorus, and danced rhythmically in rings, while the drums throbbed and the horns blared; and they danced by us in column, springing and chanting. The women shrilled applause, and danced in groups by themselves. The Masai circled and swung in a panther-like dance of their own, and the measure, and their own fierce singing and calling, maddened them until two of their number, their eyes staring, their faces working, went into fits of berserker frenzy, and were disarmed at once to prevent mischief. Some of the tribesmen held wilder dances still in the evening, by the light of fires that blazed in a grove where their thatched huts stood.

The second day after reaching Neri the clouds lifted and we dried our damp clothes and blankets. Through the bright sunlight we saw in front of us the high rock peaks of Kenia, and shining among them the fields of everlasting snow which feed her glaciers; for beautiful, lofty Kenia is one of the glacier-bearing mountains of the equator. Here Kermit and Tarlton went northward on a safari of their own, while Cuninghame, Heller, and I headed for Kenia itself. For two days we travelled through a well-peopled country. The fields of corn—always called mealies in Africa—of beans, and sweet potatoes, with occasional plantations of bananas, touched one another in almost uninterrupted succession. In most of them we saw the Kikuyu women at work with their native hoes; for among the Kikuyus, as among other savages, the woman is the drudge and beast of burden. Our trail led by clear, rushing streams, which formed the head-waters of the Tana; among the trees fringing their banks were graceful palms, and there were groves of tree ferns here and there on the sides of the gorges.

On the afternoon of the second day we struck upward among the steep foot-hills of the mountain, riven by deep ravines. We pitched camp in an open glade, surrounded by the green wall of tangled forest, the forest of the tropical mountain sides.

The trees, strange of kind and endless in variety, grew tall and close, laced together by vine and creeper, while underbrush crowded the space between their mossy trunks, and covered the leafy mould beneath. Toward dusk crested ibis flew overhead with harsh clamor, to seek their night roosts; parrots chattered, and a curiously home-like touch was given by the presence of a thrush in color and shape almost exactly like our robin. Monkeys called in the depths of the forest, and after dark tree-frogs piped and croaked, and the tree hyraxes uttered their wailing cries.

Elephants dwelt permanently in this mountainous region of heavy woodland. On our march thither we had already seen their

345

traces in the "shambas," as the cultivated fields of the natives are termed; for the great beasts are fond of raiding the crops at night, and their inroads often do serious damage. In this neighborhood their habit is to live high up in the mountains, in the bamboos, while the weather is dry; the cow and calves keeping closer to the bamboos than the bulls. A spell of wet weather, such as we had fortunately been having, drives them down in the dense forest which covers the lower slopes. Here they may either pass all their time, or at night they may go still further down, into the open valley where the shambas lie; or the may occasionally still do what they habitually did in the days before the white hunter came, and wander far away, making migrations that are sometimes seasonal, and sometimes irregular and unaccountable.

No other animal, not the lion himself, is so constant a theme of talk, and a subject of such unflagging interest round the camp-fires of African hunters and in the native villages of the African wilderness, as the elephant. Indeed the elephant has always profoundly impressed the imagination of mankind. It is, not only to hunters, but to naturalists, and to all people who possess any curiosity about wild creatures and the wild life of nature, the most interesting of all animals. Its huge bulk, its singular form, the value of its ivory, its great intelligence—in which it is only matched, if at all, by the highest apes, and possibly by one or two of the highest carnivores—and its varied habits, all combine to give it an interest such as attaches to no other living creature below the rank of man. In line of descent and in physical formation it stands by itself, wholly apart from all the other great land beasts, and differing from them even more widely than they differ from one another. The two existing species—the African, which is the larger and finer animal, and the Asiatic—differ from one another as much as they do from the mammoth and similar extinct forms which were the contemporaries of early man in Europe and North America. The carvings of our palaeolithic forefathers, etched on bone by cavern dwellers, from whom we are sundered by ages which stretch into an immemorial past, show that in their lives the hairy elephant of the north played the same part that his remote collateral descendant now plays in the lives of the savages who dwell under a vertical sun beside the tepid waters of the Nile and the Congo.

In the first dawn of history, the sculptured records of the kings of Egypt, Babylon, and Nineveh show the immense importance which attached in the eyes of the mightiest monarchs of the then world to the chase and the trophies of this great strange beast. The ancient civilization of India boasts as one of its achievements the taming of the elephant, and in the ancient lore of that civilization the elephant plays a distinguished part.

The elephant is unique among the beasts of great bulk in the fact that his growth in size has been accompanied by growth in brain power. With other beasts growth in bulk of body has not been accompanied by similar growth of mind. Indeed sometimes there seems to have been mental retrogression. The rhinoceros, in several different forms, is found in the same regions as the elephant, and in one of its forms it is in point of size second only to the elephant among terrestrial animals. Seemingly the ancestors of the two creatures, in that period, separated from us by uncounted hundreds of thousand of years, which we may conveniently designate as late miocene or early pliocene, were substantially equal in brain development. But in one case increase in bulk seems to have induced lethargy and atrophy of brain power, while in the other case brain and body have both grown. At any rate the elephant is now one of the wisest and the rhinoceros one of the stupidest of big mammals. In consequence the elephant outlasts the rhino, although he is the largest, carries infinitely more valuable spoils, and is far more eagerly and persistently hunted. Both animals wandered freely over the open country of East Africa thirty years ago. But the elephant learns by experience infinitely more readily than the rhinoceros. As a rule, the former no longer lives in the open plains, and in many places now crosses them if possible only at night. But those rhinoceros which formerly dwelt in the plains for the most part continued to dwell there until killed out. So it is at the present day. Not the most foolish elephant would under similar conditions behave as the rhinos that we studied and hunted by Kilimakiu and in the Sotik behaved. No elephant, in regions where they have been much persecuted by hunters, would habitually spend its days lying or standing in the open plain; nor would it, in such places, repeatedly, and in fact, uniformly, permit men to walk boldly up to it without heeding them until in its immediate neighborhood. The elephant's sight is bad, as is that of the rhinoceros; but a comparatively brief experience with rifle-bearing man usually makes the former take refuge in regions where scent and hearing count for more than sight; while no experience has any such effect on the rhino. The rhinos that now live in the bush are the descendants of those which always lived in the bush; and it is in the bush that the species will linger long after it has vanished from the open; and it is in the bush that it is most formidable.

Elephant and rhino differ as much in their habits as in their intelligence. The former is very gregarious, herds of several hundred being sometimes found, and is of a restless, wandering temper, often shifting his abode and sometimes making long migrations. The rhinoceros is a lover of solitude; it is usually found alone, or a bull and cow, or cow and calf may be in company; very rarely are as many as half a dozen found together. Moreover, it is comparatively stationary in its habits, and as a general thing stays permanently in one neighborhood, not shifting its position for very many miles unless for grave reasons.

The African elephant has recently been divided into a number of sub-species; but as within a century its range was continuous over nearly the whole continent south of the Sahara, and as it was given to such extensive occasional wanderings, it is probable that the examination of a sufficient series of specimens would show that on their confines these races grade into one another. In its essentials the beast is almost everywhere the same, although, of course, there must be variation of habit with any animal which exists throughout so wide and diversified a range of territory; for in one place it is found in high mountains, in another in a dry desert, in another in low-lying marshes or wet and dense forests.

In East Africa the old bulls are usually found singly or in small parties by themselves. These have the biggest tusks; the bulls in the prime of life, the herd bulls or breeding bulls, which keep in herds with the cows and calves, usually have smaller ivory. Sometimes, however, very old but vigorous bulls are found with the cows; and I am inclined to think that the ordinary herd bulls at times also keep by themselves, or at least in company with only a few cows, for at certain seasons, generally immediately after the rains, cows, most of them with calves, appear in great numbers at certain places, where only a few bulls are ever found. Where undisturbed elephant rest, and wander about at all times of the day and night, and feed without much regard to fixed hours. Morning or evening, noon or midnight, the herd may be on the move, or its members may be resting; yet, during the hottest hours of noon they seldom feed, and ordinarily stand almost still, resting—for elephant very rarely lie down unless sick. Where they are afraid of man, their only enemy, they come out to feed in thinly forested plains, or cultivated fields, when they do so at all, only at night, and before daybreak move back into the forest to rest. Elsewhere they sometimes spend the day in the open, in grass or low bush. Where we were, at this time, on Kenia, the elephants sometimes moved down at night to feed in the shambas, at the expense of the crops of the natives, and sometimes stayed in the forest, feeding by day or night on the branches they tore off the trees, or, occasionally, on the roots they grubbed up with their tusks. They work vast havoc among the young or small growth of a forest, and the readiness with which they uproot, overturn, or break off medium sized trees coveys a striking impression of their enormous strength. I have seen a tree a foot in diameter thus uprooted and overturned.

The African elephant has never, like his Indian kinsman, been trained to man's use. There is still hope that the feat may be performed; but hitherto its probable economic usefulness has for various reasons seemed so questionable that there has been scant encouragement to undergo the necessary expense and labor. Up to the present time the African elephant has yielded only his ivory as an asset of value. This, however, has been of such great value as wellnigh to bring about the mighty beast's utter extermination. Ivory hunters and ivory traders have penetrated Africa to the haunts of the elephant since centuries before our era, and the elephant boundaries have been slowly receding throughout historic time; but during the century just passed its process has been immensely accelerated, until now there are but one or two out-of-the-way nooks of the Dark Continent to the neighborhood of which hunter and trader have not penetrated. Fortunately the civilized powers which now divide dominion over Africa have waked up in time, and there is at present no danger of the extermination of the lord of all four-footed creatures. Large reserves have been established on which various herds of elephants now live what is, at least for the time being, an entirely safe life. Furthermore, over great tracts of territory outside the reserves regulations have been promulgated which, if enforced as they are now enforced, will present any excessive diminution of the herds. In British East Africa, for instance, no cows are allowed to be shot save for special purposes, as for preservation in a museum, or to safeguard life and property; and no bulls with tusks weighing less than thirty pounds apiece. This renders safe almost all the females and an ample supply of breeding males. Too much praise cannot be given the governments and the individuals who have brought about this happy result; the credit belongs especially to England and to various Englishmen. It would be a veritable and most tragic calamity if the lordly elephant, the giant among existing four-footed creatures, should be permitted to vanish from the face of the earth.

But of course protection is not permanently possible over the greater part of that country which is well fitted for settlement; nor anywhere, if the herds grow too numerous. It would be not merely silly, but worse than silly, to try to stop all killing of elephants. The unchecked increase of any big and formidable wild beast, even though not a flesh eater, is incompatible with the existence of man when he has emerged from the state of lowest savagery. This is not a matter of theory, but of proved fact. In place after place in Africa where protection has been extended to hippopotamus or buffalo, rhinoceros or elephant, it has been found necessary to withdraw it because the protected animals did such damage to property, or became such menaces to human life. Among all four species cows with calves often attack men without provocation, and old bulls are at any time likely to become infected by a spirit of wanton and ferocious mischief and apt to become mankillers. I know settlers who tried to preserve the rhinoceros which they found living on their big farms, and who were obliged to abandon the attempt, and themselves to kill the rhinos because of repeated and wanton attacks on human beings by the latter. Where we were by Neri, a year or two before our visit, the rhinos had become so dangerous, killing one white man and several natives, that the District Commissioner who preceded Mr. Browne was forced to undertake a crusade against them, killing fifteen. Both in South Africa and on the Nile protection extended to hippopotamus has in places been wholly withdrawn because of the damage done by the beast to the crops of the natives, or because of their unprovoked assaults on canoes and boats. In one instance a last surviving hippo was protected for years, but finally grew bold because of immunity, killed a boy in sheer wantonness, and had to be himself slain. In Uganda the buffalo were for years protected, and grew so bold, killed so many natives, and ruined so many villages that they are now classed as vermin and their destruction in every way encouraged. In the very neighborhood where I was hunting at Kenia but six weeks before my coming, a cow buffalo had wandered down into the plains and run amuck, had attacked two villages, had killed a man and a boy, and had then been mobbed to death by the spearmen. Elephant, when in numbers, and when not possessed of the fear of man, are more impossible neighbors than hippo, rhino, or buffalo; but they are so eagerly sought after by ivory hunters that it is only rarely that they get the chance to become really dangerous to life, although in many places their ravages among the crops are severely felt by the unfortunate natives who live near them.

The chase of the elephant, if persistently followed, entails more fatigue and hardship than any other kind of African hunting. As regards risk, it is hard to say whether it is more or less dangerous than the chase of the lion and the buffalo. Both Cuninghame and Tarlton, men of wide experience, ranked elephant hunting, in point of danger, as nearly on the level with lion hunting, and as more dangerous than buffalo hunting; and all three kinds as far more dangerous than the chase of the rhino. Personally, I believe the actual conflict with a lion, where the conditions are the same, to be normally the more dangerous sport; though far greater demands are made by elephant hunting on the qualities of personal endurance and hardihood and resolute perseverance in the face of disappointment and difficulty. Buffalo, seemingly, do not charge as freely as elephant, but are more dangerous when they do charge. Rhino when hunted, though at times ugly customers, seem to me certainly less dangerous than the other three; but from sheer stupid truculence they are themselves apt to take the offensive in unexpected fashion, being far more prone to such aggression than are any of the others—man-eating lions always excepted.

Very few of the native tribes in Africa hunt the elephant systematically. But the 'Ndorobo, the wild bush people of East Africa, sometimes catch young elephants in the pits they dig with slow labor, and very rarely they kill one with a kind of harpoon. The 'Ndorobo are doubtless in part descended from some primitive bush people, but in part also derive their blood from the more advanced tribes near which their wandering families happen to live; and they grade into the latter, by speech and through individuals who seem to stand half-way between. Thus we had with us two Masai 'Ndorobo, true wild people, who spoke a bastard Masai; who

had formerly hunted with Cuninghame, and who came to us because of their ancient friendship with him. These shy wood creatures were afraid to come to Neri by daylight, when we were
camped there, but after dark crept to Cuninghame's tent. Cuninghame gave them two fine red blankets, and put them to sleep in a
little tent, keeping their spears in his own tent, as a matter of pre-
caution to prevent their running away. The elder of the two, he informed me, would certainly have a fit of hysterics when we killed
our elephant! Cuninghame was also joined by other old friends of
former hunts, Kikuyu 'Ndorobo these, who spoke Kikuyu like the
people who cultivated the fields that covered the river-bottoms
and hill-sides of the adjoining open country, and who were, indeed,
merely outlying, forest-dwelling members of the lowland tribes. In
the deep woods we met one old Dorobo, who had no connection
with any more advanced tribe, whose sole belongings were his
spear, skin cloak, and fire stick, and who lived purely on honey and
game; unlike the bastard 'Ndorobo, he was ornamented with neither paint nor grease. But the 'Ndorobo who were our guides stood
farther up in the social scale. The men passed most of their time in
the forest, but up the mountain sides they had squalid huts on
little clearings, with shambas, where their wives raised scanty
crops. To the 'Ndorobo, and to them alone, the vast, thick forest
was an open book; without their aid as guides both Cuninghame
and our own gun-bearers were at fault, and found their way around
with great difficulty and slowness. The bush people had nothing in
the way of clothing save a blanket over the shoulders, but wore the
usual paint and grease and ornaments; each carried a spear which
might have a long and narrow, or short and broad blade; two of
them wore head-dresses *of tripe*—skull-caps made from the inside
of a sheep's stomach.

For two days after reaching our camp in the open glade on the
mountain side it rained. We were glad of this, because it meant that
the elephants would not be in the bamboos, and Cuninghame and
the 'Ndorobo went off to hunt for fresh signs. Cuninghame is as

skilful an elephant hunter as can be found in Africa, and is one of the very few white men able to help even the wild bushmen at their work. By the afternoon of the second day they were fairly well satisfied as to the whereabouts of the quarry.

The following morning a fine rain was still falling when Cuninghame, Heller, and I started on our hunt but by noon it had stopped. Of course we went in single file and on foot; not even a bear hunter from the cane-brakes of the lower Mississippi could ride through that forest. We left our home camp standing, taking blankets and a coat and a change of underclothing for each of us, and two small Whymper tents, with enough food for three days; I also took my wash kit and a book from the Pigskin Library. First marched the 'Ndorobo guides, each with his spear, his blanket round his shoulders, and a little bundle of corn and sweet potato. Then came Cuninghame, followed by his gun-bearer. Then I came, clad in khaki-colored flannel shirt and khaki trousers buttoning down the legs, with hob-nailed shoes and a thick slouch hat; I had intended to wear rubber-soled shoes, but the soaked ground was too slippery. My two gun-bearers followed, carrying the Holland and the Springfield. Then came Heller, at the head of a dozen porters and skinners; he and they were to fall behind when we actually struck fresh elephant spoor, but to follow our trail by the help of a Dorobo who was left with them.

For three hours our route lay along the edge of the woods. We climbed into and out of deep ravines in which groves of tree ferns clustered. We waded through streams of swift water, whose course was broken by cataract and rapid. We passed through shambas, and by the doors of little hamlets of thatched beehive huts. We met flocks of goats and hairy, fat-tailed sheep guarded by boys, strings of burden-bearing women stood meekly to one side to let us pass; parties of young men sauntered by, spear in hand.

Then we struck into the great forest, and in an instant the sun was shut from sight by the thick screen of wet foliage. It was a riot of twisted vines, interlacing the trees and bushes. Only the elephant paths, which, of every age, crossed and recrossed it hither and thither, made it passable. One of the chief difficulties in hunting elephants in the forest is that it is impossible to travel, except very slowly and with much noise, off these trails, so that it is sometimes very difficult to take advantage of the wind; and although the sight of the elephant is dull, both its sense of hearing and its sense of smell are exceedingly acute.

Hour after hour we worked our way onward through tangled forest and matted jungle. There was little sign of bird or animal life. A troop of long-haired black and white monkeys bounded away among the tree tops. Here and there brilliant flowers lightened the gloom. We ducked under vines and climbed over fallen timber. Poisonous nettles stung our hands. We were drenched by the wet boughs which we brushed aside. Mosses and ferns grew rank and close. The trees were of strange kinds. There were huge trees with little leaves, and small trees with big leaves. There were trees with bare, fleshy limbs, that writhed out through the neighboring branches, bearing sparse clusters of large frondage. In places the forest was low, the trees thirty or forty feet high, the bushes, that choked the ground between, fifteen or twenty feet high. In other places mighty monarchs of the wood, straight and tall, towered aloft to an immense height; among them were trees whose smooth, round boles were spotted like sycamores, while far above our heads their gracefully spreading branches were hung with vines like mistletoe and draped with Spanish moss; trees whose surfaces were corrugated and knotted as if they were made of bundles of great creepers; and giants whose buttressed trunks were four times a man's length across.

Twice we got on elephant spoor, once of a single bull, once of a party of three. Then Cuninghame and the 'Ndorobo redoubled their caution. They would minutely examine the fresh dung; and above all they continually tested the wind, scanning the tree tops, and lighting matches to see from the smoke what the eddies were near the ground. Each time after an hour's stealthy stepping and crawling along the twisted trail a slight shift of the wind in the almost still air gave our scent to the game, and away it went before we could catch a glimpse of it; and we resumed our walk. The elephant paths led up hill and down—for the beasts are wonderful climbers—and wound in and out in every direction. They were marked by broken branches and the splintered and shattered trunks of smaller trees, especially where the elephant had stood and fed, trampling down the bushes for many yards around. Where they had crossed the marshy valleys they had punched big round holes, three feet deep, in the sticky mud.

As evening fell we pitched camp by the side of a little brook at the bottom of a ravine, and dined ravenously on bread, mutton, and tea. The air was keen, and under our blankets we slept in comfort until dawn. Breakfast was soon over and camp struck; and once more we began our cautious progress through the dim, cool archways of the mountain forest.

Two hours after leaving camp we came across the fresh trail of a small herd of perhaps ten or fifteen elephant cows and calves, but including two big herd bulls. At once we took up the trail. Cuninghame and his bush people consulted again and again, scanning every track and mark with minute attention. The signs showed that the elephants had fed in the shambas early in the night, had then returned to the mountain, and stood in one place resting for several hours, and had left this sleeping ground some time before we reached it. After we had followed the trail a short while we made the experiment of trying to force our own way through the jungle, so as to get the wind more favorable but our progress was too slow and noisy, and we returned to the path the elephants had beaten. Then the 'Ndorobo went ahead, travelling noiselessly and at speed. One of them was clad in a white blanket, and another in a red one, which were conspicuous; but they were too silent and cautious to let the beasts see them, and could tell exactly where they were and what they were doing by the sounds. When these trackers waited for us they would appear before us like ghosts; once one of them dropped down from the branches above, having climbed a tree with monkey-like ability to get a glimpse of the great game.

At last we could hear the elephants, and under Cuninghame's lead we walked more cautiously than ever. The wind was right, and the trail of one elephant led close alongside that of the rest of the herd, and parallel thereto. It was about noon. The elephants moved slowly, and we listened to the boughs crack, and now and then to the curious internal rumblings of the great beasts. Carefully, every sense on the alert, we kept pace with them. My double-barrel was in my hands, and, wherever possible, as I followed the trail, I stepped in the huge footprints of the elephant, for where such a weight had pressed there were no sticks left to crack under my feet. It made our veins thrill thus for half an hour to creep stealthily along, but a few rods from the herd, never able to see it, because of the extreme denseness of the cover, but always hearing first one and then another of its members, and always trying to guess what each one might do, and keeping ceaselessly ready for whatever might befall. A flock of hornbills flew up with noisy clamor, but the elephants did not heed them.

At last we came in sight of the mighty game. The trail took a twist to one side, and there, thirty yards in front of us, we made out part of the gray and massive head of an elephant resting his tusks on the branches of a young tree. A couple of minutes passed before, by cautious scrutiny, we were able to tell whether the animal was a cow or a bull, and whether, if a bull, it carried heavy enough tusks. Then we saw that it was a big bull with good ivory. It turned its head in my direction and I saw its eye; and I fired a little to one side of the eye, at a spot which I thought would lead to the brain. I struck exactly where I aimed, but the head of an elephant is enormous and the brain small, and the bullet missed it. However, the shock momentarily stunned the beast. He stumbled forward, half falling, and as he recovered I fired with the second barrel, again aiming for the brain. This time the bullet sped true, and as I lowered the rifle from my shoulder, I saw the great lord of the forest come crashing to the ground.

But at that very instant, before there was a moment's time in which to reload, the thick bushes parted immediately on my left front, and through them surged the vast bulk of a charging bull elephant, the matted mass of tough creepers snapping like packthread before his rush. He was so close that he could have touched me with his trunk. I leaped to one side and dodged behind a tree trunk, opening the rifle, throwing out the empty shells, and slipping in two cartridges. Meanwhile Cuninghame fired right and left, at the same time throwing himself into the bushes on the other side. Both his bullets went home, and the bull stopped short in his charge, wheeled, and immediately disappeared in the thick cover. We ran forward, but the forest had closed over his wake. We heard him trumpet shrilly, and then all sound ceased.

The 'Ndorobo, who had quite properly disappeared when this second bull charged, now went forward, and soon returned with the report that he had fled at speed, but was evidently hard hit, as there was much blood on the spoor. If we had been only after ivory we should have followed him at once; but there was no telling how long a chase he might lead us; and as we desired to save the skin of the dead elephant entire, there was no time whatever to spare. It is a formidable task, occupying many days, to preserve an elephant for mounting in a museum, and if the skin is to be properly saved, it must be taken off without an hour's unnecessary delay.

So back we turned to where the dead tusker lay, and I felt proud indeed as I stood by the immense bulk of the slain monster and put my hand on the ivory. The tusks weighed a hundred and thirty pounds the pair. There was the usual scene of joyful excitement among the gun-bearers—who had behaved excellently—and among the wild bush people who had done the tracking for us; and, as Cuninghame had predicted, the old Masai Dorobo, from pure delight, proceeded to have hysterics on the body of the dead elephant. The scene was repeated when Heller and the porters appeared half an hour later. Then, chattering like monkeys, and as happy as possible, all, porters, gun-bearers, and 'Ndorobo alike, began the work of skinning and cutting up the quarry, under the leadership and supervision of Heller and Cuninghame, and soon they were all splashed with blood from head to foot. One of the trackers took off his blanket and squatted stark naked inside the carcass the better to use his knife. Each laborer rewarded himself by cutting off strips of meat for his private store, and hung them in red festoons from the branches round about. There was no let up in the work until it was stopped by darkness.

Our tents were pitched in a small open glade a hundred yards from the dead elephant. The night was clear, the stars shone brightly, and in the west the young moon hung just above the line of tall tree tops. Fires were speedily kindled and the men sat around them, feasting and singing in a strange minor tone until late in the night. The flickering light left them at one moment in black obscurity, and the next brought into bold relief their sinewy crouching figures, their dark faces, gleaming eyes, and flashing teeth. When they did sleep, two of the 'Ndorobo slept so close to the fire as to burn themselves; an accident to which they are prone, judging from the many scars of old burns on their legs. I toasted slices of elephant's heart on a pronged stick before the fire, and found it delicious; for I was hungry, and the night was cold. We talked of our success and exulted over it, and made our plans for the morrow; and then we turned in under our blankets for another night's sleep.

Next morning some of the 'Ndorobo went off on the trail of Cuninghame's elephant to see if it had fallen, but found that it had travelled steadily, though its wounds were probably mortal. There was no object in my staying, for Heller and Cuninghame would be busy for the next ten days, and would ultimately have to use all the porters in taking off and curing the skin, and transporting it to Neri; so I made up my mind to go down to the plains for a hunt by myself. Taking one porter to carry my bedding, and with my gun-bearers, and a Dorobo as guide, I struck off through the forest for the main camp, reaching it early in the afternoon. Thence I bundled off a safari to Cuninghame and Heller, with food for a week, and tents and clothing; and then enjoyed the luxury of a shave and a warm bath. Next day was spent in writing and in making preparations for my own trip. A Kikuyu chief, clad in a cloak of hyrax skins, and carrying his war spear, came to congratulate me on killing the elephant and to present me with a sheep. Early the following morning everything was in readiness; the bull-necked porters lifted their loads, I stepped out in front, followed by my led horse, and in ten hours' march we reached Neri boma with its neat building, its trees, and its well-kept flower beds.

My hunting and travelling during the following fortnight will be told in the next chapter. On the evening of September 6th we were all together again at Meru boma, on the north-eastern slopes of Kenia—Kermit, Tarlton, Cuninghame, Heller, and I. Thanks to the unfailing kindness of the Commissioner, Mr. Horne, we were given full information of the elephant in the neighborhood. He had no 'Ndorobo, but among the Wa-Meru, a wild martial tribe, who lived close around him, there were a number of hunters, or at least of men who knew the forest and the game, and these had been instructed to bring in any news.

We had, of course, no idea that elephant would be found close at hand. But next morning, about eleven, Horne came to our camp with four of his black scouts, who reported that three elephants were in a patch of thick jungle beside the shambas, not three miles away. Horne said that the elephants were cows, that they had been in the neighborhood some days, devastating the shambas, and were bold and fierce, having charged some men who sought to drive them away from the cultivated fields; it is curious to see how little heed these elephants pay to the natives. I wished a cow for the museum, and also another bull. So off we started at once, Kermit carrying his camera. I slipped on my rubber-soled shoes, and had my gun-bearers accompany me bare-footed, with the Holland and the Springfield rifles. We followed foot-paths among the fields until we reached the edge of the jungle in which the elephants stood.

This jungle lay beside the forest, and at this point separated it from the fields. It consisted of a mass of rank-growing bushes, allied to the cotton-plant, ten or twelve feet high, with only here and there a tree. It was not good ground in which to hunt elephant, for the tangle was practically impenetrable to a hunter save along the elephant trails, whereas the elephants themselves could move in any direction at will, with no more difficulty than a man would have in a hay-field. The bushes in most places rose just above their backs, so that they were completely hid from the hunter even a few feet away. Yet the cover afforded no shade to the mighty beasts, and it seemed strange that elephants should stand in it at mid-day with the sun out. There they were, however, for, looking cautiously into the cover from behind the bushes on a slight hill crest a quarter of a mile off, we could just make out a huge ear now and then as it lazily flapped.

On account of the wind we had to go well to one side before entering the jungle. Then in we went in single file, Cuninghame and Tarlton leading, with a couple of our naked guides. The latter showed no great desire to get too close, explaining that the elephants were "very fierce." Once in the jungle, we trod as quietly as possible, threading our way along the elephant trails, which crossed and re-crossed one another. Evidently it was a favorite haunt, for the sign was abundant, both old and new. In the impenetrable cover it was quite impossible to tell just where the elephants were, and twice we sent one of the savages up a tree to locate the game. The last time the watcher, who stayed in the tree, indicated by signs that the elephant were not far off; and his companions wished to lead us round to where the cover was a little lower and thinner. But to do so would have given them our wind, and Cuninghame refused, taking into his own hands the management of the stalk. I kept my heavy rifle at the ready, and on we went, in watchful silence, prepared at any moment for a charge. We could not tell at what second we might catch our first glimpse at very close quarters of "the beast that hath between his eyes the serpent for a hand," and when thus surprised the temper of "the huge earth-shaking beast" is sometimes of the shortest.

Cuninghame and Tarlton stopped for a moment to consult; Cuninghame stooped, and Tarlton mounted his shoulders and stood upright, steadying himself by my hand. Down he came and told us that he had seen a small tree shake seventy yards distant; although upright on Cuninghame's shoulder he could not see the elephant itself. Forward we stole for a few yards, and then a piece of good luck befell us, for we came on the trunk of a great fallen tree, and scrambling up, we found ourselves perched in a row six feet above the ground. The highest part of the trunk was near the root, farthest from where the elephants were; and though it offered precarious footing, it also offered the best lookout. Thither I balanced, and looking over the heads of my companions I at once made out the elephant. At first I could see nothing but the shaking branches, and one huge ear occasionally flapping. Then I made out the ear of another beast, and then the trunk of a third was uncurled, lifted, and curled again; it showered its back with earth. The watcher we had left behind in the tree top coughed, the elephants stood motionless, and up went the biggest elephant's trunk, feeling for the wind; the watcher coughed again, and then the bushes and saplings swayed and parted as three black bulks came toward us. The cover was so high that we could not see their tusks, only the tops of their heads and their backs being visible. The leader was the biggest, and at it I fired when it was sixty yards away, and nearly broadside on, but heading slightly toward me. I had previously warned every one to kneel. The recoil of the heavy rifle made me rock, as I stood unsteadily on my perch, and I failed to hit the brain. But the bullet, only missing the brain by an inch or two, brought the elephant to its knees; as it rose I floored it with the second barrel. The blast of the big rifle, by the way, was none too pleasant for the other men on the log and made Cuninghame's nose bleed. Reloading, I fired twice at the next animal, which was now turning. It stumbled and nearly fell, but at the same moment the first one rose again, and I fired both barrels into its head, bringing it once more to the ground. Once again it rose—an elephant's brain is not an easy mark to hit under such conditions—but as it moved slowly off, half stunned, I snatched the little Springfield rifle, and this time shot true, sending the bullet into its brain. As it fell I took another shot at the wounded elephant, now disappearing in the forest, but without effect.

On walking up to our prize it proved to be not a cow, but a good-sized adult (but not old) herd bull, with thick, short tusks weighing about forty pounds apiece. Ordinarily, of course, a bull, and not a cow, is what one desires, although on this occasion I needed a cow to complete the group for the National Museum. However, Heller and Cuninghame spent the next few days in preserving the skin, which I after gave to the University of California; and I was too much pleased with our luck to feel inclined to grumble. We were back in camp five hours after leaving it. Our gun-bearers usually felt it incumbent on them to keep a dignified bearing while in our company. But the death of an elephant is always a great event; and one of the gun-bearers, as they walked ahead of us campward, soon began to improvise a song, reciting the success of the hunt, the death of the elephant, and the power of the rifles; and gradually, as they got farther ahead, the more light-hearted among them began to give way to their spirits and they came into camp frolicking, gambolling, and dancing as if they were still the naked savages that they had been before they became the white man's followers.

Two days later Kermit got his bull. He and Tarlton had camped about ten miles off in a magnificent forest, and late the first afternoon received news that a herd of elephants was in the neighborhood. They were off by dawn, and in a few hours came on the herd.

It consisted chiefly of cows and calves, but there was one big master bull, with fair tusks. It was open forest with long grass. By careful stalking they got within thirty yards of the bull, behind whom
was a line of cows. Kermit put both barrels of his heavy double .450
into the tusker's head, but without even staggering him; and as he
walked off Tarlton also fired both barrels into him, with no more
effect; then, as he slowly turned, Kermit killed him with a shot in
the brain from the .405 Winchester. Immediately the cows lifted
their ears, and began trumpeting and threatening; if they had come
on in a body at that distance, there was not much chance of turning
them or of escaping from them: and after standing stock still for a
minute or two, Kermit and Tarlton stole quietly off for a hundred
yards, and waited until the anger of the cows cooled and they had
moved away, before going up to the dead bull. Then they followed
the herd again, and Kermit got some photos which, as far as I know,
are better than any that have ever been taken of wild elephant. He
took them close up, at imminent risk of a charge.

The following day the two hunters rode back to Meru, making
a long circle. The elephants they saw were not worth shooting, but
they killed the finest rhinoceros we had yet seen. They saw it in an
open space of tall grass, surrounded by lantana brush, a flowering
shrub with close-growing stems, perhaps twenty feet high and no
thicker than a man's thumb; it forms a favorite cover for elephants
and rhinoceros, and is well nigh impenetrable to hunters. Fortunately this particular rhino was outside it, and Kermit and Tarlton
got up to about twenty-five yards from him. Kermit then put one
bullet behind his shoulder, and as he whipped round to charge, another bullet on the point of his shoulder; although mortally
wounded, he showed no signs whatever of being hurt, and came at
the hunters with great speed and savage desire to do harm. Then
an extraordinary thing happened. Tarlton fired, inflicting merely a
flesh wound in one shoulder, and the big, fearsome brute, which
had utterly disregarded the two fatal shots, on receiving this flesh
wound, wheeled and ran. Both firing, they killed him before he
had gone many yards. He was a bull, with a thirty-inch horn.

By this time Cuninghame and Heller had finished the skin and skeleton of the bull they were preserving. Near the carcass Heller trapped an old male leopard, a savage beast; its skin was in fine shape, but it was not fat, and weighed just one hundred pounds. Now we all joined, and shifted camp to a point eight or nine miles distant from Meru boma, and fifteen hundred feet lower among the foot-hills. It was much hotter at this lower level; palms were among the trees that bordered the streams. On the day we shifted camp Tarlton and I rode in advance to look for elephants, followed by our gun-bearers and half a dozen wild Meru hunters, each carrying a spear or a bow and arrows. When we reached the hunting grounds, open country with groves of trees and patches of jungle, the Meru went off in every direction to find elephant. We waited their return under a tree, by a big stretch of cultivated ground. The region was well peopled, and all the way down the path had led between fields, which the Meru women were tilling with their adze-like hoes, and banana plantations, where among the bananas other trees had been planted, and the yam vines trained up their trunks. These cool, shady banana plantations, fenced in with tall hedges and bordered by rapid brooks, were really very attractive. Among them were scattered villages of conical thatched huts, and level places plastered with cow dung on which the grain was threshed; it was then stored in huts raised on posts. There were herds of cattle, and flocks of sheep and goats; and among the burdens the women bore we often saw huge bottles of milk. In the shambas there were platforms, and sometimes regular thatched huts, placed in the trees; these were for the watchers, who were to keep the elephants out of the shambas at night. Some of the natives wore girdles of banana leaves, looking, as Kermit said, much like the pictures of savages in Sunday-school books.

Early in the afternoon some of the scouts returned with news that three bull elephants were in a piece of forest a couple of miles distant, and thither we went. It was an open grove of heavy thorn timber beside a strip of swamp; among the trees the grass grew tall, and there were many thickets of abutilon, a flowering shrub a dozen feet high. On this the elephant were feeding. Tarlton's favorite sport was lion hunting, but he was also a first-class elephant hunter, and he brought me up to these bulls in fine style. Although only three hundred yards away, it took us two hours to get close to them. Tarlton and the "shenzis"—wild naives, called in Swahili (a kind of African chinook) "wa-shenzi"—who were with us, climbed tree after tree, first to place the elephants, and then to see if they carried ivory heavy enough to warrant my shooting them. At last Tarlton brought me to within fifty yards of them. Two were feeding in bush which hid them from view, and the third stood between, facing us. We could only see the top of his head and back, and not his tusks, and could not tell whether he was worth shooting. Much puzzled, we stood where we were, peering anxiously at the huge, half-hidden game. Suddenly there was a slight eddy in the wind, up went the elephant's trunk, twisting to and fro in the air; evidently he could not catch a clear scent; but in another moment we saw the three great dark forms moving gently off through the bush. As rapidly as possible, following the trails already trampled by the elephants, we walked forward, and after a hundred yards Tarlton pointed to a big bull with good tusks standing motionless behind some small trees seventy yards distant. As I aimed at his head he started to move off; the first bullet from the heavy Holland brought him to his knees, and as he rose I knocked him flat with the second. He struggled to rise; but, both firing, we kept him down; and I finished him with a bullet in the brain from the little Springfield. Although rather younger than either of the bulls I had already shot, it was even larger. In its stomach were beans from the shambas, abutilon tips, and bark, and especially the twigs, leaves, and white blossoms of the smaller shrub. The tusks weighed a little over a hundred pounds the pair.

We still needed a cow for the museum; and a couple of days later, at noon, a party of natives brought in word that they had seen two cows in a spot five miles away. Piloted by a naked spearman, whose hair was done into a cue, we rode toward the place. For most of the distance we followed old elephant trails, in some places mere tracks beaten down through stiff grass which stood above the head of a man on horseback, in other places paths rutted deep into the earth. We crossed a river, where monkeys chattered among the tree tops. On an open plain we saw a rhinoceros cow trotting off with her calf. At last we came to a hill-top with, on the summit, a noble fig-tree, whose giant limbs were stretched over the palms that clustered beneath. Here we left our horses and went forward on foot, crossing a palm-fringed stream in a little valley. From the next rise we saw the backs of the elephants as they stood in a slight valley, where the rank grass grew ten or twelve feet high. It was some time before we could see the ivory so as to be sure of exactly what we were shooting. Then the biggest cow began to move slowly forward, and we walked nearly parallel to her, along an elephant trail, until from a slight knoll I got a clear view of her at a distance of eighty yards. As she walked leisurely along, almost broadside to me, I fired the right barrel of the Holland into her head, knocking her flat down with the shock; and when she rose I put a bullet from the left barrel through her heart, again knocking her completely off her feet; and this time she fell permanently. She was a very old cow, and her ivory was rather better than in the average of her sex in this neighborhood, the tusks weighing about eighteen pounds apiece. She had been ravaging the shambas over night—which accounted in part for the natives being so eager to show her to me—and in addition to leaves and grass, her stomach contained quantities of beans. There was a young one—just out of calfhood, and quite able to take care of itself—with her; it ran off as soon as the mother fell.

Early next morning Cuninghame and Heller shifted part of the safari to the stream near where the dead elephant lay, intending to spend the following three days in taking off and preparing the skin. Meanwhile Tarlton, Kermit, and I were to try our luck in a short hunt on the other side of Meru boma, at a little crater lake called

Lake Ingouga. We could not get an early start, and reached Meru too late to push on to the lake the same day.

The following morning we marched to the lake in two hours and a half. We spent an hour in crossing a broad tongue of woodland that stretched down from the wonderful mountain forest lying higher on the slopes. The trail was blind in many places because elephant paths of every age continually led along and across it, some of them being much better marked than the trail itself, as it twisted through the sun-flecked shadows underneath the great trees. Then we came out on high downs, covered with tall grass and littered with volcanic stones; and broken by ravines which were choked with dense under-brush. There were high hills, and to the left of the downs, toward Kenia, these were clad in forest. We pitched our tents on a steep cliff overlooking the crater lake—or pond, as it might more properly be called. It was bordered with sedge, and through the water-lilies on its surface we saw the reflection of the new moon after nightfall. Here and there thick forest came down to the brink, and through this, on opposite sides of the pond, deeply worn elephant paths, evidently travelled for ages, wound down to the water.

That evening we hunted for bushbuck, but saw none. While sitting on a hillock at dusk, watching for game, a rhino trotted up to inspect us, with ears cocked forward and tail erect. A rhino always has something comic about it, like a pig, formidable though it at times is. This one carried a poor horn, and therefore we were pleased when at last it trotted off without obliging us to shoot it. We saw new kinds of whydah birds, one with a yellow breast, one with white in its tail; at this altitude the cocks were still in full plumage, although it was just past the middle of September; whereas at Naivasha they had begun to lose their long tail feathers nearly two months previously.

On returning to camp we received a note from Cuninghame saying that Heller had been taken seriously sick, and Tarlton had to go to them. This left Kermit and me to take our two days' hunt together.

One day we got nothing. We saw game on the open downs, but it was too wary, and though we got within twenty-five yards of eland in thick cover, we could only make out a cow, and she took fright and ran without our ever getting a glimpse of the bull that was with her. Late in the afternoon we saw an elephant a mile and a half away, crossing a corner of the open downs. We followed its trail until the light grew too dim for shooting, but never overtook it, although at the last we could hear it ahead of us breaking the branches; and we made our way back to camp through the darkness.

The other day made amends. It was Kermit's turn to shoot an elephant, and mine to shoot a rhinoceros; and each of us was to act as the backing gun for the other. In the forenoon, we saw a bull rhino with a good horn walking over the open downs. A convenient hill enabled us to cut him off without difficulty, and from its summit we killed him at the base, fifty or sixty yards off. His front horn was nearly twenty-nine inches long; but though he was an old bull, his total length, from tip of nose to tip of tail, was only twelve feet, and he was, I should guess, not more than two-thirds the bulk of the big bull I killed in the Sotik.

We rested for an hour or two at noon, under the shade of a very old tree with glossy leaves, and orchids growing on its gnarled, hoary limbs, while the unsaddled horses grazed, and the gun-bearers slept near by, the cool mountain air, though this was mid-day under the equator, making them prefer the sunlight to the shade. When we moved on it was through a sea of bush ten or fifteen feet high, dotted here and there with trees; and riddled in every direction by the trails of elephant, rhinoceros, and buffalo. Each of these animals frequents certain kinds of country to which the other two rarely or never penetrate; but here they all three found ground to their liking. Except along their winding trails, which were tunnels where the jungle was tall, it would have been practically impossible to traverse the thick and matted cover in which they had made their abode.

We could not tell what moment we might find ourselves face to face with some big beast at such close quarters as to insure a charge, and we moved in cautious silence, our rifles in our hands. Rhinoceros were especially plentiful, and we continually came across not only their tracks, but the dusty wallows in which they rolled, and where they came to deposit their dung. The fresh sign of elephant, however, distracted our attention from the lesser game, and we followed the big footprints eagerly, now losing the trail, now finding it again. At last near a clump of big trees we caught sight of three huge, dark bodies ahead of us. The wind was right, and we stole toward them, Kermit leading, and I immediately behind. Through the tangled branches their shapes loomed in vague outline; but we saw that one had a pair of long tusks, and our gun-bearers unanimously pronounced it a big bull, with good ivory. A few more steps gave Kermit a chance at its head, at about sixty yards, and with a bullet from his .405 Winchester he floored the mighty beast. I rose, and we both fired in unison, bringing it down again; but as we came up it struggled to get on its feet, roaring savagely, and once more we both fired together. This finished it. We were disappointed at finding that it was not a bull; but it was a large cow, with tusks over five feet long—a very unusual length for a cow—one weighing twenty-five, and the other twenty-two pounds.

Our experience had convinced us that both the Winchester .405, and the Springfield .300 would do good work with elephants; although I kept to my belief that, for such very heavy game, my Holland .500-.450 was an even better weapon.

Not far from where this elephant fell Tarlton had, the year before, witnessed an interesting incident. He was watching a small herd of elephants, cows and calves, which were in the open, when he saw them begin to grow uneasy. Then, with a shrill trumpet, a cow approached a bush, out of which bounded a big lion. Instantly all the cows charged him, and he fled as fast as his legs could carry him for the forest, two hundred yards distant. He just managed to reach the cover in safety; and then the infuriated cows, in their anger at his escape, demolished the forest for several rods in every direction.

To the Uasin Gishu

From the giraffe camp we went two days' journey to the 'Nzoi River. Until this Uasin Gishu trip we had been on waters which either vanished in the desert or else flowed into the Indian Ocean. Now we had crossed the divide, and were on the Nile side of the watershed. The 'Nzoi, a rapid muddy river, passing south of Mount Elgon, empties into the Victoria Nyanza. Our route to its bank led across a rolling country, covered by a dense growth of tall grass, and in most places by open thorn scrub, where here and there, in the shallow valleys or depressions, were swamps. There were lions, and at night we heard them; but in such long grass it was well nigh hopeless to look for them. Evidently troops of elephants occasionally visited these plains, for the tops of the little thorn-trees were torn off and browsed down by the mighty brutes. How they can tear off and swallow such prickly dainties as these thorn branches, armored with needle-pointed spikes, is a mystery. Tarlton told me that he had seen an elephant, while feeding greedily on the young top of a thorn-tree, prick its trunk until it uttered a little scream or whine of pain, and it then in a fit of pettishness revenged itself by wrecking the thorn-tree.

Game abounded on the plains. We saw a couple of herds of giraffes. The hartebeests were the most plentiful and the least shy; time after time a shall herd loitered until we were within a hundred yards before cantering away. Once or twice we saw topi among them; and often there were mixed herds of zebras and hartebeests. Oribi were common, and sometimes uttered a peculiar squealing whistle when they first saw us. The reedbuck also whistled, but their whistle was entirely distinct. It was astonishing how close the reedbuck lay. Again and again we put them up within a few feet of us from patches of reeds or hollows in the long grass. A much more singular habit is the way in which they share these retreats with dangerous wild beasts; a trait common also to the cover-loving bushbuck. From one of the patches of reeds in which Kermit and I shot two hyenas a reedbuck doe immediately afterward took flight. She had been reposing peacefully during the day within fifty yards of several hyenas! Tarlton had more than once found both reedbuck and bushbuck in comparatively small patches of cover which also held lions.

It is, by the way, a little difficult to know what names to use in distinguishing between the sexes of African game. The trouble is one which obtains in all new countries, where the settlers have to name new beasts; and is, of course, primarily due to the fact that the terms already found in the language originally applied only to domestic animals and to European beasts of the chase. Africanders, whether Dutch or English, speak of antelope, of either sex, as "buck." Then they call the males and females of the larger kinds bulls and cows, just as Americans do when they speak of moose, wapiti, and caribou; and the males and females of the smaller kinds they usually speak of as rams and ewes.

While on safari to the 'Nzoi I was even more interested in honey birds which led us to honey than I was in the game. Before starting for Africa John Burroughs had especially charged me to look personally into this extraordinary habit of the honey bird; a habit so extraordinary that he was inclined to disbelieve the reality of its existence. But it unquestionably does exist. Every experienced hunter and every native who lives in the wilderness has again and again been an eyewitness of it. Kermit, in addition to his experience in the Sotik, had been led by a honey bird to honey in a rock, near Lake Hannington. Once while I was tracking game a honey bird made his appearance, chattering loudly and flying beside us; I let two of the porters follow it, and it led them to honey. On the morning of the day we reached the 'Nzoi, a honey bird appeared beside the safari, behaving in the same manner. Some of the men begged to be allowed to follow it; while they were talking to me the honey bird flew to a big tree fifty yards off, and called loudly as it flitted to and fro in the branches; and sure enough there was honey in the tree. I let some of the men stay to get the honey; but they found little except comb filled with grubs. Some of this was put aside for the bird, which ate the grubs. The natives believe that misfortune will follow any failure on their part to leave the honey bird its share of the booty. They also insist that sometimes the honey bird will led a man to a serpent or wild beast; and sure enough Dr. Means was once thus led up to a rhinoceros. While camped on the 'Nzoi the honey birds were almost a nuisance; they were very common, and were continually accompanying us as we hunted, flying from tree to tree, and never ceasing their harsh chatter. Several times we followed birds, which in each case led us to bee trees, and then perched quietly by until the gun-bearers and porters (Gouvimali shone on such occasions) got out the honey—which we found excellent eating by the way.

Our camp here was in a beautiful country, and game, for the most part Uganda kob and singsing waterbuck, often fed in sight of the tents. The kob is a small short-haired waterbuck, with slightly different horns. It is a chunky antelope, with a golden-red coat; I weighed one old buck which I shot and it tipped the beam at two hundred and twenty pounds; Kermit killed a bigger one, weighing two hundred and forty pounds, but its horns were poorer. In their habits the kob somewhat resemble impalla, the does being found in bands of twenty or thirty with a single master buck; and they sometimes make great impalla-like bounds. They fed, at all hours of the day, in the flats near the river, and along the edges of the swamps, and were not very wary. They never tried to hide, and were always easily seen; in utter contrast to the close-lying, skulking, bohor reedbuck, which lay like a rabbit in the long grass or reeds. The kob, on the contrary, were always anxious themselves to see round about, and, like waterbuck and hartebeest, frequently used the ant-heaps as lookout stations. It was a pretty sight to see a herd of the bright red creatures clustered on a big ant-hill, all the necks outstretched, and all the ears thrown forward. The females are hornless. By the middle of November we noticed an occasional new-born calf.

The handsome, shaggy-coated, singing waterbuck had much the same habit as the kob. Like the kob they fed at all hours of the day, but they were more wary and more apt to be found in country where there were a good many bushes or small trees. Waterbuck and kob sometimes associated together.

The best singing bull I got I owed to Tarlton's good eyesight and skill in tracking and stalking. The herd of which he was master bull were shy, and took the alarm just as we first saw them. Tarlton followed their trail for a couple of miles, and then stalked them to an inch, by the dexterous use of a couple of bushes and an ant-hill; the anthill being reached after a two hundred yards' crawl, first on all fours and then flat on the ground, which resulted in my getting a good off-hand shot at a hundred and eighty yards. At this time, about the middle of November, some of the cows had new-born calves. One day I shot a hartebeest bull with horns twenty-four inches long, as it stood on the top of an ant-heap. On going up to it we noticed something behind a little bush, sixty yards off. We were puzzled what it could be, but finally made out a waterbuck cow; and a minute or two later away she bounded to safety, followed by a wee calf. The porters much appreciated the flesh of the water-buck. We did not. It is the poorest eating of African antelope—and among the big antelope only the eland is good as a steady diet.

One day we drove a big swamp, putting a hundred porters across it in line, while Kermit and I walked a little ahead of them along the edges, he on one side and I on the other. I shot a couple of bushbuck, a ewe and a young ram; and after the drive was over he shot a female leopard as she stood on the side of an ant-hill.

There were a number of both reedbuck and bushbuck in the swamp. The reedbuck were all ewes, which we did not want. There were one or two big bushbuck rams, but they broke back through the beaters; and so did two bushbuck ewes and one reed-buck ewe, one of the bushbuck ewes actually knocking down a beater. They usually either cleared out while the beaters were still half a mile distant, or else waited until they were almost trodden on. The bushbuck rams were very dark colored; the hornless ewes, and the young, were a brilliant red, the belly, the under side and edges of the conspicuous fluffy tail, and a few dim spots on the cheek and flanks, being white. Although these buck frequent thick cover, forest, or swamp, and trust for their safety to hiding, and to eluding observation by their stealthy, skulking ways, their coloration has not the smallest protective value, being on the con-trary very conspicuous in both sexes, but especially in the females and young, who most need protection. Bushbuck utter a loud bark. The hooves of those we shot were very long, as is often the case with water-loving, marsh-frequenting species. There is a cu-rious collar-like space around the neck on which there is no hair. Although if anything smaller than our white-tail deer, the bush-buck is a vicious and redoubtable fighter, and will charge a man without hesitation.

The last day we were at the 'Nzoi the porters petitioned for one ample meal of meat; and we shot a dozen buck for them—kongoni, kob, and singsing. One of the latter, a very fine bull, fairly charged Kermit and his gun-bearer when they got within a few yards of it, as it lay wounded. This bull grunted loudly as he charged; the grunt of an oryx under similar circumstances is almost a growl. On this day both Kermit and I were led to bee trees by honey birds and took some of the honey for lunch. Kermit stayed after his boys had left the tree, so as to see exactly what the honey bird did. The boys had smoked out the bees, and when they left the tree was still smoking. Throughout the process the honey bird had stayed quietly in a neighboring tree, occasionally uttering a single bubbling cluck. As soon as the boys left, it flew straight for the smoking bee tree, uttering a long trill, utterly different from the chattering noise made while trying to attract the attention of the men and lead them to the tree; and not only did it eat the grubs, but it also ate the bees that were stupefied by the smoke.

Next day we moved camp to the edge of a swamp about five miles from the river. Near the tents was one of the trees which, not knowing its real name, we called "sausage tree"; the seeds or fruits are encased in a kind of hard gourd, the size of a giant sausage, which swings loosely at the end of a long tendril. The swamp was half or three-quarters of a mile across, with one or two ponds in the middle, from which we shot ducks. Francolins—delicious eating, as the ducks were also—uttered their grating calls near by; while oribi and hartebeest were usually to be seen from the tents. The hartebeest, by the way, in its three forms, is much the commonest game animal of East Africa.

A few miles beyond this swamp we suddenly came on a small herd of elephants in the open. There were eight cows and two calves, and they were moving slowly, feeding on the thorny tops of the scattered mimosas, and of other bushes which were thornless. The eyesight of elephants is very bad; I doubt whether they see more clearly than a rather near-sighted man; and we walked up to within seventy yards of these, slight though the cover was, so that Kermit could try to photograph them. We did not need to kill another cow for the National Museum, and so after we had looked at the huge, interesting creatures as long as we wished, we croaked and whistled, and they moved off with leisurely indifference. There is always a fascination about watching elephants; they are such giants, they are so intelligent—much more so than any other game, except perhaps the lion, whose intelligence has a very sinister bent—and they look so odd with their great ears flapping and their trunks lifting and curling. Elephants are rarely absolutely still for any length of time; now and then they flap an ear, or their bodies sway slightly, while at intervals they utter curious internal rumblings, or trumpet gently. These were feeding on saplings of the mimosas and other trees, apparently caring nothing for the thorns of the former; they would tear off branches, big or little, or snap a trunk short off if the whim seized them. They swallowed the leaves and twigs of these trees; but I have known them merely chew and spit out the stems of certain bushes.

After leaving the elephants we were on our way back to camp when we saw a white man in the trail ahead; and on coming nearer whom should it prove to be but Carl Akeley, who was out on a trip for the American Museum of Natural History in New York. We went with him to his camp, where we found Mrs. Akeley, Clark, who was assisting him, and Messrs. McCutcheon and Stevenson who were along on a hunting trip. They were old friends and I was very glad to see them. McCutcheon, the cartoonist, had been at a farewell lunch given me by Robert Collier just before I left New York, and at the lunch we had been talking much of George Ade, and the first question I put to him was, "*Where* is George Ade?" for if one unexpectedly meets an American cartoonist on a hunting trip in mid-Africa there seems no reason why one should not also see his crony, an American playwright. A year previously Mr. and Mrs. Akeley had lunched with me at the White House, and we had talked over our proposed African trips. Akeley, an old African wanderer, was going out with the especial purpose of getting a group of elephants for the American Museum, and was anxious that I should shoot one or two of them for him. I had told him that I certainly would if it were a possibility and on learning that we had just seen a herd of cows he felt—as I did—that the chance had come for me to fulfill my promise. So we decided that he should camp with us that night, and that next morning we would start with a light outfit to see whether we could not overtake the herd.

An amusing incident occurred that evening. After dark some of the porters went through the reeds to get water from the pond in the middle of the swamp. I was sitting in my tent when a loud yelling and screaming rose from the swamp, and in rushed Kongoni to say that one of the men, while drawing water, had been seized by a lion. Snatching up a rifle I was off at a run for the swamp, calling for lanterns; Kermit and Tarlton joined me, the lanterns were brought, and we reached the meadow of short marsh grass which surrounded the high reeds in the middle. No sooner were we on this meadow than there were loud snortings of a heavy animal galloping across our front. It now developed that there was no lion in the case at all, but that the porters had been chased by a hippo. I should not have supposed that a hippo would live in such a small, isolated swamp; but there he was on the meadow in front of me, invisible, but snorting, and galloping to and fro. Evidently he was much interested in the lights, and we thought he might charge us; but he did not, retreating slowly as we advanced, until he plunged into the little pond. Hippos are sometime dangerous at night, and so we waded through the swamp until we came to the pool at which the porters filled their buckets, and stood guard over them until they were through; while the hippo, unseen in the darkness, came closer to us, snorting and plunging—possibly from wrath and insolence, but more probably from mere curiosity.

Next morning Akeley, Tarlton, Kermit, and I started on our elephant hunt. We were travelling light. I took nothing but my bedding, wash kit, spare socks, and slippers, all in a roll of waterproof canvas. We went to where we had seen the herd and then took up the trail, Kongoni and two or three other gun-bearers walking ahead as trackers. They did their work well. The elephants had not been in the least alarmed. Where they had walked in single file it was easy to follow their trail; but the trackers had hard work puzzling it out where the animals had scattered and loitered along feeding. The trail led up and down hills and through open thorn scrub, and it crossed and recrossed the wooded watercourses in the bottoms of the valleys. At last, after going some ten miles we came on sign where the elephants had fed that morning, and four or five miles further on we overtook them. That we did not scare them into flight was due to Tarlton. The trail went nearly across wind; the trackers were leading us swiftly along it, when suddenly Tarlton heard a low trumpet ahead and the to right hand. We at once doubled back, left the horses, and advanced toward where the noise indicated that the herd was standing.

In a couple of minutes we sighted them. It was just noon. There were six cows, and two well-grown calves—these last being quite big enough to shift for themselves or to be awkward antagonists for any man of whom they could get hold. They stood in a clump, each occasionally shifting its position or lazily flapping an ear; and now and then one would break off a branch with its trunk, tuck it into its mouth, and withdraw it stripped of its leaves. The wind blew fair, we were careful to make no noise, and with ordinary caution we had nothing to fear from their eyesight. The ground was neither forest nor bare plain; it was covered with long grass and a scattered open growth of small scantily leaved trees, chiefly mimosas, but including some trees covered with gorgeous orange-red flowers. After careful scrutiny we advanced behind an ant-hill to within sixty yards, and I stepped forward for the shot.

Akeley wished two cows and a calf. Of the two best cows one had rather thick, worn tusks; those of the other were smaller, but better shaped. The latter stood half facing me, and I put the bullet from the right barrel of the Holland through her lungs, and fired the left barrel for the heart of the other. Tarlton, and then Akeley and Kermit followed suit. At once the herd started diagonally past

379

us, but half halted and faced toward us when only twenty-five yards distant, an unwounded cow beginning to advance with her great ears cocked at right angles to her head; and Tarlton called "Look out; they are coming for us." At such a distance a charge from half a dozen elephant is a serious thing; I put a bullet into the forehead of the advancing cow, causing her to lurch heavily forward to her knees; and then we all fired. The heavy rifles were too much even for such big beasts, and round they spun and rushed off. As they turned I dropped the second cow I had wounded with a shot in the brain, and the cow that had started to charge also fell, though it needed two or three more shots to keep it down as it struggled to rise. The cow at which I had first fired kept on with the rest of the herd, but fell dead before going a hundred yards. After we had turned the herd Kermit with his Winchester killed a bull calf, necessary to complete the museum group; we had been unable to kill it before because we were too busy stopping the charge of the cows. I was sorry to have to shoot the third cow, but with elephant starting to charge at twenty-five yards the risk is too great, and the need of instant action too imperative, to allow of any hesitation.

We pitched camp a hundred yards from the elephants, and Akeley, working like a demon, and assisted by Tarlton, had the skins off the two biggest cows and the calf by the time night fell; I walked out and shot an oribi for supper. Soon after dark the hyenas began to gather at the carcasses and to quarrel among themselves as they gorged. Toward morning a lion came near and uttered a kind of booming, long-drawn moan, an ominous and menacing sound. The hyenas answered with an extraordinary chorus of yelling, howling, laughing, and chuckling, as weird a volume of noise as any to which I ever listened. At dawn we stole down to the carcasses in the faint hope of a shot at the lion. However, he was not there; but as we came toward one carcass a hyena raised its head seemingly from beside the elephant's belly, and I brained it with the little Springfield. On walking up it appeared that I need not have shot at all. The hyena, which was swollen with elephant meat, had gotten inside the huge body, and had then bitten a hole through the abdominal of tough muscle and thrust his head through. The wedge-shaped head had slipped through the hole all right, but the muscle had then contracted, and the hyena was fairly caught, with its body inside the elephant's belly, and its head thrust out through the hole. We took several photos of the beast in its queer trap.

After breakfast we rode back to our camp by the swamp. Akeley and Clark were working hard at the elephant skins; but Mrs. Akeley, Stevenson, and McCutcheon took lunch with us at our camp. They had been having a very successful hunt; Mrs. Akeley had to her credit a fine maned lion and a bull elephant with enormous tusks. This was the first safari we had met while we were out in the field; though in Nairobi, and once or twice at outlying bomas, we had met men about to start on, or returning from, expeditions; and as we marched into Meru we encountered the safari of an old friend, William Lord Smith—"Tiger" Smith—who, with Messrs. Brooks and Allen, were on a trip which was partly a hunting trip and partly a scientific trip undertaken on behalf of the Cambridge Museum.

From the 'Nzoi we made a couple days' march to Lake Sergoi, which we had passed on our way out; a reed-fringed pond, surrounded by rocky hills which marked about the limit to which the Boer and English settlers who were taking up the country had spread. All along our route we encountered herds of game; sometimes the herd would be of only one species; at other times we would come across a great mixed herd, the red hartebeest always predominating; while among them might be zebras, showing silvery white or dark gray in the distance, topis with beautifully colored coats, and even waterbuck. We shot what hartebeests, topis, and oribis were needed for food. All over the uplands we came on the remains of a race of which even the memory has long since vanished. These remains consist of large, nearly circular walls of stones, which are sometimes roughly squared. A few of these circular enclosures contain more than one chamber. Many of them, at least, are not cattle kraals, being too small, and built round hollows; the walls are so low that by themselves they could not serve for shelter or defence, and must probably have been used as supports for roofs of timber or skins. They were certainly built by people who were in some respects more advanced than the savage tribes who now dwell in the land; but the grass grows thick on the earth mounds into which the ancient stone walls are slowly crumbling, and not a trace of the builders remains. Barbarians they doubtless were; but they have been engulfed in the black oblivion of a lower barbarism, and not the smallest tradition lingers to tell of their craft or their cruelty, their industry or prowess, or to give us the least hint as to the race from which they sprang.

We had with us an ox wagon, with the regulation span of sixteen oxen, the driver being a young Colonial Englishman from South Africa—for the Dutch and English Africanders are the best ox-wagon drivers in the world. On the way back to Sergoi he lost his oxen, which were probably run off by some savages from the mountains; so at Sergoi we had to hire another ox wagon, the South African who drove it being a Dutchman named Botha. Sergoi was as yet the limit of settlement; but it was evident that the whole Uasin Gishu country would soon be occupied. Already many Boers from South Africa, and a number of English Africanders, had come in; and no better pioneers exist to-day than these South Africans, both Dutch and English. Both are so good that I earnestly hope they will become indissolubly welded into one people; and the Dutch Boer has the supreme merit of preferring the country to the town and of bringing his wife and children—plenty of children—with him to settle on the land. The homemaker is the only type of settler of permanent value; and the cool, healthy, fertile Uasin Gishu region is an ideal land for the right kind of pioneer homemaker, whether he hopes to make his living by raising stock or by growing crops.

At Sergoi Lake there is a store kept by Mr. Kirke, a South African of Scotch blood. With a kind courtesy which I cannot too highly appreciate he, with the equally cordial help of another settler, Mr. Skally—also a South African, but of Irish birth—and of the District Commissioner, Mr. Corbett, had arranged for a party of Nandi warriors to come over and show me how they hunted the lion. Two Dutch farmers, Boers, from the neighborhood, had also come; they were Messrs. Mouton and Jordaan, fine fellows both, the former having served with De Wet during the war. Mr. and Mrs. Corbett—who were hospitality itself—had also come to see the sport; and so had Captain Chapman, an English army officer who was taking a rest after several years' service in Northern Nigeria.

The Nandi are a warlike pastoral tribe, close kin to the Masai in blood and tongue, in weapons and in manner of life. They have long been accustomed to kill with the spear lions which become man-eaters or which molest their cattle overmuch; and the peace which British rule has imposed upon them—a piece so welcome to the weaker, so irksome to the predatory, tribes—has left lion killing one of the few pursuits in which glory can be won by a young warrior. When it was told them that if they wished they could come to hunt lions at Sergoi eight hundred warriors volunteered, and much heartburning was caused in choosing the sixty or seventy who were allowed the privilege. They stipulated, however, that they should not be used merely as beaters, but should kill the lion themselves, and refused to come unless with this understanding.

The day before we reached Sergoi they had gone out, and had killed a lion and lioness; the beasts were put up from a small covert and despatched with the heavy throwing spears on the instant, before they offered, or indeed had the chance to offer, any resistance. The day after our arrival there was mist and cold rain, and we found no lions. Next day, November 20th, we were successful.

We started immediately after breakfast. Kirk, Skally, Mouton, Jordaan, Mr. and Mrs. Corbett, Captain Chapman, and our party were on horseback; of course we carried our rifles, but our duty was merely to round up the lion and hold him, if he went off so far in advance that even the Nandi runners could not over take him. We intended to beat the country toward some shallow, swampy valleys twelve miles distant.

In an hour we overtook the Nandi warriors, who were advancing across the rolling, grassy plains in a long line, with intervals of six or eight yards between the men. They were splendid savages, stark naked, lithe as panthers, the muscles rippling under their smooth dark skins; all their lives they had lived on nothing but animal food, milk, blood, and flesh, and they were fit for any fatigue or danger. Their faces were proud, cruel, fearless; as they ran they moved with long springy strides. Their head-dresses were fantastic; they carried ox-hide shields painted with strange devices; and each bore in his right hand the formidable war spear, used both for stabbing and for throwing at close quarters. The narrow spear heads of soft iron were burnished till they shone like silver, they were four feet long, and the point and edges were razor sharp. The wooden haft appeared for but a few inches; the long butt was also of iron, ending in a spike so that the spear looked almost solid metal. Yet each sinewy warrior carried his heavy weapon as if it were a toy, twirling it till it glinted in the sun rays. Herds of game, red hartebeests and striped zebra and wild swine, fled right and left before the advance of the line.

It was noon before we reached a wide, shallow valley, with beds of rushes here and there in the middle, and on either side high grass and dwarfed and scattered thorn-trees. Down this we beat for a couple of miles. Then, suddenly, a maned lion rose a quarter of a mile ahead of the line and galloped off through the high grass to the right; and all of us on horseback tore after him.

He was a magnificent beast, with a black and tawny mane; in his prime, teeth and claws perfect, with mighty thews, and savage heart. He was lying near a hartebeest on which he had been feasting; his life had been one unbroken career of rapine and violence;

and now the maned master of the wilderness, the terror that stalked by night, the grim lord of slaughter, was to meet his doom at the hands of the only foes who dared molest him.

It was a mile before we brought him to bay. Then the Dutch farmer, Mouton, who had not even a rifle, but who rode foremost, was almost on him; he halted and turned under a low thorn-tree, and we galloped past him to the opposite side, to hold him until the spearmen could come. It was a sore temptation to shoot him; but of course we could not break faith with our Nandi friends. We were only some sixty yards from him, and we watched him with our rifles ready, lest he should charge either us, or the first two or three spearmen, before their companions arrived.

One by one the spearmen came up, at a run, and gradually began to form a ring around him. Each, when he came near enough, crouched behind his shield, his spear in his right hand, his fierce, eager face peering over the shield rim. As man followed man, the lion rose to his feet. His mane bristled, his tail lashed, he held his head low, the upper lip now drooping over the jaw, now drawn up so as to show the gleam of the long fangs. He faced first one way and then another, and never ceased to utter his murderous grunting roars. It was a wild sight; the ring of spearmen, intent, silent, bent on blood, and in the centre the great man-killing beast, his thunderous wrath growing ever more dangerous.

At last the tense ring was complete, and the spearmen rose and closed in. The lion looked quickly from side to side, saw where the line was thinnest, and charged at his topmost speed. The crowded moment began. With shields held steady, and quivering spears poised, the men in front braced themselves for the rush and the shock; and from either hand the warriors sprang forward to take their foe in flank. Bounding ahead of his fellows, the leader reached throwing distance; the long spear flickered and plunged; as the lion felt the wound he half turned, and then flung himself on the man in front. The warrior threw his spear; it drove deep into the life, for entering at one shoulder it came out of the opposite flank, near the thigh, a yard of steel through the great body. Rearing, the lion struck the man, bearing down the shield, his back arched; and for a moment he slaked his fury with fang and talon. But on the instant I saw another spear driven clear through his body from side to side; and as the lion turned again the bright spear blades darting toward him were flashes of white flame. The end had come. He seized another man, who stabbed him and wrenched loose. As he fell he gripped a spear head in his jaws with such tremendous force that he bent it double. Then the warriors were round and over him stabbing and shouting, wild with furious exultation.

From the moment when he charged until his death I doubt whether ten seconds had elapsed, perhaps less, but what a ten seconds! The first half dozen spears had done the work. Three of the spear blades had gone clear through the body, the points projecting several inches, and these, and one or two others, including the one he had seized in his jaws, had been twisted out of shape in the terrible death struggle.

We at once attended to the two wounded men. Treating their wounds with antiseptic was painful, and so, while the operation was in progress, I told them, through Kirke, that I would give each a heifer. A Nandi prizes his cattle rather more than his wives; and each sufferer smiled broadly at the news, and forgot all about the pain of his wounds.

Then the warriors, raising their shields above their heads, and chanting the deep-toned victory song, marched with a slow, dancing step around the dead body of the lion; and this savage dance of triumph ended a scene of as fierce interest and excitement as I ever hope to see.

The Nandi marched back by themselves, carrying the two wounded men on their shields. We rode to camp by a roundabout way, on the chance that we might see another lion. The afternoon waned and we cast long shadows before us as we rode across the vast lonely plain. The game stared at us as we passed; a cold wind blew in our faces, and the tall grass waved ceaselessly; the sun set behind a sullen cloud bank; and then, just at nightfall, the tents glimmered white through the dusk.

Tarlton's partner, Newland—also an Australian, and as fine a fellow as Tarlton himself—once had a rather eerie adventure with a man-eating lion. He was camped near Kilimakiu, and after nightfall the alarm was raised that a lion was near by. He came out of his tent, more wood was thrown on the fire, and he heard footsteps retreating, but could not make out whether they were those of a lion or a hyena. Going back to his tent he lay down on his bed with his face turned toward the tent wall. Just as he was falling to sleep the canvas was pushed almost into his face by the head of some creature outside; immediately afterward he heard the sound of a heavy animal galloping, and then the scream of one of his porters whom the lion had seized and was dragging off into the darkness. Rushing out with his rifle he fired toward the sounds, shooting high; the lion let go his hold and made off, and the man ultimately recovered.

It has been said that lions are monogamous and that they mate for life. If this were so they would almost always be found in pairs, a lion and a lioness. They are sometimes so found; but it is much more common to come across a lioness and her cubs, an old lion with several lionesses and their young (for they are often polygamous), a single lion or lioness, or a couple of lions or lionesses, or a small troop, either all lions or all lionesses, or of mixed sexes. These facts are not compatible with the romantic theory in question.

We tried to get the Nandi to stay with us for a few days and beat for lions; but this they refused to do, unless they were also to kill them; and I did not care to assist as a mere spectator at any more lion hunts, no matter how exciting—though to do so once was well worth while. So we moved on by ourselves, camping in likely places. In the swamps, living among the reeds, were big handsome cuckoos, which ate mice. Our first camp was by a stream bordered by trees like clove-trees; at evening multitudes of yellow-billed pigeons flew up its course. They were feeding on olives, and were good for the table; and so were the yellow-billed mallards, which were found in the occasional pools. Everything we shot at this time went into the pot—except a hyena. The stomachs of the reedbuck and origi contained nothing but grass; but the stomachs of the duikers were filled with berries from a plant which looked like the deadly nightshade. On the burned ground, by the way, the oribi, which were very plentiful, behaved precisely like tommies, except that they did not go in as large troops; they made no effort to hide as they do in thick grass; and as duikers, steinbucks, and reedbucks always do. We saw, but could not get a shot at, one topi with a white or blazed face, like a South African blesbok. While beating one swamp a lion appeared for an instant at its edge, a hundred and fifty yards off. I got a snap shot, and ought to have hit him, but didn't. We tried our best to get him out of the swap, finally burning all of it that was not too wet; but we never saw him again.

We recrossed the high hill country, through mists and driving rains, and were back at Londiani on the last day of November. Here, with genuine regret, we said good-bye to our safari; for we were about to leave East Africa, and could only take a few of our personal attendants with us into Uganda and the Nile Valley. I was really sorry to see the last of the big, strong, good-natured porters. They had been with us over seven months, and had always behaved well—though this, of course, was mainly owing to Cuninghame's and Tarlton's management. We had not lost a single man by death. One had been tossed by a rhino, one clawed by a leopard, and several had been sent to hospital for dysentery, small-pox, or fever, but none had died. While on the Guaso Nyero trip we had run into a narrow belt of the dreaded tsetse fly, whose bite is fatal to domestic animals. Five of our horses were bitten, and four of them died, two not until we were on the Uasin Gishu; the fifth, my zebra-shaped brown, although very sick, ultimately recovered, to the astonishment of the experts. Only three of our horses lasted in such shape that we could ride them in to Londiani; one of them being Tranquillity, and another Kermit's white pony, Huan Daw, who was always dancing and curvetting, and whom in consequence the saises had christened "merodadi," the dandy.

The first ten days of December I spent at Njoro, on the edge of the Mau escarpment, with Lord Delamere. It is a beautiful farming country; and Lord Delamere is a practical and successful farmer, and the most useful settler, from the stand-point of the all-round interests of the country, in British East Africa. Incidentally, the home ranch was most attractive—especially the library, the room containing Lady Delamere's books. Delamere had been himself a noted big-game hunter, his bag including fifty-two lions; but instead of continuing to be a mere sportsman, he turned his attention to stock-raising and wheat-growing, and became a leader in the work of taming the wilderness, of conquering for civilization the world's waste spaces. No career can be better worth following.

During his hunting years Delamere had met with many strange adventures. One of the lions he shot mauled him, breaking his leg, and also mauling his two Somali gun-bearers. The lion then crawled off into some bushes fifty yards away, and camp was pitched where the wounded men were lying. Soon after nightfall the hyenas assembled in numbers and attacked, killed, and ate the mortally wounded lion, the noise made by the combatants being ear-rending. One another occasion he had heard a leopard attack some baboons in the rocks, a tremendous row following as the big dog baboons hastened to the assistance of the one who had been seized and drove off the leopard. That evening a leopard, evidently the same one, very thin and hungry, came into camp and was shot; it was frightfully bitten, the injuries being such as only baboons inflict, and would unquestionably have died of its wounds. The leopard wherever possible takes his kill up a tree, showing extraordinary strength in the performance of this feat. It is undoubtedly due to fear of interference from hyenas. The 'Ndorobo said that no single hyena would meddle with a leopard, but that three or four would without hesitation rob it of its prey. Some years before this time, while hunting north of Kenia Lord Delamere had met a Dr.

Kolb, who was killed by a rhino immediately afterward. Dr. Kolb was fond of rhinoceros liver, and killed scores of the animals for food, but finally a cow, with a half-grown calf, which he had wounded charged him and thrust her horn right through the middle of his body.

We spent several days vainly hunting bongo in the dense mountains forests, with half a dozen 'Ndorobo. These were true 'Ndorobo, who never cultivate the ground, living in the deep forests on wild honey and game. It has been said that they hunt but little, and only elephant and rhino; but this is not correct as regards the 'Ndorobo in question. They were all clad in short cloaks of the skin of the tree hyrax; hyrax, monkey, bongo, and forest hog, the only game of the dense, cool, wet forest, were all habitually killed by them. They also occasionally killed rhino and buffalo, finding the former, because it must occasionally be attacked in the open, the more dangerous of the two; twice Delamere had come across small communities of 'Ndorobo literally starving because the strong man, the chief hunter, the breadwinner, had been killed by a rhino which he had attacked. The headman of those with us, who was named Mel-el-lek, had himself been fearfully injured by a wounded buffalo; and the father of another one who was with us had been killed by baboons which had rallied to the aid of one which he was trying to kill with his knobkerry. Usually they did not venture to meddle with the lions which they found on the edge of the forest, or with the leopards which occasionally dwelt in the deep woods; but once Melellek killed a leopard with a poisoned arrow from a tree, and once a whole party of them attacked and killed with their poisoned arrows a lion which had slain a cow buffalo near the forest. On another occasion a lion in its turn killed two of their hunters. In fact they were living just as palaeolithic man lived in Europe, ages ago.

Their arms were bows and arrows, the arrows being carried in skin quivers, and the bows, which were strung with zebra gut, being swathed in strips of hide. When resting they often stood on one leg, like storks. Their eyesight was marvellous, and they were extremely skilful alike in tracking and in seeing game. They threaded their way through the forest noiselessly and at speed, and were extraordinary climbers. They were continually climbing trees to get at the hyrax, and once when a big black and white Colobus monkey which I had shot lodged in the top of a giant cedar one of them ascended and brought it down with matter-of-course indifference. He cut down a sapling, twenty-five feet long, with the stub of a stout branch left on as a hook, and for the rope used a section of vine which he broke and twisted into flexibility. Then, festooned with all his belongings, he made the ascent. There was a tall olive, sixty or eighty feet high, close to the cedar, and up this he went. From its topmost branches, where only a monkey or a 'Ndorobo could have felt at home, he reached his sapling over to the lowest limb of the giant cedar, and hooked it on; and then crawled across on this dizzy bridge. Up he went, got the monkey, recrossed the bridge, and climbed down again, quite unconcerned.

The big black and white monkeys ate nothing but leaves, and usually trusted for safety to ascending into the very tops of the tallest cedars. Occasionally they would come in a flying leap down to the ground, or to a neighboring tree; when on the ground they merely dashed toward another tree, being less agile then the ordinary monkeys, whether in the tree tops or on solid earth. They are strikingly handsome and conspicuous creatures. Their bold coloration has been spoken of as "protective"; but it is protective only to town-bred eyes. A non-expert finds any object, of no matter what color, difficult to make out when hidden among the branches at the top of a tall tree; but the black and white coloration of this monkey has not the slightest protective value of any kind. On the contrary, it is calculated at once to attract the eye. The 'Ndorobo were a unit in saying that these monkeys were much more easy to see than their less brightly colored kinsfolk who dwell in the same forests; and this was my own experience.

When camped in these high forests the woods after nightfall were vocal with the croaking and wailing of the tree hyraxes. They are squat, woolly, funny things, and to my great amusement I found that most of the settlers called them "Teddy bears." They are purely arboreal and nocturnal creatures, living in hollows high up in the big trees, by preference in the cedars. At night they are very noisy, the call consisting of an opening series of batrachian-like croaks, followed by a succession of quavering wails—eerie sounds enough, as they come out of the black stillness of the midnight. They are preyed on now and then by big owls and by leopards, and the white-tailed mongoose is their especial foe, following them everywhere among the tree tops. This mongoose is both terrestrial and arboreal in habits, and is hated by the 'Ndorobo because it robs their honey buckets.

The bongo and the giant hog were the big game of these deep forests, where a tangle of undergrowth filled the spaces between the trunks of the cedar, the olive, and the yew or yellow-wood, while where the bamboos grew they usually choked out all other plants. Delamere had killed several giant hogs with his half-breed hounds; but on this occasion the hounds would not follow them. On three days we came across bondo; once a solitary bull, on both the other occasions herds. We never saw them, although we heard the solitary bull crash off through the bamboos; for they are very wary and elusive, being incessantly followed by the 'Ndorobo. They are as large as native bullocks with handsomely striped skins, and both sexes carry horns. On each of the three days we followed them all day long, and it was interesting to trace so much as we could of their habits. Their trails are deeply beaten, and converge toward the watercourse, which run between the steep, forest-clad spurs of the mountains. They do not graze, but browse, cropping the leaves, flowers, and twigs of various shrubs, and eating thistles; they are said to eat bark, but this our 'Ndorobo denied. They are also said to be nocturnal, feeding at night, and lying up in the daytime; but this was certainly not the case with those we came across. Both of the herds, which we followed patiently and cautiously for hours without alarming them, were feed-

ing as they moved slowly along. One herd lay down for a few hours
a noon; the other kept feeding until mid-afternoon, when we
alarmed it; and the animals then went straight up the mountain
over the rimrock. It was cold rainy weather, and the dark of
the moon, which may perhaps have had something to do with the
bongo being on the move and feeding during the day; but the
'Ndorobo said that they never fed at night—I of course know
nothing about this personally. Leopards catch the young bongo
and giant hog, but dare not meddle with those that are full-grown.
The forest which they frequent is so dense, so well-nigh impenetrable, that half the time no man can follow their trails save by
bending and crawling, and cannot make out an object twenty
yards ahead. It is extraordinary to see the places through which
the bongo pass, and which are their chosen haunts.

While Lord Delamere and I were hunting in vain Kermit was
more fortunate. He was the guest of Barclay Cole, Delamere's
brother-in-law. They took eight porters and went into the forest accompanied by four 'Ndorobo. They marched straight up to the
bamboo and yellow-wood forest near the top of the Mau escarpment. They spent five days hunting. The procedure was simply to
find the trail of a herd, to follow it through the tangled woods as
rapidly and noiselessly as possible until it was overtaken, and then
to try to get a shot at the first patch of reddish hide of which they
got a glimpse—for they never saw more than such a patch, and
then only for a moment. The first day Kermit, firing at such a
patch, knocked over the animal; but it rose and the tracks were so
confused that even the keen eyes of the wild men could not pick
out the right one. Next day they again got into a herd; this time
Kermit was the first to see the game—all that was visible being a
patch of reddish, the size of a man's two hands, with a white stripe
across it. Firing he killed the animal; but it proved to be only half
grown. Even the 'Ndorobo now thought it useless to follow the
herd; but Kermit took one of them and started in pursuit. After a
couple of hours' trailing the herd was again overtaken, and again

Kermit got a glimpse of the animals. He hit two; and selecting the trail with most blood they followed it for three or four miles, until Kermit overtook and finished off the wounded bongo, a fine cow.

Kermit always found them lying up during the middle of the day and feeding in the morning and afternoon; otherwise his observations of their habits coincided with mine.

The next ten days Kermit spent in a trip to the coast, near Mombasa, for sable—the most beautiful antelope next to the koodoo. The cows and bulls are red, the very old bulls (of the typical form) jet black, all with white bellies; like the roan, both sexes carry scimitar-shaped horns, but longer than the roans. He was alone with his two gun-bearers, and some Swahili porters; he acted as headman himself. They marched from Mombasa, being ferried across the harbor of Kilindini in a dhow, and then going some fifteen miles south. Next day they marched about ten miles to a Nyika village, where they arrived just in the middle of a funeral dance which was being held in honor of a chief's son who had died. Kermit was much amused to find that this death dance had more life and go to it than any dance he had yet seen, and the music—the dirge music—had such swing and vitality that it almost reminded him of a comic opera. The dancers wore tied round their legs queer little wickerwork baskets, with beans inside, which rattled in the rhythm of their dancing. Camp was pitched under a huge baobab-tree, in sight of the Indian Ocean; but in the middle of the night the ants swarmed in and drove everybody out; and next day, while Kermit was hunting, camp was shifted on about an hour's march to a little grove of trees by a brook. It was a well-watered country, very hilly, with palm-bordered streams in each valley. These wild palms bore ivory nuts, the fruit tasting something like an apple. Each village had a grove of cocoanut palms, and Kermit found the cool cocoanut milk delicious after the return from a long day's hunting.

Each morning he was off before daylight, and rarely returned until after nightfall; and tired though he was he enjoyed to the full the walks campward in the bright moonlight among the palm groves beside the rushing streams, while the cicadas cried like katydids at home. The grass was long. The weather was very hot, and almost every day there were drenching thunder-storms, and the dews were exceedingly heavy, so that Kermit was wet almost all the time, although he kept in first-rate health. There were not many sable and they were shy. About nine or ten o'clock they would stop feeding, and leave their pasture grounds of long grass, taking refuge in some grove of trees and thick bushes, not coming out again until nearly five o'clock.

On the second day's hunting Juma spied a little band of sable just entering a grove. A long and careful stalk brought the hunters to the grove, but after reaching it they at first saw nothing of the game. Then Kermit caught a glimpse of a head, fired, and brought down the beast in its tracks. It proved to be a bull, just changing from the red to the black coat; the horns were fair—in this northern form they never reach the length of those borne by the sable bulls of South Africa. He also killed a cow, not fully grown. He therefore still needed a full-grown cow, which he obtained three days later; this animal when wounded was very savage, and tried to charge.

We now went to Nairobi, where Cuninghame, Tarlton, and the three naturalists were already preparing for the Uganda trip and shipping the stuff hitherto collected. Working like beavers we got everything ready—including additions to the Pigskin Library, which included, among others, Cervantes, Goethe's "Faust," Molière, Pascal, Montaigne, St. Simon, Darwin's "Voyage of the Beagle," and Huxley's "Essays"—and on December 18th started for Lake Victoria Nyanza.

Uganda, and the Great Nyanza Lakes

When we left Nairobi it was with real regret that we said good-by to the many friends who had been so kind to us; officials, private citizens, almost every one we had met—including Sir Percy Girouard, the new governor. At Kijabe the men and women from the American mission—and the children too—were down at the station to wish us good luck and at Nakuru the settlers from the neighborhood gathered on the platform to give us a farewell cheer. The following morning we reached Kisumu on Lake Victoria Nyanza. It is in the Kavirondo country, where the natives, both men and women, as a rule go absolutely naked, although they are peaceable and industrious. In the native market they had brought in baskets, iron spade heads, and food, to sell to the native and Indian traders who had their booths round about; the meat market, under the trees, was especially interesting.

At noon we embarked in a smart little steamer, to cross the lake. Twenty-four hours later we landed at Entebbe, the seat of the English Governor of Uganda. Throughout our passage the wind hardly ruffled the smooth surface of the lake. As we steamed away from the eastern shore the mountains behind us and on our right hand rose harsh and barren, yet with a kind of forbidding beauty. Dark clouds hung over the land we had left, and a rainbow stretched across their front. At nightfall, as the red sunset faded, the lonely waters of the vast inland sea stretched, ocean-like, west and south into a shoreless gloom. Then the darkness deepened, the tropic stars blazed overhead, and the light of the half moon drowned in silver the embers of the sunset.

Next morning we steamed along and across the equator; the last time we were to cross it, for thenceforth our course lay northward. We passed by many islands green with meadow and forest, beautiful in the bright sunshine, but empty with the emptiness of death. A decade previously these islands were thronged with tribes of fisher folk, their villages studded the shores, and their long canoes, planks held together with fibre, furrowed the surface of the lake. Then, from out of the depths of the Congo forest came the dreadful scourge of the sleeping sickness, and smote the doomed peoples who dwelt beside the Victorian Nile, and on the coasts of the Nyanza Lakes and in the lands between. Its agent was a biting fly, brother to the tsetse whose bite is fatal to domestic animals. This fly dwells in forests, beside lakes and rivers; and wherever it dwells after the sleeping sickness came it was found that man could not live. In this country, between, and along the shores of, the great lakes, two hundred thousand people died in slow torment, before the hard-taxed wisdom and skill of medical science and governmental administration could work any betterment whatever in the situation. Men still die by thousands, and the disease is slowly spreading into fresh districts. But it has proved possible to keep it within limits in the regions already affected; but only by absolutely abandoning certain districts, and by clearing all the forest and brush in tracts which serve as barriers to the fly, and which permit passage through the infected belts. On the western shores of Victoria Nyanza, and in the islands adjacent thereto, the ravages of the pestilence were such, the mortality it caused was so appalling, that the Government was finally forced to deport all the survivors inland, to forbid all residence beside or fishing in the lake, and with this end in view to destroy the villages and the fishing fleets of the people. The teeming lake fish were formerly a main source of food supply to all who dwelt near by; but this has now been cut off, and the myriads of fish are left to themselves, to the hosts of water birds, and to the monstrous man-eating crocodiles of the lake, on whose blood the fly also feeds, and whence it is supposed by some that it draws the germs so deadly to human kind.

When we landed there was nothing in the hot, laughing, tropical beauty of the land to suggest the grisly horror that brooded so near. In green luxuriance the earth lay under a cloudless sky, yielding her increase to the sun's burning caresses, and men and women were living their lives and doing their work well and gallantly.

Our safari started on its march north-westward to Lake Albert Nyanza. We had taken with us from East Africa our gun-bearers, tent boys, and the men whom the naturalists had trained as skinners. The porters were men of Uganda; the askaris were from the constabulary, and widely different races were represented among them, but all had been drilled into soldierly uniformity. The porters were well-clad, well-behaved, fine-looking men, and did their work better than the "shenzis," the wild Meru of Kikiu tribesmen, whom we had occasionally employed in East Africa; but they were not the equals of the regular East African porters. I think this was largely because of their inferior food, for they ate chiefly yams and plantains; in other words inferior sweet potatoes and bananas. They were quite as fond of singing as the East African porters, and in addition were cheered on the march by drum and fife; several men had fifes, and one carried nothing but one of the big Uganda drums, which he usually bore at the head of the safari, marching in company with the flag-bearer. Every hour or two the men would halt, often beside one of the queer little wicker-work booths in which native hucksters disposed of their wares by the roadside.

Along the road we often met wayfarers; once or twice bullock carts; more often men carrying rolls of hides or long bales of cotton on their heads; or a set of Bahima herdsmen, with clear-cut features, guarding their herds of huge-horned Angola cattle.

All greeted us most courteously, frequently crouching or kneeling, as is their custom when they salute a superior; and we were scrupulous to acknowledge their salutes and to return their greetings in the native fashion, with words of courtesy and long drawn e-h-h-s and a-a-h-s. Along the line of march the chiefs had made preparations to receive us. Each afternoon, as we came to the spot where we were to camp for the night, we found a cleared space strewed with straw and surrounded by a plaited reed fence. Within this space cane houses, with thatched roofs of coarse grass, had been erected, some for our stores, one for a kitchen, one, which was always decked with flowers, as a rest-house for ourselves, the latter with open sides, the roof upheld by cane pillars so that it was cool and comfortable, and afforded a welcome shelter either from the burning sun if the weather was clear, or from the pelting, driving tropical storms if there was rain. The moon was almost full when we left Kampalla, and night after night it lent a half unearthly beauty to the tropical landscape.

Sometime in the evenings the mosquitoes bothered us; more often they did not; but in any event we slept well under our nettings. Usually at each camp we found either the head chief of the district, or a sub-chief, with presents; eggs, chickens, sheep, once or twice a bullock, always pineapples and bananas. The chief was always well dressed in flowing robes, and usually welcomed us with dignity and courtesy (sometimes, however, permitting the courtesy to assume the form of servility); and we would have him in to tea, where he was sure to enjoy the bread and jam. Sometimes he came in a rickshaw, sometimes in a kind of wickerwork palanquin, sometimes on foot. When we left his territory we made him a return gift.

We avoided all old camping grounds, because of the spirillum tick. This dangerous fever tick is one of the insect scourges of Uganda, for its bite brings on a virulent spirillum fever which lasts intermittently for months, and may be accompanied by partial paralysis. It is common on old camping grounds, and in native villages. The malarial mosquitoes also abound in places; and repeated attacks of malaria pave the way for black water fever, which is often fatal.

The first day's march from Kampalla led us through shambas, the fields of sweet potatoes and plantations of bananas being separated by hedges or by cane fences. Then for two or three days we passed over low hills and through swampy valleys, the whole landscape covered by a sea of elephant grass, the close-growing, coarse blades more than twice the height of a man on horseback. Here and there it was dotted with groves of strange trees; in these groves monkeys of various kinds—some black, some red-tailed, some auburn—chattered as they raced away among the branches; there were brilliant rollers and bee-eaters; little green and yellow parrots, and gray parrots with red tails; and many colored butterflies. Once or twice we saw the handsome, fierce, short-tailed eagle, the bateleur eagle, and scared one from a reedbuck fawn it had killed. Among the common birds there were black drongos, and musical bush shrikes; small black magpies with brown tails; white-headed kites and slate-colored sparrow-hawks; palm swifts, big hornbills; blue and mottled kingfishers, which never went near the water, and had their upper mandibles red and their under ones black. Barbets, with swollen, saw-toothed bills, their plumage iridescent purple above and red below; bulbuls, also dark purple above and red below, which whistled and bubbled incessantly as they hopped among the thick bushes, behaving much like our own yellow-breasted chats; and a multitude of other birds, beautiful or fantastic. There were striped squirrels too, reminding us of the big Rocky Mountain chipmunk or Say's chipmunk, but with smaller ears and a longer tail.

Christmas day we passed on the march. There is not much use in trying to celebrate Christmas unless there are small folks to hang up their stockings on Christmas Eve, to rush gleefully in at dawn next morning to open the stockings, and after breakfast to wait in hopping expectancy until their elders throw open the doors of the room in which the big presents are arranged, those for each child on a separate table.

Forty miles from the coast the elephant grass began to disappear. The hills became somewhat higher, there were thorn-trees, and stately royal palms of great height, their stems swollen and bulging at the top, near the fronds. Parasitic ferns, with leaves as large as cabbage leaves, grew on the branches of the acacias. One kind of tree sent down from its branches to the ground roots which grew into thick trunks. There were wide, shallow marshes, and although the grass was tall it was no longer above a man's head. Kermit and I usually got two or three hours' hunting each day. We killed singing waterbuck, bushbuck, and bohor reedbuck. The reedbuck differed slightly from those of East Africa; in places they were plentiful, and they were not wary. We also killed several hartebeests; a variety of the Jackson's hartebeest, being more highly colored, with black markings. I killed a very handsome harnessed bushbuck ram. It was rather bigger than a good-sized white-tail buck, its brilliant red coat beautifully marked with rows of white spots, its twisted black horns sharp and polished. It seemed to stand about half way between the dark-colored bushbuck rams of East and South Africa and the beautifully marked harnessed antelope rams of the west coast forests. The ewes and young rams showed the harness markings even more plainly; and, as with all bushbuck, were of small size compared to the old rams. These bushbuck were found in tall grass, where the ground was wet, instead of in the thick bush where their East African kinsfolk spend the daytime.

At the bushbuck camp we met a number of porters returning from the Congo, where they had been with an elephant poacher named Busherri—at least that was as near the name as we could make out. He had gone into the Congo to get ivory, by shooting and trading; but the wild forest people had attacked him, and had killed him and seven of his followers, and the others were straggling homeward. In Kampalla we had met an elephant hunter named Quin who had recently lost his right arm in an encounter with a wounded tusker. Near one camp the head chief pointed out two places, now overgrown with jungle, where little villages had stood less than a year before. In each case elephants had taken to feeding at night in the shambas, and had steadily grown bolder and bolder until the natives, their crops ruined by the depredations and their lives in danger, had abandoned the struggle, and shifted to some new place in the wilderness.

We were soon to meet elephant ourselves. The morning of the 28th was rainy; we struck camp rather late, and the march was long, so that it was mid-afternoon when Kermit and I reached our new camping place. Soon afterward word was brought us that some elephants were near by; we were told that the beasts were in the habit of devastating the shambas, and were bold and truculent, having killed a man who had tried to interfere with them. Kermit and I at once started after them, just as the last of the safari came in, accompanied by Cuninghame, who could not go with us as he was recovering from a bout of fever.

In half an hour we came on fresh sign, and began to work cautiously along it. Our guide, a wild-looking savage with a blunt spear, went first, followed by my gun-bearer, Kongoni, who is excellent on spoor; then I came, followed by Kermit, and by the other gun-bearers. The country was covered with tall grass, and studded with numerous patches of jungle and small forest. In a few minutes we heard the elephants, four or five of them, feeding in thick jungle where the vines that hung in tangled masses from the trees and that draped the bushes made dark caves of greenery. It was difficult to find any space clear enough to see thirty yards ahead. Fortunately there was no wind whatever. We picked out the spoor of a big bull and for an hour and a half we followed it, Kongoni usually in the lead. Two or three times, as we threaded our way among the bushes, as noiselessly as possible, we caught glimpses of gray, shadowy bulks, but only for a second at a time, and never with sufficient distinctness to shoot. The elephants were feeding, tearing down the branches of a rather large-leafed tree with bark like that of a scrub oak and big pods containing beans; evidently these beans were a favorite food. They fed in circles and zigzags, but toward camp, until they were not much more than half a mile from it, and the noise made by the porters in talking and gathering wood was plainly audible; but the elephants paid no heed to it, being evidently too much accustomed to the natives to have much fear of man. We continually heard them breaking branches, and making rumbling or squeaking sounds. They then fed slowly along in the opposite direction, and got into rather more open country; and we followed faster in the big footprints of the bull we had selected. Suddenly in an open glade Kongoni crouched and beckoned to me, and through the bush I caught the loom of the tusker. But at that instant he either heard us, saw us, or caught a whiff of our wind, and without a moment's hesitation he himself assumed the offensive. With his huge ears cocked at right angles to his head, and his trunk hanging down, he charged full tilt at us, coming steadily, silently, and at a great pace, his feet swishing through the long grass; and a formidable monster he looked. At forty yards I fired the right barrel of the Holland into his head, and though I missed the brain the shock dazed him and brought him to an instant halt. Immediately Kermit put a bullet from the Winchester into his head; as he wheeled I gave him the second barrel between the neck and shoulder, through his ear; and Kermit gave him three more shots before he slewed round and disappeared. There were not many minutes of daylight left, and we followed hard on his trail, Kongoni leading. At first there was only an occasional gout of dark blood; but soon we found splashes of red froth from the lungs; then we came to where he had fallen, and then we heard him crashing among the branches in thick jungle to the right. In we went after him, through the gathering gloom, Kongoni leading and I close behind, with the rifle ready for instant action; for though his strength was evidently fast failing, he was also evidently in a savage temper, anxious to wreak his vengeance before he died. On we went, following the bloody trail through the dim cavernous windings in the dark, vine-covered jungle; we heard him smash the branches but a few yards ahead, and fall and rise; and stealing forward Kermit and I slipped up to within a dozen feet of him as he stood on the other side of some small twisted trees, hung with a mat of creepers. I put a bullet into his heart, Kermit fired; each of us fired again on the instant; the mighty bull threw up his trunk, crashed over backward, and lay dead on his side among the bushes. A fine sight he was, a sight to gladden any hunter's heart, as he lay in the twilight, a giant in death.

At once we trotted back to camp, reaching it as darkness fell; and the next morning all of us came out to the carcass. He was full grown, and was ten feet nine inches high. The tusks were rather short, but thick, and weighed a hundred and ten pounds the pair. Out of the trunk we made excellent soup.

Several times while following the trail of this big bull we could tell he was close by the strong elephant smell. Most game animals have a peculiar scent, often strong enough for the species to be readily recognizable before it is seen, if in forest or jungle. On the open plains, of course, one rarely gets close enough to an animal to smell it before seeing it; but I once smelled a herd of hartebeest, when the wind was blowing strongly from them, although they were out of sight over a gentle rise. Waterbuck have a very strong smell. Buffalo smell very much like domestic cattle, but old bulls are rank. More than once, in forest, my nostrils have warned me before my eyes that I was getting near the quarry whose spoor I was on.

After leaving the elephant camp we journeyed through country for the most part covered with an open forest growth. The trees

were chiefly acacias. Among them were interspersed huge candelabra euphorbias, all in bloom, and now and then one of the brilliant red flowering trees, which never seem to carry many leaves at
the same time with the gaudy blossoms. At one place for miles the
open forest was composed of the pod-bearing, thick-leafed trees on
which we had found the elephants feeding; their bark and manner
of growth gave them somewhat the look of jack-oaks; where they
made up the forest, growing well apart from one another, it reminded us of the cross-timbers of Texas and Oklahoma. The grass
was everywhere three or four feet high; here and there were
patches of the cane-like elephant grass, fifteen feet high.

It was pleasant to stride along the road in the early mornings,
followed by the safari, and we saw many a glorious sunrise. But as
noon approached it grew very hot, under the glare of the brazen
equatorial sun, and we were always glad when we approached our
new camp, with its grass-strewn ground, its wickerwork fence, and
cool, open rest house. The local sub-chief and his elders were usually drawn up to receive me at the gate, bowing, clapping their
hands, and uttering their long-drawn e-h-h-s; and often banana
saplings or branches would be stuck in the ground to form avenues
of approach, and the fence and a rest-house might be decorated
with flowers of many kinds. Sometimes we were met with music,
on instruments of one string, of three strings, of ten strings—rudi-
mentary fiddles and harps; and there was a much more complicated
instrument, big and cumbrous, made of bars of wood placed on two
banana stems, the bars being struck with a hammer, as if they were
keys; its tones were deep and good. Along the road we did not see
habitations or people; but continually there led away from it, twisting through the tall grass and the bush jungles, native paths, the
earth beaten brown and hard by countless bare feet; and these,
crossing and recrossing in a network, let to plantation after plantation of bananas and sweet potatoes, and clusters of thatched huts.

In the afternoon, as the sun began to get well beyond the
meridian, we usually sallied forth to hunt, under the guidance of

some native who had come in to tell us where he had seen game that morning. The jungle was so thick in places and the grass was everywhere so long, that without such guidance there was little successful hunting to be done in only two or three hours. We might come back with a buck, or with two or three guinea-fowl, or with nothing.

There were a good many poisonous snakes; I killed a big puff-adder with thirteen eggs inside it; and we also killed a squat, short-tailed viper, beautifully mottled, not eighteen inches long, but with a wide, flat head and a girth of body out of all proportion to its length; and another very poisonous and vicious snake, apparently of colubrine type, long and slender. The birds were an unceasing pleasure. White wagtails and yellow wagtails walked familiarly about us within a few feet, wherever we halted and when we were in camp. Long-tailed, crested colys, with all four of their red toes pointed forward, clung to the sides of the big fruits at which they picked. White-headed swallows caught flies and gnats by our heads. There were large plantain-eaters; and birds like small jays with yellow wattles round the eyes. There were boat-tailed birds, in color iridescent green and purple, which looked like our grakles, but were kin to the bulbuls; and another bird, related to the shrikes, with bristly feathers on the rump, which was colored like a red-winged blackbird, black with red shoulders. Vultures were not plentiful, but the yellow-billed kites, true camp scavengers, were common and tame, screaming as they circled overhead, and catching bits of meat which were thrown in the air for them. The shrews and mice which the naturalists trapped around each camping place were kin to the species we had already obtained in East Africa, but in most cases there was a fairly well-marked difference; the jerbilles for instance had shorter tails, more like ordinary rats. Frogs with queer voices abounded in the marshes. Among the ants was one arboreal kind which made huge nests, shaped like beehives or rather like big gray bells, in the trees. Near the lake, by the way, there were Goliath beetles, as large as small rats.

Ten days from Kampalla we crossed the little Kafu River, the black, smooth current twisting quickly along between beds of plumed papyrus. Beyond it we entered the native kingdom of Unyoro. It is part of the British protectorate of Uganda, but is separate from the native kingdom of Uganda, though its people in ethnic type and social development seem much the same. We halted for a day at Hoima, a spread-out little native town, pleasantly situated among hills, and surrounded by plantations of cotton, plantains, yams, millet, and beans. It is the capital of Unyoro, where the king lives, as well as three or four English officials and Episcopalian and Roman Catholic missionaries. The king, accompanied by his prime minister and by the English commissioner, called on me, and I gave him five o'clock tea; he is a Christian, as are most of his chiefs and headmen, and they are sending their children to the mission schools.

A heron, about the size of our night heron but with a longer neck, and with a curiously crow-like voice, strolled about among the native houses at Hoima; and the kites almost brushed us with their wings as they swooped down for morsels of food. The cheerful, confiding little wagtails crossed the threshold of the rest-house in which we sat. Black and white crows and vultures came around camp; and handsome, dark hawks, with white on their wings and tails, and with long, conspicuous crests, perched upright on the trees. There were many kinds of doves; one pretty little fellow was but six inches long. At night the jackals wailed with shrill woe among the gardens.

From Hoima we entered a country covered with the tall, rank elephant grass. It was traversed by papyrus-bordered streams, and broken by patches of forest. The date-palms grew tall, and among the trees were some with orange-red flowers like trumpet flowers, growing in grape-shaped clusters; and both the flowers and the seed-pods into which they turned stood straight up in rows above the leafy tops of the trees that bore them.

The first evening, as we sat in the cool, open cane rest-house, word was brought us that an elephant was close at hand. We found him after ten minutes' walk; a young bull, with very small tusks, not worth shooting. For three-quarters of an hour we watched him, strolling about the feeding, just on the edge of a wall of high elephant grass. Although we were in plain sight, ninety yards off, and sometimes moved about, he never saw us; for an elephant's eyes are very bad. He was feeding on some thick, luscious grass, in the usual leisurely elephant fashion, plucking a big tuft, waving it nonchalantly about in his trunk, and finally tucking it into his mouth; pausing to rub his side against a tree, or to sway to and fro as he stood; and continually waving his tail and half cocking his ears.

At noon on January 5th, 1910, we reached Butiaba, a sandpit and marsh on the shores of Lake Albert Nyanza. We had marched about one hundred and sixty miles from Lake Victoria. We camped on the sandy beach by the edge of the beautiful lake, looking across its waters to the mountains that walled in the opposite shore. At mid-day the whole landscape trembled in the white, glaring heat; as the afternoon waned a wind blew off the lake, and the west kindled in ruddy splendor as the sun went down.

At Butiaba we took boats to go down the Nile to the Lado country. The head of the water transportation service in Uganda, Captain Hutchinson, R.N.R., met us, having most kindly decided to take charge of our flotilla himself. Captain Hutchinson was a mighty hunter, and had met with one most extraordinary experience while elephant hunting; in Uganda the number of hunters who have been killed or injured by elephants and buffaloes is large. He wounded a big bull in the head, and followed it for three days. The wound was serious and on the fourth day he overtook the elephant. It charged as soon as it saw him. He hit it twice in the head with his .450 double-barrel as it came on, but neither stopped nor turned it; his second rifle, a double 8 bore, failed to act; and the elephant seized him in its trunk. It brandished him to and fro in the air several times, and then planting him on the ground knelt and stabbed at him with its tusks. Grasping one of its forelegs he pulled himself between them in time to avoid the blow; and as it rose he managed to seize a hind leg and clung to it. But the tusker reached round and plucked him off with its trunk, and once more brandished him high in the air, swinging him violently about. He fainted from pain and dizziness. When he came to he was lying on the ground; one of his attendants had stabbed the elephant with a spear, whereupon the animal had dropped the white man, vainly tried to catch his new assailant, and had then gone off for some three miles and died. Hutchinson was frightfully bruised and strained, and it was six months before he recovered.

Of Ants and Elephants
[Editor's title]

In this camp [on the Nile] we had to watch the white ants, which strove to devour everything. They are nocturnal, and work in the daytime only under the tunnels of earth which they build over the surface of the box, or whatever else it is, that they are devouring; they eat out everything, leaving this outside shell of earth. We also saw a long column of the dreaded driver ants. These are carnivorous; I have seen both red and black species; they kill every living thing in their path, and I have known them at night drive all the men in a camp out into the jungle to fight the mosquitoes unprotected until daylight. On another occasion, where a steamboat was moored close to a bank, an ant column entered the boat after nightfall, and kept complete possession of it for forty-eight hours. Fires, and boiling water, offer the only effectual means of resistance. The bees are at times as formidable; when their nests are disturbed they will attack every one in sight, driving all the crew of a boat overboard or scattering a safari, and not

411

infrequently killing men and beasts of burden that are unable to reach some place of safety.

The last afternoon, when the flotilla had called to take us farther on our journey, we shot about a dozen buck, to give the porters and sailors a feast, which they had amply earned. All the meat did not get into camp until after dark—one of the sailors, unfortunately, falling out of a tree and breaking his neck on the way in—and it was picturesque to see the rows of big antelope—hartebeest, kob, waterbuck—stretched in front of the flaring fires, and the dark faces of the waiting negroes, each deputed by some particular group of gun-bearers, porters, or sailors to bring back its share.

Next morning we embarked, and steamed and drifted down the Nile; ourselves, our men, our belongings, and the spoils of the chase all huddled together under the torrid sun. Two or three times we grounded on sand bars; but no damage was done, and in twenty-six hours we reached Nimule. We were no longer in healthy East Africa. Kermit and I had been in robust health throughout the time we were in Uganda and the Lado; but all the other white men of the party had suffered more or less from dysentery, fever, and sun prostration while in the Lado; some of the gun-bearers had been down with fever, one of them dying while we were in Uganda; and four of the porters who had marched from Koba to Nimule had died of dysentery—they were burying one when we arrived.

At Nimule we were as usual greeted with hospitable heartiness by the English officials, as well as by two or three elephant hunters. One of the latter, three days before, had been charged by an unwounded bull elephant. He fired both barrels into it as it came on, but it charged home, knocked him down, killed his gun-bearer, and made its escape into the forest. In the forlorn little graveyard at the station were the graves of two white men who had been killed by elephants. One of them, named Stoney, had been caught by a wounded bull, which stamped the life out of him and then literally dismembered him, tearing his arms from his body. In the African wilderness, when a man dies, his companion usually brings in something to show that he is dead, or some remnant of whatever it is that had destroyed him; the sailors whose companion was killed by falling out of the tree near our Lado camp, for instance, brought in the dead branch which had broken under his weight; and Stoney's gun-bearer marched back to Nimule carrying an arm of his dead master, and deposited his grewsome burden in the office of the district commissioner.